Rural Development

Hutchinson University Library   **Hutchinson University Library for Africa**

General Editors

Michael Crowder
Paul Richards

307.72

**Hutchinson University Library for Africa
and other titles of interest**

The African City
Anthony O'Connor

African Philosophy: Myth and Reality
Paulin J. Hountondji

African Women: Their Struggle for Economic Independence
(in Association with Zed Press)
Christine Obbo

Agricultural Development and Nutrition (by arrangement with FAO and
UNICEF)
Edited by Arnold Pacey and Philip Payne

The Development of African Drama
Michael Etherton

The Development Process: A Spatial Perspective
Akin Mabogunje

Forced Migration: The Impact of the Export Slave Trade on African
Societies
Edited by J. E. Inikori

A History of Africa
J. D. Fage

Indigenous Agricultural Revolution: Ecology and Food Production in
West Africa
Paul Richards

Peasants and Proletarians: The Struggles of Third World Workers
Edited by Robin Cohen, Peter C. W. Gutkind and Phyllis Brazier

Politics and Administration in Nigeria
Ladipo Adamolekun

Rural Development: Theories of Peasant Economy and Agrarian Change
Edited by John Harriss

Rural Settlement and Land Use
Michael Chisholm

Twelve African Writers
Gerald Moore

West Africa Under Colonial Rule
Michael Crowder

Rural Development

*Theories of peasant economy
and agrarian change*

Edited by John Harriss

Hutchinson University Library
Hutchinson University Library for Africa

London Melbourne Sydney Auckland Johannesburg

HUTCHINSON UNIVERSITY LIBRARY FOR AFRICA

Hutchinson Education

An imprint of Century Hutchinson Ltd

62-65 Chandos Place, London WC2N 4NW

Century Hutchinson Australia Pty Ltd
PO Box 496, 16-22 Church Street, Hawthorn, Victoria 3122, Australia

Century Hutchinson New Zealand Limited
PO Box 40-086, Glenfield, Auckland 10, New Zealand

Century Hutchinson South Africa (Pty) Limited
PO Box 337, Bergvlei, 2012 South Africa

First published 1982
Reprinted 1984, 1985, 1986

Set in Times
by TJB Photosetting, South Witham, Lincs.

Printed and bound in Great Britain by
Anchor Brendon Limited, Tiptree, Essex

British Library Cataloguing in Publication Data
Rural development.
   1. Underdeveloped areas – Economic conditions
   I. Harriss, John
   330.9172'4   HC59.7

ISBN 0 09 144791 7

Contents

6 *Contents*

Tables

Figures

Preface

In the last decade 'Rural Development' has acquired a central role in the theory and practice of development. In the late 1960s there was a wave of optimism about food supplies and about the prospects for agricultural development in Third World countries, as a result of the introduction of new high-yielding varieties of the major foodgrains, in the so-called 'green revolution'. This optimism rapidly gave way in the 1970s to concern both about the long-term trends of food production in many countries, and especially to concern about the persistence and the deepening of rural poverty. It was in this context that a 'new strategy' for development was fostered, especially by the World Bank. This strategy was deliberately aimed at the problem of poverty, and emphasized *rural* development as a broad and comprehensive process, rather than the goal simply of 'increasing production'. It has given rise to a very large number of development projects in the rural areas of much of the Third World. At the same time the research infrastructure which produced the 'green revolution' technology has been expanded and there is now a network of internationally staffed and funded research institutes, covering a wide range of crops and aimed at raising the productivity of agriculture in diverse environments.

Over the same period there has been mounting scholarly and political interest in the study of 'peasant' economies and societies, reflected in the publication of new journals and books, and responding both to the problems which gave birth to the 'new strategy' and to its results.

The aim of this collection of readings is to give an introduction to analyses of agrarian systems, and of the processes of change within them, and to the reasoning (and the ideologies) on which policies for rural development have been based. It is critical, explicitly or implicitly, of a great deal that has been done in the name of 'rural development', and of the understandings on which projects and plans, and even research programmes, have been founded. The book draws almost entirely on the recent literature of 'peasant studies', and it marks, perhaps, the differences of emphasis and of understanding which have developed since the publication in 1971 of Teodor Shanin's reader on *Peasants and Peasant Societies* (Penguin).

There is a sense in which this book is the result of more than ten years of collective enterprise in teaching about rural development and agrarian change at the University of East Anglia. The undergraduate course which is now called 'Rural Development' has a strong claim to be considered the oldest course of the School of Development Studies, for it was taught even before the foundation of the School itself in 1973, in the days when some of the present faculty were simply members of the 'Overseas Development Group' in the School of Social Studies. Since the late 1960s Raymond Apthorpe, Tony Barnett, David Feldman, Rayah Feldman, Keith Hart, Chris Scott, David Seddon and Anne Sharman have all been involved at different times in teaching the course, as well as Deryke Belshaw and myself. As responsibility for the course has passed from person to person many modifications have been made in its style and content; but there has been continuity and I believe that we have all learned from each other and from our students, so that what is taught is the result of the interactions of a number of people over a decade.

All of us have experienced difficulties in finding suitable basic texts to accompany the course, and some of us have spent many hours at photo-copying machines preparing material for students. This book does not go all the way to satisfying the needs of our course – no one book could possibly do that – but I believe that it does bring together an important set of basic materials, while also summarizing the current state of debate on many issues. It is most unlikely that any one of the members of the School of Development Studies who has taught 'Rural Development' would have made the same selection of readings, but I think that there would be a fair degree of overlap between our different choices. The responsibility for this selection, and for the discussion of it, is mine; and it is my belief and hope that the book will be found useful by others who are involved in teaching about and learning about agrarian change, and in *doing* it, at various levels.

Chris Scott (now of the London School of Economics) and Gavin Williams (of St Peter's College, Oxford) both made valuable comments and suggestions on the contents of the book; and Raymond Apthorpe (now of the Institute of Social Studies at The Hague), Barbara Harriss (of the London School of Hygiene and Tropical Medicine), Judith Heyer (of Somerville College, Oxford) and Gavin Williams all took time and trouble, when they were very busy with other things, to comment on the editorial sections. I am very grateful to all of them. I am especially grateful, also, to Paul Richards of University College, London, both for encouraging the publication of the book and for his extensive comments upon the manuscript with reference to the African literature. I would also like to thank an anonymous reviewer for useful criticism; and Mark Cohen of Hutchinson Education for his keen and sympathetic interest in the project.

I would like to dedicate this book to the memory of Professor Athole Mackintosh, to whose imagination and drive we owe the foundation of the School of Development Studies.

John Harriss
Madras, South India

Acknowledgements

Hutchinson Education and the editor are grateful to the following authors and their publishers for permission to reproduce the articles included in this book:

B. F. Johnston, P. Kilby and Oxford University Press, New York, for ' "Unimodal" and "bimodal" strategies of agrarian change', from *Agriculture and Structural Transformation* (1975)

Michael Lipton and Professor V. S. Vyas for 'Why poor people stay poor', originally delivered as the Vikram Sarabhai Memorial Lecture at the Indian Institute of Management, Ahmedabad, India, in January 1981

T. J. Byres and Frank Cass & Co. Ltd for 'Agrarian transition and the agrarian question', from *Journal of Peasant Studies*, vol. 4 no. 3 (1977)

Stuart Corbridge for 'Urban bias, rural bias, and industrialization'

V. I. Lenin and Lawrence & Wishart Ltd for 'The differentiation of the peasantry', from *The Development of Capitalism in Russia*, vol. 3 of *Lenin's Collected Works (1960)*

Göran Djurfeldt and *Acta Sociologica, Scandinavian Review of Sociology* for 'Classical discussions of capital and peasantry', vol. 24 no. 3 (1981)

Henry Bernstein and *Review of African Political Economy* for 'Notes on capital and peasantry', from no. 10 (1977)

M. Taussig and *Latin American Perspectives* for 'Peasant economics and the development of capitalist agriculture in the Cauca Valley, Colombia', from vol. 5 no. 3 (1978)

T. Shanin for 'Polarization and cyclical mobility', from *The Awkward Class*, Oxford University Press (1972)

Mark Harrison and Frank Cass & Co. Ltd for 'Chayanov's theory of peasant economy', from *Journal of Peasant Studies*, vol. 2 no. 4 (1975) and vol. 4 no. 4 (1977); and for 'Towards a practical theory of agrarian transition', from vol. 7 no. 1 (1979)

Michael Lipton for 'Game against nature' from the texts of two talks given on the BBC Third Programme in 1968

Krishna Bharadwaj and the Department of Applied Economics, University of Cambridge, for 'Production conditions in Indian agriculture' from the book of the same title published by Cambridge University Press (1974)

Benjamin White and Sage Publications for 'Population, involution and employment in rural Java', from *Development and Change*, vol. 7 no. 2 (1976)

C. D. Scott and Frank Cass & Co. Ltd for 'Peasants, proletarianization and the articulation of modes of production', from *Journal of Peasant Studies*, vol. 3 no. 3 (1976)

Philip Raikes and Frank Cass & Co. Ltd for 'The state and the peasantry in Tanzania', from *Journal of Peasant Studies*, vol. 5 no. 3 (1978)

Gavin Williams and Sage Publications Inc (USA) for 'Taking the part of peasants', from *The Political Economy of Contemporary Africa*, ed. P. Gutkind and I. Wallerstein (1976)

General introduction

John Harriss

'Rural Development' as policy and as process

'Rural Development' has emerged as a distinctive field of policy and practice, and of research, in the last decade, and particularly over the eight or nine years since the inception of the 'new strategy' for development planning by the World Bank and UN agencies. This strategy came to be formulated as a result of the general disenchantment with previous approaches to development planning at national and sectoral levels, and it is defined by its concern with equity objectives of various kinds – especially the reduction of inequalities in income and employment, and in access to public goods and services, and the alleviation of poverty. It is this focus on distributional issues which has marked out 'Rural Development' as a distinct field, because an overwhelming majority of poor people in the developing countries of Africa and Asia live in rural areas. The World Bank, indeed, recently defined Rural Development as '...a strategy designed to improve the economic and social life of a specific group of people – the rural poor'.

The term 'Rural Development' thus refers to a distinct approach to interventions by the state in the economies of underdeveloped countries, and one which is at once broader and more specific than 'agricultural development'. It is broader because it entails much more than the development of agricultural production – for it is in fact a distinct approach to the development of the economy as a whole. It is more specific in the sense that it focuses (in its rhetoric, and in principle) particularly on poverty and inequality. Although there is a substantial overlap between the field of conventional agricultural economics and the concerns of 'Rural Development', the kinds of studies which are required to understand the factors affecting 'Rural Development' are not contained within the discipline of agricultural economics. Not only does 'Rural Development' include attention to other aspects of rural economies as well as agriculture, but the analysis of distributional issues demands an inter-disciplinary approach in which the broader social and political factors interacting with economic processes are subjected to examination. Conventional agricultural economics tends to focus upon the analysis of the efficiency of the use of resources in production and marketing, and to treat the social and political factors which are of central importance in the practical activity of 'Rural Development', simply as *ceteris paribus* conditions (or, in other words, they are assumed to be constant).

The expression '*rural development*' may also be used, however, to refer to processes of change in rural societies, not all of which involve action by governments. In this case the activity of 'Rural Development', a form of state intervention, must be considered simply as one of the forces concerned – although it is one which has become of increasing importance. The aim of this book is *not* to say how 'Rural Development' – the form of state intervention – should be done, nor to offer a guide to 'Rural Development' policies, for these are tasks which have been attempted elsewhere[1]*. In the end this book does have quite a lot to say about the 'practice' of 'Rural Development', and it includes materials which examine certain of the assumptions on which 'Rural Development' strategies are based, for such plans must of course contain some theory of agrarian change. But the main objective of the book is to present a collection of articles which together provide a basis for the analysis of the processes which make rural societies and economies what they are and substantially determine the changes that take place within them. The intention is to set out materials which will provide frameworks for understanding the nature of the phenomena with which the practitioners of 'Rural Development' are dealing, and which will also supply a basis for understanding and evaluating interventions by development agencies and planners. In this book the activity of 'Rural Development' is treated as part of the problem, for the interventions of the state profoundly affect agrarian societies, and not always in ways which conform with the stated objectives of those interventions. Some of the articles included in the book are very critical of much that has been done in the name of 'Rural Development'.

Three approaches to the understanding of agrarian change

We use the term 'agrarian change' to mean change in the total system of relationships concerned in agrarian economies and

* Superior figures refer to the Notes which appear at the end of chapters.

societies. This system includes technological and environmental factors and relationships as well as social and cultural ones; and a wide range of processes affect such systems and may contribute to bringing about changes within them. The idea of an 'agrarian system' referred to here is a broader one than that of a 'farming system' (see Ruthenberg, 1980), which denotes a more restricted set of technical factors and relationships. Much of the research now being carried on at international research institutes, in the wake of the 'green revolution', is focused on 'farming systems' in this more restricted sense. Although it is now fashionable at least to pay lip-service to social and political considerations, more often than not treatment of them is only 'tacked on' to farming systems research, and they do not enter sufficiently into the definition of objectives and the procedures of this research. One of the purposes of this book is to contribute to challenging the technocratic emphasis in much current farming systems research.

The natural environment supplies one set of factors affecting agrarian systems – of more immediate and direct relevance than they are in the case of industrial societies; and these and the way in which they work are intimately related to the technologies employed by people in making use of natural resources. Demographic factors, the density of population and the trends of population growth, are also likely to affect these relationships. But an analysis which took into account only these environmental, technological and demographic processes would be seriously deficient, for the economics of farming and of other production activities, and the way in which these are affected by markets and by the connections between the rural economy and the rest of the national economy, or with world markets, must also be included. We must also ask how these factors are affected by the social structures of rural producers and by their values or their 'culture'. Satisfactory analyses of processes of change in rural societies have somehow to embrace all of these issues. As Michael Lipton mentions in an article in Part Three of this book, attempts to understand agrarian societies and rural economies from the viewpoints of single disciplines suffer from serious limitations, and it was in the context of such studies that a perception of the need for inter-disciplinary research was born.

Approaches to the study of agrarian problems none the less reflect the major paradigms of social science research in general, and we might distinguish very broadly 'systems' approaches, 'decision-making models' and structural/historical' views, acknowledging that not all studies fit neatly into these categóries.[2] All three of these broad approaches are represented in the contents of this book, although they are far from being equally represented for reasons which are explained later.

1 Systems approaches

Amongst the 'systems' approaches we may include studies which emphasize environmental, technological and demographic factors and which seek to explain their inter-relationships within farming systems. A notable example of such an approach is Boserup's *The Conditions of Agricultural Growth* (1965) which presents the bold thesis that increasing population density explains the development of increasingly intensive systems of cultivation, involving also changes in technology and in social institutions. This has been found to be a powerful model, even though it was originally built up on the basis of quite flimsy evidence, and it has influenced a good deal of subsequent research. In a modest way, for example, Chambers and Harriss (1977) sought to explain variations between villages in a small region of South India in terms of the inter-relations of environment (especially the availability of irrigation water) and population density, and found certain fairly distinct patterns of variation of wage rates, labour relationships and rural livelihoods that could be related to the basic dynamic of environment and population. A more substantial and important piece of work which has strong affinities with the approach exemplified by Boserup is Allen's examination of the cultivation systems of several parts of Africa (Allen, 1965), in which he advances a concept of environmental carrying capacity in explaining the inter-relationships of human populations, environment and agricultural techniques.

Another notable study which makes use of certain basic ecological concepts, and examines the same inter-relationships, is Geertz's analysis of the economic history of Indonesia (1963; see also the article by White in Part Four of this book), in which he accounts for the differences between the patterns of development in Java on the one hand, and in the Outer Islands on the other, in terms of their contrasted environmental and demographic contexts. Geertz's study is more than an 'ecological' analysis, however, for he also examines these contrasts between Java and the Outer Islands historically and in relation to Dutch colonial policy. Geertz argues that the physical conditions of Java have allowed production to be increased so as to keep pace with the rapidly growing population, though at constant levels of output per head. This has required the use of more and more labour-intensive cultivation practices and also some 'sharing of poverty' – as in the sharing out of access to land or of opportunities for wage work. He describes this whole pattern as one of 'involution' – in the sense that there has been incréasing elaboration of existing social and economic structures – in contrast with the kind of transformation of older structures, and increasing inequality, which has occurred in parts of the Outer Islands.[3]

Geertz's interest in the historical development of cultivation systems at a very broad level is matched by that of some historians who have also sought to explain long-term patterns of agrarian development (an excellent example is Elvin's study of China, 1973). Kjekshus has developed the ecological/demographic approach with reference to East Africa (Kjekshus, 1977); while the relationships of environment, technology and population have long interested geographers, and some of the best geographical writing seeks to explain agrarian change in terms of the relationships of the natural environment and economic and social factors. A classic is Farmer's study of the agrarian development of Sri Lanka (1957); and for Africa there is a valuable collection edited by Prothero (1972).

This approach, emphasizing the systemic relationships of environmental, technological and demographic conditions, and social responses to them, does not figure very prominently in the contents of this book. Taussig, however, in his article in Part Two presents a fine comparison of cultivation systems in the Cauca Valley in Colombia, which demonstrates the ecological 'logic' of a peasant farming system in favourable contrast with a 'modern' system introduced by development agencies which seems to be less efficient ecologically.

There are other 'systems' approaches, including attempts to make rigorous use of general systems theory in the analysis of the agricultural sector (see review by Biggs *et al.*, 1977), and some efforts to model rural societies as '[systems] of interdependent socio-economic elements geared to the dictates of the farming calendar and with built in mechanisms to ensure [their] survival in the face of recurrent natural hazards' (Biggs and Burns, 1976, p.194). This last has some connection with the 'systems' approach found in many studies by sociologists and social anthropologists, where peasant communities are represented as stable systems. This is in the 'functionalist' vein of social science, in which all regular patterns of social behaviour are perceived as having some 'function' to perform in relation to the creation and maintenance of order in societies. A notable example of such work in agrarian studies is that of G. M. Foster (1965), who suggested that peasant behaviour can be understood in terms of 'the image of limited good'. What he meant by this is that given the technology at their disposal and the material conditions of their lives, all valued goods or qualities must appear to peasants – in many instances quite correctly – to be available in only limited supply, so that an increase in the amount going to one person must mean less for others. Many features of peasant society and culture may be understood as 'mechanisms' which function in such a way as to share out resources, to prevent the development of gross inequalities, and thus roughly to maintain a state of equilibrium within the community as a whole. Foster emphasizes the logic of the structure and culture of peasant society in relation to the material conditions in which peasants live, and he argues that once those material conditions are changed then society and culture will undergo change too (in a sense he says to those who would change peasants: 'Make it rational for them to change their behaviour and values. Don't try to change values on their own'). Foster's work remains important as one explanation of a popularly held view of the behaviour of peasants, and of why they may fail to act in ways which would appear sensible – or economically 'rational' – to a Western observer.

The difficulty with such approaches to the study of agrarian societies is that because they emphasize the systemic quality of the local community, regulated by values, they can only really explain change as something which comes about as the result of 'external' forces acting upon the local society. Thus Scarlett Epstein's famous study of economic development and social change in part of South India (1962) describes and explains the contrasting responses in two villages to the development of an irrigation system by the state. Here the village is held to be 'encapsulated' by the wider society or the state (this is a term of the anthropologist F. G. Bailey). It is an approach which both ignores the relationship of mutual determination between locality and state – in which each exercises some determining influence on the other (and which is well demonstrated in the article by Raikes in Part Five of this book) – and neglects processes of change which may be 'internal' to peasant society (on which see the paper by Shanin in Part Three).

2 Decision-making models

The second set of approaches to the study of agrarian change which we may distinguish is that which we described briefly as 'decision-making models'. We include here the many studies of farm economics in the neo-classical mould which are concerned with the allocation of resources on the farm and with the farmers' responses to markets and to innovations[4]. We also include a number of studies by sociologists and social anthropologists who, in reacting to the kinds of problems of the functionalist method briefly referred to in the last paragraph, have tried to set up alternative models in which individuals are seen as making choices about their values and their actions, and thus as changing their own societies. There is a strong interest in this literature in the concept of entrepreneurship[5]. Studies such as these – those of neo-classical economists as well as the sociological studies – are focused upon individuals, and they may be very illuminating. A good example is the substantial literature which explains the ways in which farmers have responded to modern agricultural technology, in terms of their access to resources and the uncertainty of the environments in which they have to make production decisions, or in terms of their attitudes towards and relationships with the bureaucracy[6]. As Apthorpe (1977) puts it, these kinds of social science studies have become quite good at explaining 'the success or failure of the individual within the system' – but in this case 'the system' itself is left out of the analysis. We may reach an excellent understanding of the farmers' responses to imperfect factor markets, for example, but what explains the reasons for and the operations of those markets is left out of the analysis (compare the articles by Lipton and by Bharadwaj in Part Three of this book).

3 Structural/historical approaches

The third approach, which we distinguished and described as that of 'structural/historical studies', attempts to come to grips with precisely this kind of problem. These studies start with examination of the process of production itself. They are thus concerned with the inter-relationships of people and the 'natural' environment, and with the relationships of people in the process of production ('natural' in quotation marks because in this approach the 'natural' environment is seen also as the creation of the interactions of people and the physical environment over historical time). Unlike the 'systems' studies referred to earlier this approach places the ownership and control of resources at the centre of analysis. Some of these studies, indeed, have sought to show how particular forms of ownership have led to ecologically harmful systems of land use[7]. The structures of social relationships and of conflict – or the social classes – which are based upon differences in the ownership and control of resources by different groups of people, are critically important in studies of this kind, and may be seen as one of the major sources of change. But this approach also considers exchange and the sales of inputs and marketing of products within the agrarian economy, and a strong historical theme is that of the 'commoditization' of production and of the incorporation of small-scale producers into markets (whereby instead of producing mainly for their own use or to satisfy the requirements of those with political authority, small producers begin to produce for exchange, and come to depend upon purchases for at least some of the things that they require: see Bernstein in Part Two for a discussion of this process, and Bharadwaj in Part Three for an account of the implications of the different market relationships of different groups of rural producers). The process of commoditization and the development of capitalism, or the linking up of rural household producers with capitalist production in various ways (see Scott, in Part Four), is perhaps the dominant process of change in contemporary agrarian societies.

The 'structural/historical approaches are thus concerned with the relationships between expanding capitalism and various forms of production which, on the face of things at least, might be described as 'non-' or 'pre-capitalist'. One school of thought, which has some grounding in parts of Marx's writing, holds that it is of the very nature of capitalism to absorb or abolish other forms of production. Other scholars argue that there are often circumstances in which capitalism does not destroy other forms or modes of production, and they speak of the 'articulation' of capitalism with other modes of production. 'Articulation' here means rather more than simply 'linkage', and it implies that there is some intervention by the social practices of capitalism within those of the other mode or modes of production, and vice versa. Sometimes the relationship has been seen purely in functional terms – and the persistence of pre-capitalist forms has been 'explained' in terms of the functional requirements of capitalism (such as the supply of cheap labour, or cheap raw materials). But there are serious logical and theoretical objections to this way of conceptualizing the relationship (see Bernstein in Part Two); and it should be seen rather in terms of processes of struggle between conflicting classes.[8]

The structural/historical approaches are necessarily historical, for to speak as we have done of 'commoditization' does not imply a process which must work itself out in a particular way and which can be known from purely theoretical reasoning. It is a process which may take many specific forms in different contexts. The approach also seeks to grasp the relationships between 'whole' and 'part' in such a way as to understand their mutual determination, and it particularly considers the relationships between agrarian society and the rest of the state of which it is a part (see the introduction to Part Five, and Raikes, in that part). The 'individual' does not disappear in these analyses, but the social character of the individual is emphasized. The approach is Marxist, but not all 'Marxist' studies are like this, and not all studies which are like this would call themselves Marxist[9]. This is the approach which is reflected most strongly in the readings in this book. It seems to be most appropriate for studies relating to rural development (both as policy and as process) because it is inherently inter-disciplinary, and because of all the approaches that we have reviewed it is the one which is most centrally concerned with issues of distribution, and with poverty.

The central debate

The concept of the peasantry

Although the structural/historical approach is strongly represented in this book its contents are wide-ranging, and different perspectives on a variety of issues are included within the readings. The Introduction to each part serves to point to these different perspectives and to the topics on which the readings give some comment, and also to indicate further reading. But there is a central debate which underlies the selection of readings and which links together the contents of the book as a whole. This is the debate between what may be broadly characterized as 'the differentiation perspective' on the one hand, and the notion of a 'specific peasant economy' on the other.[10] Before introducing the main lines of the debate, however, we should consider what is meant by 'peasant', 'peasant society' or 'peasantry', for these familiar terms have been given various definitions, and some have argued that they are actually devoid of analytical content.[11] Here peasants are considered to be rural producers who produce for their own consumption and for sale, using their own and family labour, though the hiring and selling of labour power is also quite possible and compatible with peasant society. Peasants possess a degree of independent control over the resources and the equipment that they use in production – in other words they are not quite like workers in a factory owned by somebody else. Peasant society is not homogeneous and may be marked by quite considerable inequalities. Peasants may also be described as a 'part society' defined by their subordinate relationships to external markets, the state and the dominant culture. The peasantry are subordinate to other classes within the state and may be required to yield some tribute to them.[12]

'Differentiation' or a specific peasant economy?

The debate to which we have referred is on these lines. On one side – that which we have referred to as 'the differentiation perspective' – there are those who argue that, with increasing commoditization and commercialization in agrarian societies, a process is set in motion whereby rural producers are set apart into distinct classes. This is a process of change which tends to create a small agrarian bourgeoisie or class of capitalist farmers, either from former landlords or from amongst the richer peasants, and a large class of agricultural labourers who might or might not retain small allotments of land for their own use. In between there is a 'middle peasantry' or a class of more or less self-sufficient household producers, who use mainly their own family labour and are little involved in selling their labour power, and who have sufficient resources to provide for their own livelihood requirements. This class tends to be squeezed out progressively as the process of differentiation proceeds. (The classic statement of differentiation is given in the reading from Lenin in Part Two; and it is discussed in the article by Djurfeldt in the same part).

On the other side of the debate are those who argue *not* that the development of commodity production is unimportant, but that the distinctive peasant economy, that of small producers who are not separated from their means of production and who retain a degree of control over land and family labour, survives. Most of those who take this position argue that peasants survive essentially because they are able to supply goods more cheaply than capitalist producers (see, for example, Djurfeldt in Part Two and Williams in Part Five). Taussig (in Part Two) explains how peasant producers may be more efficient users of 'capital' than large-scale farmers; while this assumption underlies one current orthodoxy of rural development policy (see Johnston and Kilby, and Lipton, in Part One). Some of the adherents of this position tend to argue as if the peasantry is homogeneous and composed of comparable household farm units; and they say that if there is 'differentiation' amongst the peasantry then this is brought about by cyclical processes so that there is no long-term, developing trend of polarization of classes. This was the position of the Russian economist A. V. Chayanov, whose work spanned the first quarter of this century and who tried most systematically to establish a theory of peasant economy (see Djurfeldt in Part Two and Shanin and Harrison in Part Three). Others, however, accept the existence of persistent inequalities in peasant society, and concede that a secular process of differentiation may take place, but still maintain that 'peasants', in the sense of household producers retaining some degree of independent control over their land and labour, may survive. This is rather the position adopted by Shanin (Part Three) and certainly by Williams (Part Five). Other writers have explained how, in spite of the development of capitalist agriculture, tendencies towards the polarization of peasant classes may be weakened, because of factors such as the break-up of large units at inheritance and the reproduction of small-scale holdings by the interventions of merchants' and moneylenders' capital – or in the more recent past of state capital.[13] The persistence of small peasant farms may serve the interests of capital very well. Vergopoulos (see the introduction to Part Two) and Bernstein (Part Two) refer to this, and Taussig gives an historical example.

The two positions that we have sketched out are not necessarily or absolutely opposed, except at their extremes, though when it comes to the practice of economic development by the state their implications for the appropriate direction of policy, and for rural household producers, are very different (compare Byres in Part One and Williams in Part Five). We offer no 'solution' to this debate, and we suggest that for analytical and for practical purposes both perspectives have a great deal to offer. It would be foolish to ignore the implications of tendencies towards different-iation amongst rural producers – not least for examining the reasons for and the effects of different kinds of interventions in the form of Rural Development programmes. Equally, to ignore the persistence of peasant producers, and not to seek out the reasons for it, would be damaging to any serious study of agrarian problems.

The contents of the book have been ordered in this way. The papers in the first section together lay out the most influential amongst current theories concerning strategies for Rural Development. They refer to strategies in the normative sense – of what *should* be done; but implicit within such normative conceptions there are positive theories concerning what is actually happening in agrarian societies undergoing processes of change. In relation to the debate which we have just discussed, Byres as an exponent of 'the differentiation perspective' stands opposed to both Johnston and Kilby, and to Lipton, who put forward ideas which are finally grounded in conceptions of peasant economy. The two sides of the debate are developed in greater depth in the next two sections and they are finally considered again in the context of state intervention in Part Five. In between, in Part Four, some specific attention is given to agricultural labour. Scott's paper, in this part, picks up the theme of the relationships between capitalism and peasants from Part Two; while White depicts the condition of the mass of the peasantry of Java, existing at the margins of the capitalist mode of production.

Notes

1 Discussions of Rural Development policies and some practical ideas concerning their implementation will be found in: Binswanger and Ruttan (eds.) (1978); Chambers (1983); Chenery *et al.* (1974); De Wilde *et al.* (1967); Hayami and Ruttan (1971);

Hunter, Bunting and Bottrall (eds.) (1976); Johnston and Kilby (1975); Lele (1975); and Mellor (1976).

2 This categorization roughly distinguishes *objects* for analysis and different *theories*. 'Systems' approaches include those concentrating on socio-technical systems, or on the social systems of agrarian communities, and which imply a form of holistic analysis. 'Decision-making' approaches focus rather on individuals and they employ techniques of micro-economic analysis and imply the theoretical perspectives of methodological individualism (on which see Alavi, 1973). 'Structural/historical' approaches share some of the attributes of 'systems' studies, but they have an historical emphasis, and, as is explained in the text, they may have a more or less explicit foundation in Marxian methodology.

3 For a useful critique of Geertz's notion of 'involution', see Aass (1980).

4 A very influential work, drawing on the results of such studies, is Schultz (1964), discussed by Lipton in his article in Part Three of this book. An important collection of articles is that edited by Wharton (1969); and for Africa a useful source is Collinson (1972). Reference may also be made to basic texts in agricultural economics: e.g. Found (1971); Upton (1973).

5 Barth (1966) is one influential source of 'decision-making approaches' in social anthropology; and Long (1977) in his introductory text on the sociology of rural development is particularly good on this theme. For extended studies in this vein see: Long (1968); Moerman (1968); Ortiz (1973). A classic study of the entrepreneurship of African farmers is Hill's study of the cocoa farmers of Ghana (1963; and see also Hill, 1970). Alavi (1973) gives a powerful critique of this approach.

6 Two classic studies of innovation adoption are by Griliches and by David (in Rosenberg, ed., 1971). On the new technology associated with the 'green revolution' see Wharton (1971).

7 Djurfeldt and Lindberg (1975) describe land-use problems in South India in this way; and Blaikie, Cameron and Seddon (1980) explain an ecological crisis in Nepal. In Africa, studies of the Sahel draw out the theme of the relationships between forms of ownership and environmental damage. See: Glantz (ed.) (1976); Meillassoux (1974).

8 The literature on 'articulation' is complex and it cannot be discussed in detail here. The 'functional' view of the relationships

between capitalism and other modes of production is implicit in some of the work of Meillassoux (e.g. 1972) and in Laclau's critique (1971) of the dependency theory advanced by Gunder Frank (which entails the view that the appearance of capitalism signals the disappearance of other modes of production). The theory of articulation as a process of class struggle has been developed especially by P–P. Rey (1973) (and see discussion in Foster-Carter, 1978). This theory of articulation has been referred to in a review of African agrarian studies by Cliffe (1976); and in a notable study of Jamaica by Post (1978). Recently Taylor (1979) has attempted to develop a theory of 'restricted and uneven development' based on a concept of articulation (see criticism by Mouzelis, 1980); while Wolpe, in his introduction to a collection of studies, provides an important review and critique of the way in which the concepts both of 'mode of production' and of 'articulation' have been used in contemporary neo-Marxist writing (Wolpe, 1980).

9 'Structural/historical' studies which would probably not be called 'Marxist' by their authors include Hill (1972; 1977) on Nigeria; Hopkins (1973) on West Africa in general; and Washbrook (1976, ch.1) and Baker (forthcoming) on South India. On Africa, in more explicitly Marxist vein, see also Bundy (1979); Heyer, Roberts and Williams (eds.) (1981); Kitching (1980); Meillassoux (ed.) (1971); Palmer and Parsons (eds.) (1977); and for a more introductory treatment, Mabogunje (1980, Part Two). On Indonesia see Kahn (1980).

10 Boesen, in a recent article (1980) suggests another categorization of agrarian studies; but we prefer this simple characterization because it seems to us best to reflect the debate that has actually influenced thinking about agrarian policy.

11 A most important critique of the concept of 'peasantry' is that by Ennew, Hirst and Tribe (1977).

12 A classic discussion of the concept of 'peasantry' is in Redfield (1956). See also papers in Shanin (ed.) (1971), and Wolf (1966). On the concept of 'peasantry' in Africa, see Bundy (1979), ch. 1.

13 For discussions on the break-up of large units, see Hill (1972) for a Nigerian case, and Attwood (1979) for a detailed study from Western India. On the interventions of merchants' and moneylenders' capital, see studies by Banaji (1977a; 1977b) and Roseberry 1978); Harriss, B. (1981) and Harriss, J. (1982) on

South India; Patnaik (1976); Sau (1976) for an overview with some specific reference to North India; Harris, R. L. (1978) for a review of Latin American studies on this issue; Cowen (in Heyer *et al.*, eds., 1981) on East Africa, and Harriss, B. (1979) for the case of the Sahel.

References

Rural development

Binswanger, H., and Ruttan, V. W. (1978), *Induced Innovation: Technology, Institutions, and Development*, Baltimore: Johns Hopkins University Press

Chambers, R. (1983), *Putting the Last First: Priorities in Rural Development*, London: Longman

Chenery, H. *et al.* (1974), *Redistribution with Growth*, New York and London: Oxford University Press

De Wilde, J. C. *et al.* (1967), *Agricultural Development in Tropical Africa*, Baltimore: Johns Hopkins University Press

Hayami, Y., and Ruttan, V. W. (1971), *Agricultural Development: An International Perspective*, Baltimore: Johns Hopkins University Press

Hunter, G., Bunting, H., and Bottrall, A. (eds.) (1976), *Policy and Practice in Rural Development*, London: Croom Helm

Johnston, B. F., and Kilby, P. (1975), *Agriculture and Structural Transformation*, New York: Oxford University Press

Lele, U. (1975), *The Design of Rural Development*, Baltimore: Johns Hopkins University Press for the World Bank

Mellor, J. (1976), *The New Economics of Growth*, Ithaca: Cornell University Press

World Bank (1975), *Rural Development: Sector Policy Paper*, Washington

'Systems' approaches

Aass, S. (1980), 'The relevance of Chayanov's macro theory to the case of Java', in E. J. Hobsbawm *et al.* (eds.), *Peasants in History: Essays in Honour of Daniel Thorner*, Calcutta, etc.: Oxford University Press for Sameeksha Trust

Allan, W. (1965), *The African Husbandman*, Westport, Conn.: Greenwood Press

Biggs, S. D., and Burns, C. (1976), 'Transactions modes and the distribution of farm output', in J. L. Joy and E. Everitt (eds.), *The Kosi Symposium: The Rural Problem in North-East Bihar*, Brighton: Institute of Development studies

Biggs, S. D., Chong Kwong Yuan, and Langham, Max R. (1977), *Agricultural Sector Analysis*, ADC Teaching and Research Forum no. 11, September, New York and Singapore: Agricultural Development Council Inc.

Boserup, E. (1965), *The Conditions of Agricultural Growth*, London: Allen & Unwin

Chambers, R., and Harriss, J. (1977), 'Comparing twelve South Indian villages: in search of practical theory', in B. H. Farmer (ed.), *Green Revolution?*, London: Macmillan

Elvin, M. (1973), *The Pattern of the Chinese Past*, London: Eyre Methuen

Epstein, T. S. (1962), *Economic Development and Social Change in South India*, Manchester: Manchester University Press

Farmer, B. H. (1957), *Pioneer Peasant Colonisation in Ceylon*, London: Oxford University Press for the Royal Institution of International Affairs.

Foster, G. M. (1965), 'Peasant society and the image of limited good', *American Anthropologist*, 67, 2, pp.293–315

Geertz, C. (1963), *Agricultural Involution*, Berkeley: University of California Press

Kjekshus, H. (1977), *Ecology Control and Economic Development in East African History: The Case of Tanganyika 1850–1950*, London: Heinemann

Prothero, R. M. (1972), *People and Land in Africa South of the Sahara*, New York and London: Oxford University Press

Ruthenberg, H. (1980), *Farming Systems in the Tropics* (3rd edn.), London: Oxford University Press

'Decision-making models'

Alavi, H. (1973), 'Peasant classes and primordial loyalties', *Journal of Peasant Studies*, 1, 1, pp.22–62

Apthorpe, R. (1977), 'A comment on Andrew Pearse's review of Global–2', *Development and Change*, 8, pp.370–3

Barth, F. (1966), *Models of Social Organisation*, London: Royal Anthropological Institute, Occasional paper 23

Berry, S. (1975), *Cocoa, Custom and Socio-Economic Change in*

Rural Western Nigeria, London; Oxford University Press

Collinson, M. P. (1972), *Farm Management in Peasant Agriculture: A Handbook for Rural Development Planning in Africa,* London: Praeger

David, P. (1971), 'The mechanisation of reaping in the ante-bellum West', in N. Rosenberg (ed.) *The Economics of Technological Change,* Harmondsworth: Penguin

Found, W. C. (1971), *A Theoretical Approach to Rural Land Use Patterns,* London: Edward Arnold

Griliches, Z. (1971), 'Hybrid corn and the economics of innovation', in N. Rosenberg (ed.), *The Economics of Technological Change,* Harmondsworth: Penguin

Hill, P. (1963), *Migrant Cocoa Farmers of Southern Ghana,* London: Cambridge University Press

Hill, P. (1970), *Studies In Rural Capitalism,* London: Cambridge University Press

Long, N. (1968), *Social Change and the Individual,* Manchester: Manchester University Press

Long, N. (1977), *An Introduction to the Sociology of Rural Development,* London: Tavistock

Moerman, M. (1968), *Agricultural Change and Peasant Choice in a Thai Village,* Berkeley: University of California Press

Ortiz, S. (1973), *Uncertainty in Peasant Farming,* London: Athlone Press

Schultz, T. W. (1964), *Transforming Traditional Agriculture,* New Haven, Conn.: Yale University Press

Upton, M. (1973), *Farm Management in Africa,* London: Oxford University Press

Wharton, C. R. (ed.) (1969), *Subsistence Agriculture and Economic Development,* London: Frank Cass

Wharton, C. R. (1971), 'Risk, uncertainty and the subsistence farmer', in G. Dalton (ed.), *Economic Development and Social Change,* New York: American Museum of Natural History

'Structural/historical' approaches

Baker, C. J. (forthcoming), *The Tamilnad Countryside,* London: Oxford University Press

Blaikie, P., Cameron, J., and Seddon, D. (1980), *Nepal in Crisis: Growth and Stagnation at the Periphery,* London: Oxford University Press

Bundy, C. (1979), *The Rise and Fall of the South African Peasantry*, London: Heinemann

Cliffe, L. (1976), 'Rural political economy of Africa', in P. Gutkind and I. Wallerstein (eds.), *The Political Economy of Contemporary Africa*, Beverley Hills and London: Sage Publications

Djurfeldt, G., and Lindberg, S. (1975), *Behind Poverty: The Social Formation in a Tamil Village*, Scandinavian Institute of Asian Studies Monograph Series, no.23, London: Curzon Press

Foster-Carter, A. (1978), 'The modes of production controversy', *New Left Review*, 107, pp.47–77

Glantz, M. N. (ed.) (1976), *The Politics of Natural Disaster: Sahel Drought*, London: Praeger

Heyer, J., Roberts, P. and Williams, G. (eds.) (1981), *Rural Development in Tropical Africa*, London: Macmillan

Hill, P. (1972), *Rural Hausa: A Village and a Setting*, London: Cambridge University Press

Hill, P. (1977), *Population, Prosperity and Poverty in Rural Kano, 1900 and 1970*, London: Cambridge University Press

Hopkins, A. G. (1973), *An Economic History of West Africa*. London: Longman

Kahn, J. (1980), *Minangkebau Social Formations: Indonesian Peasants and the World Economy*, London: Cambridge University Press

Kitching, G. (1980), *Class and Economic Change in Kenya: The Making of an African Petite Bourgeoisie 1905–1970*, New Haven, Conn. and London; Yale University Press

Klein, M. A. (ed.) (1980), *Peasants in Africa: Historical and Contemporary Perspectives*, Beverly Hills and London: Sage Publications

Laclau, E. (1971), 'Feudalism and capitalism in Latin America', *New Left Review*, no. 67; reprinted in E. Laclau, *Politics and Ideology in Marxist Theory*, London: New Left Books, 1977

Mabogunje, A. L. (1980), *The Development Process: A Spatial Perspective*, London: Hutchinson

Meillassoux, C. (ed.) (1971), *The Development of Indigenous Trade and Markets in West Africa*, London: Oxford University Press

Meillassoux, C. (1972), 'From reproduction to production: A Marxist approach to economic anthropology', *Economy and Society*, 1, 1, pp.93–105

Meillassoux, C. (1974), 'Development or exploitation: is the Sahel famine good business?', *Review of African Political Economy*, 1, pp.27–33

Mouzelis, N. (1980), 'Modernisation, underdevelopment, uneven development: prospects for a theory of Third-World formations', *Journal of Peasant Studies* 7, 3, pp.353–74

Palmer, R., and Parsons, N. (eds.) (1977) *The Roots of Rural Poverty in Central And Southern Africa*, London: Heinemann

Post, K. (1978), *Arise Ye Starvelings! The Jamaica Labour Rebellion of 1938 and its Aftermath*, The Hague, Boston and London: Martinus Nijhoff

Rey, P-P. (1973), *Les alliances de classes*, Paris: Maspero

Taylor, J. G. (1979), *From Modernisation to Modes of Production: A Critique of the Sociologies of Development and Underdevelopment*, London: Macmillan

Washbrook, D. A. (1976), *The Emergence of Provincial Politics: The Madras Presidency 1880–1920* (ch.1: 'The political economy of Madras'), London: Cambridge University Press

Wolpe, H. (ed.) (1980), *The Articulation of Modes of Production*, London: Routledge & Kegan Paul

The debate about the peasantry

Attwood, D. (1979), 'Why some of the rich get poorer', *Current Anthropology* 20, 3, pp.495–516

Banaji, J. (1977a), 'Capitalist domination and the small peasantry: Deccan districts in the late nineteenth century', *Economic and Political Weekly*, special number, August 1977, pp.1375–1404

Banaji, J. (1977b), 'Modes of production in a materialist conception of history', *Capital and Class* 7, 3, pp.1–44

Boesen, J. (1980), 'On peasantry and the "modes of production" debate', *Review of African Political Economy*, 15-16, pp.154–61

Deere, C. D., and de Janvry, A. (1979), 'A conceptual framework for empirical analysis of peasants', *American Journal of Agricultural Economics*, 61, 4, pp.601–11

Ennew, J., Hirst, P., and Tribe, K. (1977), ' "Peasantry" as an economic category', *Journal of Peasant Studies*, 4, 4, pp.295–322

Friedman, H. (1980), 'Household production and the national economy: concepts for the analysis of agrarian formations', *Journal of Peasant Studies*, 7, 2, pp.158–84

Harriss, B. (1979), 'Going against the grain', *Development and Change* 10, 3, pp.363–84

Harriss, B. (1981), *Transitional Trade and Rural Development: The Nature and Role of Agricultural Trade in a South Indian District*, New Delhi: Vikas

Harriss, J. (1982), *Capitalism and Peasant Farming: Agrarian Structure and Ideology in northern Tamil Nadu*, Bombay: Oxford University Press

Harris, R. L. (1978), 'Marxism and the agrarian question in Latin America', *Latin American Perspectives*, Issue 19, V, 4, pp.2–26

Latin American Perspectives (1978), Issues 18 and 19, V, 3 and 4, *Peasants, Capital Accumulation and Rural Underdevelopment*

Patnaik, U. (1976), 'Class differentiation within the peasantry: an approach to the analysis of Indian agriculture', *Economic and Political Weekly*, Review of Agriculture, September 1976, pp. A82–A101

Redfield, R. (1956), *Peasant Society and Culture*, Chicago: Chicago University Press

Review of African Political Economy (1981), special issue on 'The peasant question in Kenya

Roseberry, W. (1978), 'Peasants as proletarians', *Critique of Anthropology*, 11, pp.3–18

Sau, R. (1976), 'Can capitalism develop in Indian agriculture?', *Economic and Political Weekly*, Review of Agriculture, December 1976, pp. A126–A136

Shanin, T., (ed.) (1971), *Peasants and Peasant Society*, Harmondsworth: Penguin

Part One

Analyses of agrarian change and rural development 'strategies'

Introduction

Three paths of agrarian change

It is generally considered that there are three main ways whereby predominantly agrarian societies are, or may be, transformed, so that they become *less* exclusively agricultural, their agricultural systems become more productive and their peoples generally better off. They may be transformed by the development of capitalist farming, probably involving the establishment of relatively large-scale units of production (though possibly also involving the break-up of older 'feudal' estates) and absorbing most of the peasant sector.[1] Alternatively transformation may take place through the establishment under state initiative of large-scale co-operative, collective or state farms. Thirdly, although some theorists recognize only the first two alternatives, others clearly distinguish the possibility that transformation may come about on the basis of capital-intensive, small-scale farming. Some of the exponents of this third alternative refer to the cases of Japan and Taiwan as models, and they refer to evidence for the 'efficiency' of small farms.[2]

These three 'paths' are both descriptions of the actual processes of transformation in different countries, and they may also be elaborated into normative theories of how societies may be changed. For a long time the principal axis of debate has really been between those who have argued for the necessity of the development of large-scale units of production – and advocacy of this line has united both some Marxists and some liberal economists[3] – and on the other side those who have argued that transformation can be based on small-scale peasant family farms, and who are often labelled as 'populists' or 'neo-populists'. The use of this label in itself derives from the controversy which took place in Russia around the turn of this century, between the 'neo-narodnik' or 'neo-populist' champions of the efficiency of peasant family labour farms, and their Bolshevik critics who believed both that the differentiation of such producers into distinct classes was a reality in the Russian countryside, and that it was a necessary development for the transformation of the economy. This debate is referred to in the article by Shanin in Part Three while Lenin's book *The Development of Capitalism in Russia*, from which the reading in Part Two has been taken, was partly written in order to refute the neo-populist argument. The work of the leading Russian neo-populist economist, A. V. Chayanov, is discussed by Djurfeldt in Part Two and by Harrison in Part Three.[4]

Contemporary 'populism'

The lines of the contemporary debate about rural development in the Third World do not follow exactly the same contours. The prevailing ideology amongst development theorists and planners is that 'Rural Development' based generally on fairly small family farms, should be the main objective of development programmes. There are rather few of them at present who positively advocate a strategy of developing relatively large-scale farms, though this was an argument proposed, for example, by economists at the Punjab Agricultural University in India in the 1960s, and it still has some advocates (e.g. Sinha, 1973). Indeed in South Asia in early 1980 it seemed possible that this approach was finding fresh support, as doubts grow about the success of the small farm strategy and the effectiveness of the poverty-focused approach to development planning.

It is recognized, in any case, that no matter what might be desirable, and no matter what might be the rhetoric or the stated aims of governments and development agencies, in many countries and regions the *actual* path of change has been towards an agriculture in which the bigger farms (though not necessarily large estates) have become more prominent and have cornered the lion's share of the resources made available for development.[5] In other words what has actually been happening has been more like the first path of transformation referred to earlier. It is what Johnston and Kilby, in the first reading in this part, refer to as a 'bimodal' strategy of agrarian change where there is a dualistic size structure of farm units, and in which resources are concentrated on a small, highly commercialized sub-sector of the agrarian economy with large farms (including large-scale plantations, mixed farms, and others).

Johnston and Kilby's argument is that in the circumstances of most developing countries such a 'bimodal' strategy is likely to be less effective as a means of achieving the goals of development than a 'unimodal' approach based on the mass of relatively small farms, and requiring a divisible, improved technology (that is, an improved technology which can be divided into 'packages' of a size suitable for use on small farm units). A most important point of theirs is that with such a strategy the growth of output is not incompatible with redistribution of assets. This theme also appears in *Redistribution with Growth* (Chenery *et al.*, 1974) – the book which perhaps more than any other explains and substantiates current orthodoxies of development planning. Finally, however, the authors of *Redistribution with Growth* remain ambiguous on whether redistribution must *precede* growth.

Johnston and Kilby's may be seen as one version of the contemporary 'populist' position, but they show a lively awareness of the importance of the linkages between agriculture and non-agricultural sectors of the economy.[6] An important reason for their advocacy of the 'unimodal' strategy is that they believe that in this way stronger mutual stimuli will be set up between agriculture and non-agriculture and that the overall structural transformation of the economy (on lines like those outlined at the beginning of this introduction) will be stimulated. This reading from Johnston and Kilby's book also includes a summary of conventional discussions of the role of agriculture in economic development; and it critically reviews the concept of 'surplus labour' which played a prominent part in earlier models of economic growth.

Contemporary 'populism' and urban bias

Michael Lipton is another contemporary 'populist' who strongly believes that transformation should be based on the relatively efficient small family farms, and that such a strategy for development represents an optimal use of the poor countries' most abundant resources. Like Johnston and Kilby he is well aware that this is not what is actually happening in most developing countries, but whereas they comment only briefly on the reasons for the frequent dominance of the 'bimodal' strategy, Lipton seeks to explain it – and the persistence of poverty in spite of substantial economic growth in most developing countries – in terms of a concept of 'urban bias'.[7] This concept is outlined in the second reading in this part. 'Urban bias', it appears, is more of a master metaphor than a well-substantiated theory, though Lipton's claims for it are very wide-ranging. In essence the notion of 'urban bias' suggests that the principal class conflict in the developing countries is between all urban people on one side and all rural people on the other; and that the power of the former is generally such as to divert the major share of available resources to themselves.[8] This 'urban class' has co-opted the small élite of richer farmers as allies in order to ensure cheap supplies of food and raw materials, which explains the persistence of agricultural regimes that might be described as 'bimodal' (Corbridge, in the last reading in the part, comments on this model of class conflict in Lipton's writing). The net effects of such an 'urban bias' in the allocation of resources are not only inequitable but also inefficient – for according to Lipton, capital used in agriculture shows higher returns (as measured technically by sectoral capital/output ratios) than that used in non-agriculture. In spite of this very rarely has more than 20 per cent of public funds for development gone to agriculture. Within the agricultural sector the small family farms are most efficient, primarily because of the intensive use of labour upon them; but again, assistance has flowed mainly to the larger farmers allied to the 'urban class'. Lipton's prescriptions for agricultural and rural development are quite similar to those of Johnston and Kilby.

'Populism' and land reform

The belief that small farms are most 'efficient' (see Bharadwaj in Part Three for a critical discussion of this view) is a powerful argument in favour of land reforms which progressively redistribute land from holdings above a certain 'ceiling' to those which are below the minimum efficient farm size (see Lipton, 1974). Such reforms are often felt to be a *sine qua non* for rural development, and in many parts of the world (especially in Latin America and large parts of Asia) without such redistributive land reforms it is doubtful whether the contemporary 'populist' strategy for rural development can possibly be effective (though this objection tends to be underestimated – for example by Johnston and Kilby). Much has been written about the political feasibility of such reforms, but the fact remains that examples of successful reforms are few and far between.[9] The examples of Japan and Taiwan are sometimes put forward as instances of countries in which successful land reforms have been carried out, but it is forgotten that in both cases the reforms were carried out by an occupying power.[10]

Criticisms of the current orthodoxy of Rural Development (1)

Doubts as to the real viability of the small family farm based approach to rural transformation, as it has been advocated by development agencies, are not confined to concern about the feasibility of distributive land reforms. Some critics argue that the rhetoric of this strategy ill conceals its real effects, which are to subordinate peasant production to capital and to the state. Such critics argue that 'It is of the nature of rural development itself, that is of the intervention of public agencies in peasant production, that it should tend to distribute resources to the better off, and subject peasant producers to state control and to agro-capital' (Williams, 1981).[11] Principally what is argued is that in practice the small family farm approach intensifies the dependence of small producers upon markets and that in the process many of them become 'compulsively involved' in the market. This is a term of Bharadwaj's and it is explained in the reading in Part Three, while Bernstein further explains the implications of the process referred to in his remarks on 'the simple reproduction squeeze' in the reading in Part Two. Here Bernstein refers to the fact that household producers, because they are concerned with producing for their own livelihoods and for the reproduction of their means of producing their livelihoods (that is, with 'the needs of simple reproduction'), and not with obtaining 'profits', may go on producing in circumstances in which capitalist firms would go out of business for lack of adequate returns to investment (see Saith and Tankha, 1972, for an exposition of this point). When household producers face a decline in the prices of commodities that they produce in relation to those that they require, they may react by producing *more* at the lower price. Similarly, in order to secure a plot of land to meet their subsistence needs they may pay higher than average rents; or they may have to sell their food crop 'after harvest in order to meet immediate cash needs, subsequently having to buy food at higher prices (etc.)'. These are instances of 'compulsive involvement' in markets – and as Bernstein says, it may act 'as one of the mechanisms of intensifying the labour of the household to maintain or increase the supply of commodities without capital incurring any costs of management and supervision of the production process'. This kind of 'squeeze' of peasant household producers may be set in motion by programmes of 'Rural Development'.

Criticisms 2: the imperative of industrialization

A distinct line of criticism of the current orthodoxy of rural development is put forward by Byres in our third reading in this part. Byres rejects contemporary 'populism' not only as sham (he actually describes it as 'pipe-dreams') but because he finds that the whole reasoning on which it is based is opposed to the establishment of industrialization, which is 'the route-way from backwardness'. As he explains in the reading in this part, he believes that 'development' requires the urban bourgeoisie to have undisputed hegemony in society in order fully to develop the productive forces of industry. He argues that the existence of 'urban bias' in development policy and implementation is, however, extremely difficult to sustain empirically; and he believes that Lipton's alternative, 'rural bias', is both a closer approximation to the state of affairs in many countries, and that it is wrong in principle.[12] To an extent Byres has defined his position in opposition to Lipton's, and as he has recently explained it (Byres, 1979, pp. 221–2) a central issue (perhaps *the* central issue) concerns the long-run as opposed to the short-run implications of different investment strategies. Byres's argument is that while it may be true (as Lipton maintains) that resources invested in agriculture *now* will yield a better rate of return than investments outside agriculture, this is to take only a short-run view. Such investments will frequently have less effect on the long-run prospects for growth in an economy as a whole, than those in capital goods industries:

'The one form of investment has a once-for-all effect, the other a continuing effect on the level of income and consumption. This crucial difference is obscured by theories which treat investment simply in terms of the foregoing of present consumption in return for a future increase in consumption: here investment is always treated as though it was a direct investment in consumption goods industries. Moreover, notions of the marginal productivity of capital or of investment (so far as I am aware) are always expressed in terms of a once-for-all effect on the income-stream, and do not include the specific multiplier influence on future income-levels of investment in capital goods industries' (Dobb, 1955, pp. 150–1). Dobb could well have been writing of Lipton's treatment of sectoral capital-output ratios and their implications. Lipton does not come to terms at all with the kind of reasoning developed by Dobb (Byres. 1979, p. 222).

Equally, it is perhaps a moot point as to whether Byres, or Dobb, takes sufficiently into account the opportunity cost of tying up resources *now*.[13] Further, Byres's faith in industrialization as 'the route-way from backwardness' seems to ignore the substantial evidence which suggests that contemporary industrialization in Third World countries, in circumstances of dependency upon advanced capitalist economies, is by its very nature unlikely to create employment.[14]

Given his belief in the progressive and dynamic character of industrialization, however, the central question for Byres in the analysis of the transformation of agrarian economies is that of the extent and nature of the development of capitalism in agriculture. The third reading in this part is a discussion of this process in the context of contemporary Egypt.

The final reading here is a critique of both Byres and Lipton by Stuart Corbridge. Unlike other critics of the 'urban bias' thesis Corbridge attacks the internal consistency of Lipton's arguments. He shows that the possibility of the existence of 'urban' and 'rural' classes has to be rejected, and that with this 'urban bias' collapses. He proceeds to show how unconsidered are Byres's assertions concerning industrialization. Byres does not actually argue the case, nor specify the type of industrialization, so that 'at face value Byres's thesis reduces to the stark assertion that industrialization is a "good thing" '. Further, there is an implicit equation of socialist construction with industrialization in Byres's work: 'the transition to socialism [is to be] bullied along by the progressive development of the forces of production (especially heavy industry)'. This economistic view is highly questionable.[15] Finally, Corbridge argues that Byres and Lipton do not represent 'the two ends of the spectrum of development thinking', as sometimes seems to have been supposed; and 'The collapse of the concept of urban class bias does not guarantee the validity of rural class bias any more than the failure of Byres's industrialization teleology justifies a unitary and necessary path of development led by agriculture.' Corbridge's observations on the construction of socialism are followed up with specific relation to the development of agriculture in a socialist economy, by Djurfeldt in Part Two, and by Williams and Harrison in Part Five.[16]

Notes

1 The idea that the development of agriculture in a capitalist economy implies concentration of land into relatively large-scale holdings probably owes a good deal to understandings of the historical experience of England. The distinctive nature of that experience is not generally appreciated.

2 For a more detailed exposition of paths of agrarian change on similar lines see Griffin (1973). On the Japanese model Johnston and Kilby (1975) are useful; on Taiwan see Ranis (1978). See also other references listed under 'Rural development' in the notes following the general introduction to this book.

3 For discussion of the convergences between liberal and Marxist theorists over the concept of and requirements for 'development', see Williams (1978) and Philipps (1977).

4 On the Russian Debate referred to here, Shanin's book *The Awkward Class* (1972), from which an excerpt appears in Part Three, will be found useful; but reference should also be made to criticisms by Littlejohn (1973) and by Cox (1979). Chayanov's *Theory of Peasant Economy* was published in translation in 1966; and it has been subjected to a number of important critical discussions: see Harrison (1975, 1977); Littlejohn (1977); and Ennew, Hirst and Tribe (1977). On the peasantry and the policy debates of the 1920s in the Soviet Union, see also Erlich (1960) and Lewin (1968).

5 On this point see: Feder (1976); Griffin (1974, 1980); Pearse (1980).

6 On the linkages between agriculture and non-agriculture see also Mellor (1976).

7 Lipton first put forward the idea of 'urban bias' in a study of agricultural development policy in India (1968). It is developed more fully in a book (1977), and in the context of an important paper on agrarian reform (1974).

8 The idea of 'urban bias' and of such a class conflict found expression in the proposals made by Charan Singh for the development of the Indian economy in the period of the Janata government (1977–9).

9 Outstanding studies of land reform are those by Warriner (1969) and by the contributors to the volume edited by Lehmann (1974). Bell's paper in that book considers the political feasibility of redistributive land reform. See also Herring (forthcoming).

10 On land reform in Japan see Dore (1959); and on Taiwan see

Apthorpe (1979). On the political importance of land reform in the context of US foreign policy, as a means for containing communism, the papers of the US expert Wolf Ladejinsky (1977) give a fund of insights.
11 For critical studies in this vein see: Feder (1976); articles in the *Review of African Political Economy*, no. 10, 1977; Heyer, Roberts and Williams (eds.) (1981); George (1976); Lappe and Collins (1977, 1979); and Bennholdt-Thomsen (1980). See also Mabogunje (1980), ch. 5.
12 Byres's ideas are explained in several papers (1972, 1974), as well as in the article included here and in his long critique of Lipton's book on 'urban bias' (1979). In further connection with the 'urban bias' thesis, an important issue in the debate concerns the terms of trade between agriculture and non-agriculture, and these have been discussed in relation to India in a most stimulating way by Ashok Mitra (1977). Mitra's conclusions rather support Byres's view that public policy has frequently been marked by 'rural bias' rather than by 'urban bias'. Byres discusses marketable surplus and economic development (1974); on this see also Nadkarni (1979).
13 Byres certainly does not deal here with alternative arguments such as those of Mao Tse-tung in his 'On the ten great relationships' (1956) – discussed by Gray (1972).
14 On industrialization in the Third World, see Kay (1975); Obregon (1980); Santos (1979); and Mabogunje (1980), Part III.
15 For a major critique of economism and of its implications for the construction of socialism, see Corrigan, Ramsay and Sayer (1978).
16 It is unfortunate that constraints of space have not allowed the inclusion of more material on socialist agriculture in this book. For an introduction on the Soviet Union see Nove (1969, ch. 5 especially); and on China see articles by Gray (1969, 1971, 1972), and the edition of *World Development* edited by Unger (1978). Nolan has drawn some comparisons between China and the Soviet Union (1976).

References

Paths of agrarian change

Chenery, H., *et al.* (1974), *Redistribution with Growth*, New York and London: Oxford University Press

Feder, E. (1976), 'McNamara's little green revolution: World Bank scheme for self-liquidation of Third World peasantry', *Economic and Political Weekly*, 3 April 1976, pp. 532–41

Griffin, K. (1973), 'Policy options for rural development', *Oxford Bulletion of Economics and Statistics*, 35, 4, pp. 239–74

Griffin, K. (1974), *The Political Economy of Agrarian Change*, London: Macmillan (2nd edn published 1980)

Johnston, B. F. and Kilby, P. (1975), *Agriculture and Structural Transformation*, New York: Oxford University Press

Lipton, M. (1968), 'Strategy for agriculture: urban bias and rural planning', in P. Streeten, and M. Lipton (eds.), *The Crisis of Indian Planning*, London: Oxford University Press

Lipton, M. (1974), 'Towards a theory of land reform', in D. Lehmann (ed.), *Agrarian Reform and Agrarian Reformism*, London: Faber

Lipton, M. (1977), *Why Poor People Stay Poor: Urban Bias in World Development*, London: Temple Smith

Mellor, J. (1976), *The New Economics of Growth*, Ithaca: Cornell University Press

Pearse, A. (1977), 'Technology and peasant production: reflections on a global study', *Development and Change*, 8, 2, pp. 125–59

Pearse, A. (1980), *Seeds of Plenty; Seeds of Want: A Critical Analysis of the Green Revolution*, London: Oxford University Press

Philipps, A. (1977), 'The concept of "development"', *Review of African Political Economy*, no. 8, pp. 7–20

Ranis, G. (1978), 'Equity and growth in Taiwan: how "special" is the "special case"?', *World Development*, 6, 3, pp. 397–409

Sinha, J. N. (1973), 'Agrarian reforms and employment in densely populated agrarian economies: a dissenting view', *International Labour Review*, 108, 5, pp. 395–421

Williams, G. (1978), 'Imperialism and development: a critique', *World Development*, 6, pp. 925–36

The Russian debates

Chayanov, A. V. (1966), *The Theory of Peasant Economy*, Homewood, Ill.: Richard D. Irwin

Cox, T. (1979), 'Awkward class or awkward classes? Class relations in the Russian peasantry before collectivisation', *Journal of Peasant Studies*, 7, 1, pp. 70–85

Ennew, J., Hirst, P., and Tribe, K. (1977), ' "Peasantry" as an

economic category', *Journal of Peasant Studies*, 4, 4, pp. 295–322
Erlich, A. (1960), *The Soviet Industrialisation Debate 1924–1928*, Cambridge, Mass.: Harvard University Press
Harrison, M. (1975), 'Chayanov and the economics of the Russian peasantry', *Journal of Peasant Studies*, 2, 4, pp. 389–417
Harrison, M. (1977), 'Resource allocation and agrarian class formation', *Journal of Peasant Studies*, 4, 2, pp. 127–61
Lewin, M. (1968), *Russian Peasants and Soviet Power: A Study of Collectivisation*, London: Allen & Unwin
Littlejohn, G. (1973), 'The peasantry and the Russian revolution', *Economy and Society*, 2, 1, pp. 112–25
Littlejohn, G. (1977), 'Chayanov and the theory of peasant economy', in B. Hindess (ed.), *Sociological Theories of the Economy*, London: Macmillan
Shanin, T. (1972), *The Awkward Class*, London: Oxford University Press
Solomon, S. G. (1977), *The Soviet Agrarian Debate: A Controversy in Social Science, 1923–29*, Boulder, Colorado: Westview Press

Land reform

Apthorpe, R. (1979), 'The burden of land reform in Taiwan: an Asian model land reform re-analysed, *World Development*, 7, 4/5, pp. 519–30
Dore, R. (1959), *Land Reform in Japan*, London: Oxford University Press
Herring, R. (forthcoming), *Land to the Tiller: Agrarian Reform in South Asia*, New Haven, Conn.: Yale University Press
Ladejinsky, W. (1977), *Agrarian Reform as Unfinished Business*, New York: World Bank
Lehmann, D. (ed.) (1974), *Agrarian Reform and Agrarian Reformism*, London: Faber
Stavenhagen, R. (1970), *Agrarian Problems and Peasant Movements in Latin America*, New York: Doubleday
Warriner, D. (1969), *Land Reform in Principle and in Practice*, London: Oxford University Press

Critics of 'Rural Development'

Bennholdt-Thomsen, V. (1980), 'Investment on the poor: analysis of World Bank policy', *Social Scientist*, 8, 7 and 8, (91 and 92), pp. 3–20, 32–51

Feder, E. (1976), 'McNamara's little green revolution: World Bank scheme for self-liquidation of Third World peasantry', *Economic and Political Weekly*, 3 April 1976, pp. 532–41

George, S. (1976), *How the Other Half Dies: The Real Reasons for World Hunger*, Harmondsworth: Penguin

Heyer, J., Roberts, P., and Williams, G. (1981), *Rural Development in Tropical Africa*, London: Macmillan

Kay, G. (1975), *Development and Underdevelopment: A Marxist Analysis*, London: Macmillan

Lappé, F., and Collins, J. (1977), *Food First*, Boston: Houghton Mifflin

Lappé, F., and Collins, J. (1979), 'Whom does the World Bank serve?' *Economic and Political Weekly*, XIV, 19, pp. 853–6

Mabogunje, A. L. (1980), *The Development Process: A Spatial Perspective*, London: Hutchinson

Review of African Political Economy (1977), 10

Saith, A., and Tankha, A. (1972), 'Economic decision making of the poor peasant household', *Economic and Political Weekly*, annual number, February 1972

Williams, G. (1981), 'The World Bank and the peasant problem', in Heyer *et al.* (eds.), *Rural Development in Tropical Africa*, London: Macmillan

Critics of Rural Development: towards a socialist agriculture

Byres, T. J. (1972), 'Industrialisation, the peasantry and the economic debate in post-independence India', in A. V. Bhuleskar (ed.), *Towards a Socialist Transformation of the Indian Economy*, Bombay: Popular Prakashan

Byres, T. J. (1974), 'Land reform, industrialisation and the marketed surplus in India: an essay on the power of urban bias', in D. Lehmann (ed.), *Agrarian Reform and Agrarian Reformism*, London: Faber

Byres, T. J. (1979), 'Of neo-populist pipe dreams: Daedalus in the Third World and the myth of urban bias', *Journal of Peasant Studies*, 6, 2, pp. 210–44

Corrigan, P., Ramsay, H., and Sayer, D. (1978), *Socialist Construction and Marxist Theory: Bolshevism and its Critique*, London: Macmillan

Dobb, M. (1955), *On Economic Theory and Socialism*, London: Routledge & Kegan Paul

Gray, J. (1969), 'The Economics of Maoism', in H. Bernstein (ed.), *Development and Underdevelopment*, Harmondsworth: Penguin, 1972

Gray, J. (1971), 'The Chinese model', in A. Nove and D. Nutti (eds.), *Socialist Economics*, Harmondsworth: Penguin, 1972

Gray, J. (1972), 'Mao Tse-tung's strategy for the collectivisation of Chinese agriculture', in E. de Kadt and G. Williams (eds.), *Sociology and Development*, London: Tavistock, 1974

Hinton, W. (1966), *Fanshen: A Documentary of Revolution in a Chinese Village*, New York: Monthly Review Press; Harmondsworth: Penguin, 1972

Lewin, M. (1966), *Russian Peasants and Soviet Power: A Study of Collectivisation*, London: Allen & Unwin, 1968

Mitra, A. (1977), *Terms of Trade and Class Relations*, London: Frank Cass

Nadkarni, M. V. (1979), 'Marketable surplus, market dependence and economic development', *Social Scientist*, 83, pp. 35–50

Nolan, P. (1976), 'Collectivisation in China: some comparisons with the USSR', *Journal of Peasant Studies*, 3, 2, pp. 192–220

Nove, A. (1969), *An Economic History of the USSR*, Harmondsworth: Penguin

Obregon, A. Q. (1980), 'The marginal pole of the economy and the marginalised Labour Force', in H. Wolpe (ed.), *The Articulation of Modes of Production*, London: Routledge & Kegan Paul

Santos, M. (1979), *The Shared Space: The Two Circuits of the Urban Economy in Underdeveloped Countries*. London: Methuen

Unger, J. (1978), 'Chinese rural institutions and the question of transferability', *World Development*, 6, 5, special issue

1 'Unimodal' and 'bimodal' strategies of agrarian change*

B. F. Johnston and P. Kilby

Introduction

Because of their structural and demographic characteristics, late-developing countries face a fundamental choice between a strategy aimed at the progressive modernization of the entire agricultural sector and a crash modernization strategy that concentrates resources in a highly commercialized subsector. We refer to the first alternative, well illustrated by the patterns of agricultural development in Japan and Taiwan, as a 'unimodal strategy'. The second alternative, which results in a development pattern based on a dualistic size structure of farm units, as in Mexico or Colombia, is labelled a 'bimodal strategy'.

We will be arguing that a unimodal strategy has significant advantages because it is consistent with maximum mobilization of a late-developing country's resources of labour and land. Because the non-agricultural sectors are so small in relation to the number of farm households, agriculture is subject to severe demand constraints. The resulting purchasing power constraint limits the extent to which expansion of the agricultural sectors' output can be based on increased use of purchased inputs, whether imported or manufactured domestically. These considerations underscore the importance of the dynamic forces that determine the rate and character of technical change, especially the process of generating a sequence of divisible innovations that leads to widespread increases in the productivity of land and labour. The success of individual farm units in allocating resources so as to minimize costs is clearly an essential ingredient of an efficient agricultural strategy. It is, however, the nature of technical innovations and their diffusion among farmers that are decisive in minimizing the cost of the sector-wide expansion of farm output and in determining the pattern of development. It will be suggested that the patterns

*This chapter is an extract from Johnston and Kilby (1975), ch 4.

of agricultural development associated with the unimodal and bimodal alternatives differ a great deal in the contributions that they make to achieving three major objectives of an agricultural strategy: advancing structural transformation (see p. 37), raising the welfare of the farm population, and fostering changes in rural attitudes and behaviour that will have beneficial effects on the process of modernization.

Although the concept of 'strategy' has become fashionable in development economics, few attempts have been made to define it. A useful general definition is that a strategy is a mix of policies and programmes that influences the pattern as well as the rate of growth. Particular attention is given here to the differential effects of the patterns of agricultural development associated with a unimodal as contrasted with a bimodal strategy. Any strategy for agricultural development will embrace some combination of (a) programmes of institution building related to such activities as agricultural research and rural education and farmer training, (b) programmes of investment in infrastructure, including irrigation and drainage facilities and rural roads, (c) programmes to improve product marketing and the distribution of inputs, and (d) policies related to prices, taxation, and land tenure. Its 'efficiency' will depend in part on promoting optimal use of available resources, and still more on modifying existing constraints.

In brief, the emphasis is on action to change the production possibilities available to farmers by modifying their institutional, technical, and economic environment. An underlying premise is that decentralized decision-making by individual producers has especially significant advantages in agriculture. The price mechanism performs a critical function in harmonizing decentralized decisions and in harnessing the powerful motive of profit. Although the role of market mechanisms in resource allocation is emphasized, we also stress the interactions between the activities of individual producers and government programmes and policies. Of special significance is the role of government in undertaking research and farmer-training programmes to favourably alter input-output relations while public investments in infrastructure enlarge the scope for applying profitable innovations. In addition, governments may find it desirable to adopt policies to make prices reflect more adequately the social costs and benefits of using resources in different types of productive activities.

Our stress on strategy differs sharply from the conventional approach of agricultural planning which has emphasized the setting of production targets for individual commodities. We would emphasize that a fundamental requirement of a suitable analytical approach to the design of an agricultural strategy is simultaneous consideration of the *objectives* to be furthered and the *means* (policies and programmes) by which those objectives are to be attained. It is also essential for the choice of objectives and of means to be guided by explicit recognition of certain *constraints* that can only be gradually eliminated, especially those imposed by the structural and demographic situation in a late-developing country. The critical factors limiting agricultural development and the pace of structural transformation are technological capabilities, availability of investable funds and foreign exchange, and the level of farm purchasing power. It is our argument that a unimodal agricultural strategy aimed at the progressive modernization of the bulk of a nation's cultivators, as contrasted to a bimodal crash modernization effort concentrated upon a small subsector of large-scale mechanized farms, minimizes the extent to which the above constraints impede the development of agriculture and the process of transformation. It does so through its effects on: (a) the disbursement pattern of farm cash receipts, (b) the allocation of investment resources, (c) the kinds of new technological knowledge that are produced, and (d) the proportion of the nation's producers that has access to the new modes of production.

It is clearly an oversimplification to concentrate on the polar extremes represented by unimodal and bimodal alternatives. There are good reasons, however, for focusing initially on the choice between those two extreme alternatives. Governments, like most bureaucratic organizations, are disposed to concentrate on coping with the agenda of pressing problems rather than on developing long-run strategies. Consequently, the 'choice' of an agricultural strategy will often be made by default. Moreover, there are often strong political pressures that tend to bias the outcome toward a bimodal strategy. For both reasons, it is especially important to arrive at a clear understanding of the nature of the alternatives and of their differential effects on the pattern of agricultural development and on overall economic growth.

Choice criteria: the multiple objectives of an agricultural strategy

What criteria should guide this choice between a unimodal and bimodal strategy? We propose that the efficiency of alternative strategies should be assessed in terms of their contributions to attaining three major objectives: first, facilitating the process of structural transformation and growth in national product; second, enhancing the welfare of the farm population; and third, promoting changes in attitudes and behaviour in rural communities that have a favourable impact on the process of social modernization.

Objectives of an agricultural strategy

Because agriculture and its inter-relations with other sectors bulk so large in late-developing countries, it is essential to assess alternative agricultural strategies in terms of their intersectoral effects as well as their direct effects on the expansion of farm output and incomes. Hence, the *first objective* of an agricultural strategy focuses on the need to achieve a rate and pattern of output expansion in the agricultural sector that will promote overall economic growth and structural transformation and take full advantage of positive interactions between agriculture and other sectors. This objective encompasses what has often been referred to as agriculture's 'contributions' to development: (a) providing increased supplies of food and raw materials to meet the needs of the expanding nonfarm sectors, (b) earning foreign exchange through production for export, and (c) providing a net flow of capital to finance a considerable part of the investment requirements for infrastructure and industrial growth.

The problems involved in achieving a net flow of resources from agriculture clearly represent the most difficult area of competitiveness between this first objective of fostering structural transformation and the second objective of improving the well-being of the rural population.

The expansion in the absolute and relative importance of commercial production in agriculture is, of course, an aspect of structural transformation and increasing sectoral interdependence. The growth of a marketable surplus of farm products, expansion of foreign exchange earnings, and increased availability of resources for capital formation are necessary conditions for the development of a diversified modern economy. At the same time the growth of farm cash income associated with structural transformation means increased rural demand for inputs and consumer goods that can provide an important stimulus to domestic industry. The strength of that stimulus and the associated feedback effects will be strongly influenced, however, by the composition of rural demand.

A broadly based expansion of farm cash income generating demand for low-cost and relatively simple inputs and consumer goods can be expected to foster efficient, evolutionary growth of domestic manufacturing that is characterized by relatively low import content and which leads to the strengthening and diffusion of entrepreneurial and technical competence. Basic to all of these inter-relations between agricultural development and overall economic growth is the creation of an integrated national economy characterized by increased specialization and growing interdependence among sectors. This requires the development of flexible and sensitive market networks and continuing improvement in transportation and other types of infrastructure.

The *second objective*, achieving broadly based improvement of the welfare of the rural population, is important simply because such a large fraction of the population of developing countries is destined to live and die in farming communities. Achievement of that objective depends in the long run on altering the predominantly agrarian structure of these economies. The possibility of enlarging the income of the agricultural sector, and still more the *average* income of farm households, is determined mainly by the rate and character of structural transformation, particularly as manifested in the decline of the relative and, eventually, absolute size of the farm workforce and the associated growth of commercial demand for agricultural products.

Inequality in income distribution is a conspicuous feature of most less-developed countries and a matter for particular concern because the poverty of the low-income groups is so extreme. The extent to which such inequality in income distribution will be either reduced or exacerbated will be determined mainly by whether the demand for labour increases more or less rapidly than the country's workforce. At issue is the growth of demand for labour in all sectors; but the increase in demand for labour in agriculture, including the employment opportunities available to family members working on their own or rented land, is of special significance. And the extent to which the expansion of farm output will lead to widespread increases in income-earning opportunities will, for reasons considered shortly, hinge on the development and diffusion of divisible innovations.

Certain dimensions of welfare can be furthered most effectively by direct action through government programmes, notably public health and related activities.

Rural works programmes can provide supplementary employment and income for some of the most disadvantaged elements of the rural population. But the indirect contribution of such programmes to the expansion of farm output and income, through the construction of roads, irrigation works, and other useful infra-structure, is likely to be more important. Considerable planning and technical supervision is required, however, to ensure the usefulness of employment-oriented projects of that nature. Because of those organizational problems and the fiscal constraints which limit their magnitude, such programmes apparently have not had a very large effect on under- and unemployment in rural areas. For the rural works programme in Bangladesh (then East Pakistan), which was one of the more ambitious undertakings of this type and one that was financed to a large extent by P. L. 480 grain imports, Walter Falcon reports an annual reduction of agricultural un-employment of only about 3.5 per cent.[1]

Judgements will differ concerning the importance of the *third objective*, that is, fostering a pattern of agricultural development that will have a favourable impact on social modernization as a result of inducing changes in rural attitudes, behaviour, and institutions. The evolutionary development of a variety of social institutions is clearly a significant feature of structural trans-formation. Salient examples pertaining to agriculture include the creation and strengthening of agricultural experiment stations; expansion of educational facilities and programmes for training farmers; establishing irrigation associations or other groups that enable farmers to concert their behaviour when group action is advantageous; and strengthening the organizations – private, public, or co-operative – that distribute credit and inputs and market farm products.

The need for 'institutional progress' is especially significant in countries undertaking a unimodal strategy of agricultural develop-ment. Hence, the interactions between technical and economic change at the farm level and institutional, attitudinal, and behavioural change merit attention in assessing the differential effects of alternative strategies. Broader participation in the modernization of agriculture implies a more widespread familiarity with calculations of costs and returns and with the evaluation and selective adoption of innovations. Such opportunities for 'learning by doing' foster the development and spread of managerial competence that facilitates the recruitment and training of the entrepreneurs and skilled workers required in a modernizing economy.

It is also to be expected that broad participation of the farm population in improved income-earning opportunities will influence the rural power structure and political institutions. This has obvious implications with respect to political and financial support for rural schools and other institutions to serve farming communities. There are, of course, reciprocal interactions between the effects of the pattern of rural development on the distribution of political power and the influence of the power structure on the choice of strategy for agricultural development.

There is one other area in which the inter-relations between the pattern of agricultural development and changes in rural attitudes and behaviour is potentially of very great significance. Many years ago John Stuart Mill asserted that an agricultural system based on peasant proprietorship would have a beneficial effect on the 'prudence' as well as the 'industry' of the rural population and would therefore 'discourage an improvident increase in their numbers. . . .'[2]

The key question concerns the way in which the modernization of agriculture will affect the spread of the knowledge, incentives, and motivation essential to the practice of family planning. It is certainly a reasonable hypothesis that conscious action to limit family size will take hold more readily if rural households are actively involved in a process of economic and technical change, whether as owner cultivators or as tenants, rather than being relegated to a 'surplus population-supporting sector' with slight opportunity to better their condition. The analysis of the relationships between various economic factors and fertility change in Taiwan seems to provide considerable support for that hypothesis. In her concluding comments, Eva Mueller declares that:

Where agricultural improvement is confined to a minority of cultivators . . . the expansion of economic horizons will be more limited than in Taiwan. Only a minority will then experience the rising aspirations that in Taiwan seem to be contributing so importantly to acceptance of family planning in rural areas. The majority of farmers will have no experience with progress and no reason to raise their sights. They will continue to feel that yield-raising farm investments, a better education for their children, and modern consumer goods and services are not 'for them'. The transformation of household preferences which we observed in Taiwan will be much less extensive.[3]

Clearly, there is a marked contrast between the rapid reduction in birth-rates during the past two decades in Taiwan, and also South Korea, and the slight changes that have taken place in other developing countries.[4] This can probably be attributed in part to relatively well-organized family-planning programmes in those two countries. But the changes in rural attitudes and motivation resulting from broad participation in development and the widespread influence of education and other modernizing institutions and of the mass media undoubtedly strengthened the direct effects of family planning programmes. There are also indications that those factors and the rising aspirations which they have engendered have also contributed to more spontaneous reductions in fertility. One fact is beyond dispute. Given the structural-demographic characteristics of late-developing countries, there is no hope of bringing birth-rates into tolerable balance with the sharply reduced death-rates that now prevail unless conscious limitation of family size becomes widespread in rural areas.

Competitiveness and complementarity among objectives

To argue, as we have done in this section, that the choice of agricultural strategy should be guided by explicit attention to their effects on a set of objectives is a somewhat unorthodox approach – but one that is now receiving much attention. Richard Musgrave sums up the orthodox approach, which is in accord with the compensation principle of welfare economics, with the statement that policy makers should opt for 'the efficient choice' and then supplement that decision with 'the necessary distribution adjustment through a tax-transfer mechanism.'[5] But where poverty is widespread and tax revenues are severly limited, distributional adjustments through a tax-transfer mechanism cannot be carried out on a significant scale even if the political climate is favourable.

It has become a common practice to admonish policy makers in low-income countries to make development decisions by assigning appropriate weights to (a) growth of output, (b) employment expansion, and (c) income distribution goals. This is in accord with the predilection of economists to assume that there are invariably trade-offs between output and equity goals. This is, of course, true at the margin. Additional funds allocated to a programme of nutritional improvement will, at least indirectly, be at the expense of reduced allocations for some other programme such as agricultural research, farmer training, or investments in infrastructure.

Although it is necessary to consider trade-offs in making decisions with respect to particular policies or programmes, the trade-offs that arise in connection with the set of policies required to implement a unimodal strategy will be small compared to the situation under the bimodal alternative. In the latter case, for example, a truly massive (and usually politically not feasible) programme of rural public works would be required for unemployment relief to offset the labour-displacing effects of a capital-intensive expansion path. But within the framework of a unimodal strategy, the need to generate additional employment via a works programme would be much less. Moreover, the prospects for planning and financing rural public works projects that will have favourable effects on output are better in the context of a unimodal pattern of development; and in that context it is legitimate to give greater weight to output effects than employment creation.

The *crux* of our argument is that it is wrong to assume that the choice between unimodal and bimodal strategies necessarily involves a sacrifice with respect to the economic objective of increasing output in order to further the social objectives of expanding employment opportunities and reducing inequalities in income distribution. Given the economic constraints that condition the choice of means for promoting agricultural development, progressive modernization of the rural sector is, in general, the most efficient means of attaining the threefold objectives of an agricultural strategy.

Economic constraints and the choice of means

A major thesis of ours is that sequences of innovations *can* be generated and diffused that will foster the widespread increases in productivity that characterize a unimodal strategy and thus avoid the polarization of agriculture into subsectors using drastically different technologies.

A central element of a unimodal strategy is the development and diffusion of highly divisible innovations that promote output expansion within an agrarian structure made up of operational units relatively equal in size and necessarily small because of the large number of holdings relative to the cultivated area. The divisibility factor, by rendering new technology applicable to these small units, permits the progressive modernization of an increasing proportion of a country's farmers. There will, of course, be differences in the speed and efficiency with which farmers seize new opportunities depending on their initial resources, ability, and desire. Moreover, technical progress will inevitably have an uneven impact on different regions and types of farming. Such differences, however, are much less significant than those that result from the polarization of agriculture into modern and traditional sectors employing drastically different technologies.

Progressive modernization based on widespread adoption of a sequence of innovations compatible with the constraints imposed by structural-demographic characteristics makes it possible to exploit the large potential that exists for augmenting the productivity of the agricultural sector's internal resources of labour and land.

If purchased inputs are primarily divisible inputs such as seed and fertilizer, the new technologies can be widely adopted in spite of the purchasing power constraint. Spread of such inputs coupled with changes in farming practices and growth of farm cash income will generate demands for improved equipment to increase the precision as well as reduce the time required for various farming operations; but with progressive modernization this demand will be directed toward simple and inexpensive implements. And if output expansion results from widespread increases in productivity among the small farm units which necessarily predominate when the farm labour force is large relative to the total cultivated area, the capital requirements for investment in labour-saving farm equipment will be limited. The relative profitability – private and social – of outlays for fertilizer and other current inputs as compared to capital equipment will be influenced by the type of agricultural strategy pursued. For example, electric- or diesel-powered pumpsets in India and Pakistan have represented an innovation that has been essentially complementary to the internal resources of labour and land; and in spite of the lumpiness of the investment, the practice of selling tube-well water to near-by farmers makes the input provided quite divisible. The institution of contract ploughing can make the *services* of tractors divisible, and under certain circumstances, especially in semi-arid regions, mechanical cultivation can be complementary to yield-increasing inputs. And when the decision to hire tractor services is made by the farmer or tenant operating a unit of average size, that is, small, there is a good chance that the input will also be a complement to the labour of family members in contrast to the labour-displacing consequences when tractor mechanization is introduced in a large operational unit.

Our emphasis on framing a strategy aimed at promoting more productive utilization of the abundant supply of labour in the agricultural sector is not to be equated with the notion of a 'labour surplus' in the sense that there are individuals with zero marginal product. It is common to speak of a 'labour surplus' in traditional agriculture when the population of working age appears to be larger than the number of 'full-time workers' that would be required to maintain the level of production even with existing technologies. But those labour force concepts appropriate to a modern industrial economy are not really applicable. Particularly for the unpaid family labour that accounts for most of the rural workforce, there is no institutionally determined workday and no clear dichotomy between 'work' and 'leisure'.

For any given 'stock' of farm labour – in a household or in the sector – the actual 'flow' of labour inputs into agricultural production is determined by a 'subjective equilibrium' in the allocation of labour time. And the activities other than farming embrace pursuits such as handweaving and other types of cottage industry as well as leisure and a variety of 'non-economic' activities – litigation, ceremonies, hunting, and so on – many of which are readily *compressible* if altered circumstances make it attractive to increase the allocation of labour time to farming. In addition, agriculture is usually characterized by large seasonal variation in the demand for labour and farm work. Consequently, there is often considerable scope for increasing the number of hours worked per day, the number of work-days per year, and even the pace of work. The increase in time devoted to farming activities may also result from a reduction in the allocation of labour to cottage industries as the products of those industries are replaced by purchased goods. In brief, there is 'slack' that can be drawn into production if there is an increase in the marginal product attributable to additional inputs of labour or an increase in the marginal valuation that workers place on increments to income.

The prevalence of this labour slack in agriculture is a consequence of the economic structure and rapid growth of labour force in developing countries which make it inevitable that the farm workforce will continue to grow in absolute size for many years. In fact, 'labour slack' is merely a shorthand expression to describe a situation where the labour of a large part of the rural population of working age has a low opportunity cost. And because of rapid population growth the opportunity cost of labour is held down, or pushed even lower, unless a country's development strategy is generating new opportunities for productive employment at a pace more rapid than the rate of expansion of the labour force. The phenomenon is, of course, not confined to agriculture. Certain labour-intensive service trades characterized by easy entry also absorb part of the labour force that is unable to find jobs in firms that provide regular wage employment. But with the exception of some of the semi-industrialized countries in Latin America, agriculture is the dominant 'self-employment' sector and absorbs the majority of the annual additions to the labour force.

Because of the existence of labour slack, the impact on farm output of yield-increasing innovations goes beyond their effects on output per unit of labour input. Under a unimodal strategy, technical change and associated investments in infrastructure are likely to induce fuller use of farm labour and land as well as enlarged use of such inputs as fertilizer, because of the complementarity between the internal and external inputs. Taiwan's experience gives an indication of the quantitative importance of more productive seed-fertilizer combinations and investments in infrastructure which increased the returns to additional labour inputs. Investments in irrigation and drainage not only raised yields directly, they also facilitated multiple cropping, thereby raising the year-round utilization of both labour and land. Those who have argued that 'labour surplus' (in the sense of a zero marginal product) is an important feature of a traditional agriculture have often implied that the agricultural sector can be neglected in a development strategy. It should be clear from the foregoing that we are definitely not suggesting that agriculture can be neglected, but rather that a strategy of progressive modernization will have especially important advantages under those conditions.

If a strategy of progressive modernization has significant advantages in achieving both the economic and social goals of development, how are we to account for the fact that so many developing countries appear to be pursuing bimodal strategies?

In the absence of institutional arrangements to generate and diffuse innovations capable of raising yields on small farm units, a concentration of resources in a sub-sector of large and capital-intensive farms may appear to be the only feasible alternative. Tractors and their associated equipment constitute an innovation that is readily transferred. Their introduction is a powerful means of enlarging the area under cultivation, and it may also facilitate expansion of the planted area by increased multiple cropping. The large international corporations manufacturing tractors have considerable competence and strong incentive to promote sales and to organize distribution and service facilities in developing countries, and the local climate of opinion often favours special encouragement for the introduction of tractors because they are seen as a symbol of modernity.

Although the agricultural sector is necessarily subject to a severe purchasing-power constraint until considerable structural transformation has taken place, a sub-sector of large farm units that accounts for most of the increase in commercial production is able to escape that constraint. (This means, of course, that the remaining farm units will continue to be subject to a purchasing-power constraint that is now more binding.) It is also easy for such farms to realize the economies of scale associated with the use of tractors. In addition, reliance on rapid expansion of output by a 'modern' sub-sector of large and 'progressive' farm enterprises bypasses the problems and costs associated with involving a large fraction of the farm population in the modernization process.

This type of bias toward 'reinforcing success' is often linked with the assumption that there is necessarily a sizable trade-off between growth and equity goals. William Nicholls, for example, asserts that Brazil 'must unfortunately face a hard choice between equity and productivity', and he argues that 'the present large holdings' must be relied upon to satisfy the growth of commercial demand.[6] Moreover, there is frequently a failure to recognize the extent to which bimodal and unimodal strategies are mutually exclusive alternatives. Although a unimodal strategy has important economic and social advantages under the conditions that characterize a late-developing country, logical arguments and historical evidence will obviously not be the only factors determining a country's pattern of agricultural development. It is also necessary to take account of political factors.

Political constraints

It was suggested earlier that it is a gross oversimplification to speak of a situation in which policy makers 'opt for a unimodal or bimodal strategy'. In a remarkably perceptive essay, Colin Leys notes that 'the process of "choice" rarely consists of an explicit "moment" at which some appropriate person or committee reviews the alternatives, weighs their pros and cons and consciously selects one of them. It is, generally, a continual process of options foregone, through the passage of time, and through the taking of other decisions which have the often unforeseen consequence of closing off possibilities in spheres not considered at all in the context of the decision.'[7]

Of equal importance is the need to recognize that decisions and policies are shaped by all sorts of conflicting interests. If there is any overriding concern it is preoccupation with staying in power, not the comparatively abstract goal of development.

To the outsider the problem of poverty might appear to be a supreme challenge and a spur to sacrifice and selfless action. But there is a large element of truth in the observation by Leys that the political and administrative élites in most developing countries 'are rarely eager for measures that would entail redistribution of wealth or any threat to their own status or prospects'. After all this tends to be true of élites in all countries, the principal difference in less-developed countries being the more limited force of 'institutions which can hold these tendencies in check and make the élite give the public value for its privileges'.[8]

Notes

1 Walter P. Falcon's estimate of the employment impact of that programme is reported in Falcon (1973).
2 Stuart Mill (1870), ch. 7, concluding paragraph.
3 Mueller (1971), pp. 37–8. In a more recent paper, Professor Mueller (1973) examines additional evidence on linkages between agricultural and demographic change. She notes that much of the evidence is contradictory but continues to stress the role of rising aspirations.
4 The contrast with Brazil and Mexico, where the pattern of agricultural development has been bimodal, is striking. In

Taiwan there was a decline in the birth-rate from 41 to 36 per 1000 between 1947 and 1963 and a further decline to 26 per 1000 by 1970. In South Korea, the decline was from 45 to 30 per 1000 between 1950 and 1970. In contrast, the reduction in Brazil over the same twenty-year period was only from 41 to 38 per 1000 and the decline in Mexico was from 44 to 41 per 1000. See Kocher (1973), pp. 64–5. Clearly many factors contribute to those contrasts. Some would stress the absence of family planning programmes in Mexico and Brazil and the role of the Catholic Church and other cultural infuences; but the French peasantry that impressed Mill by its 'prudence' was predominantly Catholic yet it practised family planning on a significant scale at a time when birth control technology was very primitive.

5   Musgrave (1969).
6   Nicholls (1971).
7   Leys (1971), p. 137.
8   ibid., p. 125.

References

Falcon, W. P. (1973), 'Agricultural employment in less developed countries: general situation, research approaches, and policy palliatives', mimeo, Economic Staff Working Paper no. 113, April, Washington, DC: International Bank for Reconstruction and Development

Johnston, B. F., and Kilby, P. (1975), *Agriculture and Structural Transformation*, New York: Oxford University Press

Kocher, J. E. (1973), 'Rural development, income distribution, and fertility decline', Occasional Paper of the Population Council, New York

Leys, C. (1971), 'Political perspectives', in D. Seers and L. Joy (eds.), *Development in a Divided World*, Harmondsworth: Penguin

Mueller, E. (1971), 'Agricultural change and fertility change: the case of Taiwan', mimeo, Ann Arbor: University of Michigan

Mueller, E. (1973), 'The impact of agricultural change on demographic development in the Third World', in *Demographic Growth and Development in the Third World*, Belgium: International Union for the Scientific Study of Population

Musgrave, R. A. (1969), 'Cost-benefit analysis and the theory of public finance', *Journal of Economic Literature*, 7, 3, September, p. 804

Nicholls, W. H. (1971), 'The Brazilian food supply: problems and prospects', *Economic Development and Cultural Change,* 19, 3, April, pp. 387–8

Stuart Mill, J. (1870), *Principles of Political Economy*, 5th edn, book 2, New York

2 Why poor people stay poor*

Michael Lipton

Introduction: the urban bias argument

In essence, the urban bias hypothesis is that the main reason why poor people stay poor in developing countries is as follows. Small, interlocking urban élites – comprising mainly businessmen, politicians, bureaucrats, trade-union leaders and a supporting staff of professionals, academics and intellectuals – can in a modern state substantially control the distribution of resources. In the great majority of developing countries, such urban élites spearheaded the fight against the colonizing power. Partly for this reason the urban élites formed, and have since dominated, the institutions of independence – government, political parties, law, civil service, trade unions, education, business organizations, and many more. But the power of the urban élite, in a modern state, is determined, not by its economic role alone, but by its capacity to organize, centralize and control. Hence urban power in developing countries – by comparison with early modern development in England in 1740–1820, or somewhat later in continental Europe – has been out of all proportion to the urban share in either population or production. Rural people, while much more numerous than urban people, are also much more dispersed, poor, inarticulate and unorganized. That does not make them quiescent, but it does diffuse their conflicts. On the whole, rural groups fight each other locally; nationally they seek to join or to use urban power and income, not to seize that power and income for the rural sector.

Consequently, the natural operation of personal and group self-interest has led in almost all developing countries to far wider disparities between urban living standards – themselves highly unequal – and rural living standards than prevailed in Northwest

*This paper is taken from the text of the Vikram Sarabhai Memorial Lecture, delivered by Michael Lipton at the Indian Institute of Management, Ahmedabad in January 1981.

Europe, Japan, or the USA during their periods of early modern development. Resources – investment, doctors, teachers, clean water – are allocated between city and country in ways not merely inequitable but also inefficient. Not only could large amounts of resources, typically distributed, do much more to help poor people if shifted from city to village, because the city starts much less poor and more internally unequal: the equity point; but in most poor countries it is also demonstrable that such a shift – of doctors, public investment, cash – actually generates more results (more saved lives, more returns to investment) in rural than in urban areas: the efficiency point.

So it is not a case of efficiency versus equity, but of both versus power. The actions of the powerful, in almost all developing countries, have shifted income-per-person – inefficiencies and inequities notwithstanding – from rural to urban areas. Agriculture, with 70 per cent of workers and 40–45 per cent of GNP, has in most poor countries received barely 20 per cent of investment – but has, directly and indirectly, been induced or forced to contribute considerably more to saving. Public action renders farm products cheaper and farm purchases dearer, in domestic markets, than they would have been if such action were neutral. Education, while geared towards urban needs, transfers bright rural children to urban areas. (On the whole, however, the scope for rural–urban migration to correct gross rural–urban income disparities has proved very small in Africa and Asia, outside the Middle East.) The urban élite, for all the well-meaning talk of rural development, is in practice driven to concentrate the action heavily on the cities.

This has disappointing effects on employment, growth and poverty – partly because urban growth is increasingly costly and not very employment-intensive; partly because, with capital and skills scarce, urban bias means that largely rural, high-yielding, labour-intensive alternatives and the supporting administration and institutions especially are under-financed or overlooked; and partly because of the limited scope for successful townward migration. Cumulative *public* action to improve urban infrastructure, incentives and institutions – action itself responsive to *private* organization and voice, both far better developed in the towns – renders the movement townwards of yet more *private* capital, skills, and capacities to generate income disparity and to apply political pressure for yet more urban advance relatively to the rural areas.

But the struggle is not hopeless. Fortunately, the internal inconsistencies of urban-biased growth – and its rising. cost, intensified by growing scarcities of both energy and aid – strengthen the forces, within state machines as well as among popular protest movements, seeking to reverse urban bias. However, as I will argue shortly, there is no evidence of the required massive switch to rural emphases in the past decade or so.

Before completing this compressed account of how urban bias keeps poor people poor, I must sketch another, equally important, side of the argument. Inequalities *within* rural areas also owe much to the urban-biased nature of development policy. The cities want to receive, preferably cheap, surpluses from the rural areas: surpluses of food; surpluses of savings over rural investment; surpluses of exportables over imports, to provide foreign exchange for industrial development; surpluses of 'human capital', in the shape of rural-born doctors, teachers, engineers and administrators, as children brought up largely at rural expense, but as adults serving largely urban needs. Who, in the rural areas, can provide such surpluses? Clearly, the better-off, especially the big farmers. Provide a small farmer, meeting only half his family food needs, with the extra irrigation, or the improved health, or the educated knowledge, to grow more food, and his family will consume the gains themselves. Provide similar inputs to a large farmer, and the resulting output will be sold – and the receipts, very probably, saved for reinvestment in urban activities. This, too, is inefficient (as well as inequitable), because it is the *small* farmer who saturates each acre, each kilogram of fertilizer, with more effort, and thus grows more output per acre-year than the large farmer.[1] But it is the large farmer who gets most of the goodies. That's the 'urban alliance'. The towns get their cheap surpluses, food, exportables, etc., even if not made very efficiently and equitably. The rural better-off get most of what is going by way of rural investment, price support, subsidies, etc., even if not much of these. The rural poor, though efficient, get mainly pious words, though often sincere ones.

Let me stress that there is no conspiracy afoot. Most of the time, the process and its results involve neither corruption nor dishonesty. The politicians (and the businessmen, labour leaders and academics) who proclaim their attachment to, say, minor irrigation investment and land reform to help the rural poor, but who then somehow end up spending much more on urban roads than pumpsets, while permitting massive evasion of land reform – these people are not being dishonest. They are responding to pressures; and urban pressures (for good roads and cheap food from big farmers) are stronger than rural pressures.

Counter arguments: prices and subsidies

That account is of course oversimplified. Those who wish to decide whether it is right will, I hope, look at the evidence in my book,[2] and judge for themselves. Three sorts of argument have been advanced against the urban bias hypothesis: that it is wrong; that it is old; and that it has been outdated by corrective, pro-rural pressures and actions.

I can't do justice here to the interesting arguments advanced against the existence of urban bias, but would say only that those who have argued against the hypothesis have some explaining to do. Why, if there is no urban bias, has growth in poor countries since 1945 – very fast growth by historical standards – been consistent with *both* widespread rural-agricultural stagnation (in terms of output-per-person), *and* the failure of prices to move dramatically in favour of agriculture?[3] Why, if there's no urban bias, have the much higher rates of return in many areas on agricultural investment and its rural support in the wake of the 'green revolution', not induced bigger or more massive flows of public and private funds, both into investment in 'green revolution' areas, and into research to make 'green revolutions' possible elsewhere? I shall not, therefore, say more about the view – rather rare and frankly a bit odd – that urban bias as an explanation of persistent poverty, is just wrong or unimportant.

I fully accept, however, a second sort of criticism of the urban bias hypothesis: that it is not new. This I have never claimed for it; indeed I have been at pains to stress its ancestry, including thinkers as diverse as Mahatma Gandhi, Mao Tse-tung, Karl Kautsky, Alfred Marshall, Frantz Fanon, Theodore Schultz – and Alexander Chayanov, whose central contributions I have not, in the past, given their deserved place.

What is worrying – or rather, a sort of temptation to premature relaxation – is the third sort of criticism: that urban bias has been recognized and largely eliminated. I wish this were true. Unfortunately the evidence does not support such a hopeful view. Two examples will suffice: agriculture's share in investment; and the movement of the inter-sectoral terms of trade.

India is unusual, in that the 1970s have seen a rise in the share of agriculture (in the broad sense) in investible resources to about 23–25 per cent, from the 18–20 per cent prevailing in the 1960s. Even in India, such a small change hardly matches the dramatic rise in the relative profitability of agricultural investment in the wake of the high-yielding varieties – let alone the much greater impact on *non*-agricultural costs of higher fossil-fuel prices. These should mean a big shift in India to farm investment, because fossil-fuel forms a much smaller part of Indian farm costs (including fertilizer) than (a) of costs of non-farm production in India, or (b) of the costs of farm production in much more energy-intensive countries from which India buys cotton – or grain, when grain imports again become necessary.

One major reason why India's agricultural investment share has risen so slowly is the decision to use extra food output only to replace imported foodgrains and to build up stocks, rather than to add significantly to the inadequate intake of large sections of the population. The other side of the same coin – to which I return later – is the concentration of access to, and subsidies for, agricultural innovation upon larger farmers. These deliver the extra food for urban consumption, but do not provide much extra demand to encourage much further investment in food-growing: neither direct demand for their family consumption (because, as they already eat enough, they spend the extra 'green revolution' incomes not on extra food, but mainly on urban products, thus increasing urban sales, selling prices, and incomes); nor even, to any great extent, indirect demand by farm employees. Large farmers, after as before the introduction of HYVs, put in much less labour-per-acre (which is why they produce rather less output-per-acre than do small farmers). True enough, large farmers hire a larger proportion of the labour they do use, whereas small farmers rely to a greater extent on family labour. But this is cancelled out by the bigger farmer's lower use of total labour – of all sorts – per acre. Especially since much of the bigger farmer's urban efforts go into seeing that politicians divert such resources as do go to rural areas into subsidies for his own labour-replacing innovations – in weedicides, reaper-binders, modern rice mills, the impact on employment, and hence even indirectly on demand for food, of a large-farm-based 'green revolution' has been disappointingly small. So, therefore, is the very modest rise in the farm sector's share of investment.

But India has done better, in correcting the urban-rural balance, than most developing countries. There, as I showed in my book, agriculture's share of total investment lagged far behind its share in output and employment during the 1950s and 1960s and did not show any uptrend. The FAO's *State of Food and Agriculture* (1978 and 1979 vols.) showed that no significant increase in agriculture's share of total investment had taken place in the late 1960s or middle 1970s, either, in the great majority of poor countries with available data. (Investment in fertilizer plant, however desirable, is not – unlike irrigation – investment in agriculture, but in industrial production, for import avoidance or replacement.)

What, then of relative prices? In analysing urban bias, we must not claim that it is proved by movements of the terms of trade against farm products – or disproved by the opposite tendency. The movement of the farm-nonfarm terms of trade depends on three things: supply, demand, and changes (publicly or privately induced) in market power and market structure. Much the most important of these three is the movement of agricultural supply, in part due to medium-term trends such as the expansion of output in the wake of HYVs, but in much greater part due to fluctuations. Whether or not (as Irving Fisher believed) the US business cycle was a money-supply-based 'dance of the dollar', most of the year-to-year movement in the terms of trade in South Asia is certainly a rainfall-supply-based dance of the monsoons. Second, and less important, are changes in the demand for farm products: less important as a cause of changes in the farm-nonfarm terms of trade, especially in a developing country where farming is dominated by cereal production and consumption, because the demand for food changes much more slowly (either in trends in fluctuation) than does income-per-person, which itself changes much more slowly than does agricultural supply.

The third cause of changes in the terms of trade between agriculture and the rest of the economy lies in changes in actions by government or by private monopoly power, to alter the structure, or size, of supply or demand for farm products. Only such action is relevant to urban bias. Changes in the terms of trade between agriculture and non-agriculture could suggest changing urban bias *only* to the extent that they are due to changes in government (or cartel) actions affecting those terms of trade – for example, changing tariffs on non-farm inputs – rather than to exogenous change in demand or supply alone.

The careful recent analysis by Kahlon and Tyagi[4] shows that, since the mid 1960s and right through the 1970s the terms of trade of India's farm sector have usually been worsening. But this tells us little about urban bias. The only way to link terms of trade to urban bias directly is not by looking at 'movement' in those terms – which on its own (apart from depending heavily on the choice of base-year and the type of index-number) is likelier to reflect rainfall-induced components of supply than is government action. Rather it is by asking: if we take a three or four-year average, and suppose that farmers – instead of exchanging their marketed surplus for non-farm goods at prices affected by non-neutral actions (of the state, and of private monopolies and cartels which are incomparably more important in industry than in agriculture) – were able to exchange at *world prices* the typical bundle of their products, for a typical bundle of their purchases of non-farm products: how much more, or less, of the latter would they have obtained, as compared with transactions actually taking place at national prices?[5] In the late 1960s, S. P. Lewis found that in Pakistan the farmers could have bought about 50 per cent more at border prices than at actual prices. In other words, non-neutral actions to affect the terms of trade were robbing the Pakistani farmer of about one-third of the value of his surplus. I have not seen similar calculations for India, but I should imagine that the degree of surplus extraction from farmers through prices alone was rather more for rice, and rather less for wheat. Probably the depression of farm prices hurts the whole rural sector, including deficit farmers and landless labourers, whose job prospects (and wage rates) suffer when price disincentives depress farm production: in the case of *food* prices, labourers paid in cash (not in food) gain, but it is hard to believe that any substantial rural group can long benefit from the artificial extraction, via price manipulation, of resources out of the farm sector.

We need to be careful about data suggesting that government action is changing farmers' share of the cake. For example, subsidies on fertilizers may be 'subsidies' on a price initially raised by protective tariff, to cover the high costs of domestic production. Or they may be far below comparable subsidies to non-farm inputs. Or they may leak to import licencees, contractors, or other urban middlemen. The usual impact, if the subsidized fertilizer is scarce, is to steer it to bigger farmers, who can more easily run the bureaucratic obstacle course to the subsidized prize. That makes the fertilizer not cheaper, but even scarcer and dearer, for small farmers, while it increases the share of the fertilizers going to surplus farmers, who use it to grow more food, exportables, and raw materials for delivery to the urban sector.

Another example, of the non-obvious impact of government action apparently helpful to farmers, is the large increase in the flow of credit to Indian agriculture, consequent on the shift from co-operative credit to nationalized commercial bank credit. First, this increase must be discounted to allow for inflation, and for the much greater cash input-costs (per acre and per unit of output) implicit in the new seed-fertilizer packages. Second, the increase has gone mainly to better-off farmers, and the share that has reached small farmers may (we do not know) merely have replaced, not supplemented, non-institutional credit. Third, and above all, *deposits* in the Indian banks *by* rural people exceed, and have increased faster than, *loans* by the Indian banks *to* rural people. So the shift of responsibility for Indian rural credit from co-operatives to banks has, on balance, taken credit out of the rural sector, not put credit in.

There have been major improvements in public policy towards Indian agriculture since the mid 1960s, especially in research. Foodgrain self-sufficiency, even if so far only in good years and at low caloric levels, is a big achievement. But we should not be too hasty in assuming that urban bias is dying. Certainly it is alive and well and living in Africa. All the old discredited anti-rural myths of South Asia two decades ago are rampant still in Africa, especially among European 'advisers': the myth of the irrational conservatism of peasants, as opposed to the fact of their rational, income-seeking, risk-averse, but innovative behaviour; the myth of the greater efficiency of large farmers, as opposed to the fact that yields, and returns to capital, are higher on smaller farms with most crops and most technologies; the myth that it is scientific to apply 'Western' and capital-intensive methods to increasingly land-scarce, maintenance-skill-starved, and possibly labour-surplus rural environments; the myth that purely technical agronomic or water or engineering research, conducted in field stations conveniently near the capital city, can yield useful results without economic experimentation in the farmer's field and without feedback from the farmer himself. Small wonder that output-per-worker on the farm, about 75 per cent of the output-per-worker off the farm in Europe during its early development and about 35 per cent now in Asia and Latin America, is only some 20 per cent in Africa now;

that farm investment and research in Africa are exceptionally small relative to investment in other sectors, especially in lavish urban infrastructure; and that, unaffected by much serious application of research that really pays the small farmer, African food output per person has fallen quite sharply in the 1970s, contrary to the more hopeful trends in several of the rather less urban-biased environments of Asia.

Four paths to reduced poverty

I have given a brief outline of the urban bias argument, and some reasons for scepticism that the supply of urban bias has decreased. On the other hand, the demand for its major modification is becoming more urgent. There are four possible paths to reduced rural poverty – and rural poverty is the origin of urban poverty, both because the growing army of rural poor seek (at least temporarily) to enter urban life but tend to increase the misery and congestion and excess labour supply on the semi-jobless urban fringe; and because the under-use of the human resources of small farmers and landless labourers prevents the rural sector from generating a lasting, soundly based, efficiently (because labour-intensively) produced, farm surplus for exchange on fair terms with urban products, and permits only a big-farm surplus, costly because intensive in its use of capital and energy, but (due to inadequate, urban-biased incentives) too small and too unreliable to serve as a firm base for urban growth.

The four paths to reduced rural poverty are: rapid growth plus 'trickle-down'; intra-rural redistribution; urban-to-rural redistribution; or forms of growth specific to the rural poor. As for the first path, *very* rapid growth does trickle down to the *quite* poor. Abundant evidence shows than in several partial 'success stories' of the past two decades, really fast growth has sharply cut the proportion of people below a (constant) poverty line, as workers and small farmers seized their chances. This has happened in big countries – Brazil (after 1970), Nigeria, Kenya, Mexico, Indonesia and Thailand – apart from the 'Gang of Four' (Taiwan, South Korea, Hong Kong, Singapore) so often presented, rather ignorantly, to justify independent free-market capitalism.[6] Also *regions* of rapid growth, such as India's Punjab, Bangladesh's Comilla, and Sri Lanka's Jaffna, show real rural 'trickle-down'. But even rapid growth probably doesn't reach the *very* poor – the 15–20 per cent of South Asians in absolute caloric need. These are landless, asset-less, uneducated people; overwhelmingly rural (or rural-based); often ill; often younger siblings in big families with only one earner. They usually can't respond by *working* harder for the crumbs, as they 'trickle-down' from the rapid growth on the rich man's table. Moreover, very rapid growth – the sort that trickles down – is not likely in the oil-less 'NOPEC countries' of Asia and Africa. They are squeezed three ways. OPEC imposes spiralling energy prices; the West's leaders, largely dogmatic monetarists 'high' on redemption by recession, are unlikely to expand imports or aid substantially; and the Soviet bloc, far from poor in wealth or oil, is persistently mean about aid and (in effect) protectionist about Third World exports. 'NOPEC' will do well to achieve even a modest growth in real income-per-person in the next decade.

So abysmal rural poverty is unlikely to be relieved by the first of the four paths, 'trickle-down' from rapid overall growth. What of the second path, redistribution from the rural rich to the rural poor? I remain convinced of the case for radical redistribution of rights in land, and/or individual or joint ownership by the rural poorest of new non-farm assets. However, first, it is not the unnatural wickedness of the kulaks that stops land reform, but the reluctance of the urban, and international, community to finance the compensation loan (to enable the beneficiaries to compensate the landowners), and to forgo the urbanized surpluses that big farmers provide. Second, why should these so-called big farmers – in Asia not mainly the few really rich landowners of Bihar and Hambantota and the Pakistan Punjab, but mainly poor 'kulaks' with four or five acres in Bangladesh or Java or Sri Lanka's Wet Zone – be singled out to have their aspirations reduced? Why should a five-acre farmer be told that he may not aspire to own a radio, but must give his alleged 'excess land' to the rural poor, by a desk-wallah in Delhi, Sussex or Washington, whose annual increment far exceeds the farmer's annual income, and who lives, works or even researches in a complex containing a significant area of sprinkler-irrigated lawn or garden? In any event population growth – and in some cases sales and transfers in anticipation of land reform – are already breaking down some of the large landholdings. I don't want to talk land reform down. It is efficient, because it transfers land to those who use it more labour-intensively, and produce more crops per year, of higher unit value, and with higher yield-per-acre. It is equitable, and in a few places in South Asia (and many in Latin America) it is hard to envisage a cure for rural poverty that does *not* involve the subdivision, among poor labourers and handkerchief-farmers, of large parts of presently underfarmed giant holdings. However, it is really unpersuasive for very wealthy urban people, like us, to lecture five-acre 'kulaks' about their duty to give land to the poor. We had better pay for that transfer ourselves, and not obstruct it (in the interests of maintaining the short-run food and savings surplus that big farmers supply, albeit less efficiently than small farmers could eventually do, to the cities) by laws that are at once evasive and easily evaded.

So, of the four paths to reduce rural poverty, the first two share rather limited prospects, and the trends of the 1980s seem set against them. Economic growth looks unlikely to be fast enough to 'trickle down' very far. Population growth is subdividing rural land and assets, leaving – at least in South Asia – few obvious large concentrations of wealth for redistribution to the poorest; anyway, with urban wealth (and internal inequality) so much greater than rural, and with increasing rural aspirations to the services and treatment that urban people take for granted, I think there will be growing resistance to paternalist *urban* proposals for selective, purely intra-*rural*, redistribution. The landless, the one-acre man and the five-acre man have their conflicts of interest, of course. But I sense, in the air, a feeling that they are beginning to recognize that these conflicts are enormously outweighed by their *shared* interest – in getting better prices, more productive investment, more security, and a larger share of doctors, good teachers, waterproof houses, administrators, and scientific research, out of an urban élite whose wealth and income (and whose advantages over the poor around them) far outweigh, for urban capital and labour and bureaucracy alike, those of most 'big' farmers.

HYVs and the case for rural-to-urban redistribution

So the first two paths won't do. The fourth path – growth via techniques offering special gains to the rural poor – might seem, to us urbanites, an attractive way to avoid the rigours of the third, urban-rural redistribution. One such set of techniques, indeed, may appear to make irrelevant many of these conflicts, intra-rural and rural-urban alike. It is the spread, potential and impact of the high-yielding cereal varieties (HYVs). In ever more areas and crops, the HYVs are transforming rural Asia and much of Latin America (though they remain relatively neglected in most parts of Africa, at least at the level of research in farmers' fields).

Contrary to the published fears of many technologically illiterate social scientists – including me, before I did some overdue homework on the subject – the agronomic features of HYVs render them a potentially ideal innovation for the rural poor.[7] First, these seeds tend to produce what the poor – landless workers and deficit farmers – consume, buy and grow: coarse grains, not very tasty but cheap, and yielding many calories per acre. Second, HYVs attain their high levels of production mainly via extra human effort-per-acre, both directly in harvesting and threshing, and indirectly by raising the attractiveness of water-control and fertilizer application; all this increases both employment and wage rates, yet HYVs do not require costly items of fixed capital that only wealthy farmers can afford. Third, contrary to prevailing mythology, most HYVs – certainly most of those introduced in the last ten years or so – *reduce* risk, because they are better able to thrive despite inadequate or badly-timed water or sunlight, more responsive even to low levels of management and inputs, and better designed to resist (or to tolerate) insect and disease attack. This reduction in risk, too, should be specially helpful to the poorest farmers, because poor people are least able to take risks – and therefore least able to incur costs for seeds and fertilizers if the returns are at all doubtful.

So HYVs look like an ideal example of our 'fourth path': a technology particularly good for the rural poor. Yet it has not worked out quite like that. HYVs, by their contribution to food output, *have* saved many lives, almost all belonging to poor people (the rich eat too much anyway). But all the features of HYVs, listed above as specially favourable to the rural poor, have been somehow frustrated; bigger farmers gained most. In exploring why, we learn how the fourth path to the prevention of rural poverty – the path of poor-specific innovation – is very unlikely to lead to the destination unless the third path, of urban-to-rural resource redistribution, is taken first.

How has each of the three 'pro-poor' features of HYV innovation fared in practice? First, HYVs have indeed raised food output, especially of poor people's foods: coarser varieties of wheat and rice.[8] But, due to the actions of urban-biased nation-states, not much of the extra food has gone to increase poor people's caloric intakes. Instead the extra food has been used mainly to achieve food self-sufficiency – to replace food imports (or even to permit exports), so as to provide foreign exchange for non-food imports, especially imports of oil to nourish the endless 'energy sink' of modern capital-intensive industrial growth. Extra food output has also been used to build up large public stocks; stocks are a sensible but mainly town-orientated precaution against later shortages, and a less 'townish' policy would have helped farmers to store the grain by big advance purchases – thereby (since on-farm stored grain losses are in fact very small) reducing the huge food losses, and saving the huge transport and fuel costs involved in sudden seasonal and 'good year' upsurges of grain flows from farms to centralized grain stores. Moreover, misguided research emphases on cereal varieties with 'high protein' (when what the poor desperately need is calories), and on taste and cooking qualities (sought after mainly by richer consumers and the farmers who sell to them), have directed some research efforts away from the crucial search for high, safe yields of calories-per-acre at fairly low production cost.

What of the second 'pro-poor' feature inherent in HYV technology: the production benefits via extra employment income? Again, urban priorities, and their alliance with surplus farmers' interests, have diverted many of the benefits, this time from owners of labour to owners and hirers of equipment. How splendid it was, in the rural Punjab in the early 1970s to hear the bigger farmers' complaints of 'labour shortage' in the wake of HYVs! This complaint meant that, to get their harvesting and threshing done in time, these farmers had to hire many extra workers – usually poor migrants, often from Eastern UP – and to bid up their wages. For a few seasons, the gains from HYVs were substantially shared by the rural poorest, as per the blueprint. But the migrants were not enough; wages, for a while, went really high, and the bigger farmers successfully pressed the urban State for subsidies on labour-replacing equipment – tractors, threshing machines, reaper-binders, even sometimes combine-harvesters: equipment that does little or nothing to raise output but cuts labour-costs and hence employment. Such subsidies were (and are) often hidden – as cheap credit, as special access to foreign exchange, as subsidized fuel or electricity – but their effect remains the same. Today, the rural poor face new threats, of subsidies (or consciously loss-making State provision) for combine-harvesters once more, and for modern rice mills – neither of which, as a rule, is commercially viable in South Asia without such open or concealed help. If governments find it too hard to resist the pressures from big farmers against higher labour-costs, and the linked pressure (for food from big farmers) coming from trade unionists and urban employers – or if States are actually part of these pressures! – then its surely far better to 'cut labour costs' by supporting or subsidizing extra migration to, or employment in, the affected rural areas, rather than by spending the same money to create a bogus viability for 'unemployment machines'.[9] In any event, urban bias has greatly reduced the employment benefits of HYVs, because labour-replacing forms of irrigation, draught-power, and post-harvest technology – embodied in devices often produced or installed by city people – have been subsidized.

What of the third 'pro-poor' feature of the more recent HYVs: their risk-reducing benefits? If all farmers know about that feature, then the poor (being the most risk-averse) can expect the biggest proportionate gain from it. But education, agricultural extension, and seed and fertilizer distribution are all urban-managed institutions. All are grossly under-financed in most of rural Asia and Africa. Hence it is the better-off rural people who get hold of the few resources available. It is well known that access to education extension and inputs is heavily skewed to the better-off. With these benefits comes the information that alone can inform the farmer about the features and requirements of a new variety. Lacking such information, the small farmer faces very high *subjectively assessed* risks in innovating with a new HYV, even if its objective risk, to those 'in the know', is much lower than that of older varieties. But access to information is planned in the towns, and scarce – and therefore seldom found among poor farmers – in the villages. Of course, once poor farmers see how better-off farmers cut their risks and raise their output with a new variety of (say) wheat, the poor can follow the innovation; but by that time the extra supply of output, due to the better-off early adopters, has glutted local markets and greatly reduced the benefits to the later and poorer innovators.

It looks, then, as if the path to reduced poverty via 'trickle-down' from rapid growth is almost closed to most poor countries in the early 1980s; the path through redistribution of *rural* resources to the rural poor has limited access; and the path through pro-poor technology, as indicated by the experience of the HYVs, can lead to reduced rural poverty only if the path of urban-to-rural redistribution is taken first. Otherwise urban incomes, interests and power are likely to prevent even 'appropriate' techniques from reaching the rural poor.

How can rural-to-urban redistribution of income, assets, or power be achieved? Efficiency and equity both favour it; the existing balance of forces does not. Among factors that can help are the political organization of the rural poor; their capacity to perceive the *main* source of exploitation in the urban sector rather than in, say, landlordism and moneylending; their success in forging alliances with the rural less-poor to get more and better investments, doctors, schools, etc. for all rural people; the existence even inside the urban-orientated bureaucracies of both public-sector and private-sector organization, of groups (such as the former MFAL in India) whose career interests are helped by showing substantial benefit to the rural poor; and the growing *internal* inconsistency – in an environment of worsening urban congestion, rising oil prices, and a growing pool of overtly jobless – of a policy that encourages the diversion of outlay to relatively capital-intensive activities located in, or organized from, urban areas.

Notes

1   For conclusive recent evidence, see Berry and Cline (1979).
2   Lipton (1977).
3   For recent evidence on India, see Kahlon and Tyagi (1980).
4   ibid.
5   Raisuddin Ahmed, in a recent paper for the International Food Policy Research Institute, argues roughly as follows: in Bangladesh, when rice prices rise 10 per cent, output responds at best by rising 4 per cent; to this, employment responds at best by rising 2 per cent; therefore a 'pure', landless employee – who may well spend 70 per cent of his income on rice – must lose more by the price rise, than he gains from the extra farm employment. While logically correct, this argument rests on doubtful assumptions of partial equilibrium: can urban–rural income transfers, and their secondary (rural) spending, really harm the rural poor in the long term? See Ahmed (1979).
6   All four are in fact highly interventionist and relatively egalitarian, and have been or are heavily protectionist and aid-financed.

7   The abundant evidence for the statements in this paragraph is set out in Lipton (1979). (Readers should note, however, that some of Michael Lipton's assertions here remain controversial. For different interpretations, see Pearse, 1980; Byres, 1981.)

8   Despite recent efforts, the impact on the *poorest* people's foods – root crops, millets, sorghum, maize – remains disappointing. See Lipton (1975).

9   In other words, it is better for income-distribution, if 'the State' insists on alleviating a 'labour shortage', to do so by (say) subsidizing migration – to keep the wage *bill* up, even at the cost of artificially raising labour supply and hence of cutting the wage *rate* – than to encourage replacement of labour (and thus cutting both the wage rate and employment) by subsidizing equipment that saves labour.

References

Ahmed, R. (1979), 'Foodgrain supply, distribution and consumption policies with a dual pricing mechanism: a case study of Bangladesh', IFPRI Research Report 8, May

Berry, A. and Cline, W. (1979), *Agrarian Structure and Productivity in Developing Countries*, Baltimore, Md: Johns Hopkins University Press

Byres, T. J. (1981), 'The new technology, class formation, and class action in the Indian countryside', *Journal of Peasant Studies*, 8, 4, pp. 405–54

Kahlon, A. S. and Tyagi, D. (1980), 'Inter-sectoral terms of trade', *Economic and Political Weekly*, XV, 52, Review of Agriculture, December

Lipton, M. (1975), 'Food policy and urban bias', *Food Policy*, 1, 1, November

Lipton, M. (1977), *Why Poor People Stay Poor: Urban Bias in World Development*, London: Temple Smith

Lipton, M. (1979), 'The technology, the system and the poor: the case of the high-yielding varieties', in Institute of Social Studies, *Development of Societies: The Next Twenty-Five Years*, The Hague: Martinus Nijhoff

Pearse, A. (1980), *Seeds of Plenty, Seeds of Want*, London: Oxford University Press

3 Agrarian transition and the agrarian question*

T. J. Byres

A central episode in the history of all advanced capitalist countries has been the manner in which the agrarian question was resolved. One of the most fascinating problems in the field of social and economic history is the delineation of the complex and varied means whereby capitalism became the dominant mode of production in agriculture: growing out of simple commodity production, here via the landlord class and there via a peasantry which gradually became differentiated (so providing, at the extremes, a stratum of rich peasants who ultimately became capitalist farmers and a stratum of poor peasants who were transformed into agricultural labourers or who joined the urban proletariat); slowly penetrating the countryside; developing the forces of production in manifold ways and raising agriculture's productiveness; eroding feudal and semi-feudal relations of production and replacing them with the stark opposition of a class of capitalist farmers and one of wage labourers. This, the agrarian transition to capitalism (which, to be brief, we may call the agrarian transition), represented a *conditio sine qua non* for the resolving of the agrarian question. But, one must stress that the agrarian transition did not in itself represent a solution in a full sense. This required the working out of certain crucial class configurations. In the relatively early stages of capitalist development, before industrial capitalism can begin to realize its full potential and before, indeed, capitalism may be said truly to dominate the social formation, agriculture must perform two crucial functions. On the one hand, it must generate and release in sufficient quantity and on reasonable terms the surplus that is necessary if growth is to take place outside of agriculture; on the other hand, it must contribute to the creation of the home market that is equally essential. Thus, the agrarian question did not disappear finally until these conditions had been met, and this required that the urban bourgeoisie had undisputed hegemony in

*This chapter is taken from a review article by Byres (1977).

the social formation: the class of capitalist farmers had to yield dominance to urban/industrial interests. Until then the full unleashing of productive forces in industry could be frustrated where, through their political power, rural capitalists could maintain terms of trade which were persistently unfavourable to industry: a major factor preventing industrial growth, which was likely to be compounded, where the landed interest dominated the polity, by successful resistance to taxation (which prevents the appropriation of an investible surplus by the state). In its turn, moreover, this may have limited the development of a mass market, since it prevents the growth of urban demand and leads to no compensating increase in rural demand if, as seems likely, the benefits of favourable terms of trade do not accrue to agricultural labour (whose wages are kept low and who may be purchasers of food). It is to be emphasized, further, that this blocking of capitalist development may become apparent *before* capitalism has become dominant in the countryside, through the representation by the state of the interests of landlords and/or rich peasants.

The development of capitalist agriculture and its eventual yielding of hegemony to the urban bourgeoisie was a long-drawn-out process, sometimes stretching over centuries, which has taken a variety of historical forms. What emerges clearly from any attempt to understand the differing historical circumstances in which the agrarian question has been solved in the past is that the framework in which the analysis is contained must be a broad one. The historical roots must be traced with care; the whole social formation must be kept in mind; developments within agriculture, between agriculture and other sectors, and, indeed, within other sectors must be considered and seen in their mutually determining relationships; the emergence of new classes, shifting class relationships, and the changing hegemony of classes must be examined; the nature of the state must be at the forefront of one's analysis; and the emerging major contradictions must be identified. The appropriate framework within which these different elements may be considered is political economy. A narrowly economistic approach can only be stultifying. The task is a difficult and a complex one. It demands much of anyone who attempts it.

In those countries in which a socialist path has been attempted (in Russia and other eastern European countries, in China, etc.) the agrarian question has loomed large, inevitably, since in none of them had it been resolved satisfactorily beforehand. The classic solution to the agrarian question in such contexts has been collectivization, which has been seen as the true form of socialist agriculture. The difficulties and problems associated with such an attempted transformation are not our concern here. Again, however, we observe that the historical experience has been varied, a sufficiently long historical perspective is necessary if we are to grasp the nature of that experience and political economy is the only suitable framework for analysis.

In poor countries today the agrarian question is of paramount importance. Upon its *full* solution and (if it is solved) upon the manner of its solution the whole future social, economic and political trajectory of these countries depends. Moreover, it remains the case that, populist pipe-dreams notwithstanding (and there are a surprising number of these in the air), the two routes which are open to poor countries are via capitalism or via socialism. We may concentrate on the former since the book reviewed here is concerned with an attempted transformation via capitalism.

Where attempts to traverse the capitalist road are being made (i.e. in the vast majority of poor countries) the agrarian question has been faced and tackled over the last two decades and more, with varying degrees of realism, by a motley of regimes, which have usually mouthed populist rhetoric, on two broad fronts: the institutional and the technical. Institutional change (land reform, co-operative agriculture, community development, *ujamaa* villages, etc.) has usually had egalitarian aims as part of its ideology – aims which, in practice, have seldom been approached. In fact, one of the major effects of such policies has been to hasten the process of differentiation among the peasantry (a process, let us stress, whose historical origins lie in an earlier epoch, when colonialism created conditions in which it might spread, though not necessarily conditions in which capitalism would develop): rich peasants have been the major beneficiaries of such programmes, and one of the most significant phenomena of the last twenty-five years or so has been the emergence of rich peasants as a distinct class, capable of furthering their own class interests, and with increasing political power. A dominant aim of institutional change has been to stimulate growth in agriculture. In this it has been only partly successful, with distressing implications. Thus an attack on the technical front has proved to be a compelling necessity, and the state has undertaken to supply modern inputs and credit in large quantities in order to secure agricultural growth: the so-called 'green revolution' strategy, about which so much has been written of late. Again, the ideologists of this strategy have made egalitarian noises, pointing out, for example, that such a strategy is scale-neutral. But, from the outset it has been a betting-on-the-strong policy, and it has been the rich peasantry and sections of the landlord class who have benefited. A further turn has been given to the differentiation screw and rich peasants have become further entrenched in positions of political strength.

Capitalist agriculture can develop as landlord capitalism (capitalism from above) or as peasant capitalism (capitalism from below) or as a mixture of both forms. For many contemporary poor countries the latter is likely to be a dominant element in any possible agrarian transition, and the essential preliminary to any such agrarian transition is the development of a differentiated peasantry, from which a class of capitalist farmers and one of agricultural wage labourers can emerge. Such an agrarian transition is by no means inevitable. One of the many difficult problems involved in assessing whether or not it has taken place is that of demonstrating that the stratum of rich peasants has actually become a class of capitalist farmers, and, indeed, that a class of free wage labourers has been created. In order to do this, a mode of production approach is necessary in which the characteristics of the precapitalist mode are carefully examined, and if an agrarian transition is being posited, in which the characteristics of the new mode of production are equally carefully identified. One must not *assume* that rich peasants are capitalists, or that because differentiation has proceeded apace the capitalist mode is dominant. One must *demonstrate* that these things are so. Moreover, it is essential to recall the point made above: that the agrarian question is not solved from the point of view of the whole social formation until a regular surplus on reasonable terms (acquired through the market, taxation or savings) is made available to enable industrialization to proceed and capitalism to develop outside of agriculture. This will involve a breaking of the political power of the rich peasantry.

Such is the background necessary to a consideration of Mahmoud Abdel-Fadil's work (1975), which represents the first serious and adequate attempt to analyse the agrarian question in Egypt. From the outset Mahmoud Abdel-Fadil posits that there took place in Nasser's Egypt, between the coup of 1952 and the death of Nasser in 1970, an agrarian transition, and he sets himself the task of analysing and assessing the various dimensions of that transition.

The problem is the one Lenin addressed in *The Development of Capitalism in Russia*: can capitalism develop in a backward society? And the answer is precisely the one given by Lenin with respect to Russia: capitalism can develop (capitalism creates its own market and in the countryside grows out of a differentiated peasantry) and it has developed. Abdel-Fadil raises a number of fundamental issues. The significance of the analysis, moreover, lies beyond Egypt, since the agrarian question is a strategic issue in all poor countries (perhaps *the* strategic issue), which has attracted remarkably little treatment within an adequate framework. Admiring as one is, one is left, nevertheless, with the nagging doubt of whether, indeed, an agrarian transition has taken place in Egypt and whether, as Abdel-Fadil suggests, the agrarian question has, by and large, been solved from the viewpoint of the development of capitalism in Egypt.

For Abdel-Fadil the crucial element in the agrarian transition was the 1952 land reform. We are told, at the outset, that 'the leaders of the coup of 23 July 1952 sensed right from the very beginning, the urgent need to tackle the "agrarian question"' (1975, p. 7). It seems that their perception of the agrarian question was not the one suggested above. It was, rather, their realization that 'if their revolution were to persist, they had both to destroy the power of the entrenched class of big landlords and to win the support of small-holders and the poor rural masses' (p. 7). And so it was that a land reform programme was launched in 1952 'with the clear intention of bringing about a major redistribution of wealth, income and social power in the Egyptian countryside' (p. 7). This did not spring from a social vacuum, but was the reaction to

the mounting agrarian crisis in Egypt [which] reached a dramatic point at mid-century, as the living conditions of the mass of the landless and small peasantry has become unbearable, coupled with the dim prospects of getting employment in the industrial sector. In the years 1950–52 the so-called 'passivity' of the Egyptian peasantry was wearing thin and signs of unrest were spreading everywhere in the countryside (p. 7).

But this is the only tantalizing glimpse that we get of the conditions which gave rise to the coup of 1952: the social base which the leaders appeared to have (or might acquire), and the possible nature, therefore, of the emerging Egyptian state.

Abdel-Fadil argues that the 1952 land reform was instrumental in bringing about the demise of the old agrarian structure. It struck a mortal blow at the class of big landowners (especially absentee landowners) – the landed aristocracy who were masters of the Egyptian countryside prior to 1952 – by dispossessing them, directly and indirectly, of most of their land. The 1952 law set the upper limit on land ownership at 200 feddans (1 feddan = 1.04 acres = 0.42 hectares), but Abdel-Fadil stresses that there were two important effects. The first was the transfer of land due to expropriation by the state, which then redistributed it (including in this the sale of land by big landlords to their tenants of land in excess of the legal ceiling in plots of not more than 5 feddans, in keeping with one of the articles of the 1952 law). The second was the transfer through 'crash' or 'distress' sales of land they were legally entitled to keep by big landowners fearful of even more drastic future land-reform legislation. It is essential to take into account both effects if one is to make an adequate assessment of the nature of the new agrarian structure. That structure, let us note, is portrayed by Abdel-Fadil as being composed of a differentiated peasantry and a class of landless labourers. The former comprises four broad strata: a poor peasantry working holdings of less than 2 feddans; a stratum of small peasants with holdings of between 2 and 5 feddans; a middle peasantry with holdings of between 5 and 20 feddans; and a rich peasantry with holdings of over 20 feddans. The latter is composed of permanent wage labourers and casual farm labourers. I shall comment on this categorization below. For the moment let us concentrate on Abdel-Fadil's treatment of the effect of the 1952 land reform in relation to the agrarian structure, which is a critical element in his handling of the agrarian transition.

Before 1952 there were in Egypt 2000 landowners owning 200 feddans or more, constituting 0.1 per cent of those owning land and owning 20 per cent of the land. Immediately after the fairly speedy implementation of the 1952 law those 2000 landowners saw their total land reduced, as a result of both the effects mentioned, from 1,177,000 fedans to 354,000 feddans, i.e. from 20 per cent to 6 per cent of the total land in Egypt or to 30 per cent of the original level. That 'the power of the old ruling oligarchy, with its roots in the big estates' was broken is beyond dispute. But who were the beneficiaries? Abdel-Fadil demonstrates that as a result of the first effect (direct expropriation and sale of land in excess of the legal limit) 659,000 feddans went to swell the numbers of those owning 5 feddans or less, priority in distribution being given first to those who actually worked the land – whether owners or tenants – secondly to landless inhabitants of the village who were permanent wage labourers, and thirdly to less wealthy inhabitants (p. 8). Distribution was made in plots of 2 to 5 feddans, so that the net result of this effect of the land reform was to create a substantial stratum of what Abdel-Fadil calls 'small peasants'. This is a matter of some importance in Abdel-Fadil's analysis, but it is the second effect ('crash' or 'distress' sales) which Abdel-Fadil stresses as the truly significant one with regard to the agrarian transition. Immediately after the 1952 law some 164,000 feddans changed hands as a result of this, almost all of it purchased by those holding 20–50 feddans, Abdel-Fadil's 'rich peasants'. Medium ownerships of smaller size (5–20 feddans), or 'middle peasants', remained more or less unchanged in number and acreage, in absolute and relative terms, after the land reform. Yet more land was set free for redistribution by a law of 1961, which lowered the limit for a single owner to 100 feddans, and one of 1969 which took it down to 50 feddans, further strengthening the stratum of 2–5 feddan owners ('small peasants'). When all is said and done, however, Abdel-Fadil emphasizes that by 1970 the distribution of land ownership in Egypt was still highly skewed and that 'the most notable trend . . . has been the steady improvement in the relative position (increase in *numbers* and *acreage*) of the medium-sized properties, and in particular owners of 20 to 50 fedans', i.e. rich peasants. By then they constituted around 5 per cent of landowners and owned about 30 per cent of total cultivated area, whereas in 1952 they were under one per cent of landowners and owned just under 11 per cent of the land. For Abdel-Fadil the role of land reform in facilitating the process of differentiation among the Egyptian peasantry is of paramount importance. About this, indeed, there would appear to be little scope for disagreement. The point is demonstrated convincingly. But it is the precise implications of the process of differentiation that one wonders about, with respect to agrarian transition and the solving of the agrarian question.

It is possible that Abdel-Fadil's whole stratification schema includes mis-specifications structured around the identification of rich peasants as capitalists. One should, at this point, stress the extreme importance of the rise of a rich peasantry in a country like Egypt. It is one of the great merits of this monograph that it demonstrates this phenomenon with such clarity. But are rich peasants capitalists? The agrarian transition thesis, which implies that capitalism is dominant in the Egyptian countryside, requires that this be so. The detaching from the ranks of the rich peasantry of groups who are, in all their characteristics, rich peasants (as classically defined) but who are no more than *proto*-capitalists helps strengthen that judgement. But I would suggest that it may be premature judgement. Indeed, while in most of the monograph Abdel-Fadil is quite specific in the elision rich peasant-capitalist farmer, there are one or two points at which he hesitates a little and uses formulations which imply 'not quite'. Thus, the statement that rich peasants 'use capitalist farming methods on a significant scale' (p. 42) carries a trifle less than total conviction (if they were capitalists would they not be using capitalistic farming methods exclusively?). And so, too, does the assertion (p. 42) that 'the class of "rich peasants" is becoming increasingly identified with the formation of a class of "capitalist farmers" or "rural bourgeoisie"' ('increasingly', but not 'totally'?). These are more than mere quibbles. The last quotation implies a class-in-the-making and not a class that has been fully formed. Not only that, but, while Abdel-Fadil provides much evidence to sustain the thesis of differentiation and the emergence of a rich peasantry, he does not analyse the *process* whereby a rich peasantry is transformed into a capitalist class. Rich peasants are not capitalist farmers, and the central question in the political economy of the agrarian question is whether and how rich peasants become capitalists. It is not an easy question to investigate, but it assuredly needs separate and distinct treatment. Abdel-Fadil presents evidence on, for example, wage employment, mechanization and the growing of high-value crops (especially fruit cultivation), which is eloquent of differentiation but not necessarily of a dominant capitalism. The treatment of wage labour gives one particular pause for thought.

One of the defining characteristics of a dominant capitalism is the emergence of a class of wage labourers who are free in Marx's famous double sense: free of property and personally free to hire themselves out for work. Abdel-Fadil points out that landless labourers are divided into two groups, permanent agricultural wage-labourers and casual farm labourers, and that within the latter group we must distinguish 'farm' casual labourers (who are engaged in casual or temporary farm employment) and casual migratory or *tarahil* labourers ('who are usually recruited for the maintenance of canals and other rural public works on a temporary or seasonal basis' – p. 44). It is the last category which raises some thorny questions. It is not that the *tarahil* casual labourers are an unimportant minority, let us stress, for 'a substantial proportion of landless peasants (mostly adult males) work within [this] system' (p. 46). And what are their characteristics? Abdel-Fadil tells us (p. 48) that 'the *tarhila* system of labour-hire retains certain features peculiar to the feudal labour-service system, namely the bondage and the usurious character of the mode of labour hire.' This suggests to me that the transition to capitalism is by no means complete. He continues:

the existence of such a *reserve army of tarahil labourers* illustrates the acuteness of the crisis of transition from feudalism to capitalism in modern Egypt, for this growing mass of labourers, while separated from their principal means of production, the land, are unable as yet to find regular wage employment in the developing capitalist sector of the economy. In other words, these 'free' landless peasants are prevented from becoming a *proletariat* in the modern sense, and are thus compelled to fall back upon semi-feudal modes of exploitation based on a bonded labour-hire system (p. 48).

What does Abdel-Fadil mean here? He appears to mean that the transition to capitalism has taken place, but that it has given rise to crisis circumstances: a crisis, presumably, which will be resolved ultimately by the further development of capitalism. It seems to me, however, that another interpretation is possible. This is that the continued existence, not merely as a 'feudal remnant' but as a substantial and integral part of the relations of production in the countryside, of a 'semi-feudal' mode of exploitation suggests that capitalism is in no full sense dominant in the countryside. The phenomenon so identified by the author is, I think, widespread in the so-called Third World. Our proper identification and analysis of the problem is, therefore, of considerable significance. We are not witnessing a 'reserve army of labour' in the strict Marxist sense (i.e. a reserve army which is doubly free). The transformation of these feudally exploited labourers into a genuine proletariat is dependent upon the development of capitalism in industry on a scale sufficient to absorb them, and this, in its turn, is contingent upon the solution of the agrarian question in a full sense. Let us turn, finally, to this issue.

A careful reading of Abdel-Fadil reveals that this issue is, perhaps, the central one in the analysis. An essential conclusion drawn is that the home market necessary for the development of capitalism has been created, as it must in this kind of context, through changes in the countryside. This was the problem examined by Lenin in his *Development of Capitalism in Russia*. It is certainly an important one. After the Revolution, however, another problem, of equal significance, came to bestride the scene: a problem that was the subject of a great debate, to which Preobrazhensky, Bukharin, Trotsky and many others contributed, and which was, to a considerable degree, responsible for collectivization. This was the marketable surplus/terms of trade problem. This, too, Abdel-Fadil examines. One might add that surplus transfer also requires *taxation* of agriculture. This is touched upon by Abdel-Fadil. Abdel-Fadil's general conclusion is that the agrarian question *has* been solved:

All in all, it seems fair to say that the growth of intersectoral transactions for the purposes of agricultural production, as well as rural households' consumption, will promote industrial development further and hence will lead to a rapid expansion in the forces of production in society as a whole (p. 119).

I would want to raise some questions on this. No evidence is cited of any dramatic upsurge in industrial growth. Indeed, the reverse is indicated elsewhere in the monograph when it is pointed out, as we have seen, that industrial growth has been insufficient to absorb the large numbers of *tarahil* labourers (p. 48) and, further, that 'rural-urban migration in Egypt has proceeded at a rate far beyond the absorptive capacity of industry and particularly of the manufacturing sector' (p. 115). This at least gives one pause for thought. When, indeed, Abdel-Fadil states that 'only a sustained programme of industrial expansion could entirely relieve the landless labourers' (p. 117), might one not draw the conclusion that Egyptian industrialization has, for whatever reasons, been blocked?

In the absence of detailed evidence, it is difficult to assess fully the significance for the creation of a home market of the trends discussed by Abdel-Fadil. But a possibility does exist which he does not discuss fully, although there are hints here and there which bear upon it. That is that any 'market effect' might be neutralized by what one might call a 'surplus effect': i.e. by the inability of the industrial sector to acquire an adequate investible surplus or a marketed surplus of both food and raw materials on sufficiently favourable terms. Abdel-Fadil places considerable emphasis upon the political power acquired by rich peasants in Egypt. On this he is very convincing. Thus:

There are strong indications... that under the agrarian system of to-day, the stratum of rich peasants... carry a decisive weight in the nexus of the new agrarian power structure.... There is also clear evidence that this new privileged stratum of rich peasants (i.e. a kulak class) has gained great bargaining power in recent years (p. 49).

Abdel-Fadil stresses 'the dogged and highly successful defence of the interests of the new rural bourgeoisie by the kulak lobby in the People's Assembly' (p. 123). In view of this strong and increasing political power of the rich peasantry one might expect the defence of their interests to be focused pre-eminently upon resisting attempts by the state (which represents, too, the interests of the urban bourgeoisie and wishes to promote rapid industrialization) to appropriate the surplus upon which their material well-being depends. On the evidence presented by Abdel-Fadil this, indeed, turns out to be the case. But the question one is left asking is: how successful has been the attempt to 'protect national goals from the obstructive tactics of the rural elite' (p. 122)? Abdel-Fadil puts the view that, by and large, the attempt *has* been successful and that, therefore, the agrarian question has in essence been solved. One detects, however, some equivocation in the argument. He presents enough evidence to suggest a contrary view.

Abdel-Fadil emphasizes that the net investible surplus squeezed from agriculture to finance capital formation elsewhere in the economy is very small at 5–7 per cent of total agricultural income in, for example, 1965–70 (p. 120). The conclusion now drawn is that 'in practice there are tangible limits to the intersectoral terms of trade as an instrument for increasing state revenues, because of the possible *disincentive* effects which become operative after a certain critical level of unfavourable terms of trade to agriculture' (p. 121). As a *general* statement this is unexceptionable. But no convincing evidence is presented to the effect that the 'critical level' has been approached in Egypt. Indeed, on Abdel-Fadil's own indices no unfavourable trend emerges, while if one were to include the products which he omits from his calculations the trend would surely be a favourable one. One is left with the presumption that far from *incentives* being a critical element the factor preventing a shift in the terms of trade against agriculture is the organized political power of rich peasants, which is able to obtain subsidized inputs and to secure a truly favourable shift for themselves by moving to high-value crops. If the terms of trade are ineffective one is left with taxation as an instrument of surplus acquisition. Abdel-Fadil does not give taxation any detailed treatment but he is conclusive enough in his statements, that, for example, 'land taxation in Egypt has been allowed in the past to wither away almost to the point of insignificance' (p. 108), while 'direct taxation of farm incomes proved difficult because of both evasion and political or administrative difficulties'. In a footnote (p. 49) he further cites the example, in 1972, of the pro-rich peasant lobby successfully blocking a bill to tax fruit orchards. The upshot must surely be to cast doubt upon the position that the agrarian question has been solved in any full sense.

The differences of interpretation suggested in this article are of more than merely academic interest. They do have political implications. If, as I have suggested, the posited agrarian transition is in doubt; and if the agrarian question remains to be solved, in the sense that the Egyptian state is the uneasy representative of both the urban bourgeoisie and the rich peasantry, with the latter holding primacy and industrialization held back by an inability to acquire a sufficient investible surplus of marketable surplus on favourable terms; then, if the interests of the urban bourgeoisie are to be served at all and if some minimal process of industrialization is to be achieved, the state must ensure that urban wages are prevented from rising, for only thus are profit margins kept from being squeezed. In this kind of situation the pressure to smash organized labour, prohibit strikes and keep the labour force docile becomes overwhelming. Could it be that the developments which have taken place in Sadat's Egypt find part of their explanation in these underlying structural conditions? In these circumstances, Communist parties tempted or engineered into alliance with such regimes must, if they retain any vestige of principle, experience disaster.

References

Abdel-Fadil, M. (1975), *Development, Income Distribution and Social Change in Rural Egypt (1952–1970): A Study in the Political Economy of Agrarian Transition*, Cambridge: Cambridge University Press

Byres, T. J. (1977), 'Agrarian transition and the agrarian question', *Journal of Peasant Studies*, 4, 3, pp. 258–74

4 Urban bias, rural bias, and industrialization: an appraisal of the work of Michael Lipton and Terry Byres *

Stuart Corbridge

Michael Lipton: urban bias, urban classes and why poor people stay poor

At a time when it is beginning to be recognized that 'development' takes place within, and is constrained by, the class structures of Third World nations, Lipton's book – *Why Poor People Stay Poor* (1977) – represents a particularly challenging contribution. Lipton proposes a concept of 'urban bias' as a class explanation of the persistent poverty of much of the Third World: for Lipton the major class antagonism of poor countries is that between urban and rural populations. Clearly the theoretical and political implications of this conclusion demand that we pay his work the closest of our attention.

Lipton claims that his thesis has its genesis in a reaction to the 'industrialization by squeezing agriculture' policy which he identifies with Stalin, and later Mahalanobis (architect of the Second Indian Plan, 1956–61). Attacking this as an inefficient and inequitable ideology, sanctioned by Marxism and Marginalism alike, Lipton stresses that Third World countries should instead invest heavily in their major resource – labour-intensive agriculture. This is a necessary precursor to industrialization. So, 'if you wish for industrialisation, prepare to develop agriculture' (1977, p. 24). Both efficiency and equity goals can then be happily forged together in a progressively spiralling growth strategy. This is so because the rural sector, he argues, is a more responsive utilizer of scarce investments than the luxury-ridden, over-provided urban sector.

The novelty of Lipton's contribution to this lengthy debate on sectoral priorities lies in his attempt to account for the typical

*It is my pleasure to thank the following for their helpful and critical comments on various drafts of this paper: Graham Chapman, B. H. Farmer, Keith Griffin, Barbara Harriss, John Harriss, Barry Hindess, Steve Jones, Gerry Kearns, Michael Lipton, Muqtada, Joan Simms and John Toye.

pandering after urban-industrialization, in terms of an underlying class conflict between a dominant urban class and a largely impotent rural class. An inefficient and inequitable anti-rural strategy has been followed in most Third World countries as a consequence of their domination by urban classes issuing forth a stream of urban-biased policies.

This diagnosis of the ills of poor countries is backed up by plenty of empirical evidence. Symptomatic of urban bias are the cheap procurement prices paid by the urban sector for food, and a series of other 'price-twists' adverse to the interests of the rural class; the heavily imbalanced investment strategies favouring the urban/industrial nexus and the resultant rural skill drain; and the basic lack of health care and educational facilities that defines the rural sector. Urban bias has meant that growth and development have 'effectively' (an ambiguous word) by-passed rural society.

Nor can Lipton foresee a bright future so long as these inequities are compounded by the profligate use of resources which character-izes the urban class. Until recuperative doses of investment are switched to the rural sector, where the massive pool of under-employed family-labour-farms represents the most efficient potential user of scarce development funds, the outlook remains bleak. The possibility of such a sectoral re-allocation of resources is of course predicated, for Lipton, on the demise of the power of the urban class; for urban bias, the proximate cause of the observed inequities and inefficiencies, itself emanates from an urban class – the dominant class in the Third World.

Clearly Lipton's thesis challenges a number of cherished conceptions, alarming not only writers of Marxist persuasions but irritating too those neo-classicists who would rather wish away classes altogether. It is an argument that should elicit strong reactions.

First objection

Lipton's argument as so far presented is incomplete. What first marks him out from so many other theorists is the way he makes explicit a belief that development must mean the raising of the living standards of mankind's poorest forty per cent. Since the 'worst off one third of mankind comprises the village underclass of the Third World' (p. 28), Lipton can weave his argument around a double identity, two equations central to his whole book:

1 an identity of development with the poor masses;
2 an identity of the poor with a rural class.

These identities then sustain Lipton's fundamental assertion that it is, 'more useful, in LDCs, to conduct our analysis of class inter-action in terms of "urban" class and a "rural" class dependent on agriculture, than in terms of classes comprising capitalists, rentiers and proletarians' (p. 109).

Not surprisingly a common first objection is that equating rural with poor in this way is misplaced and misleading. Nor is textual support wanting for those wishing to press this charge on Lipton. For example, 'The WHOLE interest of the rural community is against cheap food.' Or, 'The systematic action of most governments in poor countries to keep down food prices clarifies the operation of class interests in urban bias' (both p. 67; his emphasis). But it is generally indefensible to speak of such common or undifferentiated urban and rural sectors. Sen, for example, demonstrates this clearly enough in his careful analysis of the differential impact (especially in rural areas) of the 1943 Bengal Famine (Sen, 1977); and Frankel (1971) and later writers have shown that the benefits of the 'green revolution' have not been evenly distributed across the rural sector – with the result that the landless labourers and the 'small peasantry' have become progressively more emasculated in the rural production and power stakes. Das Gupta (1977) has indicated also the strength of certain inter-sectoral linkages whereby it is the urban commercial banks which act as the chief financiers of storage granaries for the marketable surpluses of the rich rural farmers. With this direct control over the marketing of their grain the richer farmers are able to withhold produce until prices rise, while the smallholding peasants are forced, largely through debts, to sell on the market at harvest time when prices are at their lowest, thus strengthening the reproduction of the structure of intra–rural exploitation (see also Djurfeldt and Lindberg, 1975, chs. 4–6).

So, clearly, when Lipton presents a simple thesis of urban gain and rural loss damning evidence can usually be marshalled against him. Equally open to empirical appraisal in this manner is his technical formulation of urban bias, resting as it does on the empirical demonstration of relative inefficiency in the urban sector.

It would be a mistake, however, to believe that Lipton's work is concerned only to demonstrate the technical superiority of the 'small peasantry'. His major preoccupation is to argue that the principal contradiction in poor countries is between urban and rural classes. This tension then operates against the interests of the rural class through the agency of urban bias.

It might be thought that the empirical critique of sectoral homogeneity (where such a critique is possible) also damns Lipton's thesis of urban and rural classes. But for the most part Lipton is careful to allow the possibility that the rural élite benefits from urban bias and indeed participates in the 'urban class'. A system of alliances then breaches his sectoral, but not his class, divide – i.e. the rural élite belongs to the urban class. Lipton's categories, plainly, are far from conventional.

Consider the 'green revolution' again. Lipton is at pains to argue that a concentration of inputs does indeed reach the richer farmers, and that this is both inefficient and inequitable, and yet that it is still the result of urban bias. This is because the rural élite has been bought off; or, more correctly, absorbed into the urban class' by virtue of its coincident interests. Accordingly these alliances then preserve the integrity of Lipton's principal (urban/ rural) contradiction in the face of empirical difficulties. Pointing out that the rural sector is internally differentiated on many issues holds no terror for this revamped model. For precisely when Lipton allows his urban and rural classes to bridge the sectoral divide, the unelaborated empirical attack on sectoral homogeneity is circumscribed.

Second objection

Secondly, Lipton is attacked for wrongly identifying and designating his classes. These critics resist Lipton's attempts to build alliances into his analysis under the label of an 'urban class'; and they argue that the possibility of alliances between urban and rural élites, and of intra-sectoral differentiation, must place Lipton's analysis in an entirely different frame of analysis – one of (real) class alignments cutting across the rural/urban divide and merely occluded by his urban bias labelling.

This I take to be the substance of Griffin's appraisal of Lipton's book (Griffin, 1977).[1] Griffin accommodates Lipton's troublesome alliances in an analysis locating classes in terms of their relationship to the means of production. The principal contradiction then becomes not urban/rural but capital/labour. Commenting on

Lipton's devious use of alliances Griffin thus declares

Call this urban bias if you insist, but at the bottom it appears that on the one side we have the urban capitalists, members of the bureaucracy and the professions, the urban labour aristocracy and the large landowners, and on the other side we have the small farmers and tenants, landless agricultural workers and members of the so-called informal sector (1977, p. 109).

This is an objection with which I have some sympathy. Chief among its virtues is the way it resists Lipton's attempts to skirt the shock-waves of the empirical attack on his work by simply relabelling his sectors and classes on the back of a series of alliances. (So the rural élite becomes 'urban', etc.) Quoting Griffin again, this only leads to the

bizarre situation in which the people who control over half the land in rural areas are counted as beneficiaries of urban bias, whilst the people who account for over half of the labour force in urban areas are assigned to the rural classes and suffer from urban bias (1977, p. 109).

It is not only bizarre. The bulk of Lipton's thesis is only made possible by means of this semantic short-circuiting of the empirical attack on his work. Unless Lipton can demonstrate the political impotence of the rural élite to act in its own interests – which he doesn't – then 'urban bias' in such situations has no more coherent mandate than the corollary terms 'élite bias', 'rururban bias', or even 'rural bias'. And all this is quite independent of whether or not we regard such bias as emanating from a particular class.

But in other respects this second objection marks no advance beyond its predecessor. Although it seals off certain linguistic loopholes, the very structure of Griffin's critique is seriously deficient. Indeed crucial areas of Lipton's thesis are placed out of critical bounds. To demonstrate that this is the case, consider Griffin's silence on the likely status of the concept of urban bias in those instances where the formulation of plans, programmes and policies, and the resultant distribution of the spoils, might indeed be said to correspond to the rural/urban divide. That is, in those cases where the (now strengthened) direct empirical objection is precluded. This silence is not simply accidental but is necessarily imposed by the actual mode of critique employed by Griffin; and because this mode can be shown to be defective, it remains singularly inconclusive as an attack on Lipton.

For Griffin economic classes are located always and only by definite relationships to the means of production. This being the case Griffin would be loathe to allow even clear-cut evidence of an urban/rural division of interests to function as proof of the existence of an urban class (except in those freakish situations where such a division of interests coincides with an urban/rural split in terms of their relationship to the means of production). Given this definite theorization of where classes must be located – to be classes at all – even the starkest evidence of an urban/rural division of interests remains unworthy of anything but the most superfluous of comments. Silence, at such junctures, is golden. Moreover the impact of this reading is to relocate the very thrust of Griffin's critique. This is then provided not so much by its demonstrations of sectoral heterogeneity and the semantics involved in Lipton's cover-up of this fact (which is actually the critique's strength), as by its underlying claim to know the real and correct location of economic classes (which is where its difficulties begin).

These difficulties begin not with the specific conclusions of his claim (that classes are to be located by their relationship to the means of production), but with the actual mode of operation of this claim itself. Such a claim has the effect of dismissing other possible conceptions (and so locations) of classes as incorrect, not by reference to their status within particular theoretical arguments, but simply by recording their distance from the asserted real and correct location. That Griffin subscribes to such a 'realist' position is not difficult to establish. Indeed it is shown by his failure explicitly to acknowledge the fact that Lipton is operating with a conception of class fundamentally different from his own, or that it might warrant critical attention in its own terms. Where Lipton sees an urban class Griffin sees nothing at all. Hence the silence.

Of course one might well be disposed to sympathize with Griffin's irritation with Lipton, and with his own theorization of where economic classes are to be located. But this is beside the point. What we have to ask is whether such qualities present a suitable platform on which to build a conclusive mode of critique. And I think the answer must be negative. Whilst the powerful prescriptions of a 'correct' methodology and key concepts lend the realist approach a polemical self-confidence and dismissiveness, it still also shares the pitfalls of all epistemological practices. These shortcomings, of course, are the, 'ultimate circularity and dogmatism' (Hindess and Hirst, 1977, p. 13) that must persistently shadow the epistemological project of designating a uniquely privileged ('scientific') level of discourse. No matter whether this privileged level consists of the observational facts of the empiricist or the realist's key concepts, the privilege itself can only be demonstrated, 'by means of discourses that are themselves held to be privileged' (Hindess and Hirst, 1977, p. 14). Though easier to construct than a critique of a specific argument's internal logic, the external epistemological appraisal finally has only *fiat* as its guarantee.

And this is precisely how Griffin's critique is conducted at certain crucial junctures: by *fiat*. Lipton's claim that an urban/rural division of interests is evidence of the existence of urban/rural classes is silently referred to Griffin's own conceptualization of the correct location of economic classes and less than cursorily dismissed. We can see now that this must be inconclusive. Lipton has only to assert the 'reality' of his own identification of classes to complete a stalemate. Unless we are prepared to accept such indeterminacies, reducing the identification of economic classes to the dubious merits of an author's whim or Occam's razor, it is imperative that we resist Griffin's mode of criticism.

Third objection

It is important that our third objection should address itself to a consideration of the internal consistency of Lipton's argument. The failure of earlier critiques to do just this becomes yet more glaring when we realize that Lipton does provide us with a lengthy enunciation of his position.

He informs us:

the marks of a politically relevant social group are lasting common interest, actual or potential awareness of it, and an actual or potential capacity for action to further it. Let us call such a group a 'class' when its members benefit from moving, in the same direction, the one or two key, disputed variables and the associated decisions most affecting economic structure and income distribution over that period. It is then more useful, in LDCs, to conduct our analysis in terms of an 'urban' class and a 'rural' class dependent on agriculture than in terms of classes comprising capitalists, rentiers and proletarians. THE TYPE OF PRODUCT AFFECTS GROUP INTERESTS AND ACTIONS MORE THAN DOES THE RELATIONSHIP TO THE MEANS OF PRODUCTION (1977, p. 109; his emphasis).

Note that even Lipton feels the need to put 'urban' and 'rural' between quotation marks here.

In the vast majority of cases, as we have already seen, this particular conceptualization of class would certainly not locate a preponderance of undifferentiated urban and rural classes. Semantic rejoinders apart, the evidence is simply not supportive of Lipton's characterizations (for example, that rural money-wage earners always – or even usually – favour high food prices). For the most part there is no need to accuse Lipton of locating his classes by reference to the wrong economic indices to demonstrate the falsity of his claim that the chief division of interests in the Third World is that between urban and rural people.

This leaves those crucial instances where the evidence does indicate a clear-cut urban/rural division of interests. If we abandon the realist critique here, must we then accept Lipton's claim that such divisions are constitutive of urban and rural classes and so an urban bias? I think not, for Lipton's argument is still burdened by two serious deficiencies.

Firstly, any attempt to define a class as an interest group must share the inadequacies attaching to this general equation. Very briefly (for a detailed discussion see Cutler *et al.*, 1977) these inadequacies are an indeterminacy and an instability: indeterminacy in that each and every interest group, to be consistent, must then define and locate a specific class, which leads to a fruitless multiplication of classes rendering the whole concept valueless; and instability in that members of a particular class are prone to rapid and recurring shifts in their membership patterns. Indeed any individual might at the same instant be affiliated to two, possibly contradictory, class locations. This is well evinced in the particularly problematic position of the rural élite, at least in Lipton's analysis. With regard to food prices supposedly, and certainly with regard to the provision of transport and educational facilities, the rural élite is the natural leader of the 'rural class'. With regard to the provision of agricultural inputs it becomes, at the same time, part of the 'urban class'.

Plainly, in its own terms, Lipton's conception of class is untenable. Underscoring his difficulties is a second deficiency: a reductionist conception of politics. Beginning with a claimed identification of policies and plans that are made by and for urbanites, Lipton must then provide urban and rural classes to conform to his assumption that certain politics and interests must always and automatically represent certain classes.

Of course for the most part such clear-cut urban versus rural policies are rarely found. More usually both the urban and rural élites gain. So, for urban bias still to be an emanation from an urban class, Lipton than has to invoke his reductionist and semantic catch-alls, equating first a political force/interest group with a class and, secondly, rural with urban.

Implications

Now once we reject the reductionist project, and Lipton's conception of class, several important consequences follow. Firstly, the failure of Lipton's attempt to provide us with a coherent urban class must automatically lead us to reject his concept of an urban class bias. The concept evades the onslaughts of the empirical and realist critiques only to the extent that it is underwritten by a consistent and workable equation of classes with interest groups. Once this is challenged there can be no such escapes. At best 'urban bias' can exist as a purely descriptive device measuring, for example, the relative efficiencies of sectors of the economy, and inter-sectoral disparities. In this form alone would it be unobjectionable.

The aim of this section has been to show that 'urban bias', except in its toothless descriptive guise, can finally only be sustained on the shifting ground of semantics and the terrain of political reductionism. Once this ground gives way, and the possibility of urban and rural classes is similarly rejected, 'urban bias' collapses. However, because the concept of urban bias does rest so consistently and directly on unfamiliar and unusual definitions of both 'urban' and 'rural' and 'class', the finality of this conclusion will be wanting in those critiques advancing either by simple empirical barrage or by 'realist' prescriptions.

Terry Byres: rural bias, industrialization and socialism

At the other end of the spectrum Byres proclaims the virtues of industrialization. Rejecting Lipton's eulogy of the rural sector, Byres prefers to counterpose an essentially reactionary and stagnant peasant agriculture to a (latently) dynamic industrial sector. The latter, to realize its historical mission as the motor of change – the 'route away from backwardness' (Byres, 1974, p. 221) – must initially siphon off a surplus from agriculture. This means that for the first thirty years or so, to take Byres's estimate, 'the peasantry's role is unenviably Sisyphen'. It is the 'nutrient base', as Preobrazhensky put it, of development (Byres, 1972, p. 228). Unfortunately, if unsurprisingly, the peasantry resists – at least in India. Such is 'rural bias'.

This simple thesis is not without its virtues. Read in a negative sense, as a retort to Lipton's accusations of 'urban bias', Byres manages to produce some interesting and challenging evidence on the 'rural bias' of the recent terms of trade between agriculture and industry in India (see also Mitra, 1977), and on the failure of the Five Year Plans and land reforms of the 1950s to generate an agricultural surplus for industrial use (e.g. in terms of diverted savings, cheap urban wage goods, etc.). He then concludes that, 'If there has been "urban bias" in Indian planning it has proved singularly ineffective in influencing the flow of marketed surplus' (1972, p. 249). Although the evidence is challenging, however, it hardly amounts to a damning critique, even empirically, of the power of urban bias. Lipton could quite fairly grumble that Byres has ignored the sectorally inequitable provision of health and educational facilities, transport infrastructure and so on. Urban bias is not simply a synonym for the terms of trade between agriculture and industry.

The fact that Byres does not confront the whole gamut of urban bias is not simply due to evasive action on his part. Although debate with Lipton is the starting point of Byres' discussion, its main body consists in a positive attempt to stress the need for industrialization and the transfer of an agricultural surplus. As such Byres has less to say directly on the power of urban and rural bias than one might expect. Rural bias is established primarily as an adjunct to his insistence on the need for industrialization. It follows that a serious critique of Byres should not simply point out his opposition to Lipton, in the sense of confining itself to a careful weighing-up of the empirical data presented both for and against urban and rural bias. Rather it must consider the value of Byres's own thesis as an industrializer and, very importantly, the political implications of his thesis – bearing in mind that Byres writes as a socialist. The following critique examines these two related positions.

Byres and industrialization

Byres's two essays follow the same format. Both consist of a bulky exegesis of the obstacles to the extraction of a surplus from a truculent peasantry, together with an indirect consideration of the likely consequences of this for the peasantry. Both rest on the unsupported assertion that industrialization is necessary, almost sufficient indeed, for development, and that it is predicated on the availability – on favourable terms – of an agricultural surplus. Byre's stark thesis makes an easy target for Lal:

As for his [Byres's] advocacy of giving priority to the industrial sector, Lipton is surely right to protest: 'It is growth in income for, and equity among, people that counts – not priority for arbitrarily selected sectors.' To prejudice the former by insistence on the latter is indeed only explicable in terms of doctrine and ideology (Lal, 1975, p. 395).

This is a valid and telling point against Byres. It fails to counter, however, the strong arguments that could be advanced in favour of a strategy of industrial priority generating attendant increases in income and equity for all.

The case for industrialization is well known, and is usually made in terms of a series of sectoral oppositions. Stressing the virtues of industrialization, the industrializer would point to the economies of scale unattainable elsewhere; to the greater export potential of industrial goods in view of current tariff structures; and of course to the role industry has historically played in absorbing labour and sponsoring growth. To cool our passions we might then be reminded that industrialization is, nevertheless, a long-run process. A dynamic vision is needed to perceive that the fruits of growth will indeed funnel back down to the lower strata of society and to those agriculturalists whose surpluses may initially have paved the way.

It is not necessary to agree with this argument to appreciate that Byres could have supported his industrialization thesis more strongly. And one need not disagree with Byres on the need for industrialization to point out that he further fails to argue for the particular form that this industrialization will take – other than for its being capital-goods based. In a fine review, Kay is quick to point out that

[Byres's] article (1974) does not specify what type of industrialisation he proposes. In this sense Lipton is undoubtedly correct when he argues that on both efficiency and equity grounds it is not justifiable to extract an agricultural surplus for financing an inefficient and highly protected, capital-intensive and vastly underutilised industrial sector such as India and many other less-developed-countries have (Kay, 1977, p. 242–3).

Byres systematically evades the possibility that his industries might

operate in societies where capacity under-utilization is still profitable
for the possessing *bourgeoisie*. Likewise he ignores the abundant
evidence recently produced regarding the appropriateness of
technologies in Third World countries. Merely to assert the need
for heavy industry doesn't get very far.

But Kay's critique doesn't take us all the way either. The two
criticisms advanced so far are really only made possible because
Byres chooses not to argue the need for, or form of, industrialization.
Kay.should make clear that this immediately places Byres in the
same mould as the most orthodox and unthinking prophets of
industrialization. Like them Byres must then operate with a unitary
logic of industrialization which can supposedly be successfully
plugged into any society anywhere and at any time, and in any
form (provided it is capital-goods based). Even when equity considerations are appended to this sectoral growth model the difficulties
involved in this position are not by any means confined to those
concerning the appropriateness of the technology (see Williams,
1978).

In particular it is interesting that Kay's condemnation of Lipton
for his anti-socialist leanings does not also extend to Byres's thesis
regarding the imperatives of industrialization. Yet the generalized
and ahistorical nature of Byres's work precludes a consideration of
the possibility that industries operate within determinate, but not
eternal, production relations. Consequently Byres fails to problematize the possibility of a change in the class relations of an industry,
and, correspondingly, the possibility of a transformation to socialist
industry. Instead the scenario is implicitly, but eternally, capitalist
industrialization. Equity in this industrialization model would seem
to refer to a promised future convergence of income levels –
perfectly compatible with capitalism – and not to a democratization
of the relations of production and the growth of non-commodity
forms of distribution of the product.

Such a critique is unlikely to worry most industrializers, many of
whom would gladly eternalize capitalist relations of production,
but clearly it is crucial in Byres's case because his aim is socialism.
Thus if Byres is to nullify the charge of banality that attaches to the
orthodox strategy of industrialization-in-general, and also to rescue
his credibility as a socialist, then his argument has to be buttressed
by an underlying conception of socialist construction which reduces
to an insistence on the necessity of a build-up of heavy, capital-
goods based industries.

Byres and socialism

To recapitulate: at face value Byres's thesis reduces to the stark assertion that industrialization is a 'good thing'. As such it merely represents an unsophisticated reply to Lipton's insistence that a particular mode of agriculture must be given priority in most development strategies. It is then quite easy, and perfectly permissible, to dismiss Byres along the lines of either Lal or Kay. At best his suggestion that industrialization is necessary is old-hat and probably self-evident; at worst his failure to specify the whys and wherefores of such industrialization renders his work classless, ahistorical, and ultimately banal.

Nevertheless some critics, particularly those of broadly left-wing sympathies themselves, have been less than scathing in their considerations of Byres's thesis – perhaps because he claims to be a socialist. But possible personal sympathies for socialism should not be made into an *a priori* guarantee of the validity of a particular argument. If we are to follow the general practice and take seriously the possibility that Byres is a socialist, then it is imperative that we examine the theoretical consistency and political implications of his particular conception of socialism. As we have already seen, Byres insists on the need for (heavy) industrialization-in-general to the exclusion of a consideration of the class relations of production in which such industries must operate. Accordingly, if he is to escape the stigma of 'capitalist apologetic' which would normally attach to such an orthodox strategy, his conception of socialist construction must reduce to the process of industrialization itself. Heavy industry is inherently socialist. Only through such an equation can Byres evade the necessity of problematizing the role and form of industrialization or the relations of production in which it operates. Given such an equation these are self-evident.

It follows that if Byres is to be opposed to Lipton in the name of socialism it is incumbent upon Byres's supporters to demonstrate that a Marxist pedigree does exist to support the equation of socialist construction with industrialization, and to show that such a pedigree is theoretically consistent. The following section aims to review, and then to criticize, the possible arguments that could be advanced from a 'Marxist' perspective to buttress Byres's implicit conception of socialist construction. The most likely contenders here are Stalin, and a consideration of the Soviet experience in the 1930s, and the theoretical perspectives of Baran and Sweezy. But it is argued that neither present coherent, or especially Marxian, analyses.

Stalin

Byres is keen to deny any parallels between his work and Stalin's. To that end he accuses,

There is nothing necessarily sinister about 'urban bias'. The expression is simply a pejorative way of referring to those who choose the path of industrialisation. To categorise this position as 'Stalinist', to dismiss its arguments as 'doctrine' or 'ideology', is to replace logic and argument with what Myrdal aptly calls 'deprecation by terminology' (Byres, 1974, p. 222).

Of course Byres is quite right to reject such dismissals, although this warning resonates hollowly when it comes from one who fails to provide a logical argument in support of a particular mode of industrialization. Nor is it totally fair to Stalin.

Nevertheless, Byres's conception of the process of socialist construction is still reminiscent of the stance adopted by Preobrazhensky in the 1920s and Stalin in the 1930s. This involved a strategy of rapid heavy industrial growth to be based on a favourable appropriation of an agricultural surplus, drawn especially from the collective and State farms. This process represented a phase of 'primitive socialist accumulation', vital to the Soviet Union's struggle for competitiveness (with the capitalist nations) on the world market. In this struggle centralized large-scale production units, producing capital goods to supply each other's demands, were considered to be best suited to the aims of quick returns, growth, and, importantly, socialist planning and accounting.[2]

The Stalinist intrusion into Byres's discourse is most apparent, however, in his (implicit) proposition that industrialization is a prime mover in the transition to socialism. Only this proposition can distinguish Byres from the orthodox advocates of (capitalist) industrialization. Consider the relevance of Stalin's arguments here.

To justify a strategy of 'primitive socialist accumulation', Stalin had to put forward a theory of history in which the transition to socialism is bullied along by the progressive development of the forces of production (especially heavy industry). Such development creates a tension between the previously corresponding forces and relations of production (in capitalism) which must necessarily and automatically be rectified by the transformation of the relations of production until they harmonize with the newly socialist forces of production. Stalin puts this very clearly:

First the productive forces of society change and develop, and then, depending on these changes and in conformity with them, men's relations of production, their economic relations change ... however much the relations of production may lag behind the development of the productive forces they must, sooner or later, come into correspondence with – and actually do come into correspondence with – the level of the development of the productive forces (Stalin, 1938, p. 31).

At a point in time, then, socialist relations of production are automatically generated to clamp together with a set of corresponding forces of production as the socialist mode of production. In a very powerful manner this thesis sanctions a strategy of all-out development of the ('socialist') forces of production in the sure knowledge that socialist relations will follow.

Crucially, Stalin's argument that the non-correspondence of the forces and relations of production is sufficient to bring about its own rectification through the transformation of the latter, rests on a crude teleology privileging the forces of production. Within this general theory of history: 'The existence of classes and the character of the relations between them are reducible to effects of the structure of the economy' (Cutler *et al.*, 1977, p. 198–9), the class struggle operating only to sweep away the last vestiges of the earlier relations of production in times of non-correspondence. In times of correspondence, assuming that they exist, there is no class struggle in the Stalinist theme of things. Stalin (and Byres) not only depoliticize the process of socialist construction, they also obviate the necessity of socialist analyses of the current political situation. The balance of power of classes and political forces merely ebbs and flows with, and indeed reflects, the rhythms of the economy.

So the choice is clear. Defending Byres's thesis as 'socialist' means accepting a distorted form of Stalin's crude teleology. It involves relegating classes and political forces to subsidiary effects of necessary tendencies (here, industrialization) operating at the level of the economy. In short it involves, with Stalin, abandoning Marx's analysis (see Corrigan *et al.*, 1978). And, not necessarily the same thing, abandoning theoretical coherency.

Baran and Sweezy

The complementary line from Baran and Sweezy perhaps needs to be drawn more tentatively than the line from Stalin. Nevertheless it is Paul Baran to whom Byres refers when he suggests that 'the Marxist approach immediately directs attention towards the surplus and towards surplus acquisition in the context of industrialisation' (Byres, 1972, p. 243).

As we have already seen, it is only Byres's Stalinism that allows him to believe that Marxists are concerned with such unitary, abstract, and non-problematic processes as 'industrialization'. Equally, and it will be the aim of this section to show this, Byres's belief that Marxists are immediately concerned with the transfer of an agricultural surplus to industry, rests in turn on a distortion of Baran and Sweezy's own rather special reading of Marx. It is to their reading that we now turn.

The central concept in Baran and Sweezy's discourse is the economic surplus. This takes three forms:

1 *Actual economic surplus* – the current savings in all societies, e.g. as production, inventories, and foreign-exchange reserves.
2 *Potential economic surplus* – this is the vital concept and it refers to that surplus that could be generated in given technological and natural conditions, minus essential consumption.
3 *Planned economic surplus*

These concepts determine the nature of their critique of capitalism and also their conception of socialism. Briefly put, capitalism and socialism are differentiated by their varying degrees of 'rationality' as measured by their approximation to the potential economic surplus. Socialism here is the ideal wherein the full (potential) economic surplus is achieved. By comparison capitalism, especially monopoly capitalism, is wasteful and irrational, squandering resources in a haphazard fashion on inter-imperialist wars, advertising, pollution control and so forth. Lacking the vigour of early competitive capitalism, the social matrix of monopoly capitalism strangles the rational use of the surplus from an increasingly mature technology. Accordingly, sooner or later, the dictates of rationality will ensure that monopoly capitalism evolves into socialism, just as feudalism evolved into the more rational capitalism.

The problems involved in this theoretical edifice should be evident. As Culley has pointed out it rests initially on an idealistic and utopian vision of a potential economic surplus (Culley, 1977). This can only be arbitrarily defined just as the feudal, capitalist and socialist modes of production can only be arbitrarily and subjectively located in terms of their varying 'degrees of irrationality'. The historical dynamic linking this moral critique of capitalism with a utopian conception of socialism is provided by an evolutionist teleology – not unlike Stalin's – urging the transition to socialism in the name of rationality.

Aside from its internal difficulties this theorization is also far removed from Marx's. This becomes important when Byres claims a 'Marxist' pedigree for his project via Baran and Sweezy. Baran and Sweezy, unlike Marx, locate modes of production by their rationality in utilizing the economic surplus. So, instead of theorizing the class relations of possession/separation from the means of production which are constitutive of a society, Baran and Sweezy prefer to treat entities such as feudalism, capitalism and socialism monolithically, endowing each with its own rationality. One result of this failure to theorize the class relations of a given society, and also the class nature of the production of the surplus (most Marxists would anyway talk of surplus value), is that it necessarily precludes a consideration of the likelihood that inter-imperialist wars, advertising and so forth may indeed be 'rational' for the 'monopoly capitalist' or for specific political forces, if not for society as a whole.

Moreover, the transition to socialism, far from involving an active struggle to establish communal possession of the means and conditions of production and placing it under democratic control, and far from involving the eradication of the double separation of enterprise from enterprise and workers from the means of production that characterizes relations in a generalized commodity economy, is reduced to waiting on the working out of a necessary general tendency (rationality). The possibility that socialism involves the *construction* of determinate relations of production, or that political forces must be won as allies in the struggle towards socialism (or indeed that the possessors of capital might find it rational to struggle against socialist relations) finds no coherent place in Baran and Sweezy's evolutionist and essentially classless argument. A philosophical teleology is substituted for a consideration of the possibilities and necessity of political struggle; socialism is simply handed down on a plate. In short, if Byres does lay claim to Baran's analysis he cannot do so in the name of Marx.

The extent to which Byres does borrow from Baran and Sweezy

is problematic. Certainly his concern for the transfer of an agricultural surplus to industry has little in common with Baran and Sweezy's dominant project of demarcating modes of production in terms of their use of the surplus. But whilst it is possible that Byres has thus simply misunderstood Baran and Sweezy's thesis, it is more likely that he is in fact laying claim to a distorted version of Baran and Sweezy's concept of the economic surplus, and that in so doing, Byres is acting in a manner perfectly consistent with his vulgarized Stalinist conception of socialism.

In this light it is imperative to remember that industry, for Byres, is an intrinsically socialist force of production. This being so the transfer of a surplus from the non-socialist, backward agricultural sector to industry, necessarily represents, in Baran and Sweezy's terminology at least, a rational transfer of the economic surplus. And so, given his premises, Byres is being quite consistent when he insists that 'Marxists' immediately direct their attention to the transfer of a surplus – here the agricultural surplus. Despite his manifest perversion of their intentions the 'Marxists' Byres calls upon here are clearly Baran and Sweezy. It is their focus on the rationality of the use of a surplus to define modes of production, rather than on the class nature of the production of that surplus, that provides (albeit indirectly) a 'Marxist' legitimation for Byres's insistence that surplus transfer is the key issue in the transfer to socialism (industrialization). Indeed the reference to Baran only really makes sense within the framework of Byres's conception of the process of socialist construction. Stalin and Baran and Sweezy, in Byres's hands, reinforce each other.

To reaffirm: with good reason Byres claims Baran (and Sweezy) as his 'Marxist' antecedents. Combined with his Stalinist inheritance this favours the classless nature of his thesis, woven as it is around the relentless unfurling of the industrialization process. It need hardly be added that Byres also reproduces the rationalistic teleology so prominent in the work of both his counsellors. Nor can Stalin or Baran and Sweezy be claimed as either coherent or truly Marxist guarantors of his argument. Those championing Byres against Lipton in the name of socialism would do well to look a little more closely at the 'Marxist' pedigree of Byres's argument.

Conclusion

Byres's thesis can be taken in two ways. Firstly, read independently of a host of attributed supporting arguments, his thesis reduces to the assertion that industrialization is necessary, perhaps sufficient, for development. Not only does Byres fail to supply an argument to back up this claimed necessity of industrialization (which could be done), he also fails to specify fully the precise mode of this industrialization. This weak contribution is anyway confined to the debate over sectoral priorities and as such is clearly ahistorical, failing to problematize the possibility that industries must operate within determinate, but not eternal, class relations of production. In short his thesis is neither new, nor radical, nor is it especially well argued.

In spite of this Byres has been largely exempted from the academic cross-fire that greets such an ostensibly anti-socialist *bête noire* as Lipton. This exemption rests on a mistaken notion of socialist loyalty. The possibility that Byres may be well disposed to socialism cannot guarantee that his argument is automatically predicated on a consistent and coherent conception of socialism. This is the major failing of those aiming to privilege Byres's discourse in the name of socialism. As I have endeavoured to show, the theoretical perspectives that could underpin Byres's socialism are most probably provided in the form of a vulgarized Stalinism together with a similar borrowing from Baran and Sweezy. Neither are beyond criticism.

In short, Byres's thesis reduces either to the bland, and definitely not socialist, assertion that industrialization-in-general is vital (a simple retort to Lipton); or, conceivably, to the politically emasculated and theoretically deficient 'socialist' perspectives of Stalin and Baran and Sweezy. Were it not for the suggestions of certain other critics, the first possibility would perhaps be easier to believe.

Lipton and Byres : an opposition reconsidered

The thrust of the preceding analyses has not only been to examine the theoretical rigour of Lipton's and Byres's arguments in their own terms, but also to indicate that the opposition so commonly drawn between the two is largely fallacious.

If political sympathies do not always guarantee (or damn) particular arguments, neither do the inadequacies of one thesis – say Lipton's urban class bias – automatically and necessarily validate the other's (here Byres's) theory. The collapse of the concept of urban class bias does not guarantee the validity of the concept of rural class bias any more than the failure of Byres's industrialization teleology justifies a unitary and necessary path of development led by agriculture. It is the error of a crudely dualistic social theory to believe otherwise.

Far more striking than the differences between Byres and Lipton is their essential similarity; namely the subordination of their theories to the dictates of an ultimately classless and ahistorical debate on sectoral priorities. The debate between the two has acquired its very acerbity and momentum precisely because it respects this common ground. Of course the sectors that are championed do represent the 'two ends of the spectrum' (Byres, 1974, p.221) in one sense (industry versus agriculture, urban versus rural), but more pertinent is the fact that these are two ends of a very narrow spectrum, a spectrum with a common sectoral logic (and a logic both would claim to resist no doubt).[3] They are certainly not the two ends of the spectrum of development thinking, as Byres would have us believe.

Moreover the 'spectrum' to which both authors are committed offers similarly narrow political alternatives. As ever it is Lipton who spells out these possibilities most directly. Maintaining a close correspondence with his theoretical constructs, and thus neglecting the political strength of the rural élite, Lipton's professed concern for the poor and oppressed of Third World nations is suffocated beneath his demands for a simple redirection – to the rural sector – of the power and resources presently controlled by the planning oligarchy. This sectoral re-allocation is to be inspired primarily by a concerted policy of intellectual persuasion. In Lipton's world of reasonable men, advance consists in the education of self-interested parties (urban planners, élite politicians, labour and Trade Union movements) to recognize the primacy of the urban/rural contradiction and the rationality of a development strategy led by peasant agriculture. In line with the tepid gradualism of this pressure group politics, which recognizes not so much the existence of inequalities reproduced along with the reproduction of definite relations of production as inequalities stemming from the planning apparatus, Lipton outlines a number of specific political goals. These include extra pay for rural postings (government officials), longer rural postings and better incentives for rural officials to seek promotion within the public service hierarchy, the best exam entrants to be sent to the rural sector, and so forth (Lipton, 1977, pp. 340–1).

Now one would not wish to dispute the possibility that some of these reforms might have beneficial effects, but it does need to be emphasized that the limiting of Lipton's alternatives to the realm of planning reformism is a corollary of an approach which effectively privileges particular sectors. Not that Lipton would regard this as a weakness of course. Part of his aim in conflating an urban sector with an 'urban class', and then proclaiming that the principal antagonism cleaving Third World societies is that between urban and rural classes, is to offer planning reform as an ostensibly radical (i.e. 'class') alternative to Marxist political solutions. By challenging the Marxist insistence that the main enemies are capitalists and imperialists, Lipton can then take away some of the ground supporting the stress many Marxists put on the opposition between revolutionary activity and what they regard as mere tinkering within the arena of bourgeois planning.

Byres, perhaps to spare his 'socialist' blushes, refrains from offering us such detailed programmatics. But it is difficult to see how his political prescriptions could depart radically from the type of measure proposed by Lipton without contradicting the import of his industrialization thesis. By choosing to enter the debate on Lipton's terms, accepting and not resisting his sectoral constructs, Byres is constrained simply to reverse Lipton's specific conclusions (so industry replaces agriculture) but to mirror his essential logic. What makes this endeavour even less acceptable is Byres's failure then to follow Lipton's example further and at least offer us a set of arguments to support his particular assertion that industrialization is vital.[4]

To sum up: it is the suggestion of this paper that the central umbilical cord tying together the work of Lipton and Byres outweighs in importance the specific discrepancies in their arguments. Despite disclaimers to the contrary both arguments, when stripped to their essentials, are structured by a common sectoral emphasis. Given this sectoral framework, neither can coherently conceptualize sectoral differentiation or formulate political strategies consonant with the needs of the poor and dispossessed.

Notes

1 Griffin is not alone in presenting this 'second objection'. I would also include, for example, Van Arkadie (1978) and Byres (1979)

2 For another consideration of the role of the agricultural surplus

in Soviet 'primitive socialist accumulation', see Bettelheim (1967), Ellman (1975), Harrison (1978), Millar (1970) and Pollitt (1972).

3   e.g. Lipton, 'It is growth in income for, and equity among, people that counts – not priority for arbitrarily selected sectors' (Lipton, 1974).

4   Another facet of Byres's politics is his disdainful appreciation of the potentiality of a revolutionary peasantry. There is no space to examine this here; suffice to say that it is inextricably linked with his conception of industrial socialism. On this 'implicit political scenario' see Kay (1977).

References

Baran, P. (1957), *The Political Economy of Growth*, New York: Monthly Review Press

Baran, P., and Sweezy, P. (1966), *Monopoly Capitalism*, New York: Monthly Review Press

Bettelheim, C. (1967), *The Transition to Socialist Economy*, Hassocks: Harvester, (1975)

Byres, T. (1972), 'Industrialisation, the peasantry and the economic debate in post-independence India', in A. V. Bhuleskar (ed.), *Towards a Socialist Transformation of the Indian Economy*, Bombay: Popular Prakashan

Byres, T. (1974), 'Land reform, industrialisation and the marketed surplus in India : an essay on the power of urban bias' in D. Lehmann (ed.), *Agrarian Reform and Agrarian Reformism*, London; Faber

Byres, T. (1979), 'Of neo-populist pipe dreams', *Journal of Peasant Studies* 6, 2, pp. 210–44

Corrigan, P., Ramsay, H., and Sayer, D. (1978), *Socialist Construction and Marxist Theory*, London: Macmillan

Culley, L. (1977), 'Economic development in neo-Marxist theory', in B. Hindess (ed.), *Sociological Theories of the Economy*, London: Macmillan

Cutler, A., Hindess, B., Hirst, P., and Hussain A. (1977), *Marx's Capital and Capitalism Today*, vol.1, London: Routledge & Kegan Paul

Das Gupta, B. (1977), *Agrarian Change and the New Technology in India*, Geneva: UNRISD

Djurfeldt, G., and Lindberg, S. (1975), *Behind Poverty*, London: Curzon Press

Ellman, M. (1975), 'Did the agricultural surplus provide the resources for the increase in investment in the USSR during the First Five Year Plan?', *Economic Journal*, 85, pp. 844–3

Frankel, F. (1971), *India's Green Revolution*, Princeton: Princeton University Press

Griffin, K. (1977), 'Review of Lipton's *Why Poor People Stay Poor*', *Journal of Development Studies*, 14, 1, pp. 108–9

Harrison, M. (1978), 'Survey : the Soviet economy in the 1920s and 1930s', *Capital and Class*, 5, pp. 78–94

Hindess, B., and Hirst P. (1977), *Mode of Production and Social Formation*, London: Macmillan

Kay, C. (1977), 'Review of Lehmann (ed.)', Journal of Peasant Studies, 4, 4, pp. 241–44

Lal, D. (1975), 'The agrarian question' *South Asian Review*, 8, 4, pp. 389–400

Lipton, M. (1974), 'Towards a theory of land reform' in D. Lehmann (ed.), *Agrarian Reform and Agrarian Reformism*, London:Faber

Lipton, M. (1977), *Why Poor People Stay Poor: A Study of Urban Bias in World Development*, London: Temple Smith

Marx, K. (1865), *Capital*, vol. III, Moscow: Progress Publishers, 1974

Millar, J. (1970), 'Soviet rapid development and the agricultural surplus hypothesis', *Soviet Studies*, July, pp. 77–93

Mitra, A. (1977), *Terms of Trade and Class Relations*, London: Frank Cass

Pollitt, B. (1972), 'The Soviet economic debate in the twenties', *Marxism Today*, 16, 4, pp. 161–25

Sen, A. K. (1977), 'Starvation and exchange entitlements', *Cambridge Journal of Economics*, 1, 1, pp. 33–59

Stalin, J. (1938), *Dialectical and Historical Materialism*, Moscow: Red Star Press, 1972

Van Arkadie, B. (1978), 'Review article: town versus country', *Development and Change*, 8, 3, pp. 409–15

Williams, G. (1978), 'Imperialism and development : a critique' *World Development*, 6, 7/8, pp. 925–6

Part Two

Structural analysis of agrarian change: capital and peasantry

Introduction

We commented earlier (in our introduction to Part One) that in spite of the possible attractions, in principle, of the contemporary 'populist' small farm strategy of rural transformation, even its protagonists concede that this is not what is actually happening in much of the Third World. Rather do we find evidence of the development of a more capitalistic pattern of agriculture, at least in the sense that there is a good deal of evidence for relatively rapid progress on a small number of larger farms, as compared with stagnation on many small farms (see introduction to Part One, note 5, p. 44). To understand processes of change in agrarian societies it is necessary to examine the development of capitalist commodity production, and its implications.

'Differentiation' in perspective

It should be said right at the outset that in spite of the expectations both of some Marxists and of some liberal economists that the development of capitalism in agriculture, as in industry, must necessarily mean the increasing concentration and centralization of production into larger units, this has *not* been what has actually happened historically, even in some of the most advanced capitalist economies. Mann and Dickinson (1978) have recently sought to explain this in terms of the Marxist theory of value; while Vergopoulos (1978) has documented it historically in the context of southern Europe in particular. He writes:

family farming is the most successful form of production for putting the maximum volume of surplus labour at the disposal of urban capitalism. It also constitutes the most efficient way of restraining the prices of agricultural products. The peasant who is working for himself does not necessarily consider himself to be a capitalist, or an entrepreneur, whose activities depend on the ability to obtain a positive rate of profit. On the contrary, although the head of his agricultural concern, he sees himself, more often than not, as a plain worker who is entitled to a remuneration which will simply assure him his livelihood. Moreover, in the framework of domestic economy the problem of ground-rent does not arise . . . . For capitalists contemporary family farming is not an economic space which has to be penetrated and conquered, but an 'exotic' whole which has to be subdued as such (1978, p. 446, p. 452).

It seems likely that these observations have a wide general relevance, but it should be noted also that in the circumstances of much of Asia and Latin America, at least, rural societies are characterized not only by family farms but also by a very large number of *marginal* farms – that is farms which are not adequate to supply the livelihoods of the families operating them – as well as by large numbers of landless households (Washbrook estimates that of all the rural households in the Madras Presidency, which covered a substantial part of South India, perhaps as many as 85 per cent fell into these categories of marginal and landless, even at the end of the nineteenth century; Washbrook, 1976, ch. 1). Far from being 'squeezed out' by the development of capitalist farming, large numbers of marginal farmers may continue to exist and to provide the base for the deep entrenchment of merchant/money-lending capital in these societies.[1] Such households do not have the positive characteristics ascribed to family farms by the populists, and which might be deduced also from Vergopoulos's writing. These farms are subject to exploitation (for example, through what Bernstein in our third reading in this Part calls 'the simple reproduction squeeze' which we discussed in our Introduction to Part One) and their characteristics are to be understood in terms of their relationships with developing capitalism, diverse as these may be.

Lenin commented that 'Infinitely diverse combinations of elements of this or that type of capitalist evolution are possible', and Bernstein notes in his article here that the many different paths of possible development 'indicate the heterogeneity of forms of peasant production, the dangers of facile generalization, and the need in investigating particular peasantries to examine their relations with other forms of production and the overall development of commodity relations'. This might be taken as a charter; and the fact that the development of capitalist commodity relations does not imply a necessary process of centralization and concentration of agricultural production certainly does not negate the importance of understanding the implications of the deepening and the widening of commodity relations in agrarian societies.

We concentrate here in general upon the theme of capital and peasantry. It should also be noted, however, that there is a developing literature on pre-capitalist societies, especially in Africa, which examines their economic foundations. It is the product particularly of modern French anthropology, and it responds partly to the exaggerated ideas of 'equality in poverty' which characterize some of the older ethnographic studies. In the concept of the 'lineage mode of production', developed by anthropologists of the new school, attention is drawn to labour exploitation within 'families' – in societies which were once supposed to be in a blissful state of primitive communism (see Seddon, ed., 1978). This literature also examines the role of exchange in the pre-capitalist societies of Africa and it is critical of anthropological approaches which are based on a distinction between 'market economies' and economies of 'reciprocity and redistribution' (see Dupre and Rey, in Seddon, ed., 1978; and in Wolpe, ed., 1980). Finally it is concerned with the 'articulation' of these pre-capitalist modes of production with capitalism (see general introduction).

Lenin's statement of 'differentiation'

Our first reading is a passage from Lenin's classic *The Development of Capitalism in Russia*, in which he summarizes the results of his detailed examination of the existing statistical evidence on the rural economy of late nineteenth-century Russia. Lenin concluded that a process of 'differentiation' of the peasantry was taking place and was developing 'the latter's extreme groups at the expense of the middle peasantry [creating thereby] two new types of rural inhabitants... the rural bourgeoisie or the well-to-do peasantry [and] the rural proletariat, the class of allotment-holding wage-workers'. This is the key text on which many subsequent analyses of the differentiation of the peasantry have been based.[2] Although, as we have observed, and as will be seen in other readings in this part, there is good reason to be sceptical of the necessity for the process described by Lenin to take place, or certainly for it to complete itself, there is no doubt that the existence of socio-economic differentiation amongst rural households is a fact of great importance in most agrarian societies. Lenin's work teaches us to be critical of suggestions that rural producers are an homogeneous mass; and it should teach us to be critical, too, of the notion which appears in some writing on rural development that there is a sequence of stages from 'customary societies' up to 'successful, commercial, sophisticated modernizing groups'.[3] Lenin's work reminds us that the very existence of such 'commercial . . . modernizing groups' may imply the existence also of much less 'successful' groups of marginal farmers and landless people. Readers should note that Lenin's statement of the process of differentiation in this passage is much less dogmatic than some of his followers have assumed, and he concedes that

When we said above that the peasant bourgeoisie are the masters of the contemporary countryside, we disregarded the factors retarding different-iation: bondage, usury, labour-service etc. Actually the real masters of the contemporary countryside are often enough not the representatives of the peasant bourgeoisie, but the village usurers and the neighbouring landowners.

This strikingly recalls the arguments of some recent writers who have found that the continuing development of merchant/money-lending capital constrains the development of agrarian capitalism.[4]

His analysis of the differentiation of the peasantry was directly relevant to Lenin's assessments of the political tendencies of different groups within the peasantry. Recently there has been a good deal of analysis of agrarian revolutions, rebellions and political action, which has sought to establish which class or alliance of classes amongst the peasantry has mobilized to oppose oppression. A theory which has won a good deal of support is that which holds that it is the middle peasantry which is initially most militant, because of its relative independence from control by the dominant class of landlords, rich peasants, or capitalist farmers; though this fraction of the peasantry is *not*, finally, a revolutionary class. Leadership must, it is thought, pass eventually from the middle peasants to the poor peasantry and the landless in order for oppressive regimes to be successfully overthrown and replaced by a more democratic and egalitarian order. Understanding of the differentiation that exists within the peasantry is essential in the analysis of agrarian politics.[5]

Lenin, Kautsky and Chayanov

In the next reading Djurfeldt critically reviews the classical studies not only of Lenin, but also of Kautsky and of Chayanov. Djurfeldt suggests not that 'there was no differentiation' but that models based on Lenin's understanding of late nineteenth-century Russia are not adequate for explaining the actual historical development of agriculture in much of the West. Kautsky, the German social democrat who was perhaps the leading Marxist theoretician at the end of the nineteenth century, published his work *Die Agrarfrage*[6] in 1899, shortly before *The Development of Capitalism in Russia* appeared. Kautsky was engaged at that time in a bitter debate about the stance and strategy of the German Socialist Party, and in the context of the debate he was concerned to demonstrate that 'capitalism must succeed' more or less along the lines indicated by Marx. But as Djurfeldt points out 'There was a remarkable dualism in Kautsky', for while his teleological conception of capitalist development led him to interpret his evidence in terms of a model of concentration and centralization of production, the richness of his observations made him almost uneasily aware that Western agriculture in the late nineteenth century was *not* developing in the way which might have been anticipated from Marx's analysis in *Capital*. This was partly because of increasing international competition, especially in the grain trade, which created a crisis of profitability for European capitalist agriculture and produced conditions in which, relatively speaking, the so-called 'middle peasants' were able to thrive. In some respects Kautsky almost anticipated conclusions like those of Vergopoulos, to which we referred earlier.

Kautsky was aware of the possibility that agro-capital and co-operative societies could bring about vertical concentration of production in agriculture without expropriating the peasants: 'this industrialisation of agriculture does not entirely eliminate the smallholder, it binds him to the monopsonistic power of the factory and converts him into a serf of industrial capital.' Bernstein further discusses this process in the next reading.

Djurfeldt is less sympathetic to Lenin's analysis, finding that the actual historical development of Western agriculture is not reflected in Lenin's writings as it is in Kautsky's. Lenin does distinguish two roads to capitalist agriculture – the so-called 'Prussian' path of development from within a landlord economy, and the 'American' path in cases where there is no landlord class. Djurfeldt suggests that the unilinearity of Lenin's original model (as laid out in *The Development of Capitalism*) is but little modified, and that subsequent history has proved him to have been largely wrong. Djurfeldt has perhaps missed the reservation which Lenin himself expressed, and which we quoted above (though it is true that Lenin did not much develop the suggestion made in that passage).

Chayanov, however, though he was circumspect in his criticisms of Lenin, suggested alternative explanations for the patterns of socio-economic disparity that Lenin observed in the statistical data – explanations in terms of various processes of cyclical mobility (explained in the reading by Shanin in Part Three). Further, he drew attention to the same processes of vertical concentration observed by Kautsky, and developed the explanation of them. Chayanov also believed that this kind of concentration, in co-operative organization subordinated to state control, would constitute the best path for the socialist development of agriculture. Djurfeldt puts forward the view that this strategy, rejected in the Soviet Union, has been shown to have been successful in China.[7]

Peasants as 'disguised proletarians'

In the third reading here, Bernstein offers a broad discussion of the problem of the peasantry. He rejects one contemporary view, which is that there is a distinct 'peasant mode of production' which may be 'articulated' (or linked up) with the capitalist mode of production (his argument is explained in paragraphs 39 and 40). He also expresses some scepticism about the concept of a specific peasant economy; while at the same time he makes it quite clear that in his view 'differentiation' is not a *necessary* process: 'Differentiation in class terms is another dimension of the intensification of commodity relations [but] not a necessary condition or effect of [this] intensification . . . this will depend on the concrete conditions in which intensification occurs.' Bernstein analyses the process of 'commoditization' of a society of household producers, the logic of whose operations is (as we saw in the introduction to Part One) to produce for subsistence and to provide for the costs of their reproduction. The autonomy of the process of reproduction of such households is disrupted when they come to require cash (for example, in order to pay taxes to the government) or when they need to produce for sale in order to purchase things which are required for their survival. Such households are liable to become dependent upon capitalists for their reproduction (and may become subject to 'the simple reproduction squeeze' which we discussed earlier, in the introduction to Part One).

Bernstein's central argument is that in this kind of relationship with capitalism the household *form* of production may well survive and remain intact, and that this frequently serves the interests of capitalists very well. Such producers therefore become 'wage-labour equivalents' (or 'disguised proletarians' as Roseberry has it; 1978) – in the sense that although they retain a nominal independence through the possession of some of their means of production, capital exercises a substantial degree of control over what is produced and how it is produced, and finally appropriates so much of the produce of the households as to leave them with the equivalent only of a bare wage.[8] The peasantry thus constitutes a distinct form of production which may be preserved intact through its relationship with capital and the state.[9]

The 'efficiency' of peasant agriculture

Djurfeldt and Bernstein do not reject the possibility of differentiation and neither of them disputes the analytical importance of distinguishing between classes in agrarian societies – but they do show how and why peasant household production may persist in a capitalist economy. In the last paper in this part Michael Taussig extends this argument, in a study of the development of capitalist agriculture in the Cauca Valley in Colombia. What is especially striking about this paper is Taussig's defence of the 'efficiency' of the peasant agriculturalists of the valley by comparison with the large-scale capitalist farmers: 'The "capital" efficiency of small peasant producers is higher than that of capitalist farmers and their energies are far less taxed as peasant farmers than as wage labourers on capitalist farms.' The paper *documents* this important point,[10] which is made in more general terms by Williams (in Part Five), as well as by Vergopoulos, with a different emphasis, in the work to which we referred earlier. Taussig also shows how class differentiation amongst the peasantry of the Cauca Valley is mitigated by the demographic and social factors that determine household size, and by inheritance. It is not that socio-economic inequalities are unimportant (differentiation as a static pattern), but that any trend towards the polarization of peasant classes is weakened by the processes described. But the peasant production of the Cauca Valley does not exist in isolation from the capitalist production of the region, nor does it exist in isolation from the state. Taussig emphasizes how non-capitalist institutions may be necessary for capitalist development, and he shows that though capitalist farming is less efficient than peasant production '(because of its monopoly over land) it compensates for its inefficiencies by being able to take advantage of peasant efficiencies'. The relationship between capitalism and peasant agriculture has been significantly affected by the 'green revolution', as in recent years the state and international development agencies have encouraged the peasants of the valley to change over from their low-capital, low-energy farming system, which was based on perennial crops, to planting seasonal seed crops. Taussig explains the *harmful* effects of the 'green revolution' package both on the 'capital' efficiency of peasant farming and on its ecological efficiency, but he suggests that it may be intended (in spite of these effects) to shore up peasant production, or 'to reinstate the subsidy that is peasant farming', in circumstances in which, because of its declining land base, the original peasant farming system had begun to decline. This paper well illustrates the 'problem' that the peasantry pose, both practically and to different theoretical schemes.

Notes

1 On the role of merchant capital see Kay (1975) for a theoretical discussion; and for substantive studies see: Amin (1982); Banaji (1977a); Harriss, B. (1981); Harriss, J. (1982); Patnaik (1976); Roseberry (1978); Sau (1976).

2 A valuable discussion of Lenin's scheme is in Alavi (1965). See also Patnaik (1976); and Deere and de Janvry (1979).

3 Such a suggestion appears, for example, in Hunter, Bunting and Bottrall (eds.) (1976)

4 See note 1 above.

5 The 'middle peasant' thesis was originally put forward by Alavi (1965), and it was developed by Wolf in his study of *Peasant Wars of the Twentieth Century* (1969). For a recent critique of wider relevance than its immediate focus in Western India see Charlesworth (1980). For studies of peasant political action in India see Desai (ed.) (1979): and Hardiman (1981). Useful studies of peasants and peasant politics in Africa are to be found in Beckman (1976); Bernstein (1981); Beer and Williams (1975); Iliffe (1979), especially ch. 9; Kitching (1980); O'Brien (1971); Van Hekken and Van Velsen (1972). See also Raikes and Williams in Part Five, below.

6 *Die Agrarfrage* has never been translated into English, though

Banaji (1976) has recently translated a selection of passages.
7 See: Gray (1971, 1972); Nolan (1976).
8 The concept of peasant household producers as wage-labour equivalents is founded on the distinction that Marx made between the 'formal' and 'real' subsumption of labour into capital. For discussion see: Banaji (1977a); Harriss, J. (1982).
9 Hyden, in a controversial study of Tanzania (1980) presents a different perspective on the peasantry, which does, however, share Bernstein's emphasis on the persistence of peasant production. Hyden sees the autonomy of the Tanzanian peasantry – and its continuing resistance to 'capture' by the market and by the state – as constituting a major problem standing in the way of the development of the country.
10 Taussig's discussion of 'efficiency' in terms of energy expenditure is relevant to the wider debate in energy efficiency in tropical agriculture: see Merrill (ed.) (1976); Pimental, D. and M. (1979); and also Ruthenberg (1980). His discussion of work in the Cauca Valley may also be compared with other anthropological studies of 'the social construction of work': see Wallman (1979).

References

Alavi, H. (1965), 'Peasants and revolution', *Socialist Register 1965*, reprinted in A. Desai (ed.), *Peasant Struggles in India*, Bombay: Oxford University Press, 1979

Amin, S. (1982), 'Small peasant commodity production and rural indebtedness: the culture of sugar cane in eastern U.P., *c.* 1880–1920', in R. Guha (ed.) *Subaltern Studies 1: Writings on South Asian History and Society*, Delhi: Oxford University Press

Banaji, J. (1975), 'India and the colonial mode of production: comment', *Economic and Political Weekly*, 6 December 1975, pp. 1887–92

Banaji, J. (1976), '*The Agrarian Question* (by Karl Kautsky): translation and summary of selected parts', *Economy and Society*, 4, 1, pp. 1–49; reprinted in H. Wolpe (ed.), *The Articulation of Modes of Production*, London: Routledge & Kegan Paul, 1980

Banaji, J. (1977a), 'Capitalist domination and the small peasantry: Deccan districts in the late nineteenth century', *Economic and Political Weekly*, special number, August 1977, pp. 1375–1404

Banaji, J. (1977b), 'Modes of production in a materialist conception of history', *Capital and Class*, 7, 3, pp. 1–44

Beckman, B. (1976), *Organising the Farmers: Cocoa Politics and National Development in Ghana*, Uppsala: Scandinavian Institute of African Studies

Beer, C. E. F. and Williams, G. (1975), 'The politics of the Ibadan peasantry', *African Review*, 5, pp. 235–56

Bernstein, H. (1981), 'Notes on state and peasantry: the Tanzanian case', *Review of African Political Economy*, 21, pp. 44–62

Charlesworth, N. (1980), 'The "middle peasant thesis" and the roots of rural agitation in India, 1914–1947', *Journal of Peasant Studies*, 7, 3, pp. 259–80

Deere, C. D. and de Janvry, A. (1979), 'A conceptual framework for the empirical analysis of peasants', *American Journal of Agricultural Economics*, 61, 4, pp. 601–11

Desai, A. R. (ed.) (1979), *Peasant Struggles in India*, Bombay: Oxford University Press

Friedman, H. (1980), 'Household production and the national economy: concepts for the analysis of agrarian formations', *Journal of Peasant Studies*, 7, 2, pp. 158–84

Gray, J. (1971), 'The Chinese model', in A. Nove and D. Nutti (eds.), *Socialist Economics*, Harmondsworth: Penguin, 1972

Gray, J. (1972), 'Mao Tse-tung's strategy for the collectivisation of Chinese agriculture', in E. De Kadt and G. Williams (eds.), *Sociology and Development*, London: Tavistock, 1974

Hardiman, D. (1981), *Peasant Nationalists of Gujarat: Kheda District 1917–1934*, Delhi: Oxford University Press

Harriss, B. (1981), *Transitional Trade and Rural Development: The Nature and Role of Agricultural Trade in a South Indian District*, New Delhi: Vikas

Harriss, J. (1982), *Capitalism and Peasant Farming: Agrarian Structure and Ideology in Northern Tamil Nadu*, Bombay: Oxford University Press

Hunter, G., Bunting, H., and Bottrall, A., (eds.) (1976), *Policy and Practice in Rural Development*, London: Croom Helm

Hyden, G. (1980), *Beyond Ujamaa in Tanzania: Underdevelopment and an Uncaptured Peasantry*, London: Heinemann

Iliffe, J. (1979), *A Modern History of Tanzania*, Cambridge: Cambridge University Press

Kay, G. (1975), *Development and Underdevelopment: A Marxist Analysis*, London: Macmillan

Kitching, G. (1980), *Class and Economic Change in Kenya: The Making of an African Petite-Bourgeoisie*, New Haven, Conn. and London: Yale University Press

Mann, S., and Dickinson, J. M. (1978), 'Obstacles to the development of a capitalist agriculture', *Journal of Peasant Studies*, 5, 4, pp. 466–81

Merrill, R. (ed.) (1976), *Radical Agriculture*, New York: Harper & Row

Nolan, P. (1976), 'Collectivisation in China: some comparisons with the USSR', *Journal of Peasant Studies*, 3, 2, pp. 192–220

O'Brien, D. Cruise (1971), *The Mourides of Senegal,* London: Oxford University Press

Patnaik, U. (1976), 'Class differentiation within the peasantry: an approach to the analysis of Indian agriculture', *Economic and Political Weekly*, Review of Agriculture, September 1976, pp. A82–A101

Patnaik, U. (1979), 'Neo-polulism and Marxism: the Chayanovian view of the agrarian question and its fundamental fallacy', *Journal of Peasant Studies*, 6, 4, pp. 375–420

Pimental, D. and M. (1979), *Energy, Food and Society*, London: Edward Arnold

Roseberry, W. (1978), 'Peasants as proletarians', *Critique of Anthropology*, pp. 3–18

Sau, R. (1976), 'Can capitalism develop in Indian agriculture?', *Economic and Political Weekly*, Review of Agriculture, December 1976, pp. A126–A36

Seddon, D. (ed.) (1978), *Relations of Production*, London: Frank Cass

Van Hekken, P. M. and Van Velsen, H. U. E. Thoden (1972), *Land Scarcity and Rural Inequality in Tanzania*, The Hague: Mouton

Vergopoulos, K. (1978), 'Capitalism and peasant productivity', *Journal of Peasant Studies*, 5, 4, pp. 446–65

Wallman, S. (ed.) (1979), *The Social Anthropology of Work*, London: Academic Press

Washbrook, D. A. (1976), *The Emergence of Provincial Politics: The Madras Presidency 1880–1920*, London: Cambridge University Press

Wolf, E. (1969), *Peasant Wars of the Twentieth Century*, London: Faber

Wolpe, H. (ed.) (1980), *The Articulation of Modes of Production*, London: Routledge & Kegan Paul

5 The differentiation of the peasantry *

V. I. Lenin

1   The social-economic situation in which the contemporary Russian peasantry find themselves is that of commodity economy. Even in the central agricultural belt (which is most backward in this respect as compared with the south-eastern border regions or the industrial gubernias), the peasant is completely subordinated to the market, on which he is dependent as regards both his personal consumption and his farming, not to mention the payment of taxes.

2   The system of social-economic relations existing among the peasantry (agricultural and village-community) shows us the presence of all those contradictions which are inherent in every commodity economy and every order of capitalism: competition, the struggle for economic independence, the grabbing of land (purchasable and rentable), the concentration of production in the hands of a minority, the forcing of the majority into the ranks of the proletariat, their exploitation by a minority through the medium of mechant's capital and the hiring of farm labourers. There is not a single economic phenomenon among the peasantry that does not bear this contradictory form, one specifically peculiar to the capitalist system, i.e. that does not express a struggle and antagonism of interests, that does not imply advantage for some and disadvantage for others. It is the case with the renting of land, the purchase of land, and with 'industries' in their diametrically opposite types; it is also the case with the technical progress of farming.

We attach cardinal importance to this conclusion not only as regards capitalism in Russia, but also as regards the significance of the Narodnik doctrine in general. It is these contradictions that show us clearly and irrefutably that the system of economic relations in the 'community' village does not at all constitute a special economic form ('people's production,' etc.), but is an ordinary petty-bourgeois one. Despite the theories that have

*This chapter is taken from Lenin (1899), ch. II, part XIII.

prevailed here during the past half-century, the Russian community peasantry are not antagonists of capitalism, but, on the contrary, are its deepest and most durable foundation. The deepest – because it is here, remote from all 'artificial' influences, and in spite of the institutions which restrict the development of capitalism, that we see the constant formation of the elements of capitalism within the 'community' itself. The most durable – because agriculture in general, and the peasantry in particular, are weighed down most heavily by the traditions of the past, the traditions of patriarchal life, as a consequence of which the transformative effects of capitalism (the development of the productive forces, the changing of all social relations, etc.) manifest themselves here most slowly and gradually.[1]

3   The sum-total of all the economic contradictions among the peasantry constitutes what we call the differentiation of the peasantry. The peasants themselves very aptly and strikingly characterize this process with the term 'depeasantising.' This process signifies the utter dissolution of the old patriarchal peasantry and the creation of *new types* of rural inhabitants.

Undoubtedly, the emergence of property inequality is the starting-point of the whole process, but the process is not at all confined to property 'differentiation'. The old peasantry is not only 'differentiating', it is being completely dissolved, it is ceasing to exist, it is being ousted by absolutely new types of rural inhabitants – types that are the basis of a society in which commodity economy and capitalist production prevail. These types are the rural bourgeoisie (chiefly petty bourgeoisie) and the rural proletariat – a class of commodity producers in agriculture and a class of agricultural wage-workers.

4   The differentiation of the peasantry, which develops the latter's extreme groups at the expense of the middle 'peasantry', creates two new types of rural inhabitants. The feature common to both types is the commodity, money character of their economy. The first new type is the rural bourgeoisie or the well-to-do peasantry. These include the independent farmers who carry on commercial agriculture in all its varied forms; then come the owners of commercial and industrial establishments, the proprietors of commercial enterprises, etc. The combining of commercial agriculture with commercial and industrial enterprises is the type of 'combination of agriculture with industries' that is specifically peculiar to *this* peasantry. From among these well-to-do peasants a

class of capitalist farmers is created, since the renting of land for the sale of grain plays (in the agricultural belt) an enormous part in their farms, often a more important part than the allotment. The size of the farm, in the majority of cases, requires a labour force larger than that available in the family, for which reason the formation of a body of farm labourers, and still more of day labourers, is a necessary condition for the existence of the well-to-do peasantry.[2] The spare cash obtained by these peasants in the shape of net income is either directed towards commercial operations and usury, which are so excessively developed in our rural districts, or, under favourable conditions, is invested in the purchase of land, farm improvements, etc. In a word, these are small agrarians. Numerically, the peasant bourgeoisie constitute a small minority of the peasantry, probably not more than one-fifth of the total number of households (which is approximately three-tenths of the population), although, of course, the proportion fluctuates considerably according to district. But as to their weight in the sum-total of peasant farming, in the total quantity of means of production belonging to the peasantry, in the total amount of produce raised by the peasantry, the peasant bourgeoisie are undoubtedly predominant. They are the masters of the contemporary countryside.

5   The other new type is the rural proletariat, the class of *allotment-holding wage-workers*. This covers the poor peasants, including those that are completely landless; but the most typical representative of the Russian proletariat is the allotment-holding farm labourer, day labourer, unskilled labourer, building worker or other allotment-holding worker. Insignificant farming on a patch of land, with the farm in a state of utter ruin (particularly evidenced by the leasing out of land), inability to exist without the sale of labour-power (='industries' of the indigent peasants), an extremely low standard of living (probably lower even than that of the worker without an allotment) – such are the distinguishing features of this type. One must assign not less than half the total peasant households (which is approximately four-tenths of the population) to membership of the rural proletariat, i.e. all the horseless and a large part of the one-horse peasants (this, of course, is only a wholesale approximate calculation, one subject to more or less considerable modifications in the different areas, according to local conditions). The grounds which compel us to believe that such a considerable proportion of the peasantry

already belong to the rural proletariat have been advanced above. It should be added that our literature frequently contains too stereotyped an understanding of the theoretical proposition that capitalism requires the free, landless worker. This proposition is quite correct as indicating the main trend, but capitalism penetrates into agriculture particularly slowly and in extremely varied forms. The allotment of land to the rural worker is very often to the interests of the rural employers themselves, and that is why the allotment-holding rural worker is a type to be found in all capitalist countries. The type assumes different forms in different countries: the English cottager is not the same as the small-holding peasant of France or the Rhine provinces, and the latter again is not the same as the Knecht in Prussia. Each of these bears traces of a specific agrarian system, of a specific history of agrarian relations – but this does not prevent the economist from classing them all as one type of agricultural proletarian. The juridical basis of his right to his plot of land is absolutely immaterial to such a classification. Whether the land is his full property (as a small-holding peasant), or whether he is only allowed the use of it by the landlord or the lord of the manor or, finally, whether he possesses it as a member of a Great-Russian peasant community – makes no difference at all. In assigning the indigent peasants to the rural proletariat we are saying nothing new. This term has already been used repeatedly by many writers, and only the Narodnik economists persist in speaking of the peasantry in general, as something anti-capitalist, and close their eyes to the fact that the mass of the 'peasantry' have already taken a quite definite place in the general system of capitalist production, namely, as agricultural and industrial wage-workers.

6   The intermediary link between these post-Reform types of 'peasantry' is the *middle peasantry*. It is distinguished by the *least* development of commodity production. The independent agricultural labour of this category of peasant covers his maintenance in perhaps only the best years and under particularly favourable conditions, and that is why his position is an extremely precarious one. In the majority of cases the middle peasant cannot make ends meet without resorting to loans, to be repaid by labour-service, etc., without seeking 'subsidiary' employment on the side, which also consists partly in the sale of labour-power, etc. Every crop failure flings masses of the middle peasants into the ranks of the proletariat. In its social relations this group fluctuates between the

top group, towards which it gravitates but which only a small minority of lucky ones succeed in entering, and the bottom group, into which it is pushed by the whole course of social evolution. We have seen that the peasant bourgeoisie *oust* not only the bottom group, but also the middle group, of the peasantry. Thus a process specifically characteristic of capitalist economy takes place, the middle members are swept away and the extremes are reinforced – the process of 'depeasantising'.

7 *The differentiation of the peasantry creates a home market for capitalism.* In the bottom group, this formation of a market takes place on account of articles of consumption (the market of personal consumption). The rural proletarian, by comparison with the middle peasantry, *consumes less*, and, moreover, consumes food of worse quality (potatoes instead of bread, etc.), *but buys more*. The formation and development of a peasant bourgeoisie creates a market in twofold fashion: firstly and mainly on account of means óf production (the market of productive consumption), since the well-to-do peasant strives to convert into capital those means of production which he 'gathers' from both landlords 'in straitened circumstances' and peasants in the grip of ruin. Secondly, a market is also created here on account of personal consumption, due to the expansion of the requirements of the more affluent peasants.

8 On the question of whether the differentiation of the peasantry is progressing, and if so at what rate, we have no precise statistics. This is not surprising, for till now (as we have already remarked) no attempt whatever has been made to study even the statics of the differentiation of the peasantry systematically and to indicate the forms in which this process is taking place. But all the general data on the economy of our rural districts indicate an uninterrupted and rapidly increasing differentiation: on the one hand, the 'peasants' are abandoning and leasing out their land, the number of horseless peasants is growing, the 'peasants' are fleeing to the towns, etc.; on the other hand, the 'progressive trends in peasant farming' are also taking their course, the 'peasants' are buying land, improving their farms, introducing iron ploughs, developing grass cultivation, dairy farming, etc. We now know *which* 'peasants' are taking part in these two diametrically opposite sides of the process.

Furthermore, the development of the migration movement is giving a tremendous impetus to the differentiation of the peasantry, and especially of the agricultural peasantry. It is well known that the migration of peasants is mainly from the agricultural gubernias (migration from the industrial gubernias is quite negligible), and precisely from the densely populated central gubernias, where there is the greatest development of labour-service (which retards the differentiation of the peasantry). That is the first point. The second point is that it is mainly the peasants in *medium circumstances* who are leaving the areas of emigration and mainly the extreme groups who are remaining at home. Thus, migration is accelerating the differentiation of the peasantry in the areas of emigration and is carrying the elements of differentiation to the new places.

9   A tremendous part, as is known, is played in our rural districts by merchant's and usurer's capital. We consider it superfluous to cite numerous facts and indicate sources relating to this phenomenon: the facts are well known and do not directly concern our theme. The only question of interest to us is the following: What relation has merchant's and usurer's capital in our countryside to the differentiation of the peasantry? Is there any connection between the relations among the various groups of peasants described above and the relations between peasant creditors and peasant debtors? Is usury a factor and a motive force of differentiation, or does it retard this differentiation?

Let us first indicate how theory presents this question. In the analysis of capitalist production given by the author of *Capital* very great significance was attached, as we know, to merchant's and usurer's capital. The main points of Marx's views on this subject are the following: first, merchant's and usurer's capital, on the one hand, and industrial capital (i.e., capital invested in production, whether agricultural or industrial), on the other, represent a single type of economic phenomenon, which is covered by the general formula: the buying of commodities in order to sell at a profit. Second, merchant's and usurer's capital always historically precedes the formation of industrial capital and is logically the *necessary* premise of its formation, but in themselves neither merchant's capital nor usurer's capital represents a *sufficient* premise for the rise of industrial capital (i.e. capitalist *production*); they do not always break up the old mode of production and replace it by the capitalist mode of production; the formation of the latter 'depends entirely upon the stage of historical development and the attendant circumstances'.

To what extent it [commercial and merchant's capital] brings about a dissolution of the old mode of production depends on its solidity and internal structure. And whither this process of dissolution will lead, in other words, what new mode of production will replace the old, does not depend on commerce, but on the character of the old mode of production itself.

Third, the independent development of merchant's capital is inversely proportional to the degree of development of capitalist *production*; the greater the development of merchant's and usurer's capital, the smaller the development of industrial capital (=capitalist *production*), and vice versa.

Consequently, as applied to Russia, the question to be answered is: Is merchant's and usurer's capital being linked up with industrial capital? Are commerce and usury, in disintegrating the old mode of production, leading to its replacement by the capitalist mode of production, or by some other system? These are questions of fact, questions that must be answered in regard to all aspects of the national economy of Russia. As regards peasant cultivation the data reviewed above contain the reply, and an affirmative reply, to this question. The ordinary Narodnik view that the 'kulak' and the 'enterprising muzhik' are not two forms of one and the same economic phenomenon, but totally unconnected and opposite types of phenomena, is absolutely without foundation. It is one of those Narodnik prejudices which no one has ever even attempted to prove by an analysis of precise economic data. The data indicate the contrary. Whether the peasant hires workers for the purpose of expanding production, whether he trades in land (recall the data quoted above on the large scale of land renting among the rich) or in groceries, or whether he trades in hemp, hay, cattle, etc., or money (usurer), he represents a single economic type, and his operations amount, at bottom, to one and the same economic relation. Furthermore, that in the Russian community village the role of capital is not confined to bondage and usury, but capital is also invested in production, is apparent from the fact that the well-to-do peasant puts his money into the improvement of his farm, into the purchase and renting of land, the acquisition of improved implements, the hiring of workers, etc., and not only into trading establishments and undertakings (see above). If capital in our countryside were incapable of creating anything but bondage and usury, we could not, from the data on production, establish the differentiation of the peasantry, the formation of a rural bourgeoisie and a rural proletariat; the whole of the peasantry would represent a fairly even type of poverty-stricken cultivators, among whom only usurers would stand out, and they only to the extent of money owned and not to the extent and organization of agricultural production. Finally, from the above-examined data follows the important proposition that the independent development of merchant's and usurer's capital in our countryside *retards* the differentiation of the peasantry. The further the development of commerce proceeds, bringing the country closer to the town, eliminating the primitive village markets and undermining the monopoly of the village shopkeeper, and the more there develop forms of credit that accord with European standards, displacing the village usurer, the further and deeper must the differentiation of the peasantry proceed. The capital of the well-to-do peasants, forced out of petty trade and usury, will flow more abundantly into production, whither it is already beginning to flow.

10 Another important phenomenon in the economy of our countryside that retards the differentiation of the peasantry is the survivals of corvée economy, i.e. labour-service. Labour-service is based on the payment of labour in kind, hence, on a poor development of commodity economy. Labour-service presupposes and requires the middle peasant, one who is not very affluent (otherwise he would not agree to the bondage of labour-service) but is also not a proletarian (to undertake labour-service one must have one's own implements, one must be at least in some measure a 'sound' peasant).

When we said above that the peasant bourgeoisie are the masters of the contemporary countryside, we disregarded the factors retarding differentiation: bondage, usury, labour-service, etc. Actually, the real masters of the contemporary countryside are often enough not the representatives of the peasant bourgeoisie, but the village usurers and the neighbouring landowners, and the more completely bondage, usury, labour-service, etc., are forced out, the more profoundly will the differentiation of the peasantry proceed. Above we have shown, on the basis of Zemstvo statistics, that this differentiation is already an accomplished fact, that the peasantry have completely split up into opposite groups.

Notes

1 cf. Marx (1865).
2 Let us note that the employment of wage-labour is not an

essential feature of the concept 'petty bourgeoisie'. This concept covers all independent production for the market, where the social system of economy contains the contradictions described by us above (see pp. 130–1) particularly where the mass of producers are transformed into wage-workers.

References

Lenin, V. I. (1899), *The Development of Capitalism in Russia* in *Collected Works*, vol. 3, London: Lawrence & Wishart 1960
Marx, K. (1865), *Capital*; vol. 1, New York: International Publishers, 1967

6 Classical discussions of capital and peasantry: a critique*

Göran Djurfeldt

The classical conception of the development of capitalism in agriculture is that, as in industry, the agrarian class-structure will tend to polarize; the petty commodity producer will tend to disappear: a *capitalist relation of production* will develop, involving an agrarian bourgeoisie and a rural proletariat. According to this classical notion, the agrarian future would be one of big estates, managed by capitalist farmers, run with machinery and other capital-intensive methods of production, and employing landless labourers.

Close to a hundred years later, history has apparently falsified this notion: In Europe, the big estates have decreased in importance. The typical unit today is the family farm. The rural proletariat has decreased, not only in absolute size, but as part of the rural labour force. In the six original countries of the EEC in 1966–7, for example, only 14 per cent of the labour force was 'non-family', i.e. mainly hired.[1] In the United States the percentage of hired labour to total farm employment has fluctuated around 25 per cent since 1910 with no discernible trend to increase.[2] Both these figures are expressed in man-year units and thus mask the fact that the modern rural proletariat is largely part-time: students, housewives, etc. drawn into agriculture during certain peak periods, as for example during the harvest of vegetables and fruits. The group of full-time agricultural labourers is surprisingly small; in the US, for example, it was estimated to have been 670,000 persons in 1972.[3]

The petty commodity-producing farmer has thus not only survived, but has become typical of Western agriculture. At the same time, agriculture has gone through a revolution in the forces of production which can be symbolized by the tractorization carried through in thirty years. The increase in productivity has at times even surpassed that in industry.[4]

Currently, there are many indications of an increasing exploitation

*This chapter is taken from Djurfeldt (1981).

of the farmer's labour. While their productivity increases faster than in the rest of the economy, their living standard increases slower, i.e. *they are producers of relative surplus value*. One indication of this is the terms of trade between agriculture and industry which seems to have a steady tendency to disfavour agriculture. Unfortunately, I have data for only three countries on this point: in the United States 1946–70 prices paid by farmers have increased much faster than the prices received;[5] the same is true for France 1946–62,[6] while in Denmark 1963–74 the consumer price index has increased much faster than the farm producer-price index.[7]

The non-fulfilment of the classical prognoses should be no deadly blow to a non-mechanistic, non-deterministic version of historical materialism. On the contrary, it is a challenge to confront the real structural development of Western agriculture with the writings of the classical Marxists on the agrarian question, in order to find out the unjustified assumptions underlying their predictions, replace them with more well-founded ones, and find out the consequences for a historical-materialist approach to the agrarian question.

The following is a modest attempt to contribute to a renewed discussion of the agrarian question.

Kautsky's *Die Agrarfrage*[8]

There is a remarkable dualism in Kautsky: on the one hand there is the classical prediction from Marx on the development of capitalism in agriculture; on the other hand, Kautsky noted trends in the agriculture of his day which did not fit with the classical conception, and which he attempted to come to grips with theoretically. Today we can see that those very trends were forebodings of the structural development of central agriculture during the twentieth century. Kautsky did not foresee this development, since he expected the early arrival of the socialist revolution. But his attempt to interpret what he observed in terms of Marxist theory is of relevance even today.

The classical expectation of concentration of land in big units was grounded, in part, on the economies of scale supposedly enjoyed by them in the use of means of production, animals of traction, labour, specialization, including the use of *Kopfarbeiter*: agronomists, agricultural engineers, etc. and in the advantages enjoyed by big units in marketing and in obtaining credit. In Marxist terms: the concentration of production brought about by capital would launch a revolution in the forces of production, epitomized by the application of science in the process of production, which would force the peasants out of production, and convert them into landless wage-labourers.

The break-through of large-scale production in agriculture is hampered by the ability of the peasants to resist competition; they are not more productive, but they have lesser needs, and they put in more labour per worker, they use their children in production, etc. But the sturdiness of the peasants can at most delay large-scale production, and cannot prevent it. Moreover, peasant sturdiness cannot explain the facts which were already evident at the close of the nineteenth century. Statistics showed that the big estates lost, and the middle peasants gained ground, while the small holdings were fragmented.

Kautsky attempts to show that these tendencies do not contradict the Marxist conception. Among other things, he points to the intensification of cultivation, which may imply that more capital-intensive production (dairy production, for example) requires less area. (This is one of Lenin's main arguments in 'New data on the development of capitalism in agriculture'; see below.)

Poor peasants in the capitalist mode of production

Furthermore, there is a tendency for the big *latifundias* to divide parts of their land into parcels, where they settle their workers; in this way they get their own labour-colonies. This process has a counterpart in many countries, for example the British Small-holding Act 1892, the Danish *husmandsbevægelse*, the Swedish *egnahemsrörelse*, etc. It is a way of decreasing the costs of labour in a capitalist enterprise, which in more recent times also has been the specific aim of land reforms in many Latin American countries. When they have their own land, labourers reproduce their labour-power on their land, and thus the capitalists need not pay them the full value of their labour-power (the value of labour-power is equal to its costs of reproduction). The same mechanism is an important foundation for South African capitalism, where labour-power is reproduced in the Bantustans, or in the border states. Home-industry (the 'putting-out system') can function in the same way: by utilizing labour bound to the home, and partly reproduced in the household, housewives, for example, the capitalist can decrease his wage-bill.[9]

Stated in the most general way, we may say that one agrarian class, the poor peasants, who by definition own too little land to reproduce themselves, and who are thereby forced to take employment – are tied in exactly this way to the rich peasants or *latifundias*. The existence of a poor peasantry, then, implies a production relation:

Poor peasantry —————— *Rich peasantry or*
(unable   *landlord class*
independently   (dependent on the
to reproduce   exploitation of
themselves)   wage-labour or
                           share-croppers)

The existence of such a tied labour-force in agriculture gives a special pattern in the development of the distribution of land: the *parallel concentration and fragmentation of land*. Kautsky calls this pattern a modification of Marx's predictions, according to which the small peasantry would be expropriated by the big landowners. But is it really a modification? We cannot say that it is, or that it was, in Europe at the turn of the century, because the force which created this pattern was international competition, especially in the grain trade, and the ensuing crisis for European capitalist agriculture. This crisis meant that the capitalist farms could not reproduce themselves with free wage-labour.

Kautsky's interpretation is somewhat different. He accepts the complaints of the capitalist farmers over a scarcity of hands, which seems theoretically ill-founded. A more plausible interpretation is that the farmers could not afford to pay the wages necessary to keep the labourers from migrating to the industrial centres, or to the United States. In other words, the farmers were forced to circumvent the 'freedom' of the labourers by settling them on the land. (The state was often instrumental in this endeavour.)

The poor peasantry is thus not an integral part of the concept of the capitalist mode of production in agriculture; it is an indicator of an atypical reproduction process. Although this mechanism may be used to corner surplus profits, for example in order to prevent land-rent from falling, it seems more likely that we find it in crisis-bound branches or enterprises which are on the verge of bankruptcy due to competition. The latter seems to have been the case in European agriculture which at that time, was hard pressed by international competition.

It must be wrong, therefore, to call this a 'modification' of the capitalist pattern of development of agriculture; it should rather be seen as foreboding of a shift in developmental tendencies.

Kautsky saw, and to a certain extent also correctly interpreted, these new tendencies (see pp. 40 ff. in the summary, ch. 9 ff. in the German and French editions). The section about the middle peasants brings out the essence of the problem. He falsely attributes the problem to a shortage of labour, but from this false premise, a factually correct proposition is deduced: those farms which are least dependent on the exploitation of hired labour, the middle peasants, according to the Marxist definition, are least affected by the crisis, and are best able to reproduce themselves when prices are lowered due to foreign competition.

Kautsky is also able to show, by means of German statistics, that the middle peasants at this time were increasing their command of area. This stands in bright contrast to his assertion that the middle peasants are most affected by usury and commercial exploitation. It also contradicts studies which have shown that, since they can independently reproduce themselves, the middle peasants are relatively less prone to being exploited. If they are caught in the claws of the usurer or merchant they are, however, liable to be expropriated, and they take a variety of precautions to protect themselves. So, for example, kin-group solidarity has been shown to be stronger among middle peasants than among rich or poor peasants. They may also form societies for mutual protection (co-operatives).[10]

Marx's prediction of the expropriation of the middle peasantry, rests, not on its vulnerability to exploitation, but on an argument transposed from industry: the capitalist development of the productive forces, and their ensuing socialization, implies a concentration of capital, and an increasing scale of production, which in the long run will tend to eliminate the smaller units. But neither Marx nor Kautsky foresaw the development which was to come, and which meant that the middle peasantry became bearers of a revolution in the agrarian productive forces.

Periodization of agricultural development

The most prophetic parts of Kautsky's book are the two chapters, 'Overseas competition and the industrialisation of agriculture' and 'Conclusions'; but I would like to read them together with his introductory remarks on feudalism, and peasants and industry (chs. II and III). In these chapters we can see the basic outline of a *periodization* of the relation between urban-based, industrial capitalism and agriculture. There are three periods:[11]

1   First comes the breaking-up of the autonomous reproduction of peasant agriculture, which is characteristic of the feudal and other precapitalist mode of production. This occurs before capital has entered agrarian production, as such. Industry ruins home-industry, converts the peasant into a commodity-producer (and -consumer), and subverts him to usurious and commercial capital.

This is a form of articulation, which we find today in many of the Third World countries, an articulation between the capitalist mode of production and a pre-capitalist, peripheral agriculture. This form of subversion, requires, as Hamza Alavi has put it, a bourgeois revolution: it requires private property and thus a crushing of the autonomy of the pre-capitalist mode of production. Or in Marx's words:

the form of landed property with which the incipient capitalist mode of production is confronted does not suit it. *It first creates for itself the form required by subordinating agriculture to capital. It thus transforms feudal landed property, clan property, small-peasant property in mark communes* – no matter how divergent their juristic forms may be – *into the economic form corresponding to the requirements of this mode of production* (1894, p. 617; my emphases).

In other words, this first transformation of pre-capitalist agriculture by capital belongs to the theory of primitive accumulation. One of the essential characteristics of large parts of the contemporary peripheral agriculture is that it still remains in this stage.

2   In European agrarian history we have a second stage; this stage is the one analysed by Marx (1894) in the section of *Capital* on capitalist ground-rent. It is typified by the capitalist tenant, who became predominant only in England. However, there, as in other countries, the further realization of this classical conception of capitalism in agriculture was hampered by the changing economic situation after about 1875.

Kautsky shares the opinion of Marx, that in this form of articulation between industry and agriculture, the level and mass of rent tend to grow, at the expense of profit and the real value of wages. The effect is a trend in the terms of trade between industry and agriculture which is favourable to the latter.

3   The third stage is evidenced by a shift in the terms of trade, which Kautsky holds to dominate after about 1875. What brings about the whole transformation is import of grain from the colonies (USA, Argentina, etc.) and from the 'Oriental despotisms', including Russia. Kautsky's analysis of the latter suffers from serious defects, but his main point is well taken: in these types of economies the mechanisms for price-determination are different from those in the capitalist mode of production:

[Once] European penetration into these countries... is established, it increases the pressure of the State on the rural communities by boosting its demand for cash. Taxes are paid in cash, or the existing level of money taxes rises sharply.... The mass of produce increases... and flows into the market.... We can hardly argue that the price of this produce is determined by costs of production. They are not produced on a capitalist basis, and their sale comes about under the pressure of the State and the usurer. High taxes and interest rates compel the peasant to rid himself of his produce at any price; the greater the sum of labour which he expends to repay his debt and the larger the mass of produce which he brings to the market, the lower will be the price he receives for it (summary, p. 43).

What are the consequences of the competition brought about by grain imports? In Kautsky's words:

In the face of competition of this sort, there can be no prosperity in an agriculture based on capitalist foundations, an agriculture which has to reckon with the *given standard of life* of the population, the *given level of wages and rents* based on the *prevailing price of land and rate of interest*, and for which a certain level of soil fertility and the available resources of manpower constitute a minimum floor (summary, p. 43 my emphases).

The factors emphasized in the quotation, are some of the constituent elements of the capitalist mode of production in agriculture, according to the classical conception. The implication is that international competition stripped this economic form of its conditions of reproduction.

Answers to agrarian crisis

And what was the reaction of the European peasants and landlords? Kautsky mentions two 'answers' to the crisis:
1   A reorientation of production towards intensive cattle and dairy farming, which is a new ecological complex, with cultivated

fodder as the characteristic innovation. This type of production has turned out to have a wide scope for expansion of the productive forces; moreover, it has been compatible with small-scale production. Thus, it is one exception to Marx's view that large-scale production is a prerequisite for an expansion of the productive forces. Now, this future development could not be perceived by Kautsky; but it seems to be one essential component of the structural development of Western agriculture in the twentieth century. This argument should not be interpreted as implying that a technical contingency (intensive cattle and dairy farming) determined the structural development in agriculture. As will soon be evident, the driving force was probably another.

2   As already mentioned rents fell, and profits fell, creating an advantage for the middle peasantry, and resulting in a flow of capital *out of agriculture*, and *into agro-industry*. Kautsky mentions dairies, butcheries, breweries, sugar refineries, starch factories, which became objects of investment for the landlords and capitalist tenants.

In tracts where the peasants commanded a surplus, they followed the landlords and the capitalists and invested in the same industries, but through their *co-operative societies*. As a Marxist, Kautsky was sceptical towards the emancipatory potential of the co-operative movement, but he did not foresee that, although it is not a force of emancipation, it can successfully reproduce itself in a society dominated by capitalism, given, of course, that it subordinates itself to the commanding force of this society, the market. It is remarkable that, in his arguments against the co-operative movement, Kautsky mentions exactly those factors which have made it viable:

> Such co-operatives revolutionized agriculture, but they are no solution for the peasantry. Agro-industries are subject to the same laws of concentration and centralization, to economies of scale and the law of increasing firm size (cf. the example of Nestlé[12]) like other industries Where this industrialization of agriculture does not entirely eliminate the smallholder, it binds him to the monopsonist power of the factory and converts him into a serf of industrial capital, working for its requirements (summary, pp. 44–5)

But this is exactly the role of the co-operatives: to centralize capital without expropriating the peasants, so that we get a capitalism without capitalists. In that form, co-operatives are eminently able to reproduce themselves; and they come to play exactly the same role as private capital in other countries.

Here we can perceive the general form of capitalist development in relation to agriculture. We cannot say 'in agriculture' because we now see that the capitalist mode of production has developed *outside* agriculture, in agro-industry. The developing capitalist division of labour has meant that capital has taken hold of certain production processes previously located in the farms, (making of butter, cheese, beer, butchered meat, etc.), and has moved them outside, into industry, transforming them in the process. In agro-industry, then, we get *the* capitalist mode of production.

Industry as the driving force of agricultural development

Kautsky did not foresee this development, although he possessed some of the theoretical instruments needed to analyse it, as is evident from the following:

Where shall we look for the motor force behind the transformation of [the] mode of production [of agriculture]? The answer is implicit in the whole of our analysis above. *Industry* forms the motor force, not only of its own development, but also of the development of agriculture (summary, p. 46).

More precisely we could formulate the hypothesis that agro-industrial capital (in private or co-operative form) is the motor-force of the specific structural development of Western agriculture in the twentieth century.

Although the hypothesis can be derived from Kautsky, the exact mechanism is not spelled out in him. But if the driving force is agro-industrial capital, it is tempting to say that a capitalist in the farm sector is in contradiction to the interests of this capital. The difference in the mechanism of price-formation between capitalist and family farms is crucial. As pointed out earlier, the family farmer can sell his commodities at their cost-price, while the capitalist farmer must add profit. Given that the differences in productivity on family farms and capitalist farms are within a certain margin, agro-industry will prefer a non-capitalist farm-sector. The whole lesson of European agro-history teaches us that it is strong enough to enforce its interests. We can see this if we return to the turning-point around 1875 when international competition began to be effective in breaking down capitalist agriculture. Why did it come about? It was *not a contingent effect* of a development outside the capitalist centres, in USA, Argentine, Russia, etc.; on the contrary, it was the effect of the strength of industrial capital, and its overweight in the class-struggle with the landed interests, epitomized in the English corn laws of 1846. [13] As the Marxist theory of imperialism teaches us, industrial capital at that time was interested in free trade, but not only for the reason usually pointed to: that capitalistically produced commodities would get access to the markets of India, China, etc., but also because the free import of grain would subvert the mechanism of price-formation in capitalist agriculture, since it would cheapen the elements of variable capital. The latter was an issue on which the capitalists could ally themselves with the working class, and the strength of that class may have been decisive for the outcome of the political struggle with landed interests.

It might be objected that the fact that only England, the Netherlands, and Denmark kept to the policy of free trade in grain contradicts our whole argument. The other European countries, notably France and Germany, erected custom barriers to protect 'their' agriculture against foreign competition. But, in this context, some often forgotten facts must be remembered: prices fell in the whole of Europe from the beginning of the 1870s; but import duties were imposed in Germany from 1879 and in France from 1885; moreover, *these duties far from compensated for the previous fall in prices.* [14] Thus protection did not, and it was not intended to, save landlordism; it was rather a protection of peasant agriculture (so are the current protectionist policies of Western Europe).

Chayanov versus Lenin

We have seen how the actual structural development of Western agriculture is reflected in Kautsky's writings, but the same cannot be said of Lenin.

Lenin's discussion of two roads to capitalist development of agriculture is often read as an implicit self-criticism of the more unilinear conceptions of *The Development of Capitalism in Russia*

Those two paths of objectively possible bourgeois development we would call the Prussian path and the American path, respectively. In the first case feudal landlord economy slowly evolves into bourgeois, Junker landlord economy, which condemns the peasants to decades of most harrowing expropriation and bondage, while at the same time a small minority of *Grossbauern* ('big peasants') arises. In the second case there is no landlord economy, or else it is broken up by revolution, which confiscates and splits up the feudal estates. In that case the peasant predominates, becomes the sole agent of agriculture, and evolves into a capitalist farmer. In the first case the main content of the evolution is transformation of feudal bondage into servitude and capitalist exploitation on the land of the feudal landlords – Junkers. In the second case the main background is transformation of the patriarchal peasant into a bourgeois farmer.[15]

That this reading is false is evident already from the quotation. Both these paths are starting points for a capitalist development fully in accordance with the conception we have called classical. Each path leads to the capitalist relation of production, wage-labour, relating two classes to each other: a rural proletariat and an agrarian bourgeoisie. The polarization of the rural class structure arises via *differentiation of the peasantry*, according to the paradigm of Lenin's early works. The difference between the two paths relates to the absence or presence of a landlord class. In the American case, where this element has always been absent, the rising agrarian bourgeoisie is wholly recruited from the rich peasants, while in the Prussian case, the farmer landlords come to make up a sizeable part of the nascent bourgeoisie.

Thus the unilinearity of Lenin's early model is but little modified:

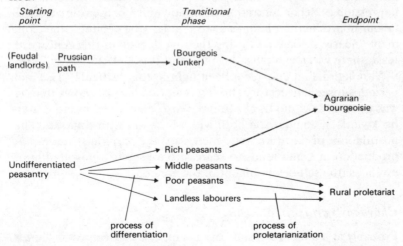

Figure 1 *Lenin's (bi)lineal model of the development of capitalism in agriculture*

Lenin held the American path to be superior, since it had a better potential for development of the productive forces:

To facilitate the development of the productive forces (this highest criterion of social progress) we must support not bourgeois evolution of the landlord type, but bourgeois evolution of the peasant type. The former implies the utmost preservation of bondage and serfdom (remodelled on bourgeois lines), the least rapid development of the productive forces, and the retarded development of capitalism; it implies infinitely greater misery and suffering, exploitation and oppression for the broad mass of the peasantry and, consequently, also for the proletariat. The second type implies the most rapid development of the productive forces and the best possible (under commodity production) conditions of existence for the mass of peasantry.[16]

As far as I can see, Lenin *never modified* his basic conception about the pattern of capitalist development in agriculture. This can be seen from his last book on the subject: *New Data on the Development of Capitalism in Agriculture* (1917) which deals with the USA. In this little pamphlet Lenin analyses American census data in order to polemicize against the populist view of agrarian development in the States. He shows that the decreasing average size of American farms in the beginning of the century was an expression of an increased capital intensification of cultivation (reorientation of production from extensive grain farming to dairy farming, for example). Thus while the area-measure gives a false impression of deconcentration of landownership, the role of wage-labour in production, Lenin's central index of a capitalist development, clearly shows that during the first decade of this century at least, there was a capitalist development in American agriculture.

Although Lenin may have been right in this particular case and period, subsequent history (briefly reviewed above) shows that he was generally off the track. In one sense, Lenin represents a step backwards in comparison both with Marx and with Kautsky. The postulation of law-like tendencies in the capitalist mode of production in Lenin tends to regress to a Hegelian postulation of essences (the self-development of the concept).

Chayanov's criticism of Lenin

Probably as a measure of self-censorship, Chayanov never criticizes Lenin directly, but it is evident that his well-known main work[17] can be read as a polemic against Lenin's unilinear differentiation theory. Chayanov does not deny that some differentiation takes place in the Russian peasantry. But he claims that it is to a large extent explained by the process that he termed demographic differentiation, according to which the volume of the family farm's activity expands and contracts with the development of the family cycle. When land is available, area also expands and contracts so that the typical cycle is: a young family starts out with little land (when ancestral property has been divided among the heirs); when the family grows, economic activity expands, to contract again when the family grows old, and when the children leave.

By analysing the works of the Russian *zemstvo* statisticians, Chayanov attempted to show that most of what Lenin took as evidence of class differentiation could be interpreted as demographic differentiation. Thus, he contends that Lenin overestimated both the extent of capitalist development in agriculture, and its rate and form of growth.

Chayanov's conception of capitalism in agriculture

The Chayanov–Lenin controversy has produced a voluminous secondary literature (see e.g. Patnaik, 1979, and Harrison, 1975). But more research and writing have to be done before we get a more conclusive analysis of Russian agrarian development before and after the revolution. What interests us here is not that issue, but the interesting fact that Chayanov had a more adequate prognosis for the development of capitalism in Western agriculture than, as we have seen, Lenin had. In 1925 Chayanov wrote:

The dynamic processes of agricultural proletarianization and concentration of production, leading to large-scale agricultural production units based on hired labour, are developing throughout the world, and in the USSR in particular, at a rate much slower than was expected at the end of nineteenth century.... Nevertheless, it is clear to everyone working in the field of agriculture that literally before our eyes the world's agriculture, ours included, is being more and more drawn into the general circulation of the world economy, and the centers of capitalism are more and more subordinating it to their leadership (1966, p. 257).

He goes on to state, in a very concise manner, his own views on the subordination of agriculture to capitalism. He seems implicitly to reason in terms of stages, very much reminiscent of those we brought out in Kautsky. Once agriculture has been drawn into commodity production, it tends to get subordinated to a combined merchant-userer's capital. He cites 'the examples of capitalist exploitation which Knop, the Moscow cotton firm, applied to the Sart cotton growers, buying up their harvests in spring, giving out advances for food, and giving them credits for seed and means of production' (p.257–8). This obviously exemplifies the extreme limits of subordination of a process of production to pre-capitalist capital, viz. merchant-userer's capital, in which the latter controls both the means of subsistence and the means of production of the immediate producers. The next step is that capitalism 'begins to actively interfere in the organization of production too. It lays down technical conditions, issues seed and fertilizers, determines the rotation, and turns its clients into technical executors of its designs and economic plan' (p.262). Hand in hand with this process, capitalism begins to penetrate into production itself, not on the farm as such, but by splitting off 'from the peasant farm individual sectors, predominantly those in the primary processing of agricultural raw material and, in general, those connected with mechanical processes' (p.262). The next stage, in Chayanov's words, is:

If to this we add in the most developed capitalist countries, such as those in North America, widely developed mortgage credit, the financing of farm circulating capital, and the dominating part played by capital invested in transport, elevator, irrigation, and other undertakings, then we have before us new ways in which capitalism penetrates agriculture. These ways convert the farmers into a labour force working with other people's means of production. They convert agriculture, despite the evident scattered and independent nature of the small commodity producers, into an economic system concentrated in a series of the largest undertakings and, through them, entering the sphere controlled by the most advanced forms of finance capitalism (p. 262).

The last sentence is important. It points to the thesis that these new forms of penetration are related to the transition in the capitalist mode of production itself, from competitive to monopoly capitalism.

Causes of vertical concentration

How does it come about that capitalist penetration takes this new form? Chayanov's answer is simple: 'it is evidently because capitalist exploitation gives a higher percentage from vertical than ·from horizontal concentration. Moreover, to a considerable extent it transfers the undertaking's risk from the owner of the capital to the farmer' (p. 263).

Can this be a full explanation for the preponderance of vertical over horizontal concentration? In so far as family farms allow agribusiness to pump out the entire surplus value created in this sector, it increases the rate of profit for capital. If it further can be assumed that the monopolies dominate technological development *in such a way* that 'middle-scale' technology, appropriate to family farms, can be developed under its aegis, the explanation holds up against logical scrutiny. Or maybe it is even possible to explain the development of 'middle-scale technology' by the preponderance of middle farmers and the demand created by them and financed by capital (as done by Bailey, 1973).

As is often noted, concentration of agricultural production meets with a difficulty not present in other branches: the cultivable area is already occupied by farmers unwilling to part with their land. This fact may also contribute to explain the non-development of a large-scale technology.

When private entrepreneurial capital is weak, the vertical concentration can take a co-operative form. According to Chayanov, 'the essence of agricultural co-operation' is:

a deep process of vertical concentration in agriculture. Moreover, it must be noted that in its co-operative forms this process goes much deeper than in its capitalist ones, since the peasant himself hands over to co-operative forms of concentration sectors of his farm that capitalism never succeeds in detaching from it in the course of their struggle (p. 264).

Chayanov goes on to state his vision of a socialist development in agriculture. Under state-capitalism, as in the Soviet Union during the New Economic Policy, it is possible to utilize these forms of vertical concentration, but subordinated to state control. With this development, the farm is 'emptied' of a series of functions, and correlated with this process:

the elements of social capital and the social economy increase quantitatively so much that the whole system changes qualitatively. It is converted from one of peasant farms that have formed co-operatives for some sectors of their economy to one of a social co-operative economy, founded on socialized capital, that leaves in the farms of its members the technical fulfilment of certain processes almost on technical commission (p. 269).

Given the considerable strength of the co-operative movement in the Soviet Union in the 1920s, it is strange that none of the contending factions in the CPSU seems to have advocated this solution to the agrarian crisis of the young worker's state. Bukharin's and the right-wing's proposal, to give free reins to kulaks, and Preobrazhensky's and the left-wing's alternative, to utilize the peasantry's surplus product for primitive socialist accumulation, both seem to miss the great potentials in a co-operative, vertical concentration. When capitalism is not the dominant mode of production vertical concentration can be steered towards a goal set by a plan for socialist development.

Conclusions

What are the conditions for development along classical lines in agriculture? From the above we can see that capitalist agriculture requires profit, which can derive from three sources:

1   *more productive land* (this is why we tend to find capitalist farmers in the West in the most fertile areas, often on old feudal estates converted into capitalist farms);

2   *a protected market* where prices are kept above cost price (many countries in the periphery have a protected grain market; it may even be possible to find a correlation between the level of protection and landlord dominance in these countries). [18]

It is implied in 2 that capitalist farmers often cannot compete in a free market. Since, in the international market, countries with different agrarian structures tend to compete between themselves, capitalist agriculture can endure in this competition only under special circumstances, the most important of which seems to be:

3   *a depressed wage-level* which may originate either from a big reserve army of labour, or from a sizeable poor peasantry. [19]

Since 2 and 3 tend to characterize countries of the periphery, we might conclude that a development along classical lines is not impossible in the periphery. A sizeable shifting out of agricultural production from centre to periphery has occurred in recent years, much of it capitalistically organized.[20] Therefore the models developed by Marx and Lenin may still be relevant to the analysis of Third World agriculture. But we must hasten to add that for capitalist farmers to prevail over the middle peasantry requires also economies of scale which, as we have seen above, cannot always be taken for granted.

Further complications must also be kept in mind: both the prices of grain in the domestic market and, to a certain extent, agrarian ownership structure, may be manipulated politically. The possibility of reproducing these conditions for capitalist development depends, then, on the political representation of the agrarian bourgeoisie, and its alliance with other classes.[21] Here the relationship between profit and rent becomes important: Under many circumstances, as we have seen, the mass of rent tends to increase at the expense of profit; moreover, it can be argued that agrarian capitalism is not as expansive in terms of productivity as is usually imagined. Therefore it cannot be taken for granted that the agrarian bourgeoisie and the landlords will be able to secure an alliance with the other ruling classes, notably with the national and international bourgeoisie. They may be pushed out of the ruling class-alliance, as they have been in the West.[22] Some have taken the World Bank's newly awakened interest for small farmers to be a sign of this.[23]

This, of course, is speculative; but one conclusion seems firmly grounded: those who take over the predictions of the classics and attempt to apply them wholesale to contemporary agriculture are engaged in a futile and dogmatic exercise.

Notes

1 OECD (1974), table 3b.
2 US Bureau of the Census (1975), p. 467.
3 McElroy (1973).
4 Economic Commission for Europe (1980).
5 US Bureau of the Census (1975), p. 488.
6 Cépede (1970) quoted in Vergopoulos (1974), p. 193
7 Monopoltilsynet (1975) quoted in Bager (1975), p. 120.
8 Stuttgart 1899; French translation 1901; reprinted in facsimile by Maspero in 1970; a summary in English made by Banaji (1976).

9 In a recent article by Philip Corrigan (1977), the importance of 'unfree' labour to the capitalist system is documented. Corrigan concludes by questioning 'free' labour as a component of the capitalist mode of production. As will be seen below, I have chosen another interpretation.

10 See the studies by Alavi (1972, 1971).

11 cf. Rey's periodization (1973), pp. 9–167.

12 Nestlé is an old concern. Already at the turn of the century 'it owned in Switzerland two big factories for making condensed milk and a factory for making malted milk. The latter, established at Vevey, processes 100,000 litres daily, produced by 12,000 cows and coming from 180 villages. These 180 villages have lost their economic autonomy and have become subjected to the house of Nestlé. Their inhabitants still appear to be proprietors (owners of the means of production), but they are no longer free peasants' (French edition, p. 423). Retrospectively, it can be seen that Nestlé was, in capitalist terms, a progressive agro-industry.

13 It is interesting to note that Perry (1973, Editor's introduction, pp. xiv-xv) sees the crisis in the 1870s as a delayed effect of the repeal of the Corn Laws in 1846.

14 Abel (1966), p. 259.

15 Lenin (1908), p. 239.

16 ibid., p. 244.

17 Chayanov (1966).

18 Boesen's (1977) study is instructive, since it shows how the structure in tobacco cultivation changed from capitalist to middle farmer dominance when deprived of market protection and thus repeated, on a micro-scale, European agrarian history.

19 Both 2 and 3 are present in the South African case of 'pure' agrarian capitalism of the Prussian variety analysed by Morris (1976). In the United States, capitalist agriculture similarly seems to presuppose the low wages of Afro-American, Mexican etc. labour.

20 See George (1976) and Lappé and Collins (1977).

21 This coupling of economic and political processes is the subject of Mitra (1977).

22 Pierre Coulomb has noted that 'bought out' might be more appropriate than 'pushed out' as a description of the elimination of landlordism in Europe. The landlord estates were gradually

sold out to peasants, financed by state credit. Thus, landed property was transformed into capital often invested, as noted above, in agro-industry (see Coulomb, 1973, pp. 55ff.).
23 Feder (1976).

References

Abel, Wilhelm (1966), *Agrarkrisen und Agrarkonjunktur*, Zweite, neubearbeitete and erweiterte Auflage, Hamburg and Berlin: Verlag Paul Parey

Alavi, Hamza (1971), 'The politics of dependence: a village in West Punjab', *South Asian Review*, 4, 2, pp. 111–28

Alavi, Hamza (1972), *Kinship in West Punjab Villages*, Contributions to Indian Sociology, new series, VI, New Delhi

Bager, Torben (1975), *Andelsbevægelsen som kooperationstype*, Copenhagen: Magisterkonferens, Sociologisk Institut

Bailey, W. R. (1973), *The One-Man Farm*, ERS 519, Washington, DC: Economic Research Unit, US Department of Agriculture

Banaji, Jairus (1976), 'A summary of Kautsky's *The Agrarian Question*', *Economy and Society*, 5, 1, pp. 2–49

Boesen, Jannik (1977), 'Dynamics of organization of production in agriculture under changing conditions of production: the case of tobacco in Tabora Region', CDR Project Paper D 77, Copenhagen

Boesen, J., and Mohele, A. T. (1979), *The 'Success Story' of Peasant Tobacco Production in Tanzania*, Uppsala: Scandinavian Institute of African Studies

Cépede, Denis (1970), 'Le transfert chrématistique – productivité, rapports des prix et domination de l'agriculture', *Cahiers de l'ISEA*, V, 5, May; cited by Vergopoulos (1974)

Chayanov, A. V. (1966), *The Theory of Peasant Economy*, ed. Daniel Thorner, Basile Kerblay and R. E. F. Smith, Homewood, Ill.: Richard D. Irwin

Corrigan, Philip (1977), 'Feudal relics or capitalist monuments? Notes on the sociology of unfree labour', *Sociology,* 11, pp. 435–63

Coulomb, Pierre (1973), 'Propriété foncière et mode de production capitaliste', *Etudes rurales*, 51, July–September, pp. 27–66

Djurfeldt, Gören (1981), 'What happened to the agrarian bourgeoisie and rural proletariat under monopoly capitalism', *Acta Sociologica, Scandanavian Review of Sociology*, 24, 3, pp. 167–91

Economic Commission for Europe (1980), *Present and Foreseeable Trends in Mechanization and their Impact on European Agriculture*, agri/mech report no. 51, vol. 1, New York: Horizon (first published by United Nations, 1973)

Feder, Ernest (1976), 'McNamara's little green revolution: World Bank scheme for self-liquidation of the Third World peasantry', *Economic and Political Weekly*, XI, 14, 3 April, pp. 532–41

George, Susan (1976), *How the Other Half Dies: The Real Reasons for World Hunger*, Harmondsworth: Penguin

Lappé, Frances Moore, and Collins, Joseph (1977), *Food First: Beyond the Myth of Scarcity*, Boston: Houghton Mifflin

Lenin, V. I. (1908), *The Agrarian Programme of Social-Democracy in the First Russian Revolution 1905–1907;* in *Collected Works*, vol. 13, Moscow: Foreign Languages Publishing House, 1962

Lenin, V. I. (1917), *New Data on the Development of Capitalism in Agriculture*, in *Collected Works*, vol. 22, London: Lawrence & Wishart

McElroy, R. C. (1973), *The Hired Farm Working Force 1972: A Statistical Report*, Washington, DC: Economic Research Service, US Department of Agriculture; abstracted in *World Agricultural Economics and Rural Sociology Abstracts*, 15, 8, abstract no. 3424

Marx, K. (1894), *Capital*, vol.III; London: Lawrence & Wishart, 1974

Mitra, Ashok (1977), *Terms of Trade and Class Relations*, London: Frank Cass

Monopoltilsynet (1979), *Forbrugerpriser og producentpriser for Landbrugsvarer*, Copenhagen

Morris, M. L. (1976), 'The development of capitalism in South African agriculture: class struggle in the countryside', *Economy and Society*, 5, 3, pp. 292–343

OECD (1974), *Agricultural Policy of the European Economic Community*, Agricultural Policy Reports, Paris

Patnaik, Utsa (1979), 'Neo-populism and Marxism: the Chayanovian view of the agrarian question and its fundamental fallacy', *Journal of Peasant Studies*, 6, 4, pp. 375–420

Perry, P. J. (1973), *British Agriculture 1875–1924*, London: Methuen

Rey, P-P. (1973), 'Sur l'articulation des modes de production', in P-P. Rey, *Les alliances de classes*, Paris: Maspero

Shanin, Teodor (1972), *The Awkward Class: Political Sociology of Peasantry in a Developing Society: Russia 1913–1925*, London:

Oxford University Press

US Bureau of the Census (1975), *Historical Statistics of the United States*, Colonial Times to 1970, bicentennial edition, Part 1, Washington DC

Vergopoulos, Kostas (1974), 'Capitalisme difforme: le cas de l'agriculture dans le capitalisme', in S. Amin and K. Vergopoulos, *La question paysanne et le capitalisme*, Paris: Editions Anthropos-Idep

7 Notes on capital and peasantry*

Henry Bernstein

Introduction

1 The purpose of these brief notes is to set out in a preliminary way some of the issues concerning the relations of capitalism and peasantry, and some of the concepts that can be employed in the analysis of these relations. To avoid unnecessary complication at this stage, questions concerning various modes of production prior to the penetration of capital are ignored, as are recent debates concerning the articulation of modes of production (stimulated by the work of C. Meillassoux and P-P. Rey in particular).

2 These notes try to avoid the following errors that often occur in discussions of this theme:

(a) an essentialist conception of capitalism in which homogenous 'interests' or 'laws of motion' of capital (in general) serve as predicates from which all else follows (see Clarke, 1977);

(b) an essentialist conception of peasantry as, notably, in concepts of a 'peasant mode of production' and its equivalents (see Ennew, Hirst and Tribe, 1977);

(c) a functionalist conception of the relations between capital and peasants in which the latter are 'reproduced' by the former (in the pursuit of its interests etc.). It is not capital nor imperialism which reproduces the peasantry – the peasantry reproduce themselves through their own labour. The question is how the conditions of production and reproduction are determined by the operations of capital (in particular social formations and at the level of world economy) and of the state;

(d) any assumption of either peasant 'irrationality' _or_ peasant 'rationality' – the latter is often counterposed for progressive

---

*This chapter is taken from Bernstein (1977). The author is indebted for a number of discussions of the agrarian question to many comrades in East Africa and Europe. In so far as these notes respond to comments and criticisms concerning a previous paper, particular thanks are due to Peter Gibbon, Gary Littlejohn, Mahmood Mamdani, Wolfgang Schoeller and Gavin Williams.

ideological reasons against the stereotypes of peasants held by e.g. many economists, 'experts' and bureaucrats, but it derives from a subjective view of the problem like that associated with the attempt to theorize a 'peasant economy' by A. V. Chayanov (see Littlejohn, 1977).

The destruction of natural economy

3 The category of natural economy suggests social formations in which the production of use-values is dominant, which does not exclude simple exchange (exchanges of material surpluses between producers at a rudimentary level of the social division of labour). The postulate of natural economy is taken as a useful abstraction from which to begin, and is not a historical observation as such; it makes no presuppositions about different forms of natural economy, nor the relations governing production and the appropriation of surplus-labour (whether on a communal or class basis) in different pre-capitalist modes of production.

4 The destruction of natural economy takes a variety of forms according to the character of pre-existing social formations, the destructive force and its historical context. Our concern is not with the kinds of destruction associated with the epoch and methods of primitive accumulation, i.e. slave raiding and trading, the collection of natural products by coerced labour, and other forms of plunder.

5 The primary focus here is on the destruction of natural economy by the penetration of commodity relations in a more or less systematic fashion. In much of Africa this process is connected with the advent of colonial rule and has occurred mostly in the present century. In many instances various means of compulsion were used to effect the initial break in the reproduction cycle of systems of natural economy, means which were supplied by the colonial state.

6 The thrust of the colonial state was to supervise the initial and necessary penetration of pre-capitalist formations, to organize the conditions of exploitation of labour and land. As is well known, there were different patterns of exploitation – land was alienated and appropriated for the production of agricultural and mineral commodities on estates run by settlers or capitalist companies, and in mines established by productive capitals of varying size and degrees of concentration. These forms of production require a continuous supply of labour, and again the state's intervention in

establishing labour reserves and ensuring a flow of migrant labour was often crucial.

7 Another pattern was the establishment of peasant commodity production which does not involve the direct separation of the producers from the means of production, nor such drastic changes in the instruments and forms of the labour process. Despite the limited *technical* changes in production, however, this process involves fundamental *social* changes in the conditions of production and exchange in which most African producers are engaged. In what follows we concentrate on this aspect of the incorporation of African social formations in the circuits of world economy.

8 The crucial moment in the penetration of natural economy by capital is the breaking of its cycle of reproduction, which is accomplished through the initial monetization of at least some of its elements. The methods used to effect this rupture are equally well known: the imposition of taxes necessitating sources of cash income: the use of *corvée* labour in public works (the creation of infrastructure necessary to the movement of commodities and the maintenance of 'law and order') or in farms organized by the state, by missions or by private capital; the forced cultivation of particular cash crops.

9 Without involving the direct expropriation of the producers, the pre-existing economic systems were undermined by the withdrawal of labour from use-value production whether in agriculture, animal husbandry, hunting or fishing, or in branches of craft activity: house building, the manufacture of tools, weapons and other artifacts. The rupture of the reproduction cycle of natural economy was also affected through the substitution, in the sphere of necessary consumption, of commodities for use-values previously produced locally or acquired through simple exchange. The needs of simple reproduction come to include the consumption of commodities and new needs develop. As Meillassoux and Rey have pointed out, this process involves the erosion of an entire culture of production and the 'disqualification' of many traditional production skills, particularly in non-agricultural activities.

The process of commoditization

10 In elaborating some of the issues and concepts relating to commoditization, there is no suggestion that this process is a uniform one, that it 'unfolds'· through a sequence of necessary

stages, nor that it is complete. Indeed the striking feature of the commoditization of African peasant economy, as it has occurred historically, is its extreme unevenness both between social formations and within them (regional differentiation). This unevenness is tied to the concrete conditions in which various capitals confront and penetrate different pre-capitalist formations, and is therefore not susceptible to general theoretical formulation. On the other hand, concepts which help distinguish the forms and extent of commoditization can contribute to the analysis of social formations in their specificity.

11 At the level of generality employed here, we are trying to pose relations between capital and peasants as simple commodity producers 'deposited' historically by the destruction of pre-capitalist modes of production. It is necessary to emphasize that simple commodity production is a *form* of production that can exist in different historical periods and in variant relations with other forms of production. In the present context, the question concerns the ways in which the conditions of existence of this form of production in Africa are established and affected by the penetration of the capitalist *mode* of production.

12 Simple commodity production designates a form of production the logic of which is subsistence in the broad sense of the simple reproduction of the production of the producers and the unit of production (descriptively, the household). The needs of simple reproduction are satisfied, at least in part, through commodity relations: on one side, the production of commodities as means of exchange to acquire elements of necessary consumption (C-M-C); on the other side the incorporation of commodities in the cycle of reproduction as items of productive consumption (e.g. tools, seeds, fertilizers) and individual consumption (e.g. food, clothing, building materials, kerosene, domestic utensils). Other more specialized elements of reproduction may also come to be realized through commodity relations; for example, the monetization of bride-price.

13 In very schematic terms, simple commodity production is distinguished from capitalist commodity production by its logic of subsistence (meeting the needs of simple reproduction), as opposed to the logic of the appropriation and realization of surplus-value and the accumulation of capital. On the other hand, the simple commodity producer is not a proletarian as (a) he/she retains some control over the organization of production (though this is

problematic as we shall see), (b) household production cannot produce the 'collective worker' in Marx's sense. The spatial concentration of peasants, when this occurs, is not equivalent to the *social* concentration of workers in capitalist production.

14 Following an initial phase of coercion to establish the conditions of peasant commodity production, commodity production becomes an economic necessity. To meet its needs for cash the household produces commodities which become, through the circuit of exchange, material elements of constant capital (raw materials) and variable capital (food).

15 Except for the limiting case of completely specialized commodity production, the peasant household continues to produce use-values (agricultural and non-agricultural) for its direct consumption alongside its production of commodities. The social organization of production and distribution within the household can vary a great deal, and this reflected in the differentiation of labour processes (along sexual lines, for example) and in different modes of distribution of use-values and income earned from the sale of commodities.

16 Once commodity relations are incorporated in the reproduction cycle of the household as an economic necessity, the question of how much of its resources (in terms of labour-time or of land) are devoted to the production of use-values and of commodities is secondary, though still important. Simple quantitative measures which might show, say, that only 20 per cent of labour-time or 20 per cent of land is devoted to commodity production, are misleading if they imply that the household is still basically a 'subsistence' unit (in the narrow sense), only marginally involved with commodity relations and therefore easily able to withdraw from them. (To the extent that a low degree of commodity production in this sense correlates geographically with labour reserve areas or socially with strata of poorer peasants, this is because the principal commodity produced in these cases is labour-power itself.)

17 So far our discussion does not necessarily indicate any form of capital other than merchant's capital which organizes the exchange of commodities produced by peasants, and consumed by them. However, the characterization of capital-peasant relations at the level of exchange is inadequate. First, it suggests the peasant as an 'independent' commodity producer, which is not the case. Second, it suggests a situation of 'superimposition' (of capitalist exchange relations on pre-capitalist forms of production) rather than a

dynamic analysis which investigates the ways in which capital attempts to regulate the conditions of peasant *production* (as well as exchange) without undertaking its direct organization.

18 There were various interests involved in the production and supply of cash crops in the colonial economics. These included the metropolitan industries which consumed the crops as elements of constant capital; the large trading companies which organized the collection of cash crops (directly or through intermediaries) and their subsequent export to the industries of the particular colonial power or to the world market; the colonial state which was interested in the extension of commodity relations for several reasons: to increase its sources of revenue (to meet the costs of administration, and of infrastructural development, and to contribute if possible to imperial investment funds), to ensure the supply of raw materials to the industries of the home country, and at the ideological level, to turn Africans into 'economic men', producers and consumers of commodities, as part of the programme of the 'civilizing mission'.

19 These various interests could not depend for the supply of commodities required – in sufficient quantities and of sufficient quality – on the apparent whims of the peasant producers (e.g. the notorious so-called backward-sloping supply curve of labour or of commodities, resistance to new cultivation practices). The industrial interests, the trading companies and the state combined to attempt to regulate what was grown, how it was grown, the quality of the produce, as well as to establish monopolistic pricing and marketing arrangements. This means in effect that the branches of the imperial trading companies and the apparatuses of the colonial state – despite their mercantile and politico-administrative form – had to perform certain functions associated with productive capital. While the immediate organization of the production process remained in the hands of the peasants, their production and reproduction was determined by the development of commodity relations, including the economic and political measures such as cultivation bye-laws, compulsory land-improvement schemes, and credit and extension services, which tied the producers more closely to particular kinds of production.

The simple reproduction 'squeeze'

20 As the logic of household economy is determined by the needs

of simple reproduction and not by a logic of accumulation regulated at the enterprise level by the operation of prices of production (realization of an average rate of profit), its economic 'behaviour' is different to that of a capitalist economy. For example, falling prices are experienced by household economy as a deterioration of the terms of exchange of the commodities it produces relative to those it needs for simple reproduction (the circuit C-M-C), which means a reduction in levels of consumption or an intensification of commodity production, or both simultaneously. This can be termed the simple reproduction 'squeeze' and it has a number of implications.

21 The simple reproduction 'squeeze' does not operate at the level of the terms of exchange only as their deterioration raises the costs of production both directly (increased costs of means of production) and indirectly (increased costs of reproducing the producers). The costs of production can also be raised in other ways – (a) by the exhaustion of both land and labour given the techniques of cultivation employed, (b) by rural development schemes which encourage or impose more expensive means of production (improved seeds, tools, more extensive use of fertilizers, pesticides, etc.) with no assurance that there will be increased returns to labour commensurate with the costs incurred. Both these points deserve fuller comment.

22 The precariousness of the material and technical basis of peasant production combines with the pressures exerted by commodity relations to determine the simple reproduction 'squeeze'. As much of peasant production in Africa is fuelled by human energy, and as techniques of land use in many cases exhaust the soil after a certain period, the intensification of production occurs (more labour-time on poorer or more distant soils) which increases the cost of production and reduces the returns to labour. Costs of production can increase both in terms of labour-time and, as indicated, in monetary terms – the replacement of means of production and acquisition of new means of production in the attempt to increase yields. The low level of development of the productive forces in peasant agriculture means that the household is extremely vulnerable to failure in any of its material elements of production. The vagaries of climate; the deterioration in soils which are not easily substitutable because of competition for land or the costs of clearing new land (a deterioration not uncommonly caused by the very techniques of cultivation promoted by

'development' schemes); the incidence of crop disease (especially of crops which represent a major investment of labour-time), of animal diseases (affecting draught animals or animals with other functions in terms of use or exchange), and of disease and death or infertility in the household (reducing the supply of labour) – all testify to the vulnerability of peasant farming.

23 As far as rural development programmes are concerned, these objectively operate to incorporate the peasantry further into commodity relations, and attempt to standardize and rationalize peasant production of commodities for the domestic and international markets. The regulations of such schemes often dictate very precisely the forms of the labour-process to be employed and represent a more direct intervention in the organization of production. They tie the producers in various ways to the use of particular techniques of cultivation, often to a greater expenditure of labour-time, and to direction and sanctions by the development agencies concerned.

24 The more commodity relations and acquisition of a cash income become conditions of reproduction, then shortfalls in production and/or income can lead to a cycle of indebtedness. Studies of peasant economy in a number of capitalist social formations have demonstrated the phenomena of 'starvation rents' (the payment by poorer peasants of higher than average rents to secure a plot of land for minimal reproduction needs), and of peasants selling their food crop after harvest in order to meet immediate cash needs, and subsequently having to buy food at higher prices. Similar in principle to the latter is the practice of crop-mortgaging (to richer peasants, local traders or larger-scale merchant's capital) in order to acquire cash in the case of emergencies.

25 The objective of the simple reproduction 'squeeze' then is to act as one of the mechanisms of intensifying the labour of the household to maintain or increase the supply of commodities without capital incurring any costs of management and supervision of the production process.

The extent of commoditization

26 Our remarks so far have concerned the establishment and extension of commodity relations described in general terms. It is necessary to introduce the concept of the *intensification* of

commodity relations which can help distinguish the various ways in which, and degrees to which, peasant production is constituted and household reproduction realized through commodity relations. 27 In any concrete analysis this entails consideration of the extent and forms of capitalist development of the economy of a social formation as a whole, that is, examining the place of peasant production in the social division of labour, its relations with other forms of production including capitalist agriculture and industry, the overall development of the circulation of commodities and money, and so on. At the level of household economy the intensification of commodity relations refers to the degree to which the reproduction cycle is realized through the production and exchange of commodities. Both these aspects can be illustrated in the case of food production and the satisfaction of food needs.

28 Peasants specializing in the commercial production of food can, in principle, consume a great proportion of their crop in the event of a poor harvest although this restricts their ability to purchase other commodities. Those peasants who specialize in cash-crops which have little or no use-value to the producers are more vulnerable to shortfalls in production, to the extent that the labour-time, land and money used in commodity production reduces the resources available for food production.

29 When food needs are satisfied on a regular basis by purchase this signifies that commodity relations have developed to a higher level. It reflects a more advanced social division of labour in which some peasants specialize in the commercial production of food, some of which is directed through to the market to peasants engaged in other branches of commodity production, or in which food is produced on capitalist farms with higher levels of productivity (of labour) and is available more cheaply than food produced within the household.

30 The coexistence of peasant and capitalist forms of production in agriculture raises the question of competition between the two. It was observed by Engels, Kautsky and Lenin that the ability of simple commodity producers both to reduce their standards of consumption and to continue to produce commodities in the face of deteriorating terms of exchange, means that they compete effectively with capitalist enterprises producing the same commodities (this being precisely the effect of the simple reproduction 'squeeze', and a form of competition involving the devalorization of peasant labour-time – see below; and Djurfeldt, this volume).

31 There is also the situation where industrial consumers of agricultural commodities promote their production by peasants (under contract agreements) to ensure a continuous and regulated supply to the factory or processing plant. This is another particular form of specialization which signifies an intensification of commodity relations, bringing small producers into a more direct relation with productive capital. The latter (like the rural development agencies already mentioned) is then able to determine to a greater degree the forms and conditions of production.

Differentiation of the peasantry

32 The differentiation of the peasantry is a subject of considerable confusion and to avoid such confusion a clear analytical distinction has to be established (although empirically, as those who have done research in rural areas of Africa will appreciate, the distinction is often less easy to establish). The distinction concerns different-iation in the sociological sense – indicators of inequality derived from a problematic in which 'social class' is constituted in terms of some or other scale of privilege and deprivation, and differentiation in the materialist sense which poses class in terms of the social relations of production.

33 On the first and more descriptive sense of differentiation, a wide range of variation in the relative wealth or poverty of households is encountered in many rural situations. In the first place these are differences in the accumulation and consumption of use-values, which in itself is unable to indicate socially significant differences at the level of production. Much of the time these differences in standards of consumption are related to factors that are random with respect to the relations of production. They include the vulnerability of individual households to disasters of the kind indicated above, sources of income outside household production (e.g. regular remittances of presents from relatives in wage or salaried employment), and the 'demographic differentiation' stressed by Chayanov which correlates the size and relative prosperity of households with their position in the cycle of generational reproduction (see also Shanin, Part Three of this volume). Advantages in the conditions of production which are initially distributed randomly (household size and composition, more fertile land, better access to sources of irrigation or transport, savings accumulated from wage-labour) can contribute to class

differentiation but this is by no means a necessary development.

34 Differentiation in the materialist sense is tied to the conditions in which wealth becomes capital, when it is not consumed individually but productively through investment in means of production. It is this which gives a content to the tripartite classification of 'poor', 'middle' and 'rich' peasants in terms of the relations of production:

(a) 'Poor' peasants unable to reproduce themselves by household production exchange their labour-power on a regular basis and come to form a category reproduced through the sale of labour-power. It was in this context that Lenin warned against 'too stereotyped an understanding of the theoretical proposition that capitalism requires the free, landless worker' (Lenin, 1899, p. 178). He was referring here to agricultural workers who retain a small plot for cultivation. The access to a small plot does not make them 'peasants' but in so far as it contributes to their subsistence reduces the wages paid by those who employ them. They constitute a rural proletariat in the process of formation.

(b) 'Middle' peasants are able to reproduce themselves through family labour and land but in specific relations with other strata of the peasantry and with other forms of production. It is these relations through which middle peasant households are constituted that determine the relative stability or instability of the reproduction of a middle peasantry.

(c) 'Rich' peasants or kulaks accumulate sufficiently to invest in production through the purchase of superior means of production and/or labour power; in short, in so far as they initiate and maintain a cycle of extended reproduction based on accumulation they come to form a category of capitalist farmers.

35 Several further comments are in order. Evidence of the exchange of labour-power is not sufficient to establish class differentiation. On one hand, it is not uncommon to find peasant households which both sell and buy labour-power for different purposes and at different moments in the annual cycle of economic activity. On the other hand, the exchange of labour-power may be concealed by forms of payment other than money-wages, and may be disguised by ostensibly 'traditional' forms of co-operation and reciprocity.

36 Differentiation in class terms is another dimension of the intensification of commodity relations to be added to our previous observations, in that the homogeneity of the conditions of household economy (as an economy of simple reproduction) is broken up as

means of production are capitalized and labour-power becomes a commodity, exchanged on a systematic basis within the rural economy. However, differentiation of the peasantry is not a necessary condition nor effect of the intensification of commodity relations – this will depend on the concrete conditions in which intensification occurs.

37 It is worth recalling the original Russian connotation of 'kulak' as an 'all-round' agent of the extension of commodity relations – an economic agent who not only operates as a commercial farmer employing labour-power but also rents out farm machinery, acts as a local merchant's and moneylending capital, investing in crop purchasing, retail business, transport and credit, and as a productive capital establishing small-scale processing and manufacturing enterprises. This is particularly important in Africa where, given the relative backwardness of circuits of exchange in many areas, capital accumulated in agriculture is often invested in mercantile and transport activities which yield a better rate of return than reinvestment in production. This can help account for the limited formation of agrarian capital and the limited differentiation of units of production simultaneously with the extension (and intensification) of commodity relations.

Capital, state and peasantry

38 The question of conceptualizing the relations of production through which peasant production is constituted has not yet been posed directly, although it has been suggested that this question is to be pursued in the relations between peasant households and capital rather than by invoking modes of production other than the capitalist mode. The latter approach, that of various versions of the 'articulation' of modes of production, is precluded for reasons which can only be briefly summarized here.

39 Fuller discussion of the arguments against a peasant or simple commodity mode of production will be found in the papers cited in the introduction (para. 2). It should be noted that formulations of a peasant or simple commodity mode of production (and some versions of a domestic mode of production) ultimately come down to relations *within* the unit of production (the household) and its mode of economic calculation (as a unit of simple reproduction). At best these formulations may elaborate the nature of simple commodity production as a *form* of production but cannot satisfy

questions, concerning the *relations* of production through which it is constituted, a problem that is not resolved by appealing to an articulated combination of peasant and capitalist modes of production.

40 Another type of articulation theory suggests that pre-capitalist modes of production are subjected to a process of 'dissolution/conservation' by the capitalist mode. In this case, the relations of production in which peasants are engaged represent particular and determinate combinations of pre-capitalist (e.g. the domestic community, the lineage mode, the feudal mode) and capitalist relations of production. While attempts to pursue a theory of articulation have been useful in emphasizing the variant modes of penetration of pre-capitalist formations by capital, and the variant forms of the development of commodity relations, they encounter several basic problems. One is that it makes little sense to talk of the 'conservation' of modes of production whose conditions of reproduction, it is admitted, have been destroyed by capitalism even if the forms of production have not been completely transformed. Second, theories of articulation tend to be functionalist in the sense that the degree and forms of 'dissolution/conservation' are held to be determined by what is functional for capital. Third, in these theories pre-capitalist modes of production and the capitalist mode 'meet' essentially at the level of exchange (although pre-capitalist ruling classes are sometimes suggested as the agency mediating capitalist relations of production).

41 Two alternative lines of approach to the relations of production have been indicated above. The first is that of investigating the relations of simple commodity producers with (various forms of) capital in varying concrete conditions. The second is that of investigating the internal differentiation of simple commodity producers (towards capitalist farmers and wage-workers). We have been at pains to emphasize that the latter 'classic model' is a special case of the first set of relations, and not its sole or necessary form of development.

42 Without providing any definitive answer to the question of the relations of production, a number of issues can be indicated within the framework employed here. One set of issues concerns how the conditions of production are determined by the circuit of capital, and the question of effective possession of the means of production and effective control of the production process. While the degree of effective control exercised by capital sometimes appears to be

virtually total (e.g. as in out-grower arrangements, and as in some rural development schemes) – and this has prompted character-izations of small commodity producers as 'semi' or 'disguised' proletarians – the process stops short of full proletarianization in that the separation of the producers and the means of production is not complete, and the individualized production of the household is not replaced by a socialized production process, 'set in motion' by capital.

43 This suggests that the content of the relations between peasants and capital has to be related to the struggle between the direct producers and capital over the conditions of labour in the sphere of production and over the distribution and realization of the product, up to the moment of complete expropriation and direct control of production by capital (which is the basis of a different kind of struggle). The resistance of peasant producers is manifested in a number of ways: refusal to adopt new cultivation practices or their sabotage (thus peasant 'conservatism'), bearing in mind that such measures introduce further elements of risk in the already precarious basis of household production; peasant 'strikes' involving the refusal to grow certain crops or cutting back on their production, i.e. attempts to withdraw at least partially from commodity relations, or to find alternative sources of cash income (e.g. labour migration); evasion of crop-grading regulations and of the terms of exchange imposed by state or other monopolistic agencies of merchant's capital (by smuggling and other forms of illicit marketing) in order to realize a higher return to labour; as well as political actions, including acts of violence, against agents of capital and state functionaries who confront the peasants.

44 On the other side, the movement of capital to determine the conditions of small commodity production and exchange can be described broadly in terms of the 'vertical concentration' of the producers. The 'classic model' of capitalist development in agriculture incorporates the expropriation of the peasantry and the horizontal concentration of means of production (land, machinery, labour-power) in units of production equivalent to industrial enterprises in their organization of production and modes of economic calculation. Vertical concentration refers to the co-ordination, standardization, and (greater or lesser) supervision of the production of numerous individual small producers through a central agency, whether this represents productive capital directly (as in out-grower arrangements), forms of merchant's capital

which thereby actively intervene in the organization of production, or whether the agency is that of a cooperative or other state-managed scheme.

45 In *The Development of Capitalism in Russia* Lenin (1899) gave examples of the process of vertical concentration in conditions in which it was more profitable for productive capital to invest in processing and manufacturing enterprises consuming commodities produced by peasants (production it could find ways of regulating) rather than undertaking the production of those commodities itself. A. V. Chayanov in the final chapter of his work on *Peasant Farm Organization* (1925) also drew attention to vertical concentration brought about by the intervention of trading capital in the conditions of production, and by certain kinds of cooperatives (refer also to Djurfeldt, this volume).

46 At this point it is useful to make more explicit the operation of state forms of capital. It is generally true that in Africa, as compared with Latin America or Asia, there has been less direct involvement in agricultural production of large-scale productive capitals (for example, international agri-business companies). The further development of commodity relations since independence cannot be discussed without considering the role of the state, of which there are two important aspects in this context. The first is that the economic role of the state has to be located in relation to the possibilities of accumulation by the ruling classes which have formed since independence, whether they are reproduced and accumulate on the basis of individual or state property or some combination of the two forms. Their reproduction as classes and their ability to accumulate are tied to the development of the economies of the particular social formations in which they exist; that is, their ability to appropriate surplus-labour and to establish an accumulation fund is closely related to the further development of commodity production within their countries. In this sense, they have a more direct interest in the development of commodity relations within *any given country* than international companies which mobilize capital and switch investments on a global basis.

47 The second aspect (related to the first) is that the state acts to promote the extension and intensification of commodity relations in conditions where it might not be immediately profitable for productive and finance capitals to do so. The lack of capital for investment on the necessary scale as well as the lack of technical and managerial expertise to help explain the major role of aid

(bilateral or multilateral as in the case of the World Bank) in the promotion of rural development schemes which provide infrastructure for the further development of commodity relations (communications, energy, storage, local processing facilities, education and health schemes), or the planning and financing of production schemes (agricultural machinery, irrigation equipment, improved seeds, fertilizers, insecticides, pesticides, etc.). In the past such schemes have concentrated on the production of export crops and have usually incorporated 'progressive farmer' incentives (which contribute to the differentiation of the peasantry). In recent years another strategy has emerged, not necessarily a contradictory one, of encouraging food production for national self-sufficiency and providing production inputs and credits to the 'poorer rural sectors'.

48 The reasons for this new emphasis can be hypothesized – the chronic state of food production, particularly the commodity production of food staples in many African countries; the political instability associated with food shortages and inflationary food prices in the cities; the cost in foreign exchange of food imports to make up the shortages in domestic production. While capital in general has an interest in the extension and intensification of commodity relations, there is also the more specific interest in extending the market of those capitals engaged in the production of agricultural inputs (see Feder 1976; also S. George, 1976), as well as the interest of the ruling class, already alluded to, in deepening the material basis of appropriation and accumulation. This means, in short, that alongside the commoditization associated with the differentiation of the peasantry and the investment of large-scale productive capitals in agriculture, a major impetus to the further development of commodity relations comes from the operation of state-managed forms of capital. These represent an alliance between the apparatuses of the state which organize the political, ideological and administrative conditions of the further penetration of capital into peasant agriculture, and the provision of the financial and technical means of this penetration by either private capitals or the particular form of finance capital represented by the World Bank and other aid agencies.

49 Rural development schemes promoted through this alliance need not have the same rationale nor the same objective effects as far as the particular forms of the development of commodity relations are concerned. In some cases they amount to a quasi-

dispossession of the producers by converting land and other means of production into state property (in the economic sense, not necessarily juridically), which is related to the struggle of the direct producers and capital/state over the effective possession of the means and organization of production (e.g. the process occurring in Tanzania from villagization). Alternatively, differentiation may be encouraged with incentives to 'progressive farmers' which consolidates and develops further private property in land and other means of production. Again, the effect may be to reproduce a relatively stable middle peasantry engaged in specialized forms of commodity production in particular relations with productive capital (this situation is analysed with great specificity in the work by M. P. Cowen on household production in Central Province, Kenya). These different possible paths of development indicate the heterogeneity of forms of peasant production, the dangers of facile generalization, and the need in investigating particular peasantries to examine their relations with other forms of production and the overall development of commodity relations.

Conclusion

56*   These notes have tried to outline in a provisional way some of the issues raised by contemporary forms of the agrarian question in Africa, issues which clearly require far more theoretical and empirical investigation. No definitive solutions have been offered but the position taken here is that peasants have to be located in their relations with capital and the state, in other words, within *capitalist relations of production* mediated through forms of household production which are the site of a struggle for effective possession and control between the producers and capital/state. It may be inferred that in this way peasants are posed as 'wage-labour equivalents' (Banaji, 1977), but in a relative sense that limits the subjugation and real subsumption of household labour by capital to the extent that the producers are not fully expropriated nor dependent for their reproduction on the sale of labour-power through the wage-form.

57   These notes are also limited by their primary focus on the level of economic relations but the conclusions at this level of analysis – that there is no single and essential 'peasantry' –

---

*   Paragraphs 50–5 have been omitted.

militates *a fortiori* against any such homogenization of peasants at the level of politics and ideology. There can be no uniform 'model' of class action by peasants nor any single and abstract formulation of the relation of peasants to revolutionary politics, whether such a formulation expresses a blanket optimism or a blanket scepticism concerning their 'revolutionary potential'.

References

Bernstein, H. (1977), 'Notes on capital and peasantry', *Review of African Political Economy*, 10, pp. 60–73

Chayanov, A. V. (1925), *Peasant Farm Organization*; in *The Theory of Peasant Economy*, ed. D. Thorner, *et al.*, Homewood, Ill.: Richard D. Irwin

Clarke, J. (1977), 'Some problems in the conceptualisation of non-capitalist relations of production', *Critique of Anthropology*, 2, pp. 59–66

Ennew, J., Hirst, P., and Tribe, K. (1977), '"Peasantry" as an economic category', *Journal of Peasant Studies*, 4, 4, pp. 295–322

Feder, E. (1976), 'McNamara's little green revolution: World Bank scheme for self-liquidation of Third World peasantry', *Economic and Political Weekly*, 3 April, pp. 532–41

George, S. (1976), *How the Other Half Dies*, Harmondsworth: Penguin

Lenin, V. I. (1899), *The Development of Capitalism in Russia;* in *Collected Works*, vol. 3, Moscow: Foreign Languages Publishing House, 1960

Littlejohn, G. (1977), 'Peasant economy and society', in B. Hindess (ed.), *Sociological Theories of the Economy*, London: Macmillan

8 Peasant economics and the development of capitalist agriculture in the Cauca Valley, Colombia*

M. Taussig

In a pattern common to many Third World countries, a sustained and dramatic upsurge has occurred in large-scale capitalist crop farming in Colombia during the past fifteen years, while macro-economic studies indicate that peasant production has remained stagnant and that peasant incomes have probably decreased (Kalmonovitz, 1974; Urrutia and Berry, 1975; and cf. Feder, 1973). Despite the fact that little faith should be placed in the aggregate data on which such analyses of peasant farming are based, numerous conclusions have been drawn concerning the evolution of rural class structure. One of the most contentious issues surrounds the question as to whether, or in what ways, the intensive development of large-scale capitalist agriculture is a cause of peasant pauper-ization, thereby augmenting the labour supply necessary for the capitalist farms and creating an ever larger rural proletariat. The question is most relevant and especially compelling for those areas of the countryside where peasants subsist alongside burgeoning agribusinesses and where peasants themselves are adopting some of the new technology and increasing their costs of production.

As yet there are no community-focused micro-economic studies which could illuminate the nature of the social changes that these sorts of peasants are undergoing in Colombia. Because macro-economic studies based on aggregate data of peasant production are quite unreliable, I therefore wish to discuss the relationship between peasant and large-scale capitalist farming by means of a case study undertaken in the south of the Cauca Valley where the development of capitalist agriculture on large holdings exists side by side with declining peasant farms and is probably more advanced than in any other part of Colombia.

As conjoined but quite distinct modes of production, it is extremely difficult to compare peasant economics with those of large-scale capitalist agriculture. Chayanov (1966) held that the

*This chapter is taken from Taussig (1978).

analytic tools used for understanding the latter were largely irrelevant for the analysis of the former, in stark opposition to the Bolsheviks, for example, who claimed that Marxist economics explained both (see Djurfeldt and Shanin, both this volume), just as many economists and anthropologists claim that neo-classical economics are sufficient to the task. Marx himself never systematically dealt with the issue, his understanding being that the peasantry was a doomed class anyway. On general principles, however, given his socio-historical approach to economic analysis, he would have fought shy of universalizing categories that applied to one mode of production, such as capitalism, to another mode of production such as peasant farming.

Sensitive to some of Chayanov's warnings, Roger Bartra (1974 and 1975) has recently presented an interesting Marxist analysis of the agrarian structure and social classes in Mexico in which he takes sharp issue with those whom he calls the 'liberal' economists of the Comité Interamericano de Desarrollo Agrícola (CIDA) studies, whose empirical findings led them to extol the efficiencies of *some* of the productivity functions of peasant farming. Arguing that peasants were more efficient than large landowners in terms of crop yield per hectare, the CIDA reports served as an unsuccessful plea for land reform as the means for increasing national food production by granting more land to peasants. But two considerations have here to be borne in mind. First, with the progressive intensification and technification of large-scale agriculture since the time of the CIDA studies, many Latin American countries such as Colombia show greater yields per hectare from large-scale crop production units than from peasant farms – a fact that is overlooked in important recent accounts of Third World agriculture (Griffin, 1974; George, 1976; Lappé and Collins, 1977). Second, the fact was never really confronted that peasants' efficiency, such as it is, usually turns on their being poor and working hard, reducing consumption and intensifying labour (see Djurfeldt and Bernstein, both this volume). Bartra's repeated observation on this second point, and one which stands as the leitmotiv of his entire work, is derived from Lenin's first preface to the *Development of Capitalism in Russia* where Lenin concurs with Kautsky in saying:

The existence of a small peasantry in any capitalist society is due not to the technical superiority of small production in agriculture, but the fact that the small peasants reduce the level of their requirements below that of wage-workers and tax their energies far more than do the latter (Lenin, 1899, p. 27).

The empirical basis for this statement came from studies of Russian and West European agriculture. As far as the southern Cauca Valley is concerned, however, the 'technical superiority' of small peasant producers over that of adjoining large-scale capitalist farms *is* an important cause for the persistent existence of small peasants, contrary to the implications of the above quotation. The 'capital' efficiency of small peasant producers is higher than that of the capitalist farmers, and their energies are far less taxed as peasant farmers than as wage labourers on the capitalist farms.

But what is meant by 'technical superiority'? As Bartra is at pains to point out, and this cannot be overstressed, everything depends on how one defines and calculates this 'technical superiority', or farming and economic efficiency. For example, and contrary to Chayanov (as well as the analysis of the peasants with which this article is concerned), Bartra decrees that peasants' unpaid household labour *can* be and *has* to be budgeted as a cost of production. Thus his manipulation of the data on Mexican peasant farming reveals exorbitant production costs and hence low efficiency in comparison with capitalist farming because of its economies of scale.

Bartra's conclusion, following Lenin and Kautsky, is that peasant efficiency is low, costs of production are high, peasant labour is intense, and peasant 'surplus labour', as invested on the peasant plot, is thus equivalent to a transfer of value from the peasantry to the capital class, in particular, via the society in general. The total elimination of the peasantry foreshadowed by such an analysis is only checked by the fact that the state (in Mexico, for example) has a serious political interest in subsidizing them. Kautsky (n.d., pp. 140, 174–5) also noted similar checks. Although this seemed to contradict the general thrust of his analysis, he was able to integrate the apparent anomaly of peasant persistence with capitalist development by pointing to the needs of large-scale farmers for a local labour pool admirably provided by poor peasants whose farming, he stated, could in no way compete with the capitalist farms. Vaguely and unsystematically, Lenin (1899, pp. 183, 185) also alluded to the same thing almost as an aside.

Unequal access to means of production by peasants and capitalist farmers is only a symptom, according to Bartra, not a cause of their unequal efficiencies. He fulminates against the 'liberal' economists for their compulsive concern with the unequal distribution of land, when it is to the inefficiencies of the peasant mode of production that attention should be directed.

The efficiencies of large-scale capitalist farming also riveted the enthusiastic attention of Kautsky and Lenin. As regards one aspect of this, for instance, Lenin wrote, '"The agricultural labourer is better off than the small peasant", says Kautsky repeatedly; the same is to be observed in Russia' (1899, p. 27). For Britain, Marx himself was far less sure. His more dialectical vision contrasts notably with the positivism of the *epigoni*. In *Capital* (vol. 1) he noted the marked deterioration in the standard of living of the British agricultural labourer associated with the rise of large-scale agriculture (1867, pp. 673–96) and typically stressed the costs of progress.

The understanding of the articulation between large-scale capitalist farming and peasant production presented by Bartra, following Lenin and Kautsky, does not, it seems to me, do justice to the ways in which they interlock to the benefit of capitalist farming where it is developing in areas of peasant agriculture as in the southern Cauca Valley over the past twenty-five years.

My argument concerning the southern Cauca Valley is as follows. In the evolution of the relationship between large-scale capitalist farming and peasant production, the former is *less* efficient than the latter on several crucial criteria. But because of its monopoly over land, capitalist farming compensates for its inefficiencies by being able to take advantage of peasant efficiencies. Contrary to Bartra's assertion, the inequality in the distribution of land *is* crucial and cannot be seen merely as a 'symptom' of unequal economic efficiencies. For it is by reducing peasant farm size below a certain minimum that gives to the capitalist class the mechanism for accumulating surplus. In other words, bigness and technology are not in themselves inherently more efficient; rather, they provide the political muscle necessary to coerce a labour force into being, as well as the discipline and authority necessary to exact surplus value from that labour (cf. Marglin, 1974).

Until the capitalist class was able to obtain the political power necessary to reduce peasant holdings to a certain small size – less than required for subsistence – wages in the capitalist sector of agriculture were high due to the fact that peasants could subsist from the use-value production of their own plots. The high cost of labour was due to the low value of labour – value of labour being defined as the value of commodities necessary to maintain and reproduce labour. Beginning around 1900, capitalist farmers used the political power channelled their way by the entry of US capital and by opening up of foreign markets forcibly to appropriate peasant land, motivated by the desire for more acreage for their crops and by their need to reduce peasant holdings to the extent that peasants were forced to become wage labourers or semi-proletarians (whose subsistence was provided in part from their peasant farming and, in some cases, from their wages as remittances to sustain the peasant farm). The employers of these semi-proletarianized peasants were able to extract a higher rate of surplus value from this type of labour force than would be possible if the costs of maintenance and reproduction of labour had to be met by capitalist production alone. This appropriation of higher rates of surplus value occurs not merely because a significant part of the rural proletariat is part-peasant and produces part of its own subsistence directly, nor merely because of the elasticity this gives to the local reservoir of labour, but also and very importantly because peasant maximization of 'capital' (as we shall see below) is greater than that of the capitalist farmers and their costs per kilogram of product are lower, even if we include unpaid labour by the peasant and members of his household as a cost of production. As the technology of the 'green revolution' penetrates the ranks of peasant cultivators themselves, due to the intervention of the Colombian government and USAID, the picture changes. The peasants' 'capital' efficiency decreases, and the rate of land loss to the large-scale capitalist farming sector increases. But even so, peasant maximization of capital is no less than that of the large-scale capitalist farmers.

Moreover, both the cash return and crop yield per kilo-calorie of human energy expended in peasant farming are greater than that which results to them from their wage-labouring on the large-scale capitalist units of crop production. This labour-energy efficiency advantage of peasant over proletarian labour also serves towards decreasing the costs of maintaining and reproducing wage labour, where such labour is also part-peasant.

It needs emphasizing that this type of articulation between the two modes of production is part of a larger determining context, that of neo-colonial underdevelopment, specifically the smallness of the domestic market and the underdeveloped division of labour.

This structural feature of peripheral economies, whose market lies at the centres of the world capitalist system, means that concern with increasing workers' purchasing power is secondary to the drive for unlimited expansion of production. Hence, reducing the value of labour or maintaining it at a low level makes for less contradictions than in advanced capitalist economies, and semi-proletarianization of the peasantry as opposed to complete proletarianization is in keeping with such a structure. Moreover, this same structural feature precludes the conditions necessary to sustain a fully fledged, 'pure' proletariat (especially in the countryside) – i.e., that class of people who have nothing to fall back on but their labour power, which they are forced to exchange on the market for wages. The petty commodity adjunct to wage labour is thus necessary to capitalists, and also to wage workers for whom a capitalist wage is rarely sufficient for survival, and this has important implications for our understanding of the lethargic development of class-based associations and of class consciousness.

In directing attention to the efficiencies of small-scale production and the diseconomies of large-scale capitalist farming, my aim is not to argue in favour of sustaining peasant agriculture as the World Bank is now trying to do in Colombia and elsewhere. Rather, I wish to demonstrate how certain sorts of efficiencies built into the peasant mode of production, as in the Cauca Valley, can serve to sustain and develop large-scale capitalist farming, especially where such farming exists alongside peasant holdings. As for efforts such as those of the World Bank to sustain peasants through expanded credit and technification in lieu of land reform, this case study indicates that the *logic* of such attempts is to strengthen and perpetuate such an articulation, while the *practical consequence* shall be to further pauperize the bulk of the peasantry into landlessness.

Capitalist development and the appropriation of peasant land

The peasant economy with which this essay is concerned is that of the Afro-American freeholders living at the southern extremity of the very fertile and large Cauca Valley in a general region known as 'Norte del Cauca', 4 degrees north of the equator and about 3000 feet above sea level. Since the abolition of slavery in 1851, this peasantry has experienced a social history evolving through two distinct phases, the understanding of which most certainly does not lie in any supposed inefficiencies of peasant farming but in the political dynamics of class struggle.

For fifty years following abolition, the ex-slaves and their descendants formed a flourishing subsistence economy squatting illegally on the vast lands of their former masters who, without avail, tried desperately to limit this peasant farming in order to reinvigorate their failing estates on a wage-labour and rent-labour basis. Armed struggle between peasants and the faction-ridden large landowning class characterized the entirety of this period (Taussig, 1974; Mina, 1975). In the late nineteenth century, the peasant economy was described in terms which leave little doubt as to the abundance of its production and the viability of its self-sufficiency – in stark contrast to the decaying *hacienda* economy throughout most of the second half of the nineteenth century. It was because the peasants could subsist so easily that they were both loath to work on the *haciendas*, and the local *hacienda* owners complained bitterly that not even high wages could woo peasants off their plots into wage-labour (Taussig, 1974; Mina, 1975). The high price of labour reflected the fact that costs of maintenance and reproduction of labour were low; 'use-value' production on the peasant plot resulted in high labour costs to the large-scale producers.

The balance of power, which slightly favoured the peasantry, swung quickly and irrevocably to the advantage of the large landowners following the War of One Thousand Days (1899–1901). This allowed for the political centralization of the republic, following which there was a large influx of US finance capital (much of which entered the Cauca Valley). With the termination of the railway between the Valley and the Pacific Ocean in 1914, the same year that the Panama Canal was completed, the Valley was provided with the means for exporting bulky tropical crops for the first time. Land values rose rapidly, and peasants were put on the defensive as a myriad of land claims were successfully prosecuted against them by large landowners. The infamous Colombian *violencia* or 'civil war' (1948–58) further accelerated the loss of peasant lands as large landowners took advantage of the frightful insecurity of those times to drive down peasant land prices and force peasants into selling. It is said by the peasants in the Norte del Cauca region that aerial spraying was then used to destroy peasant crops – a tactic repeated in other parts of Colombia in the 1960s as well (Patiño, 1975, pp. 181–3). The production of cocoa, one of the mainstays of peasant cash income, dropped by around

80 per cent in the eight years between 1950 and 1958 (Wood, 1962). With the aid of World Bank and US financing (Fedesarrollo, 1976, p. 344), the sugar plantations have been able to continue their remorseless expansion over the flatlands; whereas only 2000 metric tons of sugar were produced in this region in 1938, some 91,000 tons were produced in 1969.

Local land tax records (supported by peasant oral history) show that the modal peasant farm size decreased from 7.5 plazas in 1933 to half a plaza in 1967 (a plaza equals 0.64 of a hectare). This decrease of 15 times was accompanied by no more than a twofold natural increase of the local population (and there was little out-migration); land shortage cannot be blamed on the 'population explosion'. Peasant households did not suffer equally, for although the vast majority now have less than a subsistence-size holding of three plazas, around 5 per cent have more than ten plazas and can be classified as 'rich peasants'. By 1970, according to government census, about 80 per cent of the cultivable land was in the possession of four sugar plantations and several large-scale capitalist farmers growing other crops, while 90 per cent of holdings were less than 15 plazas.

Writing in 1954, in reference to the plantations of the centre and north of the Valley which developed earlier than those of the south, a local agronomist pointed to some of the consequences of this pattern of land distribution:

The poor peasants supply the labour closest to the plantations. As they possess their own houses they save the plantation the cost of constructing housing and the transport of a very large number of people. Moreover, their economic necessities tie them indefinitely to the plantation outside of which it would be difficult to obtain work (Mancini, 1954, p. 30).

The dual character of the labour force for plantations and large farms

Unlike most other sugar producing areas of the world, the climatic and soil conditions of the Cauca Valley permit an essentially year-round, aseasonal production. The notorious instability of labour inputs cannot be ascribed to ecological factors but to the political action of the plantation owners (Knight, 1972; Buenaventura, 1976) *and* to the partially peasant character of much of the labour force as well.

In the early 1960s the militant trade union structure was broken by the growers who fomented a dual system of labour recruitment and employment, together with a switch from growing all their cane themselves to buying more than half of it from independent large farmers by 1974. Faced with serious labour unrest and the opportunity to expand export production as never before – to fill the gap in the US sugar import quota subsequent to the embargo on Cuba – the Cauca Valley cane growers stimulated the development of the labour contractor system by which formally independent intermediaries are paid to recruit their own workers for set tasks.[1]

The workers directly employed by the plantations, day in and day out, are referred to as *afiliados* or 'permanents', and are eligible for social security benefits and membership in trade unions with very limited powers of strike. On the other hand, the casual workers employed by the labour contractors, referred to as *contratistas*, receive far lower wages, are not eligible for social security, and cannot legally form or join trade unions.

The proportion of the total plantation field force that is organized into relatively small, unstable, mobile gangs of contracted workers has oscillated between 20 per cent and 33 per cent since the early 1960s (Fedesarrollo, 1976). This has substantially lowered the cost of labour and undermined the political strength of *all* workers. It has also provided the growers with the elastic reservoir of labour needed to facilitate the co-ordination of uneven field supplies of raw material with the varying capacity of the mills – a variation which becomes all the more marked in a rapidly growing industry – and in addition, buffers changes in labour demand consequent to fluctuations in the price of sugar.

The percentage of the labour force that is organized by labour contractors is higher for the more critical tasks, such as harvesting, and it is noteworthy that the percentage is higher in the cane fields of the Norte del Cauca region than in other parts of the Valley where the density of peasants is lower and the minimum daily wage for both *afiliados* and *contratistas* on capitalist farms is higher. The majority of the *contratistas* are not only locals born in the immediate region and of peasant descent, but they depend to varying extents on their peasant farms for part of their subsistence. Many alternate between peasant farming and wage-labouring for contractors, while others have their immediate family supplying part of its subsistence needs from the peasant plot. For the remainder, who have at least some land yet whose on-farm income is almost negligible, rent-free accommodation on the peasant holding represents a substantial saving since rent otherwise would consume 25 per cent of wage income.

Around 70 per cent of the *afiliados*, or 'permanents', are immigrants from the isolated rivers and rain forests of the Pacific coast. The majority of them stay one to two years and then return to their economically self-sufficient households on the coast for a year or so before returning to the cane fields for another round of employment, usually leaving their spouses and children behind.

The remainder of the *afiliados* are locally born. Like the *contratistas*, but to a lesser extent, the majority of them have economically meaningful links with local peasant farms. On occasions, more so in the case of *afiliados* than *contratistas*, the plantation labourer will contract another peasant to work his farm in his absence, paying the latter from the wages he receives from the plantation, and one year later, for instance, the roles may well be reversed.

Over the past fifteen years, the Valley has also undergone a striking increase in the large-scale cultivation of crops other than sugar cane, and these crops are exclusively worked by the contractor system – the difference with the cane being that a high proportion of these workers are local women and children, which is an additional cause for lowering the price of labour. The contractors say they prefer women to men because they are 'more tame', will work for less, and do as they are told. They have to, because with the steady decomposition of the extended and nuclear family consequent to the development of capitalist agriculture in this region, the burden of child care and feeding falls increasingly on the women who are painfully conscious of the hungry children left at home waiting their rice at nightfall. An extremely important source of income for these women and child labourers (known as *iguazas*, in reference to migratory ducks that eat seed lying in the fields) comes from gleaning the fields of the large capitalist farms after harvest. There are people whose main source of livelihood derives from eating or selling the grain they find loose in the soil.

Hence, the majority of the wage-labourers on the capitalist farms and plantations, in this very developed region, are in reality not 'pure' proletarians with nothing to sell or subsist on but their labour power. Instead, whether *contratistas* or *afiliados*, whether locals or temporary immigrants from far-off areas, they are but part-time proletarians whose subsistence or that of their families depends on their being able to complement proletarian labour with the fruits of peasant or other non-capitalist modes of production.

This dualized social character of the wage-labour force, especially of the *contratista* fraction, greatly facilitates the predominance of the piece-rate wage system in capitalist agriculture, which in turn bolsters the labour contractor system. As compared with a time-rate method of payment, the piece-rate system offers far more opportunities to the employer to intensify labour, atomize the workforce, maintain the sense of individualization, set the workers in competition with one another, and reduce the average daily wage (cf. Marx 1867, pp. 551–8 on 'Piece wages'). Given the low rate of the latter, the wage labourers themselves prefer the piece-rate system (because of the possibility of exceeding it). Since many of the *contratistas* prefer to alternate between working their plots and working on the plantations or large farms, the *contratista* system is further reinforced.

Ease of recruitment and organization of contracted labour rely heavily on the utilization of existing social networks among the poor in general and the peasantry in particular. It is by encouraging these people to organize themselves into work groups and through co-opting their own form of organization that the contracting system depends – a further instance of how non-capitalist institutions are useful, indeed necessary, for capitalist development.

Of all types of work in the region, wage labour on the plantations and large-scale capitalist farms is held to be the most arduous and least desirable. Above all, it is the *humillación* (the humbling authoritarianism) that workers complain of most, just as the large landowners and their foremen complain of the workers' intransigence, laziness, and sabotage, and fear their sporadic, unorganized violence. Peasant farming has its problems, but not these.

Peasant agriculture

Until 1971 *all* peasant farming, regardless of size of holding, was based on the same mixture of interplanted cocoa trees, coffee trees, fruit trees, and plantains. While cocoa and coffee are predominantly cash crops, plantains and fruit occupy a smaller proportion of each holding and are only sold if there is a surplus over household consumption. The technology used was and is the same regardless of size of holding. However, since 1970–1, many peasants have been encouraged by the government's agricultural extension service Instituto Colombiano Agropecuario (ICA), which was funded by a USAID programme, to uproot the perennials and plant seasonal seed crops on open fields using tractors. In analysing the effects of this changeover from a low-capital, low-energy, and unintensive labour system, to its opposite, I will first deal with the traditional method of agriculture and then contrast it with the new, making comparisons with large-scale capitalist farming where relevant.

Traditional peasant agriculture

All crop species are interplanted one next to the other in seemingly random array, together with a large variety of tall shade trees, fruit trees, and other natural vegetation of all heights. The tall shade trees are considered essential for the health of the cocoa and coffee trees, and greatly reduce weed growth, a factor of prime importance in tropical agriculture. Firewood, house-building materials, cordage, packing, gourds, matress-fill, wrapping leaves, and many medicinal plants are also obtained from the plot, in which most peasants can name up to seventy species without much effort. Poultry and pigs are often maintained as well. Commercialized as it is, this type of agriculture preserves most of the pre-existing structure of the eco-system, as well as the fertility of the soil which is constantly nourished by the heavy tonnage of naturally falling leaf compost.

While the plantains yield fruit every eight to ten months, regardless of the time of year, cocoa and coffee are harvested every two weeks and yield for at least thirty years. Both of these have a six-month production cycle, and even at their lowest ebb may produce a little. Furthermore, the cycles of cocoa and coffee are such that they very neatly complement one another; when cocoa waxes, coffee wanes, and *vice versa* in such a manner that a fairly constant trickle of income and labour input is maintained throughout the year. There is very little, if any, capital maintenance.

It is usually considered that around three plazas of land cultivated in this manner provide a subsistence living for the peasant household. Labour requirements are very small. Most households could cope with up to six plazas on their own, and labour inputs are spaced evenly and frequently throughout the year. The two main tasks, harvesting and weeding, are very light work. The former is carried out every two weeks, while the weeding is performed once or twice a year. The only tools used are the machete and the *pala* (a light spade). Corn, when it is grown, is planted with a digging stick, and no chemicals are used.

A three-plaza plot requires on average 105 labour-days; forty-five on weeding, and sixty on harvesting. A man and his wife (to take a hypothetical case) can thus subsist by each working no more than one-sixth of the year, provided the plot is in an average state of productivity.

My survey of production of four such plots showed that at 1971 prices, the annual net income of a three-plaza (subsistence sized) farm is around 11,000 pesos (in 1970 one peso = US $ 0.05) before deducting living expenses, and categorizing unpaid household labour not as a cost but as part of that income.

This compares very favourably with the maximum income of a contracted day labourer on the sugar plantations who, at that time, received around 10,000 pesos a year working the whole year round (275 labour-days), especially in view of the fact that the spokesmen for the sugar plantations claim that among the social benefits of the sugar industry is its great use of well-paid labour. But since the sugar plantations require no more than one worker for every five plazas of land (Fedesarrollo, 1976, p. 16), it in fact generates fewer work places per unit of land than do the labour-extensive peasant farms, while the sugar worker receives no greater annual income. Furthermore, if one budgets unpaid household labour as part of income instead of as a cost of production, then the traditional-style peasant farming yields as high a net income per unit of land as is realized by the owners of the sugar plantations.

In terms of cash yield per peso invested per harvest and unit of land, then, these peasant farms are far superior either to the plantations or to other types of large-scale capitalist crop farms in the same area, even if we budget unpaid household labour as a production cost by imputing a market value to that labour.

Peasant social organization

The preceding remarks concerning the traditional-style peasant economy have been largely based on the ideal-typical three-plaza subsistence-sized holding. This discussion has to be complemented by a brief sketch of the social context in which that farming operates, because of the variation in the size of holdings and because the relationships between households, as much as between them and the wider society, determine the overall functioning and efficiency of the peasant economy.

There are striking differences in the size of household farms, all of which have been in freehold private-property plots, but mostly titleless, since the 1930s. In 1971, 5 per cent of eighty-eight households that I surveyed had more than ten plazas and could be thus classified as 'rich', while some 75 per cent had less than the three plazas required for subsistence, forcing them to seek off-farm work. At that time, two-thirds of peasants over the age of 15 gained the major part of their livelihood from work on peasant farms, either their own, or their own as well as those of neighbouring peasants for whom they worked for wages. Of the remainder, practically all the males were mainly employed as wage labourers on plantations or capitalist farms, while the females were equally divided among wage-labouring for contractors, working as servants in the nearby city of Cali, or peddling peasant produce such as bananas, citrus fruits, tomatoes, and wrapping-leaves in the rotating local markets. People frequently change occupation and often perform more than one at the same time.

Because it is often claimed that capitalist development invariably augments the differentiation of sub-classes among the peasantry, it has to be pointed out that in this region the development of class differences in terms of plot size and/or income tends to be somewhat mitigated by the demographic and social factors which determine household size. A household with many adult workers generally achieves a higher total income than a household (of the same land area) with fewer workers, as a result mainly of off-farm employment (although there is a notable tendency for labour intensity to decrease as the household's worker/consumer ratio increases). Indeed, the remittances brought back to the peasant household from off-farm wage-labour can assist the household in keeping its land. Class differences among the peasantry are also mitigated over time by the system of inheritance. Rich male peasants tend to have more children with more wives and concubines than do poor peasants. Inheritance is divided equally between all offspring. Hence, concentration of land by a rich peasant gives way to dispersion of land at his death. (cf. Shanin, this volume).

The vast majority of the peasantry live outside, but within walking distance, of the town. Kinship ties of descent and marriage tend to cluster into separate neighbourhoods known as *veredas*. And each vereda is socially composed of one or more hierarchical stem kindreds whose function is dominated by a rich peasant, invariably a male. Although the kindred is far from functioning as a perfectly harmonious and co-operative group, it does constitute a framework for the fluid sets of social relationships, reciprocity, and redistribution that interlace households into a non-market, non-capitalist mode of organization encysted within the surrounding national economy and policy.

Reciprocity between households is an important feature of peasant livelihood, while the most economically crucial aspect of redistribution within a kindred lies in the affinal relationships that centre on the rich peasant whose many wives, concubines, and children live on surrounding smaller holdings. Together with their progeny, these affines provide the bulk of the rich peasant's workforce, paid on a time basis (not a piece-rate one) with extra benefits as well. Almost one-third of the households are headed by females, and women are as likely as men to own land even when they are not heads of households. In fact, there is a strong tendency for women to concentrate and manage land in short matrilines (although the size of these joint holdings rarely approaches those of the rich peasants), and the male affines or siblings are sloughed off into wage-labour on the plantations or large capitalist farms (cf. Clarke, 1953, p. 105, on Jamaican peasants). Unlike the men, women are generally opposed, indeed violently opposed, to uprooting the perennials and adopting the far more capital-intensive mode of production now encouraged by the state and the growth of agribusiness.

The 'green revolution' in peasant agriculture, 1970–2

Since 1970–1 peasant agriculture has been largely transformed as a result of the introduction of new crops and techniques. With the uprooting of the perennials and the development of a machine-based agriculture to grow seed crops on open fields, the entire basis of production has changed, and income per unit of land has decreased. This change was wrought by the government in an attempt to introduce a modified 'green revolution' to peasant farming in lieu of land reform – in areas where peasants were contemplating invading the large estates. In principle it is almost identical with the plan for peasant development, known as the

DRI (Desarrollo Rural Integrado), now being implemented by the World Bank and other international development agencies on a far larger scale in other areas of Colombia (DNP, 1974; 1975).

The old pattern of agriculture was one of steady but little income and labour spread out evenly and frequently over the year. There was a diversity of cultigens limiting soil sterilization and pests, ensuring the stability of the hydrological cycle, and in addition, the crops cultivated were suitable to the soil and climate, particularly to the rainfall and existing drainage system. Machinery was never used, and capital inputs were negligible.

The new pattern, based on the mono-cultivation of soya, corn, or beans, is radically different. On-farm income is obtained only once every four to six months at harvest time. Capital inputs rise astronomically due to the use of tractors for the preparation of the soil and planting, the use of 'improved' varieties of seed, pesticides, and fertilizer, and also due to the necessity to pay labour drawn from outside the household. For despite the use of labour-saving machinery, the labour requirements for the new crops are some 2.3 times higher per plaza per year than for the old-style crops. Although most households could supply this extra labour themselves if it was spread out, the fact is that the labour for harvesting and weeding has to be applied in very short time periods. Furthermore, the new crops are far more likely to damage from flooding, which in turn has become more common with the uprooting of the large trees and with the elimination of the forest floor cover; and if the crop is thus damaged, it means the loss of a substantial amount, if not all, of the peasant's investment.

Those who have taken the initiative in converting to the new crops are usually males from *all* classes of the peasantry, rich, middle, and poor, and have done so for the following reasons. First, they believed that they would increase their income. They are also intensifying their on-farm labour and thus creating a partial alternative to off-farm labour. Second, the traditional cash crops of cocoa and coffee have been declining in productivity, and the peasants have not been replacing them at a rate equal to their decline. One generation ago, when the balance between subsistence and cash cropping was quite different and when the average farm size was far greater, replacement could be effected without any significant capital from the farm's own resources, but today that is rarely possible. The decline in productivity is a result of accelerated pathogenesis of the trees, probably dating from the initial ecological assault inflicted by the plantations in the early 1950s, and further aggravated by the changes in the regional ecology as the plantations and large farms increasingly use pesticides and weed-killers. Added to this, the peasants' capacity to attend to their trees has declined concomitant with their shrinking land base and incomes. In other words, the trees have declined at a faster rate than usual, while the peasants' capacity to restore them has likewise deteriorated, compounding the problem. As it requires four to six years from the time of planting before newly planted perennials are in full production, there is naturally a tendency to view the new seasonal crops with favour since they yield within a few months of planting. As long-term credit is unavailable or too expensive, the seasonal quick-return crops become all the more attractive. Third, the government's rural bank (Caja Agraria) and the government's agricultural extension service, Instituto Colombiano Agropecuario (ICA), have both been actively encouraging the peasants to convert; and for cultural reasons their efforts have inevitably been focused on the male peasants. The local ICA branch has a close working relationship with the nearby Rockefeller, Ford, and Kellogg funded Centro Internacional de Agricultura Tropical (CIAT), the spearhead of green revolution research for much of South America. Fired with enthusiasm after their visit to the 'Plan Puebla' in Mexico, which is an attempt to transfer green revolution technology to peasants, the ICA agronomists were granted USAID funds to provide peasants with low-interest loans, fertilizer, seed, and tractors at low rentals. But once the perennials were uprooted, and the first or second seed crop in the ground, this 'service' was largely withdrawn. ICA also influenced peasant opinion by being able to manipulate the local branch of the USUARIOS, the national peasants' association. Between 1971 and 1972, the Cali-based vegetable oil firm of Lloreda also advanced credit for the cultivation of soya, but when a glut followed shortly thereafter, this stopped abruptly.

For the new crops, tractors are used to prepare the soil and to plant, but quite often there are problems with the seeders, and planting is inadequate. Weeding and harvesting are largely done by hand, and on average some 40 per cent of this labour comes from outside the household and is paid on a piece-rate basis – whereas extra-household labour on the traditional-style farms is paid by the day and is far less intensive. Soya is threshed on the plot by machines rented from the townsmen, and it is often difficult to get a thresher at the right time, in which case losses can be large.

Rich peasants have acquired small second-hand tractors in company with merchants from the town and rent them out to poorer peasants for soil preparation and planting, since machine costs are no greater than having the work done manually and it is felt that tractors do a better job. Credit is obtained from the Caja Agraria and occasionally from the local grain merchants who, in exchange, demand the right to buy the harvest at some 15 per cent below the market price. The Caja demands a legal title to land, or a certificate of rental, or that there be a guarantor. In most instances, the peasants are able to persuade the local rich peasant to be the guarantor, which increases his dominance, ensures that his tractor will be used at his price, and places him in a favoured position to buy or rent the land of those peasants who fail to make a success of the new agriculture.

Farming efficiency: modern peasant and modern capitalist

Comparison of traditional-style peasant farming with large-scale capitalist has already been made. In the last few months of 1972 it was possible to make an initial assessment of the impact of the *new* peasant agricultural system in one vereda. Around one-third of the households had converted all or part of their land. About one-quarter of these had given up because of high indebtedness. Their land had either been sold, rented out, or lay fallow, bereft of the old perennials and all else but weeds. The common explanation was the heaviness of the rains, but this had not adversely affected the perennial crops that still existed.

Careful analysis of the remaining households' experience with the new crops and techniques over two years revealed the important fact that even though their yields per unit of land of soya, corn, or beans were around no more than 60 per cent of those obtained on the large-scale capitalist farms in the same area, the peasants' rate of return on capital invested was far greater than that achieved by the large-scale farmers cultivating the same crops.[2]

If we include the household's own unpaid labour on corn and soya cultivation as a cost of production (by imputing the current market value to that labour), then the rate of return on capital invested is 1.6 times higher than that of the capitalist farmers. If we do not, then it is 2.7 times as high. By the same token, the peasants' costs of production per kilogram of product are lower too.

Thus, despite the fact that the peasants operate in a markedly unfavourable factor market as compared with the capitalist farmers, it turns out that they are more efficient in their use of capital with the new capital-intensive crops. This also holds true in the comparison with the sugar plantations (though here we have to calculate the rate of profit as net income divided not by costs, as we have done above, but by *sales*, because that is how Fedesarrollo presents the data). Between 1971 and 1974, the plantations with mills recorded an annual profit ratio of 26 per cent. Peasants growing soya and corn with the new technology achieved 37 per cent (budgeting unpaid household labour as a cost) or 48 per cent (not including this labour as a cost).

The greater efficiency of the peasants on this criterion is largely due to their costs of production per unit of land being much lower, and this is related to their being more labour- than capital-intensive. In the case of soya, for example, the peasant farmer requires about forty man-days of labour per plaza per crop, while according to the Valley's development corporation (CVC, 1975, p. 34), the capitalist farmer uses only twenty. But differences in days of labour-input are only part of the explanation. Not only do peasant cultivators pay lower wages for the extra-household labour they employ than do the capitalist farmers and provide 60 per cent of the labour themselves (which they do not count as a cost of production), but they are able to organize that labour more efficiently.

Yet despite their superior efficiency in terms of capital use and product cost, the peasants' income is deteriorating, which belies any success that greater capital efficiency might imply. To begin with, it has to be emphasized that the peasant mode of production is such that the profit formula needed to facilitate a comparison with capitalist farming is not easily applicable. Normally, one of the major problems in this regard comes from the way in which one categorizes and evaluates the household's unpaid labour. One can categorize it as part of income instead of as a cost, in which case the profit looms large, but the reality is somewhat obscured. Alternatively one can categorize it as a cost, imputing – quite falsely – the market price to the amount of labour, in which case profit drops significantly. In many, if not most, peasant economies the world over, the result of the latter type of accounting procedure is a *reductio ad absurdum* in that the peasant household appears to be operating at a constant deficit despite the fact that the household persists as an economically viable unit. Hence, in either manoeuvre, the result is unsatisfactory or paradoxical, and the only conclusion can be that accounting procedures used for capitalist firms are an inadequate tool for the analysis of peasant farming, *unless* one realizes the limitations associated with the necessary manipulations of peasant budget categories. More relevant to the specific case that we are analysing is the problem of how to deal with the household's living expenses for food, clothing, health, transport, etc., which are *not* included in the foregoing comparison of peasant and capitalist farming. The difficulty arises because the peasant farm is *both* a production and a consumption unit (and a small one, at that) while the capitalist enterprise is not.

In order to have an idea of how certain productivity functions compare between peasant and capitalist farmers, it is necessary to somewhat fictionalize the peasant's budget, compute the production costs and income in stages, and initially ignore the living expenses as a production cost – a 'fiction' which the peasants themselves follow. This procedure has been adopted above, and as a result important efficiencies in favour of the peasant producer came to light. But the analysis has to then proceed by including the living expenses, if the fiction is to become a reality. Then it is seen that the peasant's profit margin dwindles to a very small or zero amount, depending on the absolute size of the plot.

Nevertheless, one must remember that this final profit or labour product of the peasant farm is critically dependent on the fact that the peasant use of capital is as efficient as it is. Furthermore, because peasant capital-use is more efficient than that achieved by the capitalist farms and plantations and because the bulk of the capitalist wage-labour force is partially self-subsistent owing to its peasant farming, the overall costs of maintenance of the capitalist wage-labour force is lower than it would be if the workers were totally dependent on the performance of the capitalist farmers.

Hence, this partially peasant-based proletariat is a cheaper proletariat; lower maintenance costs of labour tends to mean a lower price of labour, and capital savings for the capitalist sector is achieved at the same time.

Effects of the peasant green revolution, 1970–6

Compared with the traditional mode of peasant farming, the new form has resulted in 40 per cent reduction in annual income per plaza for the cultivating household, regardless of size of holding, and an enormous increase in indebtedness and dependence on the capital market. Receipt of income is now widely spaced, and the cultivators become more dependent on the non-peasant labour market for income between harvests. On-farm labour inputs are such that relations between households become more commercialized, and despite the increase in labour requirements, the new rhythm of labour inputs means that there is in effect only the same or even less work available in any given neighbourhood for people resident in that neighbourhood.[3] The sexual division of labour changes, diminishing women's power and range of employment opportunities.[4] Class differences widen and take new forms; a larger proportion of people enter the labour force of the plantations and large capitalist farms, and peasant land passes much more rapidly into the large-scale farming sector as people are forced to sell out or lease to cover their mounting debts.

The sugar plantations have taken advantage of the peasants' indebtedness and heightened dependency and in the vereda under investigation had acquired around one-third of the land that had been in peasant cultivation in 1972. There has been a notable increase in the proportion and absolute number of peasants who work for local labour contractors, despite the emigration of almost 20 per cent of the adult population – women leaving to work as servants in the city, men leaving for wage-labour work in other parts of the Colombian or Venezuelan countryside. Labour contractors now employ around half the neighbourhood's women, coming from as far away as the city of Cali to take them into the adjoining department each day. Most of the men are now spending most of their time as contracted labourers working the new sugar cane fields spreading over former peasant lands.

In 1976 around 40 per cent of all households had the major part of their land in the new crops. Experience and the great increase in coffee and cocoa prices had cooled the ardour of the remainder to follow suit, but half of those who adopted the new agriculture in 1971 had actually increased their areas planted in new crops. In nearly all such cases the increase was not the result of improved on-farm income. Instead, these households had either uprooted more of their remaining perennials in a desperate bid to pay off debts, acquired more land through inheritance, or else were being subsidized by outside sources such as plantation wage income, wife's income, or remittances from offspring working in other parts of the country. These households have tended progressively to mobilize kindred into working units on the farm, in contrast to the usual dispersion, thereby increasing the proportion of unpaid family labour.

Various capital-saving modifications may help to sustain if not slightly improve on-farm income, and there is indication that peasants are turning to more labour-intensive crops such as tomatoes which can support three to four households per plaza. The complete elimination of the local peasantry is not a foregone conclusion but modern-style peasant farming is always in jeopardy.

Energy, exploitation, malnutrition and capitalist development

The evolution from the subsistence-sized, traditional-style peasant farm to the more labour-intensive modern peasant farm, ending ultimately in wage labour on the plantations and large capitalist farms, is paralleled by a very great increase in the output of labour (and fossil-fuel) energy associated with the appropriation of surplus labour by the capitalist farmers and a high rate of malnutrition among children.

The traditional peasant farm of three plazas requires annually 105 days of labour with an annual labour-energy expenditure of around 173,000 kilocalories. The modern peasant farm requires 2.3 times more labour days per unit of land per year, and gives a lower net income. The contracted wage-labourer cutting cane on the plantations receives roughly the same annual income as the traditional peasant with three plazas but works all the year round (275 days). His labour-energy expenditure per working day is roughly 210 per cent higher than that of the peasant working the land with traditional crops, and his *annual* energy expenditure in labour is some 570 per cent higher.[5]

What is certain is that the proletarianization process has greatly increased the intensity of labour, the food requirements per worker, and the costs of maintaining nutritional balance, while delivering a generous surplus of labour time to the large landowning employers.

Lenin's statement regarding the causes of the existence of peasants in all capitalist societies (as cited in my introduction), could not be further off the mark as regards the southern Cauca Valley. 'Technical superiority' turns out to be a far more complex concept than the presence of machines, 'economies of scale', etc., suggest, and the assertion that the peasants (*qua* peasants) intensify their labour incomparably more than the wage workers, is quite the opposite of what we find. Were it not for their modes of non-capitalist sustenance, the wage-labourers and their families would be literally burnt out – consumed by the fire of their own labour.

Conclusion

This hybrid economic system generates surplus value through intensifying labour and through reducing costs for reproducing labour. The precise articulation of peasant with capitalist modes of production that makes this possible is critically dependent on the fact that peasant holdings have been reduced by the political force and physical violence of the class struggle to less than subsistence size. This reduction cannot be seen as the result of unequal efficiencies of production. The fact that the majority of peasants now have less than subsistence-sized holdings assures for the capitalist farmers a secure supply of labour for their plantations which in some crucial ways are less efficient than the tiny peasant holdings on which that labour is partially maintained and re-produced. Furthermore, the social dynamics of the labour contractor system, in many ways the pivot of the entire system, depends on the co-optation and persistence of non-capitalist forms of social organization.

In the case of the southern Cauca Valley, agribusiness has been dependent on the formation of a class of poor peasants who combine wage-labour on capitalist farming units with their own small-scale peasant production. On the one hand the capitalist farms provide the peasants with a type of subsidy through wages. But on the other hand, the semi-proletarians, as peasant producers, are supplying the capitalist farmers with a subsidy too, and it is this subsidy which allows the capitalist farmers to extract higher rates of surplus value than would be possible were the costs of maintaining and reproducing labour totally dependent on the capitalist mode of production.

This subsidy functions in several ways: first, it lowers the cost of maintenance and reproduction of the labour force; second, it saves the capitalist sector and the state from investing capital in services; third, the potential tensions in the political sphere are checked, owing to the sociological nature of the proletariat, inhibiting the steady and stable concentration and co-operation of proletarian labour, preventing the formation of trade unions, flattening out the disturbing consequences of business cycles and seasonal fluctuations in demand, and lowering political pressure on the state for services.

The size and source of this peasant subsidy to capitalist farming is dependent on the specific social and technological features of the peasant mode of production, in which a peso invested by the peasant in the peasant plot yields a greater cash return than a peso invested by the capitalist farmer in large-scale capitalist agriculture.

The role of peasant subsistence production in thus sustaining capitalist enterprise is indirect, but none the less real. One of the aims of this article has been to show how this comes about, in detail and with reference to the intricacies of peasant economics as a system of provisioning embedded in its own specific form of social organization qualitatively distinct to that of the market or capitalist organization.

The contradictions within the total system of interaction are manifold. In areas such as the Cauca Valley flatlands, where land is now extremely valuable, the capitalist farms are steadily exprop-riating local peasants of their subsistence base, and hence undermining the source of this labour subsidy. Here is where the state and international development organizations such as the World Bank and USAID step in with peasant development plans like the DRI in order to reinstitute that subsidy. As their parcels dwindle, peasants are encouraged to intensify their on-farm labour and use of land, but this only leads to an increase in their rate of land loss. Thus, to the degree that state aid fails, largely on account of trying to tie the peasant producer yet more directly to the capitalist mode of production as a grower and not as a labourer, the capitalist farms are forced to extend and to intensify their dragnet for partially self-subsistent labour to the adjoining mountain slopes and highlands, as well as the Pacific coast, thus replicating their initial phase of primitive accumulation over a far wider area.

Nevertheless a new phase is born, overlapping with its predecessor. On the one hand, the capitalist farmers and the government are increasingly forced to provide more services for a more permanent proletariat, while on the other hand, so as to curtail these costs, more and more of the hinterland migrants are now being forced to enter the local elastic reservoir of casual labour by working for labour contractors, instead of joining the permanent fraction of the workforce.

The human wreckage left in the wake of the process squats

alongside the roadways in the intensively developed rural areas, or drains into the rural slum towns. From wage-labour, gleaning, and informal income opportunities, it develops its own type of family mode of production – the 'informal economy' as it has come to be called – which *in principle* is the same species of productive system as the peasant mode of production, only less stable and productive owing to the absence of means of production such as land.

In any event, the development of large-scale capitalist farming in this area is dependent on the fact that a significant majority of its wage-labour force provides part of its subsistence costs outside of the normal capitalist institutions. Capitalist development of this sort does not so much displace peasant and other forms of non-capitalist production, but rather incorporates their very real economic efficiencies so as to balance the costs of capital investment which are otherwise largely supplied by international financing.

Notes

1   Far from being a 'backward' form of labour organization, the contractor system seems to intensify in concert with the development of large-scale capitalist farming.

2   Figures for peasant production come from my field work between 1970 and 1972, as well as in 1976. It can hardly be over-emphasized how carefully this type of work has to be done, especially for the traditional-style crops which are harvested every two weeks and are constantly fluctuating, thereby necessitating a minimum of six months monitoring every two weeks. Four traditional-style peasant plots were thus surveyed over nine months, and six modern-style plots over two years, re-examined four years later. Data for the large-scale capitalist farms comes from a variety of secondary sources pertaining to the same growing seasons as the data on peasant production, CVC (1972, 1975), the Banco de la Republica (1973), and Osorio (n.d.).

3   The new pattern of labour requirements – larger amounts over shorter periods – implies that more work is available for the neighbourhood's population. But precisely because the jobs have to be done more quickly and need more labour per unit of land, and because most farmer's requirements occur simultaneously, workers have to be recruited over a far wider area than with the traditional crops, the net result being the same or

less local employment for locally resident people. In the case of a rich peasant's corn harvest, for example, one-third of the workers came from another neighbourhood, and one-quarter came from a village ninety minutes walk away. Women workers with young offspring are faced with the difficult choice of travelling further from home and leaving the children to fend for themselves, or else not working on such occasions.

4   Generally it is male landowners who opt for the new crops, whereas before, men and women equally cultivated the perennials. Thus, sexual differences in land-use have become important, involving sexual differences in the relation to modern technology, to income, to spending pattern, and to labour-hiring practices as men become more firmly integrated into modern financing organizations and state agencies. Furthermore, women workers are forced to contend with the painful logistics of working far from the home which they have to manage, and due to the uprooting of the traditional-style plots, women pedlars are deprived of much of their sources of market-produce and hence of their accustomed livelihood.

5   There are many difficult problems in trying to assess the labour energy output in peasant farming. The figure I posit is not meant to be anything more than a very rough approximation and is not based on direct measurement of energy output but on imputed values of 3.0 calories per minute for harvesting and 4.0 kilocalories per minute for weeding, figures which I regard as the upper limit. Energy output for cane cutting on a nearby plantation has been measured by respirometry; mean output during work being 7.4 calories per minute (Spurr *et al.*, 1975). These authors note that 7.4 calories per minute is an inflated measure due to experimental stimulation of the subjects. But I have used it in my comparisons as none of the other measures of energy output for different types of work that I have come across, and on which I base my peasant energy output estimates, make a correction for subject stimulation. Daily energy output in other types of plantation jobs are probably of the same order of magnitude as cane cutting, and certainly significantly higher than in peasant farming.

References

Banco de la Republica de Colombia (1973), 'Estudio de product-ividad y costos de producción de cultivos anuales en siete zonas del pais', semestre A., 1972; semestre B., 1972, mimeo, Bogota: Banco de la Republica

Bartra, Roger (1974), *Estructura agraria y clases sociales en México*, Mexico City: Instituto de Investigaciones Sociales de la UNAM, Serie popular Era/28

Bartra, Roger (1975), 'Peasants and political power in Mexico: A theoretical model', *Latin American Perspectives*, II, Summer, pp. 125–45

Buenaventura, Nicolas (1976), *Precapitalismo en la economía colombiana*, Bogota Ediciones Los Comuneros

Chayanov, A. V. (1966), *The Theory of Peasant Economy*, ed. D. Thorner, *et al.*, Homewood, Ill.: Richard D. Irwin

Clarke, Edith (1953), *My Mother Who Fathered Me*, London: Allen & Unwin

CVC (Corporación Autónoma Regional de Cauca) (1970), 'El Valle del Cauca en la economía nacional', mimeo, Cali

CVC (1972), 'Manual de costos de producción agrícola', mimeo, Cali

CVC (1975), 'Manual de costos de producción agrícola', mimeo, Cali

DNP (Departamento Nacional de Planeación) (1974), 'Programa de Desarrollo rural integrado – esquema preliminar', in *Revista de Planeación y Desarrollo*, VI, 2, Bogota

DNP (1975), *Para cerrar la brecha*, Bogota: Ediciones del Banco de la Republica

Feder, Ernest (1973), 'Poverty and unemployment in Latin America: a challenge for socio-economic research', *The Rural Society of Latin America Today*, Scandinavian Studies on Latin America, Institute of Latin American Studies, Stockholm, 2, pp. 29–67

Fedesarrollo (1976), *Las industrias azucaeras y paneleras en Colombia*, Bogota: Poligrupo Comunicación

George, Susan (1976), *How the Other Half Dies: The Real Reasons for World Hunger*, Harmondsworth: Penguin

Griffin, Keith (1974), *The Political Economy of Agrarian Change*, Cambridge, Mass.: Macmillan

Kalmonovitz, Salomon (1974), 'La agricultura en Colombia; 1950–72', *Boletín Mensual de Estadística*, Bogota: DANE, pp. 276, 277, 278

Kautsky, Karl (n.d.), *La cuestión agraria*, Editorial Latina (first published 1898)

Knight, Rolf (1972), *Sugar Plantations and Labor Patterns in the Cauca Valley, Colombia*, Toronto: Department of Anthropology,

University of Toronto, Anthropological Series, 12

Lappé, Francis, and Joseph Collins (1977), *Food First*, Boston: Houghton Mifflin

Lenin, V. I. (1899), *The Development of Capitalism in Russia;* Moscow: Progress Publishers, 1967

Mancini, S. (1954), 'Tenencia y uso de la tierra por la industria azucarera del Valle del Cauca', *Acta Agrónomica* (Facultad de Agronomía, Palmira, Colombia), IV (1)

Marglin, Stephen (1974), 'What do bosses do? The origins and functions of hierarchy in capitalist production', *The Review of Radical Political Economics*, VI, Summer, pp. 33–60

Marx, Karl (1867), *Capital*, vol. 1; New York: International Publishers, 1967

Mina, Mateo (pseudonym for M. Taussig and A. Rubbo) (1975), *Esclavitud y libertad en el valle del río Cauca*, Bogota: Editorial La Rosca

Osorio, Miguel Angel (n.d.), 'Agricultura tradicional y moderna en Colombia', mimeo, Bogota: SENA, División de Desarrollo Social, (*c.* 1975)

Patiño, Hernando (1975), 'La luncha por la democracia y la neuva cultura en el seno de las facultades de agronomia e instituciones académicas similares', in *La tierra para él que la trabaja*, Bogota: Asocación Colombiana de Ingenieros Agronomos, pp. 140–227

SENA (Servicio Nacional de Aprendizaje) (1976), 'Investigación en socio-economía campesina; Utica, Cundinimarca, Colombia', mimeo, Bogota: SENA; Curso de Instructores de Capacitación Empresarial Campesina

Spurr, G. B., Baraca-Nieto, M., and Maksud, M. G. (1975), 'Energy expenditure cutting sugar cane', *Journal of Applied Physiology*, XXXIX, December, pp. 990–6

Taussig, Michael (1974), 'Rural proletarianization: a social and historical enquiry into the commercialization of the southern Cauca Valley, Colombia', unpublished Ph.D dissertation, University of London

Taussig, Michael (1978), 'Peasant economics and the development of capitalist agriculture in the Cauca Valley, Colombia', *Latin American Perspectives*, 18, 5, 3, pp. 62–90

Urrutia, Miguel, and Berry, Albert (1975), *La distribución del ingreso en Colombia*, Bogota: Editorial Lealon

Wood, G. P. (1962), 'Supply and Distribution of Cacao in Colombia', mimeo, Bogota: Universidad Nacional de Colombia, Facultad de Agronomía

Part Three

Analyses of the
peasant farm economy

Introduction

The readings and discussions in the first two sections of this book have been focused mainly on the structural level of analysis, and they have been concerned with the understanding of agrarian societies as 'wholes'. This has been in deliberate contrast with much earlier analysis of agrarian societies where the focus has been rather on the behaviour of individual decision-makers. In the readings in this section, however, we examine different aspects of the economy of household or family labour producers, and look more closely at processes which are internal to the household. The readings are all concerned, though in different ways, with the specificity of the peasant economy. The first two papers, by Shanin and Harrison, are about the theory of a specific peasant economy associated with Chayanov and other Russian economists, and pitched against the 'differentiation' school of thought. In the third paper Lipton discusses the characteristics of peasant production in relation to the circumstances of uncertainty in which peasants operate – what Marx referred to as the 'incidental circumstances which interrupt the process of reproduction on the peasant farm'. Lipton shows how, because of these conditions, some of the assumptions which have been used in conventional economic analysis have to be modified. Of all the papers here Lipton's is the one which most concentrates on the individual decision-maker; but the style of analysis which the paper exemplifies is not incompatible with a 'structural/historical' approach and may complement it. Still, Lipton does tend to 'take for granted' market conditions which are subjected to scrutiny in the last paper in this section, by Bharadwaj, who takes us back again to a structural level in showing the implications of the different market relationships of different groups within the peasantry. Bharadwaj also explains certain limitations of conventional economic analysis, because of the interlinkages of the markets in which peasants operate.

Cyclical processes of social mobility

We have already mentioned (in the introduction to Part One) the Russian debate of the early part of this century between those who, like Lenin, argued that capitalist development was a reality, and the neo-populist writers who believed that the family labour farms of the peasantry (Lenin's 'middle peasantry') continued to thrive. Shanin argues that 'The major fact of Russian rural history in the first quarter of this century is that the predicted development [predicted, that is, by the differentiation model] both of the class structure and of the political response of the peasants did not happen.' Shanin perhaps overstates his case but his argument is an important one. It is that the data collected by the Russian economists late in the nineteenth century and early in this, show *not* that there was no tendency of differentiation, but that there were also other processes cutting across, tending to contain differentiation within limits, and to reinforce the stability of the peasantry. These processes, including the partitioning, merger and extinction of households, as well as changes relating to the biological life-cycle of the family, had a levelling tendency which blunted the trend of differentiation. The value of Shanin's work for us is that it provides a basis for understanding the distinctive structure of peasant society – without neglecting that it is a 'part-society' inserted into the state as a whole. Shanin's critics[1] point out that the static analysis of socio-economic disparities does not in itself constitute class analysis, since 'class' is defined in terms of relationships and not in terms of categories. This criticism is well made, but the critics still do not succeed in demonstrating that the development of capitalism in Russia must necessarily have eliminated peasant production, or that the *processes* described by Shanin did not contain the process of polarization. The controversy does raise the important question as to how the relations of production in agriculture can best be studied empirically; and in the recent past this has been the subject of a major debate in India.[2] The question has also been discussed in a practical context in East Africa.

Chayanov's model of peasant economy: strengths and limitations

Shanin outlines the work of Chayanov regarding social mobility amongst the Russian peasantry, but in our next reading Harrison discusses the core of Chayanov's attempt to establish the theory of a distinctive 'peasant economy'. This is the idea that the level and nature of activity on a peasant farm is determined by the ratio between labourers and consumers within the household. It is this ratio, according to Chayanov, which above all determines the way in which the household producer (who is assumed to be a patriarch) strikes his own subjectively determined balance between the benefits of additional work and the drudgery (or disutility) associated with that work. The higher the dependency load, or the ratio of consumers to workers, the higher the level of drudgery which will be tolerated (or, perhaps, of risk which will be borne[3]). The assumptions that are made in this model are quite restrictive, especially the assumption that wage labour is not involved (although this is relaxed somewhat in the full elaboration of Chayanov's theory), and the assumption that 'the household' is an indivisible unit under the control of a single head. There is a lot of evidence from different societies that such a formulation is plain wrong, and that it seriously underestimates the independent roles of women, and of children.[4] Chayanov's theory of peasant economy has been treated in the recent past both with unstinted admiration, and with contempt – as offering mere truisms.[5] Weaknesses are summarized by Harrison in this reading, but we would emphasize the point that, by his own account of it, Chayanov's theory of a specific and distinctive 'peasant economy' stands or falls according to his success in demonstrating that accumulation is necessarily absent on family labour farms. Harrison shows that Chayanov's argument finally rests on the undemonstrated case that peasants aim to maintain a constant level of well-being.

Even though Chayanov did not succeed in establishing a theory of a distinct 'peasant economy' his work remains a source of insights. In many agrarian societies an examination of the dependency load within different households helps to reveal the dynamics of the economy. Thus Barnett, for example, in his study of the Sudanese Gezira Scheme is able to show that it is the adverse dependency load, and the lack of manpower within tenant farm families for a large part of the developmental cycle of the household, which substantially accounts for high levels of indebtedness amongst them (Barnett, 1977). More generally, we may note that there are connections between some aspects of Chayanov's theory and the arguments of anthropologists concerning both the developmental cycle in domestic groups and the relationships between different kinship structures, environment and economy.[6]

In the end, however, the relative ease with which Chayanov's theory can be criticized has probably helped to create an impression that the 'differentiation thesis' is more or less correct. We would emphasize that even telling criticism of Chayanov's theory does *not* in itself demonstrate that there is nothing specific about peasant production, or that peasant production cannot survive the development of capitalism – for two reasons referred to earlier (see Djurfeldt and Taussig in Part Two; Williams in Part Five; and the introduction to Part Two).[7]

Decision-making models: why peasants may be 'conservative'

With our third reading in this part, by Michael Lipton, we turn to a somewhat different set of issues about peasant production. One major problem for students of agrarian societies, and especially for practical 'developers', has been the apparent 'resistance to change' of many peasant household producers. There was once a beautifully simple way of explaining this, and of saying why peasant farmers do not always respond to new ideas, particularly those presented to them in government development programmes. This was the idea that they are inherently conservative or 'tradition bound' and thus naturally resistant to change. In its more extreme forms this explanation amounted to little more than the belief that peasants are stupid; while in its more modest versions it suggests (in a well-known phrase of Kusum Nair's) that they have 'limited horizons of ambition'[8] (see also our discussion of Foster's concept of 'the image of limited good', in the general introduction). The phrase 'limited horizons of ambition' is one which may still be heard from the lips of expatriate rural development project managers, who are not otherwise able to explain why it is that 'the farmers' don't do what it appears (to the managers) to be in their interests to do. This attractive idea of the 'traditional peasant' was knocked on the head by the mounting evidence in the 1960s that peasant farmers do in fact respond, for example to changes in the prices of commodities they produce, like the 'rational economic men' of the economists' models (see Jones, 1960). Then the idea was further helped on its way by the discovery of T. W. Schultz (a recent winner of the Nobel Prize for Economics) that 'peasant farmers are efficient but poor' (Schultz, 1964). In fact Schultz's claim was substantially grounded on empirical research by D. W. Hopper in a North Indian village, on the basis of which Hopper had argued that the farmers were doing just about as well as they possibly could with the technology and the resources available to them. The argument is explained by Lipton, in our third reading here.

The finding that peasant farmers are not so much conservative by nature as seriously constrained from doing anything very much different by the technology and training available to them, was of very great practical significance in the 1960s, for the 'efficient but poor' thesis served to provide a theoretical underpinning for the strategy of 'transforming traditional agriculture' by means of the introduction of new technologies together with training and extension help and the provision of infrastructure – even if necessarily on a highly selective regional basis. This development strategy was examined critically by Lipton, in an important paper on Indian agricultural planning (1968a); and in the light of his criticism of the 'efficient but poor' thesis which is summarized in the reading in this part (and explained with greater technical precision and detail in Lipton, 1968b).

Lipton's main point is that Shultz's argument depends on the assumption that small farmers are profit maximizers, whereas the reality is that because of the conditions under which they have to operate small farmers who attempted to behave like this would very soon be out of business. This is partly because of the institutional constraints within which they have to operate – Lipton mentions especially the fact that there is not a competitive land market.[9] But it is principally because peasant farmers are so much subject to conditions of risk and uncertainty that they must be 'optimizers' – who seek to strike a balance between the objective of maximizing profits or yields, and that of keeping the risks of failure to a minimum. This 'theory of the optimizing peasant' has a considerable explanatory power, and it has often been found possible to explain patterns of peasant behaviour – as for example over the adoption of innovations – in terms of the minimization of risk and uncertainty.[10] At the same time this approach takes us back to the societal level, for of course farmers are not all equally endowed and do not all have the same capacity to withstand risk. Finally then, the theory of the optimizing peasant should be absorbed into a broader, historical analysis, in serious attempts to explain 'resistance to change'.[11]

Another classic study of peasant decision-making is that by Gould (1963), making use of game theory. Gould relates actual cropping patterns of Ghanaian peasant farmers to the 'mini-max' solution predicted by the theory – that is, the solution which permits the highest possible level of output to be achieved whilst also keeping the risks of failure to a minimum. Gould appears to imply, however, that farmers have hit upon the 'right' answer by a long process of trial and error. It has now come to be appreciated that this is a gratuitous assumption, for peasant farmers are frequently quite capable of conceptualizing decision problems along game-theory lines, computing answers, and of acting on the results (see for example Karimu and Richards, 1981). Since Gould wrote, a much greater appreciation of the skill of scientific understanding of peasant farmers has been shown. It is being recognized increasingly that although their knowledge may not be codified in the same way as that of Western scientists, peasant farmers may understand a great deal that is imperfectly understood by Western science[12].

The problem of 'resistance to change' has perhaps loomed largest in relation to African farmers. Doyle has reviewed the evidence of a large number of studies, concluding that economic factors far outweigh social and cultural ones in explaining responses to planned change (Doyle, 1974). Where farmers have failed to respond to new opportunities it can generally be shown to be the result of an inadequate level of incentives, or an inadequate incentive in relation to the farmers' perceptions of the risks involved. Further, Doyle finds that shortages of capital have probably been over-emphasized in explaining the failures of development initiatives, while the significance of labour shortages and labour bottlenecks in holding up innovation has so far been underestimated.

It is noteworthy, finally, that 'decision theory' approaches have been quite prominent in the recent African literature. This is perhaps because there has been a tendency in agrarian studies generally to concentrate upon issues relating to land tenure and land distribution. Tropical Africa differs from Asia and Latin America in that, until recently, land shortage has not been a problem of such pressing importance. Theories of agrarian change emphasizing land issues may, therefore, have appeared of limited relevance, with a consequent tendency for Africanists to fill the theoretical void with explanations stressing 'mental' as opposed to 'structural' factors when attempting to account for apparently irrational unresponsiveness to technically sound agricultural innovations. Recent research (cf. Hill, 1972; 1977) tends to suggest that structural problems concerning access to land may have been underestimated: 'traditional' tenure may still prevent outright land sales but not pledging to cover debts, and an apparently viable system of shifting cultivation may embrace considerable shortages of key strategic land resources such as moist valley-bottom land ideal for dry-season crops and vital during drought. Attention to constraints of this kind, and to problems of labour supply and rural indebtedness in recent research suggests that 'decision theory' will be much less a maid-of-all-work in future.[13]

The implications of land distribution

Many important arguments about the peasant farm economy *do*, however, concern the effects of farm size and the implications of different forms of land tenure. The first of these problems is discussed by Bharadwaj in our final reading in this part. The suggestion that there is an inverse relationship between farm size and yield is, as we pointed out in the introduction to Part One, most important for contemporary 'populist' conceptions of land reform. Bharadwaj finds from her re-examination of the Indian farm-management survey data on which the claim of the 'inverse relationship' has often been based, that in so far as it is possible to demonstrate a tendency for value productivity per acre to decline with an increase in farm size, it is explained mainly by intensity of cultivation and cropping pattern. She says that this is not an original conclusion, but she goes beyond it in showing how these two factors are themselves influenced 'by the particular character of markets, by the resource position of the individual operator and by the nature and extent of his involvement in these markets'. She questions the possibility of handling the economics of Indian agriculture in terms of the conventional economics of competitive markets; and in the passage which we include here she discusses the implications of 'the unequal and diverse nature of market involvement of different groups of cultivators arising from their position in... the agrarian power structure'. It is in this context that Bharadwaj advances the idea of 'compulsive involvement' in the market, to which we referred in our introduction to Part Two.

There is an extensive technical literature on the implications of different forms of land tenure, much of it deriving from the commonsense notions of an earlier generation of economists (and from Marshall in particular) that where cultivators of land have to surrender a large part of its product to landowners who contribute little or nothing to the process of cultivation, there will be little incentive, or perhaps little possibility, for them to invest in the development of the land[14]. Others have argued that there are circumstances in which because of the sharing of risks between landowners and tenants, crop-sharing tenancy may encourage innovation and investment. Empirical evidence from some regions of Asia fails to reveal any well-defined relationship between tenancy and productivity; while in Africa the earlier belief that the establishment of individual private property rights, replacing older customary systems of land tenure, is a necessary precondition for the development of the land, is also not very well founded empirically.

There is also a thesis that in circumstances described as 'semi-feudal' where landowners exploit their tenants through usury and through control of commodity markets as well as through rent, it is likely that the landowners will be discouraged from investment in the land, and will actively discourage their tenants from so investing, because of the possibility that this would release the tenants from the debt bondage which is the landowners' main source of profits[15]. Although in its original form this thesis is hard to sustain either logically or empirically, it has helped to stimulate interest in the effects of the interlinkage of land, labour and money markets in agrarian economies, to which Bharadwaj refers in our final reading in this section.[16]

Notes

1 For criticisms of Shanin see: Cox (1979); Harrison (1977); Littlejohn (1973).
2 See: Rudra (1970, 1971); Patnaik (1971a, 1971b, 1976, 1980) and Shanin (1980). These papers refer most explicitly to methodological issues.
3 This point is argued in: Harriss, J. (1982), ch. 5.2.
4 On the independent roles of women see: Deere (1976); Edholm *et al.* (1977); Jackson (1978); and Meillassoux (1975).
5 Shanin (1972) emphasizes the insights to be derived from Chayanov's work; while Ennew, Hirst and Tribe (1977), Harrison

(1975, 1979) and Littlejohn (1977) seek to do justice to the strengths of the theory whilst also exposing its basic flaws. See also Patnaik (1979).

6 On these themes see: Douglas and Kaberry (eds.) (1969) and Goody (1958). It should be noted that arguments based on the assumed 'adaptive' potential of features of social organization are inherently dubious: see discussions in Burnham and Ellen (1979).

7 Chayanov and his colleagues also pioneered quantitative farming systems input-output analysis, and contributed to a tradition which is still very much alive and valuable. For contemporary examples see: Norman (1972); Spencer (1975).

8 The phrase appears in Kusum Nair's book on Indian agriculture: *Blossoms in the Dust*.

9 On the 'stickiness' of land markets see: Harriss, J. (1982), ch. 4.5; and Patnaik (1976).

10 On the impact of uncertainty on innovation adoption see: Wharton (1971).

11 On structural influences on decision-making see: Griffin (1974); and Weeks (1970). For an argument about the absorption of the theory of the optimizing peasant into broader, historical analysis see: Hutton and Cohen (1975).

12 An issue of the *Bulletin of the Institute of Development Studies* (Chambers, ed., 1979) gives an introduction to these developments. See also: Barker, D., *et al.* (1977); and Guggenheim, H. (1978); Karimu and Richards (1981).

13 For recent discussion of labour factors in African agrarian change see: Klein (ed.) (1980) and Meillassoux (1975). The historical significance of slavery and the slave trade is discussed by Inikori (1981) and Miers and Kopytoff (eds.) (1977).

14 Srinivasan and Bardhan (1971) argue the case about risk-sharing between landowners and tenants; Pieris (1976) discusses evidence for the relationships between tenancy and productivity in Sri Lanka and reports on the equivocal conclusions of that evidence; and Brock (1969) gives a useful discussion of land tenure in an African context. See also Biebuyck (1963); and Uchendu (1970).

15 The 'semi-feudalism' thesis was argued by Bhaduri (1973) with reference to a part of the state of West Bengal in India; and his argument has been discussed critically by Newberry (1974) and Schoer (1977).

16 On the interlinkage of markets see: Bardhan and Rudra (1978).

References

Chayanov and cyclical processes of mobility

Barnett, T. (1977), *The Gezira Scheme*, London: Frank Cass

Chayanov, A. V. (1966), *The Theory of Peasant Economy*, Homewood, Ill.: Richard M. Irwin

Cox, T. (1979), 'The awkward class or awkward classes? Class relations in the Russian peasantry before collectivisation', *Journal of Peasant Studies*, 7, 1, pp. 70–85

Deere, C. D. (1976), 'Rural women's subsistence production in the capitalist periphery', *The Review of Radical Political Economics*, 8, 1; and in R. Cohen, P. Gutkind, and P. Brazier (eds.), *Peasants and Proletarians: The Struggles of Third World Workers*, London: Hutchinson, 1979

Deere, C. D., and de Janvry, A. (1981), 'Demographic and social differentiation among northern Peruvian peasants', *Journal of Peasant Studies*, 8, 3, pp. 335–66

Edholm, F., *et al.* (1977), 'Conceptualising women', *Critique of Anthropology*, 9–10, pp. 101–130

Ennew, J., Hirst, P., and Tribe, K. (1977), '"Peasantry" as an economic category', *Journal of Peasant Studies*, 4, 4, pp. 295–322

Harrison, M. (1975), 'Chayanov and the economics of the Russian peasantry', *Journal of Peasant Studies*, 2, 4, pp. 389–417

Harrison, M. (1977), 'Resource allocation and agrarian class formation', *Journal of Peasant Studies*, 4, 2, pp. 127–61

Harrison, M. (1979), 'Chayanov and the Marxists', *Journal of Peasant Studies*, 7, 1, pp. 86–100

Harriss, J. (1982), *Capitalism and Peasant Farming: Agrarian Structure and Ideology in Northern Tamil Nadu*, Bombay: Oxford University Press

Hunt, D. (1979), 'Chayanov's model of peasant household resource allocation', *Journal of Peasant Studies*, 6, 3, pp. 247–85

Jackson, S. (1978), 'Hausa women on strike', *Review of African Political Economy*, 13, pp. 21–36

Littlejohn, G. (1973), 'The peasantry and the Russian revolution', *Economy and Society*, 2, 1, pp. 112–25

Littlejohn, G. (1977), 'Chayanov and the theory of peasant economy', in B. Hindess (ed.), *Sociological Theories of the Economy*, London: Macmillan

Meillassoux, C. (1975), *Femmes, greniers et capitaux*, Paris: Maspero; published as *Maidens, Meals and Money: Capitalism and the Domestic Community,* Cambridge: Cambridge University Press, 1981

Norman, D. W. (1972), *An Economic Survey of Three Villages in Zaria Province: 2 Input-output Study, vol. 1, Text,* Samaru, Zaria: Institute of Agricultural Research, Ahmadu Bello University

Patnaik, U. (1971a), 'Capitalist development in agriculture: a note', *Economic and Political Weekly*, Review of Agriculture, September, pp. A123–A130

Patnaik, U. (1971b), 'Capitalist development in agriculture – a further comment', *Economic and Political Weekly*, Review of Agriculture, December, pp. A190–A194

Patnaik, U. (1976), 'Class differentiation within the peasantry: an approach to the analysis of Indian agriculture', *Economic and Political Weekly*, Review of Agriculture, September, pp. A82–A101

Patnaik, U. (1979), 'Neo-populism and Marxism: the Chayanovian view of the agrarian question and its fundamental fallacy', *Journal of Peasant Studies*, 6, 4, pp. 375–420

Patnaik, U. (1980), 'Empirical identification of peasant classes revisited', *Economic and Political Weekly*, 1 March, pp. 483–8

Rudra, A. (1970), 'In search of the capitalist farmer', *Economic and Political Weekly*, Review of Agriculture, June, pp. A85–A87

Rudra, A. (1971), 'Capitalist development in agriculture – a reply', *Economic and Political Weekly*, 6 November, pp. 2291–2

Shanin, T. (1972), 'Nature and logic of the peasant economy', *Journal of Peasant Studies*, 1, 1 and 1, 2, pp. 63–80 and 186–206

Shanin, T. (1980), 'Measuring peasant capitalism: the operationalisation of concepts of political economy: Russia's 1920s–India's 1970s', in E. Hobsbawm *et al.* (eds.), *Peasants in History: Essays in Honour of Daniel Thorner,* Calcutta, etc.: Oxford University Press for Sameeksha Trust

Spencer, D. S. C. (1975), 'The economics of rice production in Sierra Leone: 1 Upland Rice', *Bulletin*, 1, Department of Agricultural Economics and Extension, Njala University College, Sierra Leone

Decision-making models

Barker, D., Oguntoyinbo, and Richards, P. (1977), *The Utility of the Nigerian Peasant Farmer's Knowledge in the Monitoring of Agricultural Resources*, London, MARC, University of London

Chambers, R. (ed.) (1979), 'Rural development: Whose knowledge counts?' *Bulletin*, Institute of Development Studies, University of Sussex, 10, 2,

Doyle, C. J. (1974), 'Productivity, technical change and the peasant producer: a profile of the African cultivator', *Food Research Institute Studies*, 13, pp. 61–76

Gould, P. (1963), 'Man against his environment: a game theoretic approach', *Annals of the Association of American Geographers*, 53, pp. 290–7

Griffin, K. (1974), *The Political Economy of Agrarian Change*, London: Macmillan

Guggenheim, H. (1978), 'Of millet, mice and men. Traditional and invisible solutions to post harvest losses in Mali', in D. Pimental (ed.), *World Food Pest Losses and the Environment*, Boulder, Colo.: West View Press

Hill, P. (1972), *Rural Hausa: A Village and a Setting*, Cambridge: Cambridge University Press

Hill, P. (1977), *Population, Prosperity and Poverty: Rural Kano 1900 and 1970*, Cambridge: Cambridge University Press

Hutton, C., and Cohen, R. (1975), 'African peasants and resistance to change', in I. Oxaal, *et al.*, *Beyond the Sociology of Development*, London: Routledge & Kegan Paul

Jones, W. O. (1960), 'Economic man in Africa', *Food Research Institute Studies*, 1, pp. 107–34

Karimu, J. A., and Richards, P., (1981), 'The northern area integrated agricultural development project: the social and economic impact of planning for rural change in northern Sierra Leone', Occasional Paper, series no. 3, Department of Geography, School of Oriental and African Studies, University of London

Lipton, M. (1968a), 'Strategy for agriculture: urban bias and rural planning', in P. Streeten, and M. Lipton, *The Crisis of Indian Planning*, London: Oxford University Press

Lipton, M. (1968b), 'The theory of the optimising peasant', *Journal of Development Studies*, 4, 3, pp. 327–51

Schultz, T. W. (1964), *Transforming Traditional Agriculture*, New Haven, Conn.: Yale University Press

Weeks, J. (1970), 'Uncertainty, risk and wealth and income distribution in peasant agriculture', *Journal of Development Studies*, 7, 1, pp. 28–35

Wharton, C. R. (1971), 'Risk, uncertainty and the subsistence farmer', in G. Dalton (ed.), *Economic Development and Social Change*, New York: American Museum of Natural History

The farm size debate

Berry, R. A. and Cline, W. R. (1979), *Agrarian Structure and Productivity in Developing Countries*, Baltimore and London: Johns Hopkins University Press

Chattopadhyay, M., and Rudra, A. (1976), 'Size-productivity revisited', *Economic and Political Weekly*, 25 September, pp. A104–A116

Rudra, A. and Sen, A. (1980), 'Farm size and labour use: analysis and policy', *Economic and Political Weekly*, Annual number, XV, 5, 6, and 7, pp. 391–4

Sen, A. K. (1975), *Employment, Technology and Development*, Appendix C, London: Oxford University Press

Saini, G. R. (1979), *Farm Size, Resource Use Efficiency and Income Distribution*, New Delhi: Allied Publishers

Implications of land distribution

Bardhan, P., and Rudra, A. (1978), 'On the interlinkage of land, labour and credit relations: An analysis of village survey data in East India', *Economic and Political Weekly*, annual number, February

Bhaduri, A. (1973), 'A study in agricultural backwardness under semi-feudalism', *The Economic Journal*, March, pp. 120–37

Biebuyck, D. (ed.) (1963), *African Agrarian Systems*, London: Oxford University Press

Brock, B. (1969), 'Customary land tenure, "individualization" and agricultural development in Uganda', *East African Journal of Rural Development*, 2, 2, pp. 1–27

Griffin, K. (1975), *Land Concentration and Rural Poverty*, London: Macmillan

Newberry, D. (1974), 'Tenurial obstacles to innovation', *Journal of Development Studies*, 11, 4, pp. 263–77

Peiris, G. H. (1976), 'Share tenancy and tenurial reform in Sri Lanka', *Ceylon Journal of Historical and Social Studies*, VI, 1, pp. 24–54

Schoer, K. (1977), 'Agrarian relations and the development of the forces of production', *Social Scientist*, 63, pp. 13–27

Srinivasan, T. N., and Bardhan, P. K. (1971), 'Cropsharing tenancy in agriculture: a theoretical and empirical analysis', *American Economic Review*, LXI, 1, pp. 58–64

Uchendu, V. (1970), 'The impact of changing agricultural technology on African land tenure', *Journal of Developing Areas*, 4, pp. 477–86

African Issues

Burnham, P., and Ellen, R. (eds.) (1979), *Social and Ecological Systems*, London: Academic Press

Douglas, M., and Kaberry, P. (eds.) (1969), ' Is matriliny doomed in Africa', in *Man in Africa*, London: Tavistock

Goody, J. (1958), *The Developmental Cycle in Domestic Groups*, Cambridge: Cambridge University Press

Inikori, J. E. (1981), *Forced Migration: The Impact of the Export Slave Trade on African Societies*, London: Hutchinson

Klein, M. A. (ed.) (1980), *Peasants in Africa: Historical and Contemporary Perspectives*, Beverly Hills and London: Sage Publications

Meillassoux, C. (1975), *Femmes, greniers et capitaux*, Paris: Maspero

Miers, S., and Kopytoff, I. (eds.) (1977), *Slavery in Africa*, Madison: University of Wisconsin Press

9 Polarization and cyclical mobility: the Russian debate over the differentiation of the peasantry *

Teodor Shanin

1 Introduction

The conception of the basic dynamics of a peasant society accepted by Russian policy-makers and, indeed, by the majority of educated Russians at the beginning of this century can be outlined in a few sentences. It was believed that, in the process of inevitable economic advance, every human society necessarily headed towards an increasing division of labour,[1] the establishment of market relations, the accumulation of capital, and social diversification. It was also believed that these processes were centred in towns but inevitably spread into the countryside. Rich peasant farms, which were larger and better equipped and had a higher capital/worker ratio, found themselves in an advantageous position as far as the optimal use of the factors of production and their further accumulation were concerned. For precisely opposite reasons, poor peasant farms were at a disadvantage in any attempt to improve their economic position. Continuing cumulation of economic advantages and disadvantages led to a polarization of peasant society into rich farmers, who increasingly acquired the characteristics of capitalist entrepreneurs, and poor farmers, who lost their farms and became landless wage-labourers in the employ of rich farmers, estate owners, or urban entrepreneurs. Some of the typical characteristics of a traditional peasant family farm could still be seen in the middle strata of the peasantry, but these would disintegrate or change in the inevitable process of economic advance. With them would disappear the survivals of the traditional peasant society. A new social structure based on capitalist farming would finally come to be established in the countryside.

This general picture of the dynamics of a peasant society was firmly established as a piece of self-evident knowledge – it had become part of the prevailing ideology, not only in the normative

*This chapter is taken from Shanin (1972).

but also in the cognitive sense.[2] It was, in turn, taken as given and constituted the basic assumption underlying the rural policies of all the rulers of the Russian state during the crucial quarter of a century which followed the 1905–6 revolution. The political perspective was that the peasantry would break down into new rural classes typical of capitalist society (i.e. capitalist farmers, wage-workers, etc.) which would demonstrate increasing self-awareness, cohesion, and tendencies to political action in support of their own interests. This expected development was in fact a precondition for the success of the policies pursued by successive Russian governments.

The major fact of Russian rural history in the first quarter of the century is that the predicted development both of the class structure and of the political response of the peasants did not happen. The richer farmers and the rural wage-earners (and/or poor peasants) on the whole failed to act as independent factions. In spite of the apparent differentiation and of polarization-processes, the villages of the Russian peasantry went on showing remarkable political cohesiveness and unity of action.

The apparent failure of accepted theories to accord with the crucial evidence of Russian rural history can be approached in three ways: first, by denying the very existence of a problem; second, by claiming that delays intervened in the processes expected; or third, by introducing new factors into the analysis. The first approach could be made by denying either the very fact of an unexpectedly high political cohesion of the Russian peasantry or denying the existence of peasant differentiation and polarization during the period. An alternative form of the first approach could be to dispose of the very premiss of class analysis by putting in doubt the correlation between socio-economic position and political attitude and action. But neither the Russian evidence available nor the indications of comparative studies would seem to make any such solutions appear reasonable. In the case of the second approach, the initial theory would be sustained, and the claim would be made that the changes predicted had not had time to take place fully. Interest and further research promoted by this attitude would therefore be focused on the factors of social inertia as the reasons behind the delay in the fulfilment of the changes predicted – i.e. on the static factors which reinforce stability. Research on these lines has, in fact, been done and has produced illuminating results in the form of studies of Russian peasant culture, of the structure of the peasant commune and so on. Finally, the accepted basic model of the dynamics of peasant societies can be challenged by re-analysing the nature of the factors accepted as relevant and their interaction. It will be apparent that this study is based on the last approach – namely, the admission of major additional factors as necessary for the understanding of the problems analysed. Particular attention is given to the *processes reinforcing the stability* of the social system – an aspect which tends to be overlooked by many theories of social change.

2 Dynamic studies and the mobility of peasant households

Statistical data published by the Russian government before the revolution tended to present the peasantry and the agriculture of the country (or of any region) as wholes. The introduction of the use of categories representing various socio-economic strata revealed illuminating correlations between the socio-economic differentiation of peasant households and some basic aspects of peasant life. Furthermore, it permitted the identification of socio-economic mobility within peasant societies by comparing peasant differentiation in consecutive years.

However, the recorded changes in the differentiation of peasant society did not fully express the extent of the socio-economic mobility of peasant households; for instance, the economic rise of of a thousand households counteracted by the decline of another 800 may be recorded merely as a rise of 200, while, in fact, 1800 units have experienced socio-economic mobility. It was the attempt to reach behind the gross data on peasant societies and/or socio-economic strata and to analyse the mobility of individual peasant households which brought 'dynamic studies' into being. This development of statistical methodology clearly reflected a conceptual change related to the increasing interest in peasant socio-economic differentiation as well as to increasing awareness of the importance of households as the basic units of peasant society. Dynamic studies involved tracing the individual histories of peasant households and analysing them statistically as mass data. The essential features of this method may be illustrated by the hypothetical example given in the following Table 1.

The basic data analysed by a dynamic study included information about the socio-economic position of each household at the beginning and at the end of the period studied, and some further information about changes which had taken place in their internal structure during the same period.[3] The households were classified by socio-economic stratum at the beginning of the study. At the next stage, every stratum was treated as a unit and the socio-economic position of each of its households at the end of the period was recorded in figures or percentages in the appropriate columns (A A1, A B1, A C1; B A1, B B1, B C1; etc.). The figures in squares A A1, B B1, C C1 (25, 265, and 15) indicate, therefore, the households which had not changed their socio-economic position in terms of the strata as defined. The other figures represent households in various degrees of ascending or descending mobility.

Table 1   *Simplified hypothetical dynamic study of a community, 1900–10**

Socio-economic stratum	Number of households			
		1910		
		A1	B1	C1
	1900	Poor	Middle	Rich
A Poor	275	25	75	175
B Middle	450	120	265	65
C Rich	125	85	25	15
All strata	850	230	365	255

*Merger, partitioning, extinction, and migration omitted.

The evidence gathered by three decades of dynamic studies of the Russian peasantry revealed clear, and somewhat surprising, uniformity and continuity in the patterns of mobility of peasant households. The basic processes and inter-relations proved qualitatively similar in dynamic studies of samples reflecting different periods, drawn from different areas, and using different categories of peasant wealth. The following pre-revolutionary study of Vyazma *uezd** presented in Table 2 will serve here as an example of such typical processes and inter-relations.

An attempt to measure the mobility of peasant society just by comparing differentiation in 1884 with that of 1900 (Table 2, part B) would have indicated that only about 10 per cent of peasant

* A former territorial administrative unit.

households had changed stratum (in terms of the arbitrary categories of wealth used) between the two dates. However, during the period 1884–1900, of the original sample of 13,880 households, 2039 households (15 per cent) had emigrated, 663 (5 per cent) had become extinct, and 1884 (14 per cent) could not be traced,

Table 2 *Peasant mobility in Vyazma Uezd. Smolensk Gub, 1884–1900**

A   *The dynamic study*

Stratum	Sown land (des.)	Number of households 1884†	Percentage of 1884 households sowing in 1900					Percentage of households undergoing stratum change 1884–1900
			Nil	Less than 3 des.	3–9 des.	More than 9 des.	Totalling 0–9+ des.	
A	Nil	1,329	49.0	26.3	23.6	1.1	100	52.0
B	Less than 3 des.	2,249	10.7	39.7	48.3	1.3	100	60.6
C	3–9 des.	5,238	4.1	19.6	68.7	7.6	100	31.3
D	More than 9 des.	418	3.2	10.6	65.3	20.9	100	79.1
All strata		9,294						44.5‡

B   *The differentiation of peasant households (%)*

Years	Households sowing				
	Nil	Less than 3 des.	3–9 des.	More than 9 des.	Totalling
1884	14.3	24.2	56.9	4.5	100
1900	9.5	24.6	59.2	6.7	100
Households changing stratum 1884–1900**	(−)4.8	(+)0.4	(+)2.3	(+)2.2	9.7

*The study is based on the records of those of the 13,880 households in the 1884 census which still actually existed in 1900.
†Only the households still accounted for in 1900.
‡Weighted average.
**Percentile points; + indicates additions to a given stratum, − indicates losses from a stratum.

Source: Rumyantsev (1906), pp. 527, 538.

making altogether 4586 (33 per cent) households which had disappeared. Furthermore, the dynamic study carried out (Table 2, part A) revealed that, of the residuum analysed, as many as 45 per cent of the households had moved into another category of peasant wealth by the end of the period. To the households which had changed position, one could legitimately add the total, or at least the larger part, of the 4586 households which had disappeared during the period of the study. This would put the proportion of households which had undergone socio-economic mobility during the period 1884–1900 at more than half, and indicates a ratio of more than 5:1 between the total mobility of peasant households and the mobility recorded for the peasant society in Table 2, part B, using identical categories of wealth.

The first general conclusion which can be drawn from the dynamic studies, is, therefore, that the mobility of peasant households, is *multidirectional* in character – i.e. it consists to a great extent of opposing movements of individual households which cancel themselves out when analysis is confined to the study of the mobility of the society as a whole. The net mobility of a peasant society can be seen as the tip of an iceberg – the summary results of socio-economic changes of much greater magnitude.

A further conclusion which can be drawn from the dynamic studies would have to be the existence of a strong *centripetal* mobility of peasant households in relation to the median wealth in the society studied – i.e. the rises of the poorer households and the descents of the wealthier ones. Moreover, as the example in Table 2 shows, the higher the relative socio-economic position of the peasant household, the greater, on the whole, is the likelihood that it will begin to deteriorate, and vice versa, the lower its position the better its chance of showing an improvement.[4] Given the existence of demonstrable centripetal forces, in a society in which socio-economic stratification does not disappear, it follows that centrifugal tendencies must be operating to countervail the centripetal forces, a conclusion which finds empirical support in the results of the 'budget studies'.* A complex multidirectional mobility, involving centripetal and centrifugal tendencies simultaneously operating among peasant households, is, therefore, at work and underlies the gross differentiation-process in peasant society. Moreover, anticipating the discussion of dynamic studies further

*Systematic studies of the economic performance of individual peasant households in terms of input/output analysis, and the statistical analysis of the data so collected.

on, the socio-economic position of substantial numbers of Russian peasant households in the period studied fluctuated with a certain specific regularity. A peasant household would, for a time, rise in socio-economic terms within the peasant community, and then after reaching some peak undergo a decline. At a later stage the same household, having reached its lowest ebb, might again start to move upward and the whole cycle would recommence. This recurring process we term cyclical mobility.[5]

Cyclical mobility represents, therefore, a specific case of multidirectional mobility in which a substantial number of units successively participate in simultaneously operating powerful and opposing trends. Figure 2 sets out the main patterns into which

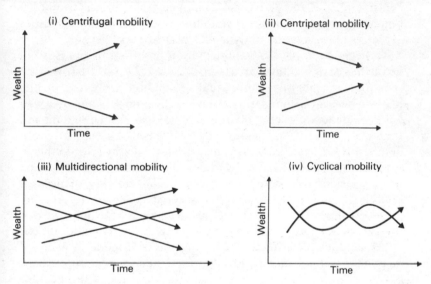

Figure 2   *Types of household mobility*

mobility of peasant households is analysed in our study – centrifugal, centripetal, multidirectional, and cyclical – as processes, i.e. as happening on a time scale. The simultaneous occurrence of opposing trends shown in sections (i) and (ii) would lead to multidirectional mobility, indicated in (iii). The process in which peasant households are caught up in turn in ascending and descending phases (i.e. cyclical mobility) is depicted in section (iv). The more complex, actual processes can be classified in terms of the typology presented.

Economic theory and the empirical evidence of the 'budget studies' lead us to accept, at least tentatively, the cumulation of economic advantages and disadvantages as a major generator of the *centrifugal* tendencies in the mobility of peasant households.[6] However, the *centripetal* tendencies evident in dynamic studies cannot be explained in these terms. For this very reason, the evidence of the dynamic studies did not make sense to many economists, and tended to be dismissed as doubtful, or, at least, as reflecting only a temporary and abnormal situation.

The focus of the following discussion will turn, therefore, to the causes of centripetal mobility and the possible reasons for which peasant households would move from being under the determining influence of centrifugal forces to being under the influence of centripetal ones and vice versa. Such analysis must go beyond the boundaries of neo-classical economics and consider broad issues of the social structure and dynamics of peasant society.

To begin with, the land-redistribution practised by the Russian peasants seems to have provided a manifest egalitarian wealth-redivision mechanism. The extent of land-redistribution by the Russian peasant communes was never fully recorded and may well have to remain for ever in the realm of guesswork.[7] The extent and frequency of land-redivision varied between regions and even between different communes in the same locality. No doubt, in some cases, land-redivision by communes would have accounted for a considerable share of the centripetal mobility of peasant households, or would even have been the major factor responsible for it. Yet, for several reasons, it fails to account for a major part of the centripetal (levelling) trend evident from the dynamic studies.

Yet another set of factors affecting the centripetal mobility of peasant households and the levelling tendencies in peasant societies can be seen, also arising out of the peculiarities of the peasant social structure and specifically of the internal dynamics of peasant households. The Russian scholars working on the dynamic studies identified them under the umbrella term 'substantive changes'.

3   'Substantive changes'

(a)   The levelling mechanism

Transmutations of peasant households resulting in their appearance and disappearance within peasant communities in Russia were given the name 'substantive changes' (*organicheskie izmeneniya*). This term covers the processes of the partitioning, merger, extinction, and migration of peasant households. These processes make apparent the intimacy of the links connecting the fortunes of the traditionally structured peasant family and the peasant farm. Partitioning results in the appearance of new peasant households. Extinction and merger led to households' disappearance. With emigration, a peasant household disappears from one community to reappear (as immigration) elsewhere. The umbrella term 'substantive changes' therefore embraces social processes of vastly differing kinds but which have one characteristic in common: their differential impact is reflected in levelling tendencies in peasant societies.

The social structure of peasant households and the demographic characteristics of the Russian peasantry were the fundamental causes of the differential effects which 'substantive changes' had on the mobility recorded for the various socio-economic strata within peasant communities. Rates of partitioning correlated with the size and the wealth of peasant households. The 'pulverizing' effect of partitioning was strongest, therefore, among the wealthier strata. On the other hand, the disappearance of peasant households through merger, extinction, and emigration correlated inversely with size and wealth. A considerable number of the poorer households were constantly being purged from peasant societies. Both partitioning and disappearance, therefore, generated levelling trends and worked in a direction running counter to economic polarization.

But careful examination of the Russian statistical data shows that the existence of *another* real and major component of mobility must be accepted; it will be referred to as the residual component of peasant households' mobility. An explanation of the causes of the appearance of this residual component will have to be found and incorporated in any satisfactory general model of the mobility of peasant households.

During the first quarter of the twentieth century a group of Russian scholars undertook the ambitious task of explaining both the residual component of the mobility of peasant households and the phenomenon of multidirectional mobility as a whole, within a unified conceptual framework which could be labelled 'biological determinism'.

(b)   Biological determinism

In our discussion of peasant social structure, a basic duality in the character of the peasant household was pointed out. The peasant household operates both as a family unit and as a production unit; it is therefore influenced by both biological and economic factors. The majority of Russian students of the peasantry can correspondingly be divided into two diametrically opposed groups – biological and economic determinists.[8] The prevailing mode of analysis was 'monistic'; an explanation of peasant social dynamics was sought by tracing them to a single major determinant, regarded as a prime mover. Only a few of the Russian scholars attempted a consistent multifactorial analysis, in which the various factors and their interaction were analysed without some rigidly preconceived conception of their importance and hierarchical ordering.

The Organization-and-Production School (or Neo-Populists)[9] represented the hard core of the Russian 'biological determinists' in our period. The 'biological determinists' seized upon the demographic changes in peasant families as the basic determinant of the overall development of peasant households. The 'ideal type' of household, within this analytical framework, was assumed to meet the essential consumption-needs of its members through its own family labour, employed on the farm. Consequently the impacts of the market and the price-mechanism (via commodities and wage-labour) were discounted or minimized, and it was held that an altogether different economic rationality had to be accepted in assessing economic alternatives. The development of the economy of the peasant household and the economic choices made were seen as determined by the consumption-needs of the family and by its available labour. Given the traditional peasant cultural framework, the biological cycle of peasant family life – birth, maturity, marriage, growth of children, ageing, and death – would lead to regular economic changes, cyclical in character. In a peasant household, 'those working mate (*sorazmeryayut*) their production to the needs of the consumers'. For example, increases in the consumption-needs of a household due to the growth of children result in additional effort by those working and in the intensity of their attempts to acquire, by buying or renting, more land, livestock, and equipment. It was argued, then, that peasant households' mobility reflected the biological cycle of the growth and decline of family units.

Table 3 *Development of the labour force and consumption-needs of a hypothetical peasant family (labour and consuming units*)*

Number of years of the family's existence	Consumption of husband	wife	1st child	2nd child	3rd child	4th child	5th child	6th child	7th child	Total consumers in family	Total workers in family	Consumer in worker ratio
1	1.0	0.8	—	—	—	—	—	—	—	1.8	1.8	1.00
2	1.0	0.8	0.1	—	—	—	—	—	—	1.9	1.8	1.06
3	1.0	0.8	0.3	—	—	—	—	—	—	2.1	1.8	1.17
4	1.0	0.8	0.3	—	—	—	—	—	—	2.1	1.8	1.17
5	1.0	0.8	0.3	0.1	—	—	—	—	—	2.2	1.8	1.22
6	1.0	0.8	0.3	0.3	—	—	—	—	—	2.4	1.8	1.33
7	1.0	0.8	0.3	0.3	—	—	—	—	—	2.4	1.8	1.33
8	1.0	0.8	0.3	0.3	0.1	—	—	—	—	2.5	1.8	1.39
9	1.0	0.8	0.5	0.3	0.3	—	—	—	—	2.9	1.8	1.61
10	1.0	0.8	0.5	0.3	0.3	—	—	—	—	2.9	1.8	1.61
11	1.0	0.8	0.5	0.3	0.3	0.1	—	—	—	3.0	1.8	1.66
12	1.0	0.8	0.5	0.5	0.3	0.3	—	—	—	3.4	1.8	1.88
13	1.0	0.8	0.5	0.5	0.3	0.3	—	—	—	3.4	1.8	1.88
14	1.0	0.8	0.5	0.5	0.3	0.3	0.1	—	—	3.5	1.8	1.94
15	1.0	0.8	0.7	0.5	0.5	0.3	0.3	—	—	4.1	2.5	1.64
16	1.0	0.8	0.7	0.5	0.5	0.3	0.3	—	—	4.1	2.5	1.64
17	1.0	0.8	0.7	0.5	0.5	0.3	0.3	0.1	—	4.2	2.5	1.68
18	1.0	0.8	0.7	0.7	0.5	0.5	0.3	0.3	—	4.8	3.2	1.50
19	1.0	0.8	0.7	0.7	0.5	0.5	0.3	0.3	—	4.8	3.2	1.50
20	1.0	0.8	0.9	0.7	0.5	0.5	0.3	0.3	0.1	5.1	3.4	1.50
21	1.0	0.8	0.9	0.7	0.7	0.5	0.5	0.3	0.3	5.7	4.1	1.39

*Physical persons were ascribed values as working and consuming units as shown in the Note to Table 3 on p. 234.
†See Chayanov (1915), pp. 4–6.

Note to Table 3

	Consumer	Worker
Male worker – head of household	1.0	1.0
Female worker – mother of family	0.8	0.8
Other members – age 17 + years	0.9	0.9
age 13–17 years	0.7	0.7
age 7–12 years	0.5	0.0
age 2–6 years	0.3	0.0
age 0–1 years	0.1	0.0

Source: Chayanov (1915), p. 4.

A full explanation of multidirectional mobility (including the residual component) was proposed on the eve of the revolution by Chayanov. The economic development of the peasant household was, in Chayanov's view, determined by (and could be operationally defined by) the changes in the consumer/worker[10] ratio. The consumer/worker ratio in a hypothetical family into which a live child was born every three years is described in Table 3.

The biological growth of the young peasant family would thus have caused a rise in the consumer/worker ratio and in 'consumption pressure'. This would lead to an increase in the intensity of labour (i.e. 'self-exploitation' among its working members) and the pulling-in (*podtyazhka*) of further factors of production by renting land, borrowing, or saving). Such processes would be recorded as a rise in the economic position of the household. At a given stage, the coming to working age of additional workers would ease the consumption pressure (in consumer/worker terms) and lead to a lowering of the drive for economic expansion. At the same time, such a development generated partitioning and heralded possible deterioration and the beginning of new cycles, with young families setting off to make a start on new small farms. Moreover, 'biological' deterioration of some of the households (e.g. the ageing of a childless couple or the emergence of a consumption pressure which could not be met because of, say, the death of the main worker) would lead to their disappearance through extinction, merger, or, in some cases, emigration.

The biological cycle of peasant family life would explain,

therefore, both the 'residual component' of peasant households' mobility and 'substantive changes'. The other known components of the mobility were explained by supporters of this view within the same conceptual framework.

Chayanov's general theory of peasant economy and mobility was empirically validated – or at least illustrated – by intensive budget studies of 101 peasant households in Starobel'sk *uezd* published in 1915. Chayanov's evidence was strongly challenged by scholars opposed to his theoretical stand, and his own views underwent change. However, he seems to have retained the essence of his views about the crucial influence of 'biological' factors on the Russian peasant economy of this period and, more important, for us here, fully restated in his later studies his initial explanation of peasant socio-economic mobility.[11]

The validity of 'biological determinist' theories and the degree of influence of peasant life-cycles on household mobility must remain, for the time being, unresolved. They can be elucidated only by further studies based on comparable data. However, to turn to our basic concern, even if we accept that biological life-cycles affected peasant mobility, the scale of the residual component of household mobility recorded does not seem to be fully explicable in these terms. For example, in the Ts.SU* dynamic study of 1924 –5 the residual component of mobility affected 34.3 per cent of peasant households, which had moved from one arbitrarily-defined socio-economic stratum to another within a year. Similar rates of change were reported for 1925–6. The annual change in the consumer/worker ratio (see Table 3 above) could not possibly account for a movement of such size. Neither can some catastrophe or external change be accepted as an explanation for such a change in this relatively peaceful period of Russian rural history. We must therefore conclude that, even were all the theories and models of the 'biological determinists' validated, such an explanation could not be regarded as adequate for explaining the whole of the 'residual component' of peasant households' mobility – or, at least, of that recorded in the Ts.SU dynamic studies.

---

*Tsentralnoe statisticheskoe upravlenie: the central statistical board created by the Soviet government after the revolution.

(c) The peculiarities of a smallholding economy

For a more satisfactory interpretation of the mobility of peasant households, it is necessary to return to our analysis of the basic social structure of the peasantry and the peculiarities of a peasant economy. Up to this point, the widespread notion of the peasant household as a highly integrated duality of family and production-unit has been accepted. According to this view, the peasant household operates as a family and, at the same time, as an enterprise in conditions of partial commodity production. We shall now isolate a third major characteristic of peasant households which is significant for our analysis. The peasant household functions as a *small* production-unit of extremely limited resources, greatly subject to the powerful forces of *nature*, the *market*, and the *state*.

The *natural fluctuations* of weather (hot and cold spells, timely or untimely rains, hail, storm, and so on) make for a more or less random succession of 'good' and 'bad' agricultural years. The impact of natural factors was probably reinforced by a relative rigidity in crop-rotation, traditional in peasant agriculture, and may have been associated with the prevalent plant and livestock diseases. To give but one example: the national figures for yields of rye – the key component of Russian peasant diet – during the three decades 1891–1921 moved between a maximum of 73 *pud* per *desyatina* in 1916, and 43, 46, and 32 respectively in the famine years 1891, 1907, and 1921.[13] Nor were such changes limited to a few extraordinary years. The record for these three decades shows five years of famine, five more as years with annual yields of less than 50 *puds* per *desyatina*; for five years, though, the yield was 65 *puds* per *desyatina* or more. The yields for localities would no doubt have fluctuated even more sharply. To the tale of natural fluctuations in yields one can add the 'natural disasters' of flood and fire.

The *terms of trade* between the rural and urban sectors (reflected in the relative prices of major agricultural and non-agricultural products on the open market) strongly influenced peasant households' economies. Practically every peasant household was involved in some exchange operations; at the minimum, it had to sell its produce at least to pay taxes and to buy some industrial goods, including equipment. At the same time, peasant wage-labour came to the market. In fact, peasant market operations were, of course, much more complex than this and varied from period to period, decreasing during the years 1917–19 and increasing afterwards. The extent of the involvement in a money economy of peasant households was subject to heated controversy at the time and has not since become clear. However, the fact of the involvement of households in market exchanges cannot be denied. For example, the 1924–5 annual budget studies – based on representative samples drawn from the main agricultural regions of the Grain-Deficient Zone, the Grain-Surplus Zone, and the North Caucasus – showed 19, 25, and 26 per cent respectively of Conventional Net Income spent as cash on purchases on the general market. The market prices significant for a peasant economy fluctuated widely and their determination was, of course, outside the scope of the peasant smallholder's economy. The changes taking place in the relative prices of industrial and agricultural products can be seen in their extreme form in the so-called 'scissors crisis', in which the movement of the exchange rate against agricultural products reached in 1923 a rate of 1:3 (taking the 1913 price levels as 1:1).[12]

The *policy* of the highly centralized Russian and Soviet states strongly influenced Russian agriculture. The economic intervention of the state involved the imposition of taxes and the granting of credits but also went further in the form of attempts at securing total control over the market through price fixing (e.g. under the 'grain monopoly' after 1915), at imposing a ban on the distilling of home-made vodka, at confiscating all agricultural surpluses (under 'War Communism', 1918–21), and even at total planning of the production of rural smallholders (in 1920). One can also include the legislation on land-reform in 1917–19 and the ban and later limitation on land-renting and the employment of wage-labour in the years 1917–28. The real ability of the state to impose its will on the peasant communities varied over time, but the fact of its influence on the peasant economy cannot, once again, be doubted.

Our specific knowledge of the impingement of these factors on the peasant economy is still extremely thin, and demands further work. However we may already draw some conclusions about certain of the general characteristics of the interaction between the external factors discussed and the economy of Russian peasant households.

The economy of Russian peasant households was typified by limited resources of labour, land, and equipment and by extremely limited money savings and access to credit. The impact of the major external forces on the peasant economy would have varied widely in extent and character by period and by area. Yet the way these forces acted tended, on the whole, to be uniform, at least in that: firstly, the impact of these external forces was overwhelmingly powerful compared to the resources of the peasant household; secondly, they appeared to the peasants as almost totally unpredictable and certainly quite uncontrollable; lastly, they tended, by their very nature, to fluctuate widely – whether in the form of sequences of 'good' and 'bad' years, of fluctuations in prices, or of seemingly arbitrary twists and turns in the state's policies and its officials' applications of them.

The massive economic vicissitudes of peasant households resulting from the impact of these external factors were expressed in two ways: first, aggregate shifts, or changes in the prosperity of the peasantry *en masse*; second, changes in the relative positions of peasant households. The general economic effect of external factors on peasant society has been discussed above. These aggregate shifts were, it seems clear, coupled with large fluctuations in the relative socio-economic positions of peasant households. Each peasant farm was strongly influenced by individual chance factors in its specific history and present family structure. The relative position depended on very small economic differentials; chance could therefore play an exaggerated role. A successful contract, a hard-working son, a useful merger, or, conversely, the illness or death of a working member, a fire, the death of a horse, the obligation to provide a dowry, or even a family quarrel culminating in partitioning, could lead to a complete change in the socio-economic position of a household. Peasants were well aware of the influence of chance factors on their life. For example, a local survey reports: 'The middle peasants say "Today I am a middle peasant, tomorrow I become a poor peasant. If the horse dies, I'll have to hire myself out." ' Far from being extraordinary occurrences, crises and strokes of luck formed an integral part of peasant life. These unique individual factors and the idiosyncratic impacts on individual households of the externally determined general economic trends must, therefore, have caused marked socio-economic mobility among peasant households.

If we accept what has been said above, a number of conclusions would seem to follow. In the conditions of a peasant economy such as we have been discussing, considerable *random oscillation* of peasant households is to be expected; it will take the form of multidirectional mobility – not, however, cyclical in nature. This 'random oscillation' of peasant households, the product of the conditions of a peasant smallholder economy facing powerful and fluctuating external pressures, should be accepted as yet another distinct and major type of mobility among peasant households on a par with that due to the cumulation of economic advantages and disadvantages, the effects of 'substantive changes', land-redivisions by communes, and the possible consequences of the biological life-cycle within the peasant family.

(d) The mobility of peasant households: a multifactorial model

Hunting for the laws of historical development and 'progress' has diverted the attention of the investigators from a study of the phenomena of repetitions, fluctuations, oscillations and cycles in social life, phenomena which attracted a great deal of attention on the part of social thinkers in the past.

This statement of Sorokin is certainly true of the last two centuries. Social scientists have been particularly interested in structural changes, i.e. those creating qualitatively new social structures and organizations. Alternatively their work has been focused on linear changes, i.e. those changes which necessarily result in and are defined by quantitative differences between the position at the beginning of the process and at the end of it, in which the extent of change correlates with its duration. Conceptually, such changes have the advantage of indubitable significance; they can be clearly discerned and they enjoy the intellectual attractiveness (often meretricious) of promising prediction – however rough – by simple extrapolation. In processes which combine linear and non-linear or cyclical changes, attention was generally given to the linear aspects of them. In our case, the attention of the students of socio-economic mobility has been attracted primarily by 'net' linear changes as defined by differences in the distribution of units at the beginning and at the end of the process, for example, polarization.

The social significance of 'repetitions, fluctuations, oscillations, and cycles' seems beyond doubt but the accepted concepts of contemporary social sciences have on the whole committed the non-structural and non-linear issues to the margins of inquiry.

The three basic reasons which barred a more realistic comprehension of socio-economic mobility of the Russian peasantry were: first, the structural/linear paradigm of the contemporary social sciences; second, the prevailing 'monistic' tendency in modes of explanation; and third, the methodological tendency to limit discussion to peasantry as a whole or to peasant village communities.

The suggested solution to our problem attempts to highlight multidirectional and cyclical processes and their impact on peasant society. It keeps in focus the dynamics of single peasant households and its reflection on peasant society. It comes to accept the fact that the mobility of peasant households reflects the interaction of qualitatively different and relatively autonomous major factors, acting simultaneously, each displaying its own momentum. The process of mobility consists, therefore, of several component processes, each with different social characteristics. Only a multifactorial model can accommodate the complexities of peasant mobility, particularly in conditions of growing market relations. The loss of the elegance of the simpler monistic models is the price to be paid for a closer approximation to reality.

An operational model of the mobility of peasant households will need further work to validate its components and to help determine their relative 'weights'. The effects of particular factors will have to be analysed within specific historical and regional frameworks; further empirical and comparative studies are therefore called for. We are, though, already able to present a prototype model, indicating the basic components of the mobility of peasant households and their interaction. Such a model of the effects of the mobility of peasant households on differentiation-processes can tentatively clarify these processes and their causes and give cohesion to our earlier treatment. Such conceptualization is, in any case, a necessary precondition for further investigations.

Figure 3 is offered to present the main components and to suggest patterns and causes of peasant household mobility, underlying the differentiation-processes found in Russian peasant society.

Figure 3, part B looks at the specific influence of each of the analytically delineated major types of factor involved in the mobility found among peasant households, and relates the predominant direction of mobility to the socio-economic strata affected. The character of each of the major components of the mobility of peasant households (and the elements of the proposed

Figure 3 *Multidirectional and cyclical mobility: the determinants of centrifugal and centripetal mobility among peasant households (a prototype model)*

A   *Types of household mobility* (following Figure 2)

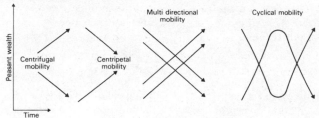

Note: The figure is a further elaboration of the typology of peasant socio-economic mobility in relation to the differentiation-process in peasant societies. Household wealth is here used mainly in the sense of means of production: land, livestock, and equipment as well as savings and reserves. On the whole, these assets correlated with available family labour.

B   *The major trends in peasant household mobility*

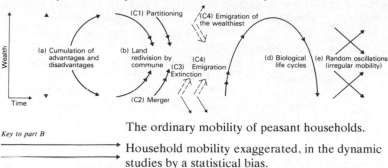

Key to part B

The ordinary mobility of peasant households.

Household mobility exaggerated, in the dynamic studies by a statistical bias.

Mobility evident in only some of the dynamic studies.

The actual process   The levelling reflection of the process

'Semi-centripetal aspects of mobility – i.e. the differential disappearance of the richest and the poorest households, leading to a levelling in the peasant community (discussed on pp. 230–1).

The directions of such centrifugal mobility as may lead to structural change and disappearance of typical characteristics of peasant economy, e.g. the emergence of enterprises engaged in capitalist production or, alternatively, the transformation of peasants into wage-labourers.

C   *The determinants of household mobility underlying differentiation processes**

I	*Centrifugal trends†*	II	*Centripetal trends‡*
a	Cumulation of economic advantages and disadvantages. (i.e. 'polarization'; see Lenin, Part Two of this volume)	b	Land-redivision administered by the communes.**
		c	Substantive changes:
			1 Partitioning.
			2 Merger.
			3 Extinction.#
			4 Emigration.#
d	Biological life cycle (?).	d	Biological life cycle (?).
e	Random oscillation (irregular mobility).		Random oscillation (irregular mobility).

*The figure aims only to show the *main tendencies* of the determinants and does not exclude differing results in the cases of individual peasant households (e.g. the partitioning of an impoverished household).

‡Centrifugal mobility may lead, in some cases, to structural changes (e.g. final proletarization or alternatively the development of a peasant household into a commodity-producing enterprise typical of a market economy) with subsequent disappearance of mobility of peasant societies.

‡A centripetal statistical bias will result from the form of presentation usually adopted in the dynamic studies.

**Land-redivision administered by communes did not occur in some areas – in particular, in Belorussia and the north-west.

#For a discussion of the specific 'semi-centripetal' characteristics of the process of extinction and emigration of peasant households see pp. 230–1.

model) has been already discussed at length and will not be repeated here. The arrows indicate the most probable directions of each type of socio-economic movement of peasant households and the semi-centripetal levelling effect of differential emigration and extinction on the peasant society. In peasant communities and peasant society the tendency towards the cumulation of economic advantages and disadvantages (a) leads to a polarizing tendency which is at least partly counteracted by commune-administered land-redivision (b). Differential 'substantive changes' (c) – the existence of a correlation between the rates of 'substantive changes' and the wealth of peasant households – has, on the whole, an additional levelling effect on peasant society, through both centripetal trends of partitioning and merger (c1 and c2) and the 'semi-centripetal effect' of disproportionately high disappearance of poor households as the result of extinction and emigration (c3 and c4). A particularly intensive emigration of the richest could, at times, have a similar effect. The powerful residual centripetal mobility in the dynamic studies which cannot be ascribed to factors (b) and (c) indicates the existence of additional components of mobility. These are explained here in terms of random oscillation (e) and the possible influence of the biological cycle (d). The centripetal tendency would have been somewhat magnified in the dynamic studies as the result of a statistical bias, created mainly by the elimination of 'substantive changes' from the records; this has been pointed out by the use of a double arrow. The operation of such a set of simultaneously acting factors in a peasant community would necessarily lead to and account for the powerful multidirectional mobility of peasant households revealed in the dynamic studies. It will also, in all probability, generate strong cyclical forces – tendencies for peasant households to be caught up successively in ascending and descending phases of socio-economic movement.

Some reasonably secure quantitative conclusions can be drawn at this stage. For example, the fact that multidirectional mobility greatly exceeded net mobility in terms of peasant communities. However, the most significant conclusion to be drawn from the Russian dynamic studies is the establishment of the very fact that massive multidirectional and, in all probability, cyclical types of household mobility were taking place among the Russian peasantry at this time; this must be accepted, whatever interpretation is adopted.

Notes

1 In the broad sense advanced by Adam Smith (1806).
2 Ideological images of reality may act merely as justifications and canonizations of political decisions taken but also as 'lenses . . . through which men see, a medium by which they interpret and report what they see' (Wright Mills, 1963, p. 406). For a recent discussion see Berger and Luckman (1967).
3 This additional information included the disappearance and creation of new peasant households through migration, extinction, partioning and merger. For a discussion of this, see below (pp. 230ff).

4 This pattern is the probable one. It does not exclude the possibility of some of the richer households continuing further enrichment and even taking a structural leap into commodity-centred or even capitalist farming.

5 Similar processes were observed in other peasant societies – see, for example, Yang (1945), p. 132, Stirling (1965), ch. 7 and Ajiami (1969). See also for centripetal trends Nash (1967).

6 Only further studies of a peasant economy and, in particular, of the problems of enrichment and capital formation could make it conclusive.

7 Robinson (1949), pp. 121–2.

8 Economic determinists: that is, orthodox Marxist and neo-classical economists.

9 Among the prominent members of this group was A. Chayanov (see Djurfeldt, Part Two, and Harrison, Part Three, this volume).

10 The word 'worker' is used here in the sense of one who works, not necessarily as a wage-worker, i.e. including those who work in their own households, in fact, the most important group here.

11 Chayanov (1966), originally published in German and then in Russian in the mid 1920s.

12 Dobb (1966), pp. 162–9.

13 A *pud* equals approximately 16.3 kg.

References

Ajiami, I. (1969), 'Social classes, family demographic characteristics and mobility in Iranian Villages', *Sociologia Ruralis*, ix, pp. 62–72

Berger, P., and Luckman, T. (1967), *The Social Construction of Reality*, London: Allen Lane

Chayanov, A. (1915), *Byudzhety krest'yan starobel'skogo uezda,*, Khar'kov

Chayanov, A. (1966), *The Theory of Peasant Economy*, Homewood, Ill.: Richard D. Irwin; originally published in German and then in Russian in the mid 1920s

Dobb, M. (1966), *Soviet Economic Development since 1917*, London: Routledge

Nash, M. (1967), 'Indian economies', *Social Anthropology*, pp. 93–101

Robinson, G. (1949), *Rural Russia under the Old Regime*, New York: Macmillan

Rumyantsev, P. (1906), 'K voprosu ob evolutsii russkogo krest' yanstva', *Ocherki realisticheskogo mirovozreniya*, pp. 527,

Shanin, T. (1972), *The Awkward Class: Political Sociology of Peasantry in a Developing Society: Russia 1913–1925*, London: Oxford University Press

Smith, Adam (1806), *The Wealth of Nations*, London

Stirling, P. (1965), *Turkish Village*, London: Weidenfeld & Nicolson

Wright Mills, C. (1963), *Power, Politics and People*, New York: Oxford University Press

Yang, M. (1945); *A Chinese Village*, Cambridge, Mass.: MIT Press, 1959

10 Chayanov's theory of peasant economy*

Mark Harrison

Introduction

Why is Chayanov important for us today? Chayanov belonged to the *neo-populist* tradition; that is, the Russian populist tradition in social science and rural statistical, agronomic and extension work, which can be dated roughly from the turn of the century.

The neo-populist tradition emphasized the viability of peasant agriculture and its ability to survive and prosper under any circumstances. For the peasantry had no necessary tendency to develop the increasing economic inequalities and class antagonisms of bourgeois industrial society: there was no tendency to create increasing groups of rich and poor or landless peasants with a more and more unstable group of middle peasants in between. The village was an overwhelmingly homogeneous community, able constantly to reproduce itself both economically and socially. Consequently, Chayanov saw the modernization of traditional small farming as lying along neither a capitalist nor a socialist road, but as a peasant path of raising the technical level of agricultural production through agricultural extension work and co-operative organization, at the same time conserving the peasant institutional framework of the family smallholding. This vision of the future has important political implications, both in the Soviet context of the 1920s and today in the context of modern underdevelopment.

One can, I think, put the modern significance of Chayanov's work as follows. Since the early 1960s a definite shift has occurred in the focus of the Cold War within the underdeveloped world. This shift has tended partly to replace military confrontation with a variety of 'hearts and minds' campaigns directed by various Western agencies and aimed at the rural bases of political power, mostly in South and South-East Asia; it has brought to these parts of the world armies of agronomists and technicians and the High

*This chapter is taken from Harrison (1975 and 1976).

Yielding Varieties Programmes of the 'green revolution'. As a result the recipient countries have experienced substantial growth in particular areas of the agricultural sector itself; there has been a stimulus to agrarian inequality and social tensions which has created all kinds of unexpected and disparate phenomena – populist anti-hoarding campaigns, sporadic village terrorism, movements of national liberation. It has been demonstrated in a number of ways that the future of peasant agriculture in the world is again in the balance. This is an important reason for the recent expansion of peasant studies in the West, and the Western republications and translations of Chayanov's work. For it appears that Chayanov and the Soviet experience with co-operative and collective farming are once more being added to the political scales.

The scope of the present paper is restricted to the most basic questions of resource allocation raised in Chayanov's work: how do peasant households allocate their labour-power? Are inequalities generated in peasant societies as a result?

Family labour and household property

Neo-populist theories of resource allocation

What distinguished Chayanov's school from all others interested in agrarian resource allocation was its highly specific theoretical position, characteristic of neo-populist social science, which is summed up in a secondary meaning of the *organization of production*. In the works of the organization of production school, the organization of production also means the peasant's activity of economic organization (or resource allocation), guided by a peasant rationality, which makes the peasant farm a fundamental organism of the national economy (Chayanov, 1912–13, vol. I, pp. VII, X; Makarov, 1920, pp. 37–8, 78).

What are the implications of the fact that peasant agricultural production is 'based on' the household economy and family property? An old variant of Marxism asserted that the answer depended on the presence of commodity or non-commodity production. Natural economy might be a reflection of gentile society, in which the 'household' was the clan itself; or it was a reflection of the subordination of the village to the manorial system. With commodity economy, the rise of the law of value destroyed the harmony of peasant society, inducing a schizophrenic coexistence within the peasant personality of the bourgeois and the proletarian 'in one person'. This contradiction was eventually realized in the transition to capitalism. Elements of this view may be traced to the present, for example, in the work of Galeski (1972, p.11).

A variant of Russian Populism held that this objective contradiction was overcome through mechanisms intrinsic to the *specific peasant culture and consciousness*. For example, laws of subsistence motivation can be found scattered through the literature, including the work of Chayanov (Shcherbina, 1900, pp. 6–10, 224; Chayanov, 1912–13, vol. I, p. XIV; Chelintsev, 1918, pp. 8, 60–2, 125–6, 161–3; Chayanov, 1966, p. 218). These laws had the force of denying the drive to accumulate and to compete; however, they did so as a matter of assertion or by reference solely to factors of consciousness.

Others went further, and attacked the very application of the law of value to peasant commodity production. Shcherbina himself raised the first doubts (quoted by Makarov, 1920, pp. 15–16). The Marxist Kosinsky made the decisive break, abandoning the notions of wages and profits, variable capital and surplus-value in his economic analysis. Kosinsky's peasants sought to maximize total factor income, not the rate of profit or the marginal product of labour (Kosinsky, 1906, pp. 81–4, 92). Chayanov introduced the notion of a trade-off between total factor income and leisure, that is utility-maximization; in the manner of Jevons he defined a short-run partial equilibrium with respect to family labour supplies, and in applying it to peasant economy called it the 'labour consumer balance' (Chayanov, 1966, pp. 68–79).

In doing so, Chayanov achieved much more. He developed a systematic theory of peasant economy based on the *specific structure of peasant economy* – the application of non-wage family labour to the family household farm. This theory was independent of *whether or not there was commodity production* (Chayanov, 1966, p. 125).

The short-run analysis of the labour-consumer balance can be stated briefly as follows. It proceeds from 'a single organizational concept of the peasant labour farm independent of the economic system into which it enters' (Chayanov, 1966, p. 42) and seeks to establish 'the living organizational ideas, the machinery of its individual economic organism which is "the subjective teleological unity of rational economic activity", i.e. running the farm' (Chayanov, 1966, p. 118). The family farm is an *organism* of the national economy. The analysis proceeds from its internally generated needs and resources, taking an explicitly subjective approach to farm organization within a given environment. The justification for this analytical *isolation* of the family economy was the initial absence of a market for wage-labour (Chayanov, 1966, pp. 11, 53).

In abstraction from external relations, the peasant family becomes the unit of production, distribution and exchange. To this atomistic, self-determining entity Chayanov applied the logic of utilitarian individualism. The labour process is dominated by the relationship between work done and income received. Increased income brings diminished marginal utility, and increased intensity or duration of labour bring increased marginal disutility. In consequence, the elasticity of demand for income with respect to income per day worked is positive but less than unity, while the elasticity of supply of labour with respect to income per day worked lies between zero and minus one.

Taking a family of given size and structure, with given tastes and facing given prices, assume an autonomous improvement in the technical conditions of production. Labour productivity per day worked is improved by dp. If the number of days worked in the year is held constant at n_0, and the level of the marginal disutility of labour is held constant with it, then the resulting increase in annual income under these conditions is measured by $n_0 dp$. This also measures the rightward shift in the MD schedule. However, it will not normally measure the equilibrium value of dx when n is variable. For as total income increases, the marginal utility of income falls and the number of days worked per year must be reduced to maintain the marginal conditions. In this case

$$dx < n_0 dp$$

Since n_0 is equal to (x_0/p_0), we can rewrite this expression as

$$\frac{dx}{dp} \cdot \frac{p}{x} < 1$$

That is, the elasticity of demand for annual income with respect to income per day worked is less than unity: our familiar friend the backward-sloping supply curve of labour.

Model 1 is a pre-Chayanov version with a long history (but remember that Chelintsev and others continued to use it right up to the end of the 1920s). In Model 1 the family has a given level of culturally determined wants; therefore there is a vertical MU schedule at x_0 on the x-axis which measures the family requirements. Labour may have increasing marginal disutility, but the subsistence requirements must be achieved at any cost. The demand for family income is therefore inelastic with respect to both the disutility of labour and the return per day worked. For $n_0 dp \lessgtr o$, $dx = o$ and the supply curve of labour slopes so far backward that it is horizontal. For subsistence, Chelintsev (1918, p. 8) wrote, is a 'definite level of family consumption at a given time and place', a 'minimum which powerfully dictates' economic behaviour. Moreover this level of subsistence,

in spite of the human tendency to 'seek after improvement', cannot be rapidly raised when the addition of incremental means [of subsistence] is associated with further expenditure of labour.... Therefore the level of consumption of the family ... found on average in each particular locality, is a constant magnitude for the given time ...

This remains, formally at least, a passage abstracted from Chelintsev's work; his writings are deficient in such features of model-building as consistently stated assumptions and hypotheses, but this is part of his major working theory.

Model 2 however is taken directly from one of Chayanov's earliest works, published in 1913. This date marks his transition from Model 1 which he had used in a work of the previous year (Chayanov, 1912–13, vol. II, pp. VII–IX; cf. Chayanov, 1966, pp. 79–89). Both these early works were concerned with the question: why do the peasants of Moscow and Smolensk provinces cultivate flax, which yields a value return per day worked lower than for most other crops (and sometimes lower than the local market day-wage)? Between one volume and the next, Chayanov had read Jevons's *The Theory of Political Economy* (1871), and was now bringing the English utilitarian counter-revolution against Ricardo and Marx home to Russian agrarian economics. In Model 2, the MU schedule is no longer vertical but downward-sloping, so that a shift to the right in the MD curve, proportional to an increase in the value productivity per day worked, results in an increase in

Model 1: 'subsistence' theory

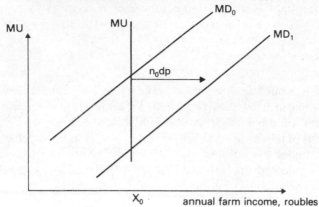

Model 2: Jevons–Chayanov 'utility' theory

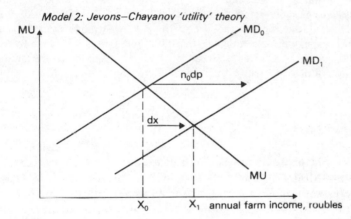

Key

MU marginal utility of income: a function of prices of goods consumed and invested, of individual preferences, and of family size standardized in terms of the adult male consumer.

MD marginal disutility of labour: a function of prices of goods produced of material resources per man and of techniques of production (i.e. physical productivity per day worked), and of family size standardized in terms of the adult male workers.

p   value return to labour per day worked.

n   days worked per year per farm.

x   annual farm income, roubles ($x = p.n$).

Figure 4 *The labour–consumer balance*

family equilibrium income which is positive but less than proportionate:

$$0 < \frac{dx}{dp} \cdot \frac{p}{x} < 1$$

The positive but less than unitary elasticity of demand for income is expressed in Chayanov's remark (1966, p. 80) that 'the rate of increment of the budget considerably lags behind the rate of increment of labour productivity ... the annual intensity of labour declines under the influence of better pay.'[1] Note that Chayanov explicitly rejected the 'reproach' that he believed in fixed subsistence; in the analysis of consumer budgets, he wrote,

the consumption rates we have quoted are precisely real rates of consumption and by no means a quantitative expression of demands themselves as such. Speaking generally, the demand for any product for personal consumption cannot be expressed by any one figure; and if, generally speaking, it can be expressed in figures, then it is in the form of a whole scale of consumption rates which corresponds to the gradual satiation of demand and its extinction, (Chayanov, 1966, p. 131).

$$\text{The condition } 0 < \frac{dx}{dp} \cdot \frac{p}{x} < 1$$

shows that peasants neither aim at a unique subsistence level of income (Model 1), nor maximize income per time period ('crude materialism'); they seek to maximize the net utility of income and leisure. Hence the cultivation of labour-intensive flax in the land-hungry provinces of Moscow and Smolensk is explained by high marginal utilities and disutilities.

This refers to current decisions; what about the long period? Model 1 was taken to be unambiguous on this point – the peasant family is motivated only to achieve the desired level of consumption, which is actually achieved, and therefore 'the whole annual income of the farm is consumed' (Chelintsev, 1918, p. 125). Where marginal utility is downward-sloping, however, wants are not entirely satisfied. and there is a rationale for net savings and investment which can be analysed in the marginalist framework, through time-preference. Unfortunately, Chayanov did not understand time-preference, and the chapter 'Peasant farm organization' which deals with this subject is one of the most opague passages in the literature. However it may be ultimately discerned that Chayanov fell back to the Model 1 criterion: optimum gross savings equals capital consumption. The family aims at 'a sufficient level of well-being in future years', and usually this will also equal the initial level. That means accepting,

– though this does not always correspond with everyday reality – that available income is divided according to the equilibrium of production and consumption evaluations or, more accurately, a desire to maintain a constant level of well-being (Chayanov, 1966, p. 218).

As they stand, these models of resource allocation are formally static. (However, they can be used to generate two distinct models of an 'evolving' economy: the evolution of the individual farm within a given region [there is a discussion of this in the paper by Shanin, above] and the evolution of the agricultural region itself.)

These propositions are important primarily because of their axiomatic basis. They are also important because of their application.

Chayanov used them to derive certain secondary propositions which purported to describe the laws of motion of the Russian peasant economy. Assuming variable supplies of non-labour inputs, as the family grows and decays the family economy will also experience a cyclical development. The addition of children to the nuclear couple will expand family needs relative to resources in terms of labour-power. The family's equilibrium will shift towards increased effort and output per worker, reduced leisure and reduced per capita income. As the children mature, the tendency is reversed. The family divides into new sets of nuclear couples, and the cycle is repeated (Chayanov, 1915, pp. 3–5; Chayanov, 1966, pp. 57–60). The population of families within a local peasant economy will thus manifest a degree of inequality in the utilization of labour-power, productivity and income per head which is 'demographic', or at any rate non-social in origin (Chayanov, 1966, pp. 66–9, 71–89).

Over time, as population pressure increases relative to the availability of non-labour inputs, the family life-cycle is repeated amid a constantly shifting structure of activities in the direction of more intensive, high-yielding products. Thus macro-demographic laws impose a second, non-social level of inequality across the national peasantry in terms of the utilization of labour-power, productivity and income per head (Chelintsev, 1928, pp. 13–16; but see Chayanov's cautionary comments, 1966, p. 142).

The evidence for all these propositions is unsound and is critically analysed elsewhere (Harrison, 1975, 1977a). From a theoretical point of view the reason is as follows. In a perversion of normal procedures, Chayanov assumed that the availability of means of production was variable in the short run and fixed in the long run. In the short run he saw the flexible supply of non-labour inputs as an essential condition for the family life-cycle to be reflected in the development cycle of the farm (Chayanov, 1966, p. 68). In the long run, however, he saw the possibilities of accumulation as limited by the technical constraints described above, and by the subsistence motivation of the peasant family (Chayanov, 1966, pp. 201, 218). In this way, strong ideological associations determined the concrete inferences which he formed from a model so axiomatic as to be trivial.

Again at a theoretical level, the inference which he drew can be summarized as follows:

(i) Peasant economy involves an intrinsic social relation: 'self-exploitation' of labour-power. The measure of self-exploitation is the number of days in the year which the peasant 'chooses' or 'compels himself' to work. The inequalities within peasant society spring from this subjective relation, and do not involve the exploitation of some people by other people.

(ii) Peasant economy reproduces itself through the family. The family is the progenitor of the family life-cycle and of population growth. It is the owner of property. As such, it expresses the fact that the aim of production is household consumption, not feudal rent or bourgeois profit. From an ideologically based conception of consumption and accumulation, Chayanov here slipped back into the world of subsistence motivation and the static economy.

(iii) Peasant economy embodies a contradiction between human needs and the forces of production. This is what generates the laws of motion of both household and economy, and which propels agricultural production towards more highly developed systems of cultivation and more valuable products. But this contradiction is not antagonistic. Not only is the scale of peasant production technically appropriate. It is also *more* appropriate, *more* efficient and *more* competitive than capitalist production. Peasants do not 'need' to earn a profit; where capitalists go bankrupt, peasants survive (Chayanov, 1927, pp. 39–44).

Out of a sense of historical fairness it should be pointed out that many peasants did not survive; first among the survivors was the emergent rural bourgeoisie.

In summary, Chayanov had a definite theory of the relationship between peasant labour-power and the means of production. It was based on a non-social view of human nature – sometimes utilitarian man, who exercises choice and whose behaviour is analysed as a set of revealed preferences; sometimes man as the agent who determines the goal of his own labour, in the sense of production for the sake of consumption – sometimes quite specifically for the sake of subsistence. All these elements are important aspects of the unity of Chayanov's work, in itself and with a whole tradition.

In fact, there were relations of production developing through the labour market, in particular the massive migrant-labour market in agriculture. These developments, while in many ways shallow and marginal in relation to the whole economy, indicate the existence of a growing network of social relations between households mediated through product and factor markets, with a number of consequences for the freedom of choice exercised by the peasants involved. For example, it is possible to detect the exercise of leisure-preference on the part of wealthy households, combined with the hiring of labour-power on their farms. Among those who supplied wage-labour, it is possible to detect under-employment or leisure-preference exercised within the context of the impossibility of finding full employment in the underdeveloped national economy (Maslov, 1930, pp. 57–63).

Within households, also, it may be that 'self-exploitation' was an unfortunate conception. We know very little about the sexual division of labour in the Russian peasantry. It seems possible however that the changing role of patriarchy had considerable impact upon the position of women and youth, as well as upon processes of class formation generally (Harrison, 1977a). However, patriarchy, an institution by no means intrinsic to peasant society, cannot be analysed through the labour-consumer balance.

Let me repeat, however, that Chayanov's utilitarianism, while set firmly within the Populist ideological tradition, was a great scientific advance. Peasants cannot be analysed either as innocent savages or as split personalities. Perhaps Chayanov was the Newton of agrarian studies. The trouble is that today we believe in relativity.

Note

1   There is a double mistake here which I did not realize when I
    cited these words. The mistake was made initially by Chayanov,
    and I repeated it. I am grateful to Mr Abu Abdullah of the Chr
    Michelsen Institute, Bergen, who pointed out the error in a
    letter to me in 1978.

    The assumptions stated by Chayanov, and repeated by me,
    are not yet sufficient to generate the results claimed – an
    inelastic demand for income and a negatively elastic supply of
    labour with respect to changes in income per day worked. The
    inelastic demand for income must be entered as an assumption,
    not claimed as a result. Once assumed, it results in Model 2
    marginal utility schedules and in the backward-sloping supply
    curve of labour. Without this assumption dx might be less than,
    equal to or greater than $n_0 dp$, and the supply curve of labour
    might be backward-bending (inclining positively over a range
    before turning backwards) rather than backward-sloping. The
    more theoretically inclined reader is referred to a rather
    compressed discussion by Blaug (1964, pp. 290–2), which I
    cited without fully grasping when my article was first published.

    How does this affect the argument which I sought to make in
    the text? Chayanov's mistake suggests that Model 2 was more
    closely related to Model 1 than I thought at first. The results of
    Model 1 depended entirely upon restrictive assumptions about
    the marginal utility schedule which I described as 'subsistence'
    motivation. But the assumptions of Model 2 are still heavily
    restrictive, more so than Chayanov recognized, so that the
    result still has the character of a special case. Chayanov's
    mistake strengthens my argument because it emphasizes the
    ideological element in his doctrine – his readiness to assume
    away the incentives to labour and accumulation beyond subsist-
    ence needs when the opportunity presents itself. Thus my
    mistake in following Chayanov on this point was not especially
    critical for the force of my argument, although it does of
    course contain its own object lesson.

References

Blaug, M. (1964), *Economic Theory in Retrospect*, London:
    Heinemann

Chayanov, A. V. (1912–13), *Len i drugie kul'tury v organizat-sionnom plane krest'yanskogo khozyaistva nechernozemnoi Rossii*, vols. I–II, Moscow

Chayanov, A. V. (1915), *Byudzhety krest'yan Starobel'skogo uezda*, Khar'kov

Chayanov, A. V. (1927), *Osnovnye idei i formy organizatsii sel' skokhozyaistvennoi kooperatm*, Moscow

Chayanov, A. V. (1966), *The Theory of Peasant Economy*, ed. and introd. by Basile Kerblay, Daniel Thorner and R. E. F. Smith, Homewood, Ill.: Richard D. Irwin

Chelintsev, A. N. (1918), *Teoreticheskie osnovaniya organizatsii krest'yanskogo khozyaistva*, Khar'kov

Chelinstev, A. N. (1928), *Russkoe sel'skoe khozyaistvo pered revolyutsiei*, 2nd edn, Moscow

Galeski, Boguslaw (1972), *Basic Concepts of Rural Sociology*, Manchester: Manchester University Press

Harrison, Mark (1975), 'Chayanov and the economics of the Russian peasantry', *Journal of Peasant Studies*, 2, 4, pp. 389–417

Harrison, Mark (1977a), 'Resource allocation and agrarian class formation', *Journal of Peasant Studies*, 4, 2, pp. 127–61

Harrison, Mark (1977b), 'The peasant mode of production', *Journal of Peasant Studies*, 4, 4, pp. 328–31

Jevons, W. S. (1871), *The Theory of Political Economy*; New York: Kelley, 1970

Kosinsky, V. (1906), *K agrarnomu voprosu*, Odessa

Makarov, N. P. (1920), *Krest'yanskoe khozyaistvo i ego evolyutsiya*, Moscow

Maslov, Pavel (1930), *Perenaselenie russkoi derevni*, Moscow–Leningrad

Shcherbina, F. A. (1900), *Krest'yanskie byudzhety*, Voronezh

Studensky, G. A. (1927), *Ocherki sel'skokhozyaistvennoi ekonomii*, Moscow

11 Game against nature: theories of peasant decision-making*

Michael Lipton

The traditional, academically respectable positivist view of the method of the social sciences would be that we don't need theories of peasant decision. A positivist, whether in social or in physical science, wants to test whether a theory *works*, whether it is good at predicting; not whether a theory *explains*, whether its assumptions are right. The aim of the theory is to produce accurate predictions. A positivist points out that, once we have tested a theory, it tells us how confidently we can predict. Suppose our theory of peasant behaviour predicts that, ninety-five times out of a hundred, peasants will respond to a 5 per cent rise in guaranteed jute prices by increasing jute output by more than 8 per cent but less than 9 per cent. And suppose this is just what happens. Then the theory is a predictive success. It does not seem to need any theory of decisions to back it up. For the positivist, the assumptions about how the peasant decides do not matter much. Indeed it doesn't matter much if the theory assumes that the moon is made of green cheese. The proof of the theorizing is in the predicting.

We might well think that extreme positivism of this sort is intellectually unsatisfying and logically unsatisfactory. But we do not yet understand much about the motives for individual decisions in simple peasant communities. And we badly need to be able to predict the consequences of policy. The planner needs to know where to put his schools, his fertilizers and his price increases. So we might still admit that the positivist approach makes good sense as a guide to research method in the short run. Forecasts based on a single discipline – economics – *work* well enough; so why complicate matters with other disciplines? But there are, in my view, decisive objections to this positivist approach.

Let us look at some of these in the light of a theory of farming behaviour. This theory asserts that farmers act as if they used their

*This chapter is taken from the texts of two talks given by Michael Lipton on the BBC Third Programme in 1968.

resources so as to make as high a return as possible – that they maximize profit. This theory is neo-classical in the technical economic sense – it is a reversion to the accounts of producers' behaviour given by the great Cambridge economists, Marshall and Pigou, in the late nineteenth century. It is also neo-classical in a broader sense, in that it restates the traditional assumption that a social science such as economics can proceed without taking much account of other social sciences. But can it?

It has become almost conventional wisdom that social scientists must co-operate when they study simple communities, if they are to bridge the gap between pre-scientific description and post-scientific planning models. But people seldom spell out how and why they should co-operate. That leaves a gap in their reasoning, and the neo-classical reaction, which I have just described, exploits that gap. Thus economists, instead of co-operating with other social scientists in a woolly way, have tried to test the unlikely but precise proposition that a Kenyan or Indian peasant, even if he can't add up, knows how to maximize profits. Putting it more cautiously, the neo-classicist says 'our evidence of the way that peasants use resources is *consistent with* the hypothesis that he behaves *as if* he maximizes profit.'

Let us look at the argument that the peasant *does* maximize profits. Its limitations will help us to see why social scientists must co-operate in underdeveloped countries.

The argument is most succinctly presented by Professor Schultz in his book, *Transforming Traditional Agriculture*. He points out that many farmers in poor countries 'continue year after year to cultivate the same type of land, sow the same crops, use the same techniques of production and bring the same skills to bear'. In this environment, unchanging over the centuries even if disturbed by the occasional unpredictable drought or flood, farm families come to inherit almost totally efficient farming methods, according to Schultz. He thus argues that 'there are comparatively few significant inefficiencies in traditional agriculture.'

This conclusion, at once startling and plausible, rests partly on data collected by David Hopper in a single Indian village, Senapur. Hopper looks at the prices prevailing in Senapur, both for the various crops grown, and for the inputs used in farming – labour, land, irrigation water and bullock-time. He then asks: how much extra profit could farmers make by rearranging their use of labour, land, water or bullocks? And he answers: hardly any.

Now there are some counter-arguments, at the technical level, against Hopper's procedure. 'Hardly any extra profit' turns out to mean 'ten per cent'; some farm inputs, (like land and labour) vary together, their influences on output are hard to disentangle, so that Hopper's assumed production relations are bound to be somewhat arbitrary. But more important is the weakness of the basic positivist assumption: that if we can say 'the evidence is not inconsistent with the hypothesis that peasants act as if they maximized profit', it is almost as good as if we had tested a theory of decisions to show that profit maximizing really *is* the key to their behaviour.

It is this positivist assumption that allows Schultz to argue that governments, by tampering with traditional allocations of traditional farm resources, can do very little to raise farm output. True enough, if the peasant is already a maximizing Economic Man in the Henry Ford mould; but quite false if he merely *acts as if* he were a maximizer, *within* rigid constraints imposed by tradition, ignorance or the need to insure against risk; for a pure profit maximizer would already be attacking these hindrances to profit if he could. If he can't or won't, then social or religious or educational change can bring about a cumulative upward movement of the economic system in a village like Hopper's Senapur. And if we neglect these opportunities – if we consistently assume that *acting like* a maximizer, under crippling constraints, is as good as *being* a maximizer – then we shall conclude, quite wrongly, that here is little scope for helping peasants to improve their traditional tools and practices. We shall be forced to conclude that only big, expensive new investments can help. But if a man is maximizing his efficiency in washing his face with one hand tied behind his back, it is cheaper to untie his hand than to buy him a sponge.

What is the general lesson for the social scientist? The peasant, as a maximizer, is constrained by social, religious and educational factors. So perhaps our normal assumption, that economic and non-economic variables are independent, is weaker in poor and primitive farm communities than in the advanced industrial societies where both economists and sociologists usually work.

There are two reasons for this. First, several non-economic determinants of economic decisions – things such as literacy, freedom from dysentery, some knowledge of technical advice available in the nearest big towns – can be assumed for almost all decision-makers in a rich industrial community. These preconditions will not hold for every decision-maker in an Indian village, and the structure of his economic decisions *may* depend on whether the preconditions hold or not. In other words, economic differences among farmers acting as producers are likelier to correlate with non-economic factors in a primitive community than in an advanced community, simply because these factors are less uniform among farmers in the primitive community.

The second reason for the stronger link between economic and non-economic variables in poor communities is this. Suppose we know the degree of interdependence among economic variables like income, prices, and output. Now social changes are likely to play more havoc with our purely economic predictions in a primitive community than in an advanced community, because of the other side of the so-called 'vicious circle of poverty'. The vicious circle has several forms. Ragnar Nurkse has argued that income per person was low in poor countries, so people could not save, so they could not finance the extra capital needed to raise productivity and income. For example, the poor farmer must spend his time growing food to feed his family. He has no food left to sell to the town, so he cannot raise the cash to dig a well. Gunnar Myrdal has identified another vicious circle: this one depends on undernourishment, which inhibits hard work and thus keeps food output low and the farmer undernourished. There is yet another vicious circle: poor farmers lack personal assets and social security, so they are reluctant to make risky investments which would raise their output. So their output stays low and they stay unwilling to experiment. Now such vicious circles have their hopeful side. Give the economic system an upward push from outside and progress reinforces itself cumulatively through the social variables we have discussed, after the initial push – just as stagnation *maintained* itself before the push. Plainly all this weakens the case for treating social variables as if they lay completely outside the economic system; for a change in social variables can cumulatively alter economic behaviour.

This brings me to my recent field work, in an Indian village several hundred miles from Hopper's. I have suggested that we cannot explain Indian or African farming without a theory of decisions. If we make do with a hypothesis that peasants act as if they maximize profit, we beg the important questions about agricultural development. Now I will look at some theories of how farmers make decisions, against the background of the Indian village of Kavathe, where I recently spent a cropping season of seven months.

Kavathe consists of about 120 farm families, owning on average 4.5 acres each. Most families own their farms; sometimes they exchange labour with their neighbours. The main crop is millet. The village is near the Indian average for poverty, as well as for indicators of development such as irrigation and distance from the nearest big town, Poona, fifty miles away. About one in four adults in Kavathe can read – again near the Indian average. There is a school attended by most children from the ages of seven to twelve, and a dispensary five miles away. There are ten castes including Brahmins and Untouchables, but eighty of the 120 families belong to the main farming caste of the region, the Marathas.

Kavathe is fairly typical, if seven hundred people can typify India's four hundred million villagers. The farmers are shrewd, open, aware of why they farm their land as they do. But after the first few weeks, when I did not learn much because I was suspected of being a spy for the tax man, it became clear that the farmers of Kavathe are motivated by many other things than the search for profit.

There are three sorts of reason for saying this. First, the farmers accept constraints on their behaviour that reduce profit – and are not even required, either by law or by the moral code. Second, you might expect that the farmers' long experience of an unchanging environment had produced agreement on practices expected to get as much profit from the land as possible: in fact, there is agreement on some very bad practice indeed. Third, there is disagreement on important aspects of farming – even among farmers with similar resources.

A typical profit-reducing constraint in Kavathe, as in the entire Hindu and Moslem world, is the way land is inherited. Father wants all his sons to get some land, to insure them against the servile and insecure status of a landless labourer. But Father also wants to give each son a fair share of good land. So he splits his holding into several plots – some good and some bad for each son. After a few generations of this, each farmer's holding is a patchwork quilt of plots, too tiny to be ploughed or weeded efficiently. Plainly, the village needs to exchange plots. Yet the peasants don't do this for themselves – and it is not because of any moral attitude or legal statute. Land confers too much status and security for the peasant to take risks with it; and it is a huge risk to swap plots, even with a neighbour. Caste similarly constrains labour from moving to the best-paid job.

So much for constraints on profit maximizing. The second objection to excessive claims for the profit motive is that the farmers of Kavathe agree on practices that reduce profit – still the farmers heap up their manure, rather than taking time to make a proper compost pit, which would preserve the nitrogen in the manure. These heaps made sense thirty years ago, when the farmers of Kavathe learned their job. Then there was plenty of land for the cows to graze in, and therefore plenty of manure – but not enough labour to dig a pit. Nowadays, though, there is plenty of labour, but a shortage of land, and things like manure-heaps do not make sense any longer.

Another reason why the farmers of Kavathe persist in some practices that reduce profit lies in the quest for security. When sowing, most farmers mix their millet seed with bean-sprouts. These are not worth much, but they are very robust in the face of water shortage. If the peasants sowed only millet they would make more profit, averaging the good years with the years of poor rainfall; but in the dry years they would go very hungry indeed.

We have seen that a theory of peasant decisions needs to explain why peasants accept constraints that reduce profit, and why they agree on practices that don't maximize profit. We must also explain why farmers adopt different practices with similar resources of land and labour. For instance, on the soils of Kavathe it pays to sow less millet per acre when the soil is good, because the plants grow strongly, and may kill each other in the fight for space and light if they are sown too thickly. Yet only one farmer in six reduces the seed rate on good soil. Half make no change and one-third actually sow more seed per acre on good soils.

Decision-makers, like the farmers of Kavathe, are not as irrational as many people think. Any consistent theory of decisions must assume they are rational; but the rationale may be unfamiliar. For many years, economists have been unhappy with the familiar profit-maximizing interpretation of business behaviour; businessmen also want status, security and leisure. Why then is this old-fashioned interpretation of plain profit maximizing still applied to the Indian farmer?

There are two reasons. First, people see the peasant as a simple man taking simple decisions in a simple environment. But if we list the inputs, techniques and outputs among which he has to choose, and the ways in which his preference may be slanted among status, income, leisure and security, we see that the decision problem is as complicated for an Indian farmer as for a steel firm or even a national planner. Second, people jump out of the colonialist into the neo-classical frying pan; if the farmer isn't an unresponsive dud, it does not follow that he is maximizing profit.

Once we allow for security in our explanation of peasant behaviour, much of it falls into place. For instance, most Indian tenants.prefer to pay a big share of the crop as rent, rather than a more moderate, fixed cash-rent. Planners do not like share-rents; apart from cutting the peasant's profit, they eat into potential farm output. A tenant will not be keen to dig a well if half the extra crop goes to the landlord as share-rent. So why does the tenant go for share-rent? Because it insures him against bad harvests, by reducing his rent liability when output is low; and against a low price for his crop, because he does not need to sell it to raise cash to pay the rent. Once the planners see that the peasant needs insurance, they will understand his readiness to pay a high crop share. Then they can try to change it, perhaps by providing alternative means of security.

There is a general principle behind all models of peasant behaviour under uncertainty: the riskier a policy is, the less will be spent on it, even if it is a fair gamble. So a fifty-fifty chance of one thousand pounds or five hundred pounds is generally worth less than the certainty of seven hundred and fifty pounds. The poorer the gambler, and the bigger the gamble, the truer this is.

This suggests new models of Indian farm behaviour. Most of them derive from an exciting contribution to social science: the theory of games. In 1944 Neumann and Morgenstern analysed repeatable conflict situations, called 'plays' of a game, between two players, each with several strategies to choose from. Let us look at a typical example, the game of Matching Pennies. On each 'play' of this game, you and I each put down a penny. Each of us can choose whether to put it down heads or tails, but neither of us can see what the other does. If both pennies are heads, or both are tails, you win both pennies. If the pennies do not match, I win both pennies. Clearly I shall lose if I pick a 'pure' strategy, say heads, on all the plays. You will find out, match my strategy by picking heads too, and win all the time. So what is my best 'mixed strategy' – that is, my best sequence of heads and tails – in such a game? This trivial question has analogies in economic, social and even international behaviour.

Neumann and Morgenstern showed that such games always have a solution – a 'best strategy', and a calculable pay-off, for each player – if both players try to attain as high a security level as possible. Each player, then is mini-maxing – minimizing maximum loss, or maximizing minimum profit; making the most unfavourable outcome as acceptable as he can. There will always be some strategy to ensure this. For instance, in the game of Matching Pennies the mini-max strategy is for me to play heads half the time and tails the other half, and to choose which to pick on each play by some chance process of selection. That way I will win half the time and lose half the time. I minimize my maximum loss – at zero.

Now what on earth has this to do with the behaviour of an Indian peasant? Well, we can interpret his search for maximum security by saying that he is playing a game against nature. That is, he'll pick a combination of crops to maximize his minimum profit. Just like that fifty-fifty combination of heads and tails, the mini-maxing peasant might pick a forty-sixty combination of wheat and millet. Player and peasant both maximize security levels.

The anthropologist Davenport[1] visited a Jamaican fishing village, and found that the fishermen had two strategies. Either they could put all their fishing pots far out to sea, or they could put some of them in close to the shore. Nature also, as it were, had two strategies: a strong current and a weak current. When the current ran weakly, it paid to put some of the pots a long way out. When the current ran strongly, it paid to put all the pots in close to shore. This is just like the Matching Pennies game, and Davenport found a mini-max solution.

This theoretical maximum-security strategy was very close to what the fishermen actually did. The theory predicts that typically seventeen captains will be fishing inshore and nine will be fishing the in-out strategy; that means putting some of the pots inshore and some far out. Observation showed that, on a typical day, eighteen captains fished inshore and eight fished the in-out strategy. This is a good fit of theory to fact – better than that produced by profit-maximizing models.

Indian peasants are even closer to the margin of survival than Jamaican fishermen. So they need a great deal of extra profit prospects to make up for even a little extra risk. Mrs Das Gupta,[2] an economist, found out the various mixtures of crops which farmers could use in several poor Indian districts. She calculated the expected (or average) yearly profit and the risk for each mixture of crops, and discovered which crop mixture the farmers actually used. Most of the time they chose the mixture which gave them the greatest security level, even if they had to give up a lot of potential profit.

There is another sort of approach to the theory of decisions: learning theory. It derives from experiments to find out how people behave in the so-called binary choice situation. Suppose you have to guess whether the experimenter is going to shout out black or white. If you guess right you win a dollar; if you guess wrong you lose a dollar. After a while, you notice that the experimenter is calling black three-quarters of the time, white one-quarter of the time, but with no detectable pattern. So what do you do? Well, most people follow the experimenter's own strategy: that is, they call black three-quarters of the time and white one-quarter of the time, just like the experimenter. This so-called 'event matching' isn't a maximizing policy; a profit-maximizer would call black all the time, and thus win as often as possible, three-quarters of the time. True, the bigger the sum involved, the more people come over to this profit-maximizing approach. But most people most of the time are event matchers – even when the sums of money involved are quite large.

This non-maximizing behaviour almost makes one despair of the human species. However, there has been an ingenious attempt to explain it. Herbert Simon, a psychologist and mathematician, has suggested that businessmen do not maximize anything, but try to obtain a satisfactory outcome on several scales, including profit and security. Simon calls this 'satisficing'. It is based on a psychological rather than an economic model of man.[3]

Can this be brought back to my Indian village? Well, almost every farmer in Kavathe has discovered a set of rules to ensure survival: what I call a survival algorithm. That is, he has found a group of practices, a group of decisions about allocating farm resources, which allows him just tolerable levels of profit, security and status. This survival algorithm allows him to muddle through in good years and bad alike. Naturally he is reluctant to change it.

Can this explain the three sorts of behaviour which led us to question profit-maximizing explanations in Kavathe? The acceptance of apparently irrational constraints is a social survival mechanism for the village as a whole. Many of these constraints stem from the caste system, even when they are not directly enjoined by it. Caste provides a social ordering within the village; if sons do the same jobs as their fathers this cuts down the squabbling that would be linked to the job competition in a poor and status-conscious society. The caste system is not entirely inflexible. Any casteman may earn more money as a skilful farmer. But caste does provide order – and divides big villages into groups of castemen, small and loyal enough to help each other in emergency. No modern Indian would deny that the caste system does more harm than good. But he is comparing it with an ideal that which cannot be created overnight. Once the administrator realizes that the caste system represents a set of personal claims on order, security and mutual support for which there is at present no substitute, he will start to construct substitutes, actively promoting social security and contract law and so on. At present, even low-caste villagers accept the caste system as a least evil – part of a communal survival algorithm that is known to work, however badly.

Fear of disrupting this algorithm also explains why all villagers are reluctant to adopt some farming innovations. Just as the American businessman fights harder to raise his market share when it has been falling, so the Indian villager needs a big incentive to take risks with an allegedly improved practice, so long as the old practices he knows and trusts do not lead to an actual fall in living standards – and they have not.

The last aspect of apparent irrationality is the persistent difference in the ways that similar peasants deploy similar resources. This also makes sense as part of a learned and inherited survival algorithm, satisficing rather than maximizing. In any situation, only one group of practices can maximize profit. But many different groups of practices can give tolerable results. And if safe tolerable results are what each poor farmer is after, each set of practices, once found, will be highly stable.

This is partly because farming is so complicated. A farmer whose neighbour gets a higher output from similar resources, may know some of the practices where he differs from his neighbour. But there is likely to be a whole batch of practices which he adopts and his neighbour does not – and vice versa. If the farmer sticks to his own algorithm in some respects, but adopts bits and pieces of his neighbour's algorithm too, the result may be a disastrous mess.

We have been struggling free of the picture of the Indian peasant as stupid, irrational and so on. The first extreme reaction was to a hardly more lifelike picture of him as a profit maximizer. There are several ways to get beyond this – game theory, learning theory, satisficing, and so on. To choose among them, we need experimental psychologists, skilled in interviewing and testing illiterates, to find out how and why villagers take farming decisions. The notion of a survival algorithm suggests that such a study would find a number of 'satisficing' groups of farmers. The groups would have stable and distinct decisions procedures, leading to stable and distinct farm practices. Distinct, because reflecting a particular set of preferences among security, profit and status. Stable, because established from long experience as giving the best chance of survival in conformity with each set of preferences. When a planner in India or Africa tries to improve farm practices, he should look for the preferences that make one group of farmers good at ploughing, another group good at weeding, and so on. The search for an all-round paragon, 'the progressive farmer', is too crude to succeed. Tested decision theories can refind it – and, in the process, advance both interdisciplinary social science and underdeveloped farming.

Notes

1   Davenport (1963).
2   Das Gupta (1966).
3   cf. the findings of Cyert and March that US firms give up profit, to raise market share, only in so far as that share has been falling.

References

Das Gupta, S. (1966), 'Oil prices in the Indian Market, 1886–1964', unpublished Ph.D thesis, London School of Economics and Political Science

Davenport, W. (1963), 'Jamaican fishing: a game theory analysis', in C. Mintz (ed.), *Yale Contributions to Caribbean Anthropology*, New Haven, Conn.: Yale University Press

12 Production conditions in Indian agriculture*

Krishna Bharadwaj

Introduction

It is not surprising that problems relating to agriculture have occupied a prominent place in discussions of the Indian economy. However, most analytical discussions in the area of 'agricultural economics' have been set out, explicitly or implicitly, as extensions of the conventional economic theory in terms of competitive markets. The researcher has yielded much too easily to the temptation of treating the cultivator and his problems of resource acquisition and utilization on the analogy of the producer of a competitive firm. Such analogies give rise to some awkward problems, for example, in handling owned inputs like family labour or owned land. Attempts to impute market prices to such inputs have resulted in the majority of cultivators showing up net losses. This has baffled the theorists and has led to such controversies as whether it is the imputation of wages to family labour or of rent to owned land that is responsible for such a result! Even when the researcher recognizes the inadequacy or irrelevance of such specific assumptions like profit-maximization or mobility of resources guided by freely fluctuating market prices, he is prone to tinkering with only those specific parts of the competitive model, keeping undisturbed the rest of the framework, rather than face the challenge at a more fundamental level of concepts, categories and the nature of economic relationships. Thus what emerges is a product of manipulating, relaxing or restricting one or more assumptions. For example, the complex nexus of socio-economic conditions that underlies the phenomenon of underutilization of agricultural labour force (the so-called 'disguised unemployment') gets neatly and elegantly summarized into a single consequence for the theory – the perfectly elastic horizontal supply curve of labour. Another attempt likewise partially to reformulate the

*This chapter is taken from Bharadwaj (1974), pp. 1–14, 18, part of ch. 7 and the summing up.

model of the agrarian economy treating it as a departure from the competitive framework is made by introducing imperfections (in the form of monopoly or monopsony elements) in specific markets while the other markets continue to enjoy their well-behaved competitive status.

The analytical challenge, however, emanates importantly from the rich variety and complexity of institutional forms manifested in the conditions of production in agriculture. The agrarian economy which is in the process of a gradual transformation is characterized by the co-existence and interaction of multiple modes of production. The analytical complexities which arise cannot be handled as deviations from or imperfections of a competitive economy. Even the treatment of production conditions as mere production 'activities' – each producing unit characterized as a sort of a black box turning inputs into outputs – is not merely restrictive but it positively hinders a meaningful understanding of a concrete situation. Property relations between individuals involved in production activity are an integral part of production relations as are the technical characteristics of production. These property relations are particularly complicated in semi-feudal agriculture where power is exercised through privilege as much as through markets.

The complexity of the network of market relations that characterizes such an economy becomes evident when we note some of the peculiar features of agrarian markets which violate the competitive premises. Under the competitive framework while markets are interlinked, this is so only through prices.[1] Each producer decides on the use of a resource – owned or purchased – by treating its market price as an opportunity cost. In the long run, each producer has open to him the possibility of buying or selling any particular resource in indefinite amounts at the prevailing price. Under a regime of complete mobility of resources and profit maximization, with a well-behaved technology, every resource will have, in equilibrium, the same marginal value productivity in all uses, which will equal the market price of the resource. The market does not discriminate between producers, and decisions of the participants in the market are thus linked by the purely impersonal forces of pricing. Each producer decides on the basis of relative prices and his own budgetary constraint what best to produce and how. The point to note however is that any choice made by him in one market (factor or product) does not directly influence the field of *feasible* choices open to him in any other market.

Discussions pertaining to production decisions in Indian agriculture have mainly been within the context of such a framework. To cite common research endeavour: production functions, popularly of the Cobb–Douglas variety, expressing output as a function of land, labour and material inputs, are fitted to cross-sectional data on holdings. Comparisons are then made between the marginal productivities of inputs derived from such fitted functions (generally valued at the geometric mean level of inputs) and the market prices of the respective inputs in order to draw out inferences about efficiency with which resources are utilized.

Some characteristics of agrarian market relations

The competitive assumptions are violated in a fundamental way in an agrarian economy in which the *extent* of market penetration, as also the *character* of markets, is very different. We may briefly mention here some of the crucial features that differentiate the agrarian markets. The point to note is that while markets have penetrated into the rural economy in a deep and significant manner, the extent and *type* of involvement in markets of the different sections of the peasantry are not at all uniform. The character of markets reflects and to a significant extent is determined by the local patterns of power. At the same time, the functioning of the markets is itself such as to reinforce the pattern of power. The situation may broadly be sketched as follows: the initial resource position defines the 'bargaining' position[2] of the participants in the various markets. The relative 'bargaining strength' (reinforced by forces of tradition, custom, social mores) determines the access to resources, the terms on which they can be obtained and the fields of feasible choices open to the individual producer in the various markets or, in short, his current production activities and his income and asset position resulting therefrom. This, in turn, influences his relative 'bargaining' position in the succeeding period.

We may distinguish, broadly speaking, three types of market involvements that may emerge, depending upon the economic position of the participant. There is, first, the category of operators with a clearly dominant 'bargaining' position like the big landlord in the land (lease) market or the money lender in the credit market. These operators are powerful enough to be able to exploit the market from a position of vantage and, more importantly, are able to shape the character of the market relations themselves through contracts which interlock markets (discussed below). Second, we can envisage the category of the economically very weak sections of the peasantry, landless agricultural labourers, very small owners or tenants, all of whom have an extremely weak 'bargaining' position in the markets. Yet they cannot avoid involving themselves in market operations. As they do not have enough land to cultivate, they have to depend upon hiring out their labour and hence submit to the vagaries of the labour market. Given the uncertainty of employment they often prefer to lease in a tiny plot of land even on extremely onerous conditions. Not having enough circulating capital to produce even their subsistence they have to rely on credit, thus depending precariously upon the credit market. The higher degree of monetization of inputs and outputs on very small farms indicates this element of compulsive involvement in markets, reflecting conditions of distress. The third category of peasants falls somewhere between these two; while not powerful enough to exploit markets like the large operators, they can be somewhat more self-reliant than the landless or very small farmers and may be able to protect themselves from markets if they turn unfavourable. They have (or can make provision for) adequate circulating capital, possess bullocks and implements of their own with some holding capacity over market supplies of output.

The economic status of the cultivating households influences the degree of land utilization, the cropping pattern, the level of employment and so on. For example, given the nature of the labour market employment on and off farm may not be treated as independent of each other and this, in turn, affects both land utilization (intensity of cultivation as well as the cropping pattern) and the level of employment. Dependence on the purchase of circulating capital and hence the need for cash resources may influence the cropping pattern on very small holdings. Given the superior bargaining position of the big landlord, he may choose to parcel out land – especially when irrigated – to the very small tenants, who in turn, will be compelled by economic necessity to cultivate their small plots intensively, applying owned inputs (particularly labour) far beyond the point of maximum net return. The landlord by so parcelling out land may be in a position to extract a maximum return.

It may be argued that the differential bargaining positions of the participants in any particular market may be fitted into the conventional models of monopoly or monopsony. What does complicate the analysis, however, is the fact that markets become interlocked through price and non-price links, given that market and social power is vested in the dominant rural classes and that the dominant party often combines multiple functions, thus enjoying a superior position simultaneously in a number of markets. When a landlord combines the functions of a lessor and a merchant, the terms of the lease are not only themselves quite stringent (given his position *vis-à-vis* the tenants in the lease market) but quite often include stipulations as to what crops the tenant ought to grow and the mode as well as terms of payment of rent. For instance, he can dictate the rent to be paid in kind and the time of payment. Thus the tenant's involvement in the lease market restricts his freedom to exercise choice in production (in terms of crops to be grown) and in the output market (to whom and when to sell the produce). If the landlord also possesses land under personal cultivation it is not unusual for him to extract underpaid or unpaid services from the tenant (or his dependents) on his own land. Similarly a moneylender-cum-merchant may extract a very high own rate of interest by giving commodity loans and stipulating suitable conditions on time and terms of repayment in kind. Again the weaker position of the borrower imposes limitations on the opportunities to phase his sales of output over time. Such interlocking of markets increases the exploitative power of the stronger sections because, while there could be limits to exploitation in any one market – due to traditions or conventions – or due to economic factors, the interpenetration of markets allows them to disperse exploitation over the different markets and to phase out exploitation over time as well. Thus there may be a traditional or conventional limit beyond which a landlord cannot exploit his monopoly position in land market in terms of the share of output owing to him under a crop-sharing system. Also, he may possibly fear that if the tenant is left with too small a share at any time, he may not put in as much of his own (labour or other) inputs as he would under slightly more favourable conditions. If the landlord also enjoys monopoly advantages as a moneylender or a merchant, he could then so work out the conditions of tenure that he secures gains from exploiting the tenant in the conjoint markets. Thus the ability of the combined functionary to exploit in interlocked markets is more than what he could achieve operating in any one individual market.

Furthermore, we cannot presume that all the operators are profit-maximizers irrespective of their economic status. In fact we may not even presume that there are objectives of production defined *a priori* and uniformly applicable to all producers. The objectives of production themselves depend upon the economic status of the operator and different operators may presumably maximize (if maximization is a universally applicable behavioural premise at all) profits or gross output, or 'farm business income' (i.e. gross revenue net of actually paid out cost); some may be governed by the need to raise mainly subsistence foods. We have observed, for example, that the very small operators who live in almost perpetual indebtedness may choose to raise as much gross value of output as possible per acre, even at the cost of having to incur debts to provide circulating capital; they may operate land intensively even to a point where the additional input costs are more than the value of additional output. On the other hand, the big cultivators, while aiming to produce a surplus, may yet prefer not to cultivate the land intensively for a number of reasons, including the existence of opportunities for making profits or for wielding social power through non-farming activities.

These are only illustrative examples to indicate that, to be meaningful, an analysis of an agrarian economy would have to be conducted within this wider context of market and non-market relations with the peculiar interlocking of markets. It is misleading when talking about individual operators, to hypothesize that each producer confronts technical data and market prices in an impersonal environment and all are equally free to take decisions in all markets. Nor is it possible to analyse the producer's behaviour in any one single market without knowing how the markets are interlinked by price and non-price relations for the fields of *feasible* choices in the different markets are not, as assumed under competition, definable *a priori* independently of each other. Detailed information in a historical, specific context about the agrarian economy under study would be required to describe the particular characteristics of its markets, the nature and extent of the involvement of the different sections of its peasantry and the implications thereof.

The factual basis and the aim of this chapter

With growing empirical investigations into agriculture, more detailed observations on its various aspects are becoming available for the research scholar to interpret in the light of his theory and, more importantly, to use to examine the validity and relevance of his theories and models when applied to specific situations. Many controversial ideas and concepts that have preoccupied development theorists like 'surplus labour', 'production and resource allocational efficiencies', are being confronted with specific observations. The data base is as yet neither sturdy nor comprehensive, partly because of the difficulties of organizing and financing data collection on a vast scale. This apart, however, there are problems connected with the nature of data themselves. As is to be expected, the form in which data are collected and presented as well as the variables on which data collection is focused cannot be viewed as neutral to the theoretical predilections of those who provide the data nor of those who use them. Given the issues on which agro-economists have been particularly engaged, the enquiries – as is illustrated by the Farm Management Surveys studies here – have concentrated chiefly on the question of technological input-output relations in agriculture. Partly due to the nature of data, their coverage, emphasis and presentation, the question which attracted by far the most intense discussion following the publication of the *Studies on the Economics of Farm Management* was the relation between farm size and productivity (namely, the alleged inverse statistical relation between yield per acre and size of holding). No doubt the question was deemed important for policy formulation, the planners emphasizing the problem of increasing output more than any other aspect of agriculture. This issue has considerable political implications as well.[3] Another area of research that received stimulus was the question of efficiency of resource allocation in agriculture, efficiency being defined in terms of factor rewards equating their respective marginal value products.

The purpose of this paper is much less ambitious than the preceding discussion may suggest. In fact, the allusion to wider issues is included partly to forewarn readers against the very limitations of this paper which is only a small step in the construction of a broader analytical framework. The limitation of the scope and of analysis primarily inheres in the empirical material it employs. We have employed here the empirical information available in the published *Studies in the Economics of Farm Management* (henceforth referred to as FMS) carried out in two selected districts in each of the six states, Bombay, Madhya Pradesh (both presently in

Maharashtra), Punjab, West Bengal, Madras and Uttar Pradesh, during the period 1954 to 1957. As mentioned already these studies emphasize the technological input-output relations and this bias, together with rather scanty information on other aspects of production, especially on property relations and on incomes originating from activities other than crop production and animal husbandry, impose severe limitations on carrying out a comprehensive and more meaningful analysis in terms of market characteristics and market involvements of different groups of peasantry. Bearing this in mind, what we have attempted in this paper is the following – although fully conscious of the limitations of treating questions such as utilization and productivity of individual inputs or of considering particular markets in isolation, we have taken this oft-beaten, conventional route. The aim in doing so is twofold: first, to see how far some of the hypotheses currently advanced in the literature are borne out by reference to the empirical data and to indicate the difficulties, if any, at a conceptual or interpretational level that may arise in applying certain of the basic premises that are explicit or implicit in such formulations; second, to bring out how the observations concerning these partial facets of the overall picture are not inconsistent with (or could be employed as the building blocks for) a more comprehensive view in terms of the unequal and diverse nature of market involvement of the different groups of cultivators arising from their position in the nexus of the agrarian economic power structure. The focus, given the nature of the FMS data, is on the farm size and productivity relations. After a close look at the debate concerning holding-size and land productivity, we conclude that the intensity of cultivation and the cropping pattern are the two most important factors explaining the tendency of the value productivity per acre to decline with an increase in farm size. These are not new results. However, in the course of our argument we indicate how the specific resource availability, the characteristics of the labour market affecting labour utilization (a significant factor in explaining intensity of cultivation) and the interlocked nature of markets constraining the area of feasible choices may be influencing decisions concerning intensity of cultivation and the cropping pattern themselves.

FMS: sampling design and coverage

The FMS adopted in their survey a multi-stage stratified random sampling procedure with villages as the primary unit and the holdings as the ultimate unit. In each state (or region) two contiguous districts were first selected representing the typical soil-complex of the region. Each district was subdivided into two fairly homogeneous zones on the basis of agricultural and climatic conditions and the villages were then selected at random with probability proportion to the cultivating population. The ultimate unit of the enquiry was the 'operational holding' comprising all the land cultivated by the selected farmer irrespective of location or ownership. The selection of holding was arrived at after ranking the holdings in each village in ascending (or descending) order according to their size. The total number of holdings was then divided into five size-groups, each containing an equal number. From each such group, holdings were selected with equal probability.

Limitations of the data

The information concentrates on input-output or technical relations in agriculture, and other aspects of production receive much less emphasis. This is reflected, first, in the rather non-discriminating, uni-dimensional, purely quantitative information that we obtain on, say, irrigation or tenancy.

A particular feature of the published FMS reports that may, to a certain extent, bias our results is that they present information as aggregated into size-groups of holdings. Such aggregation is bound to affect some results more than others. Classifying and presenting information on the basis of size-groups of holdings implicitly assumes that the characteristics of farms under study depend predominantly upon their belonging to a certain size-group. To the extent that they do not, by pooling together the information about the individual holdings falling within a single size-group, the variations in their traits will be lost, as what one gets is an average figure for the group as a whole.

It must be noted that the years under consideration, 1954-7, are prior to the emergence of the so-called 'green revolution' in India. It is likely that production relations may change significantly in their technical aspects as well as in terms of property relations. For example, the holding-size-productivity relations discussed here might alter. The new technology based on the use of improved seeds, improved techniques, on well-regulated and adequate supply of irrigation, etc., even if scale-neutral might benefit the bigger operators to a greater extent. They may be in a favourable position to exploit the new opportunities with their relatively easier access to credit and perhaps also to the essential but scarce and costly inputs like hybrid seeds, fertilizers, improved techniques of irrigation. Furthermore, with investment in agriculture turning out to be a profitable enterprise, the patterns of land-leases might alter; possibly, large owners may gradually shift towards capitalist farming relying on the use of hired labour rather than parcel out their land to petty tenants.

Land use and productivity

The inverse relation between yield per acre and size of holding

Discussions following the publication of the FMS have mainly centred around questions of productive efficiency. The one proposition which attracted considerable notice and has continued to recur in discussion is the alleged inverse relationship between yield (i.e. value of output) per acre and the size of holding. Even if such an inverse relation holds, based as it is on a static, cross-sectional comparison, it does not provide a sufficient basis to judge the relative potentialities of the different size-groups nor to predict the future patterns of size distribution that might emerge. Also, the comparison of productive efficiency is based on the productivity of an isolated input, land, thus treating it implicitly as the only limitational input. Despite these limitations, the 'inverse' relation acquired some significance as it could provide some rationale for arguing that the small farms were superior to large ones on 'purely economic' grounds. A double-edged conclusion, it could be employed, on the one hand, to support land reforms purporting to redistribute land into smaller units and, on the other, as an argument against pooling of lands into larger units. Although the political implications of the findings have not always surfaced in the debates, they possibly account for the fervour the question has generated.

There has been substantial controversy over the 'inverse relationship'. Our results for the aggregated data relating to the individual districts and for individual years between 1954 and 1957 show that in the majority of cases there appears to be an inverse relationship. However, it is not statistically significant in all cases. Although the inverse relation is not altogether unexceptionally supported, it is not yet conclusively rejected either and it may not be entirely speculative to look into explanations that have already been advanced and attempt to advance others. In fact, to draw the correct implications for purposes of analysis as well as policy formulation, it is necessary to search for factors that may explain the relatively higher value-productivity on smaller holdings as compared with the larger ones. An adequate explanation of the phenomenon would also help in assessing future possibilities – whether productivity differentials are a characteristic that could persist, making the small peasant family farms a historically viable form and perhaps even relatively a more efficient one, or whether the relative advantage rests on a specific conjuncture, subject to change and hence of a temporary nature.

Some suggested explanations

Explanations that have been advanced so far fall into one or the other of three categories: (a) differences in techniques; the small holders using technically superior methods of production (b) qualitative differences in factor endowments; either land or labour on smaller farms is intrinsically of a superior quality (c) more intensive application of other co-operant inputs like labour, bullock power or irrigation. These are not mutually exclusive analytical categories. The overlap is particularly evident when one tries to identify them empirically. Thus, if 'technique' is merely identified with a vector of inputs, then the distinction between (a) and (c) vanishes, for 'more' intensive application of inputs to land is, by definition, a different technique. To avoid this we may here interpret 'technique' as associated with a particular type of productive equipment, and hence differences in techniques as different types of productive equipment in operation. Attitudinal differences (such as diligence and interest in work) between small and large farm-operators, if present, should be ultimately reflected in one or the other of these factors. Whether the difference is in matters of risk-taking or entrepreneurial ability, it should ultimately reflect itself either in the adoption or otherwise of better techniques of production or in willingness or otherwise to apply inputs intensively. Similarly quality of management would reflect itself in (a) or (c) and while these attitudinal and behavioural factors could at best by hypothesized as underlying forces the proximate factors with which productivity can be linked will be the ones recorded under (a), (b) and (c). If higher value productivity on small farms could be ascribed to superior techniques, it would be correct to assert that the small peasant households are progressive and the relevant question about the future possibilities would be whether their relative advantage would continue in the context of techno-logical changes within any specified time horizon. If it is due to qualitatively superior inputs, the question to raise would be about the process that explains the concentration of the better-quality inputs on the small farms and whether this process would be expected to continue. If, on the other hand, the explanation is to be found in greater utilization of other inputs, the question is whether and in what sense it constitutes an efficient use of resources and what explains the unequally efficient input-combin-ation on farms in different size-groups.

If 'superior technique' is to be interpreted as better-quality or technologically advanced inputs, the present FMS data do not favour the smaller operators on that ground. If anything 'modern' equipment, which in these years made little headway in any case, is concentrated on larger holdings. There is, however, a stronger statistical ground for questioning the 'superior technique' hypothesis. Taking the per acre yields (in physical units) of individual crops, we carried out regression exercises to test the inverse relation between yield per acre and size of holding. The results show that in a majority of cases there is no significant or systematic relation between yield per acre and the size of holdings. In some cases such a relation shows up only in parts and over some size-groups, but the fact that it is not systematic should warn us against hasty generalization on the basis of linear regressions. Moreover, in the majority of cases there is no systematic and significant relation at all. There are some cases (Punjab, particularly in the case of irrigated wheat grain and American cotton) where, in fact, we note a significant positive relation between yield per acre and size of holding. If indeed the smaller holdings were characterized by 'superior technique' it should have been reflected in a productivity advantage in the case of individual crops as well. That it is not, goes against this hypothesis.

Our result concerning individual crops raises the problem of reconciling these results with the inverse relation which does not appear to be ruled out when the total yield in value terms is considered. The explanation may be found in the smaller operator's use of crop mixes and/or intensive use of land in the form of double cropping (measured by the ratio of *gross* cropped area to *net* cropped area) such that he derives a higher gross yield *per acre* on his holding. In the case of individual crops, the area actually sown is reckoned so that the intensity of cropping cannot enter into productivity comparisons. The fact that, in the case of the total *value* of crops the inverse relation weakens when productivity is measured per gross cultivated acre rather than per net acre, suggests that higher intensity of cropping on smaller farms is a contributory factor. However, as we shall see below, differences in the intensity of cultivation over farm sizes are not sufficient to explain the relationship. And the cropping pattern (a relatively greater proportion of land devoted to more lucrative crops on smaller farms) appears to be contributing to the phenomenon.

Cropping pattern and intensity of land use

It emerges from our analysis that qualitative differences in inputs, so far as they exist, would be most predominantly reflected in the cropping pattern and intensive use of land. To the extent that quality of land is not a perennial attribute, the 'quality differences' hypothesis is not entirely satisfactory; one has yet to answer the question why the large operators do not undertake quality augmenting productive investments. The differences in value productivity thus finally boil down to differences in intensity of land-use and cropping pattern. Here, we note that the intensity of land use generally, though not systematically or in all cases, varies inversely with the size of holdings. It does in Punjab and U.P. where the percentage area irrigated is generally high for the region as a whole. The relation between intensity of cropping and size of holding is inverse although not systematic in the two districts of Bombay (Ahmednagar and Nasik). In the case of Madhya Pradesh, there is no variation over size classes worth noting – in fact double cropping is almost negligible on all farm sizes. In West Bengal and Madras intensity of cropping is higher on smaller size-groups than on the larger, although the inverse tendency is not systematic. Apart from intensive land use, cropping patterns also contribute to the relative higher value productivity on smaller farms. Intensive use of land, in turn, involves the application of other inputs to land. We shall now discuss factors influencing the cropping patterns adopted by the cultivator.

Cropping pattern and the size of holding

The cropping pattern, along with intensity of cropping, may explain a number of relations observed between input uses (and productivity) and the average size of holding which appear to hold for total crop production but fail to do so at the level of individual crops. We have referred to the various resource constraints (or specific resource availabilities) which operate on different size-classes of holdings. There is a two-way relation between resources at the disposal of, or accessible to, a cultivator and his position in the factor and output markets of the rural economy: his initial resource constraints determine for him his bargaining position in the land and credit market (e.g. the terms on which he can lease in or lease out land and secure credit or loan out funds); they also determine his dependence on hiring in or out of labour or on purchase of other inputs. On the other hand his past and current involvements in market operations influence his production decisions and, through these, his future resource availabilities.

The economic status of the cultivator and his position in the nexus of relations also define for him the objectives he sets himself to achieve. There are no motivational forces which are definable *a priori* for any operator independently of the entire gamut of production and market relations in which he is involved. Thus it is futile to reduce all operators to profit maximizers, drawing upon the analogy of capitalist producers in a competitive market economy. For a large number of cultivators, profit in this sense is not the relevant category at all. Total returns (including wages for family labour, rents on owned land), i.e. gross output netted for paid out costs, may be more relevant. When the cultivator cannot even make both ends meet, it may not be the net returns but the gross yield which he seeks to maximize with the burden of debt allowed to accumulate. The 'motivational' forces at play are extremely complex and not enough research has yet gone into unravelling them.

Categories of cultivators

Relying on the limited information here available, we present a rather over-simplified categorization of cultivators into 'very small', 'small', 'middle' and 'large' which may be useful to focus on the conditions of production that are particular to these different groups. (The landless are not included here as the FMS covers farm operators). The very small farmers are, in their economic status, not far removed from the landless labourers as they too are dependent upon hiring out labour. Our discussion of cropping patterns in relation to individual regions will broadly identify these groups for the region concerned. They cannot be identified precisely given the nature of the information we have and will vary in terms of the size range of holding from region to region, so that our general discussion does not specify the size range for each group.

The 'very small' cultivators possess very little land relative to the available family labour and depend upon hiring out labour to supplement their income from land. The landless who lease-in a tiny piece of land in search of some secure income fall into this category as well. Very often they possess no bullocks and have to hire their services for payment or in exchange for labour. They have quite often to purchase seeds; the gross output of the previous harvest may only just cover or even fall short of family consumption. Also, if they have debt liabilities, the output or a part of it may have to be disposed of soon after harvest for debt repayments. Quite often, they are compelled to raise consumption loans or even loans to provide circulating capital on onerous terms of repayment – the own rate of interest on such loans turn out to be very high. The rates of hire, whether of bullock, labour or equipment, work out, on an average, higher for the very small farmers. We calculated the per hired day rate for bullock labour by the number of bullock days and found it to be higher on the very small holdings. This was the case with human labour too. Even small holdings hire in casual labour for specific operations or in peak seasons. The explanation for the higher rate for both could be that during peak seasons when the very small farmers hire in these services, the rates are higher than at other times. With regard to labour, another reason could be the somewhat specialized nature of the operations for which labour may have to be hired. Furthermore, there could be diseconomies of buying inputs in smaller quantities. The dependence of this class on the market for providing circulating capital is reflected in the index of monetization of inputs (proportion of inputs purchased). The dependence on cash expenditure is very high in their case. It declines for the holdings in the next highest size-classes and picks up again on the large holdings. The higher index of monetization of the large holdings is qualitatively a different phenomenon from that on the very small ones. While in the former case it reflects a higher degree of commercialization of production, in the latter it is more a reflection of the distress conditions under which production is carried out and market involvement assumes a compulsive character.

Given their higher availability of family labour relative to land, it may be expected that these small farms will concentrate on the relatively more labour-absorbing crops. The intensity of cultivation is higher on these holdings which means that their bullock use per acre is not lower as compared with others, and that they have to hire in a substantial part of it, if not the entire amount. Given their resource base, they are severely constrained by the need to raise cash resources even in order to keep the cycle of production going. This may explain why farmers in this group are seen to allocate a higher proportion of their area to more lucrative (i.e. yielding higher gross revenue per acre) although risky, cash crops, especially if the crops (like jute, groundnuts) require a high labour input per acre and do not require any specific investments in equipment, etc. Also it is quite often possible to get more credit more easily for cash crop production on the condition of repayment in kind. Land can be more easily leased-in and circulating capital or a part of it borrowed from the landlord on a contract to raise a cash crop on the farm. For example, in West Bengal, the FMS reports that the holdings which produced cash crops *only* (constituting only one per cent of the total number of holdings) were concentrated in the very small size-groups. Our analysis of cropping patterns, separately for individual regions, brings out a similar feature of the cropping pattern in other regions as well. Part of the food requirements of the family may be earned as wage income since labour is hired out and wages are quite often paid in kind, and in any case, food crops may not yield the high rate of gross revenue per acre that cash crops do. Of course there is a greater risk attached to lack of self-sufficiency in food. But given the tiny size of the holding, and given that even to raise the food crop he has to finance circulating capital through loans which he has to repay immediately after the harvest so that he may not be able to provide for consumption in the following periods, the operator has to depend on market purchases or on consumption commodity loans to feed the family through the year.

The next group of 'small farmers' (with somewhat larger holdings) is also characterized by relatively higher availability of family labour. They are less dependent upon the purchase of operational inputs (as reflected in the lower extent of monetization of inputs) than the very small farmers and hence are under somewhat less pressure to raise cash resources. Employment outside the farm is much lower in their case and they raise more of the subsistence food crops on the farm using family labour to cultivate the land.

The next group of bigger holdings which may be called 'middle', are somewhat more self-sufficient in terms of bullock labour, seed requirements, equipment etc.; they have a higher level of irrigation than the 'large' holdings and generally produce a surplus over subsistence. We have attempted to measure the 'technical efficiency' of different size-classes of holdings in terms of an index based on multiple inputs. We find that the 'middle' group of holdings are 'technically' more efficient in the sense defined there; namely, under certain assumptions, they can be seen to be employing input combinations closer to the 'technically minimum combinations' for given output levels. They produce a crop-mix which covers a larger variety of crops; these are mainly food crops, but the more lucrative ones. These crops, like vegetables, require considerable care in weeding, sowing, transplanting, etc. Unlike the first two groups of holdings – 'very small' and 'small' – where dependence on the market appears to be primarily a by-product of providing consumption requirements for the family (thus one could roughly characterize it as 'production for consumption' as distinguished from 'production for the market'), the middle farmers are producing, at least in part, for the market. Not all of the disposal of their output occurs under conditions of distress, at least during periods of normal climatic conditions.

The 'large' holdings produce for the market, i.e. to raise a surplus. In poorly irrigated regions the 'large' holdings have, on an average, a lower level of irrigation than the smaller groups. Intensity of cultivation is much lower. They do not depend totally upon hired labour – family labour continuing to play an important role – although the proportion of hired to family labour is higher in their case. Many of the large holdings, too, showed losses in the years under study when all costs were imputed, suggesting that perhaps even the large holdings do not strictly aim at profit-maximization (or do not at least succeed in achieving it). A reason that may be suggested (not on the grounds of internal evidence in the FMS however) and which appears to be a reasonable hypothesis is that, for the large landowner, cultivation happens to be only one source of income. His position as a large landowner in the rural economy with the powers and privileges that accrue, places him in a favourable position to extract incomes from other activities – like money-lending. The lower level of asset formation, irrigation and productive investment in general goes hand-in-hand with the low degree of labour-hire on these holdings. Investment on farm does not appear to be favoured, especially in sparsely irrigated areas. The large holdings in these poorly irrigated areas thus appear to economize on hired labour by concentrating on crops that use less labour. They also have a lower level of irrigation compared to that on smaller farms and therefore produce the sturdier varieties of cereals which can better stand climatic variations. A very small proportion of the area, or none, is devoted to the more lucrative food crops (vegetables, fruits, etc.), possibly, in part, because these require careful management of labour. Also, given the rather austere and low level of consumption which is found to prevail in the regions of poor irrigation, their marketability constitutes an additional problem. Inadequacy of preservation and transport facilities make their production for a distant market and on a large scale additionally risky.

The situation appears to change quite significantly in the case of the better irrigated regions like Punjab and UP. With land better irrigated and risks in cultivation diminished, the area under cash crops (like American cotton in Punjab and sugarcane in UP) is seen to be quite high on the large holdings, signficantly so in the case of Punjab. The intensity of cultivation shows, however, a significant inverse relation to size of holding, declining sharply on large holdings. This probably explains the significant inverse relation between value productivity per acre and the size of holding found in Punjab despite the predominance of higher value cash crops on large holdings. The relatively lower level of irrigation on these holdings and the relatively higher wage rate in the region which discourages hire of labour, may partly explain the low intensity of cultivation. With new technology inputs like fertilizers, mechanized implements, tubewell irrigation, hybrid seeds, etc., this situation may possibly change.

Summing up

We took up earlier the familiar debate on the 'inverse relation' between yield per acre and size of holding. Arguing from purely technological relations, we concluded that this inverse relation may be attributed to differences in intensity of cultivation and in cropping patterns – the smaller holdings generally cultivating land more intensively and/or producing crops of greater value per acre. This conclusion is by no means original or striking although in the current literature on the subject, cropping pattern has not received much attention. Our emphasis on these two factors, especially cropping pattern, is derived partly from a recurrent finding that a technical relation between input use (or productivity) and size of holding which appears to find support at the level of total crop production activity, fails to do so for individual crops. Intensity of cultivation and cropping pattern, we suggest, are in turn influenced by particular characteristics of markets (for both inputs and outputs), by the resource position of the individual operator and by the nature and extent of his involvement in these markets.

We tried to classify the cultivators into four categories – namely, 'very small', 'small', 'middle' and 'large'. This classification is based on the nature of their market involvement which is in turn determined by their initial resource position. We discussed the factors influencing the crop pattern of each of these groups of farmers. For example, we noted that the very small farmers who are compulsively involved in markets tend to devote a higher proportion of their area to cash crops while the small farmers who can to some extent protect themselves from markets tend to produce predominantly subsistence crops. The middle cultivators, who can secure some surplus over subsistence, appear to produce a variety of crops including crops of high value requiring careful management (like vegetables), while big farmers have a different pattern in sparsely irrigated areas as compared with the better irrigated areas like Punjab and UP. In the former, they concentrate on the sturdier but low-valued crops, while in the latter they devote a considerable proportion of their area to high-value cash crops.

Before attempting prediction or the drawing out of prescriptive inferences, it is necessary to devise suitable categories in terms of which the inter-relations within the economy may be worked out. It appears to us that a meaningful analysis of a changing agrarian economy could be carried out by studying the process of its commercialization. This process can itself be described in terms of the extent and nature of the market involvement of different groups of peasantry, the interlocked character of markets, and the way in which the power relations in the rural economy are reflected in, and are influenced by, market relations.

Notes

1   Such, in fact, is the exclusive reliance on price links that the effects of economic activities which cannot be captured by the usual market pricing processes are excluded from analysis by convenient assumptions such as absence of externalities, etc.

2   The word 'bargaining' here may be somewhat misleading in that there may not be actual bargaining taking place on the market between individuals or groups of individuals. In part, custom, tradition, social mores crystallize the relative strength of different classes of the peasantry. To a certain extent the laws of the state (concerning, say, minimum wage or tenurial contracts) may influence the terms on the market. But these in turn may themselves reflect the relative economic power of the different classes of peasantry as also the class composition of the state.

3   Incidentally, the relative efficiency of small peasant farms *vis-à-vis* the large farms was hotly debated in Marxist works on the eve of the Russian Revolution (see Shanin, Part Three of this volume).

Reference

Bharadwaj, Krishna (1974), *Production Conditions in Indian Agriculture*, Cambridge: Cambridge University Press

Part Four

Rural labour

Introduction

The extent to which labourers are ignored in studies of 'Rural Development' and in considerations of rural development 'strategies' is rather remarkable. *Redistribution with Growth*, for example, the book which supplies the theoretical underpinning for the current rural development policies of the major international development agencies, identifies rural labourers and marginal farmers as one of four 'target groups', requiring special programmes, but it finally devotes no more than two pages to them. Contemporary 'populism', in its advocacy of the virtues of small farms and of redistributive land reforms, also tends to neglect the interests of landless labour, or attempts to allow for them in what are generally rather vague proposals concerning rural public works programmes[1].

The 'employment' of the poor

The first of our readings in this section, by Ben White, explains the problems of the landless and of marginal farmers in one of the most densely populated parts of the world – Java. White uses the concepts of 'employment' proposed by Myrdal in his *Asian Drama* (1968), in which attention is drawn to three dimensions of employment: participation, duration of work, and productivity. Earlier studies of labour in rural Java have argued that the employment problem is primarily one of the limited duration of work, and have referred to the importance of 'shared poverty' and of work-sharing in Javanese society. On the basis of more detailed research on labour use than has been conducted before in Java, White questions this view, arguing that people are rather fully employed in terms of duration of work, and that women especially work very long hours (in outside production as well as in household tasks – or, in the production of consumption goods and in social reproduction). [2] The problem is one rather of the very low productivity of their work and of the very low returns to the workers themselves. White admirably documents for rural labour the point which has been well established for the urban poor in discussions of the so-called 'informal' sector in Third World cities – that 'unemployment' or 'underemployment' is a luxury that the poor cannot afford. It is in this context that the multiple occupations of many rural workers makes sense.[3] White's paper also has the merit of illustrating the importance of *seasonality* among the determinants of rural poverty (see also Chambers *et al.*, 1981).

Paternalistic labour relations

White shows how recent changes associated with the 'green revolution' have brought about a deterioration in the conditions of rural workers, partly as a result of some breakdown in the patron-client relationships which formerly helped to provide some guarantee of the labourers' livelihoods. Patron-client relationships involve an exchange of a range of possible goods and services, political loyalty and sentiments of 'respect', between the dominant partner, or 'patron' (usually a relatively large farmer or landowner), and his or her dependent 'clients'. The exchange is unequal in the sense that patrons benefit more than clients, but the relationship provides some guarantee of the clients' right to subsistence and there is an element of reciprocity within it. The survival of these relationships probably depends mainly upon the patrons' needs for retinues of clients, as for example where there are marked seasonal shortages of labour (see Chambers and Harriss, 1977); and it appears that in the changing circumstances of the 'green revolution', or of more mechanized agriculture, or simply of more labour-abundant rural economies, the patrons' needs for clients are reduced, so that these paternalistic social relationships may tend to collapse. These themes have been explored in depth by other writers. A classic statement of the principles of patron-client relationships has been given by Epstein (1967) using South Indian case material; a critical treatment has been given by Alavi (1973); and patron-client relations are the subject of a book by James C. Scott (1976), mainly illustrated with South East Asian materials, and by Van Hekken and Van Velsen (1972), on Tanzania. Frankel points out how in certain cases in India, as in Java, the introduction of the new high-yielding varieties in the 'green revolution' may have contributed to the decline of paternalism and to a deterioration in labourers' livelihoods (Frankel, 1971). Where this has occurred it is often because of changes in the organization of harvesting operations in particular, and these have been studied by Collier and others in Indonesia (1974) and by Clay in Bangladesh (1976). It is not necessarily or universally the case, however, that the 'green revolution' has brought about the collapse of paternalism (see for example, J. Harriss, 1977, for one contrary instance).

Rural wages

A closely related issue concerns the determination of rural wage rates. It has been asserted (by Griffin, 1974, for example) that in spite of its effect of increasing output, the 'green revolution' has not benefited the rural poor, and part of the evidence for this conclusion is the suggestion that in spite of the presumed increase in the demand for labour which can normally be expected to accompany·agricultural growth, real wage rates have not risen. There are some serious difficulties here both with regard to the reliability of the data on wage rates that are available and with the time periods which have been used in attempts to measure the effects of the 'green revolution', but it still seems possible that in large parts of India and in other parts of Asia the determination of wage rates cannot be explained in terms of the 'normal' framework of supply and demand.[4]

One factor affecting wage rates is the extent and nature of labourers' organizations. Some evidence from India, for example, suggests that real wages have shown some improvement in Kerala in spite of the fact that there has not been so much improvment in the productivity of agriculture in that state, and it is argued that this has been because of the strength of the agricultural labour unions there. Indeed it is on the basis of this example that *Redistribution with Growth* makes one of its few policy suggestions for the landless poor, which is simply that such organizations should be encouraged! Several writers have discussed the origins of agricultural labour unions in Kerala, drawing attention variously to the significance of the breakdown of patron-client relationships of the kind briefly described above, to the existence of possible sources of 'countervailing power' for the labourers, and to the importance of strong political and trade union movements in urban areas. See also wider discussions of the conditions of rural protest movements or for peasant rebellions.[5]

The role of women

In his article White draws attention to the amount of work which is done by women, as well as to the economic benefits which may be produced by children, and we commented in the Introduction to Part 3 on the independent roles of women in many agrarian societies. Further discussion of these important themes will be found in Boserup (1970), Deere (1976), Hafkin and Bay (1976), Meillassoux (1975), Rogers (1980) and Sharma (1980).

Proletarianization

Our second reading in this part, by Christopher Scott, turns to a distinct set of themes, and it refers back to the interest in the relationships between capitalist and non-capitalist production which appears in the article by Taussig in Part Two, and elsewhere in this book. Scott is concerned with the creation of a proletariat and the formation of labour markets. He points out (in an introduction to the paper which we have not reprinted here) – that the conventional dualistic models of development economics – which postulate the existence of distinct 'traditional' and 'modern' sectors in underdeveloped economies – assume that the process of 'development' entails movement from a situation of abundant labour (in the 'traditional' sector) to one of relative scarcity (in the 'modern' sector). The reverse was the case in the area of Peru to which this paper refers, where for a long time sugar estates made use of a system of debt bondage in order to raise labour in the adjacent highlands, and even then suffered from seasonal shortages of supply. In the recent period, however, as a result of absolute increases in population, of increasing proletarianization in the highlands, and the creation of slums in the coastal towns, the estates now have a relative abundance of labour. And whereas before they sought to create a stable, regular workforce, one of the effects of the organization of labour in trade unions has been to stimulate the estates to employ more casual labour.

The story that Scott tells, of the formation of a labour market involving coercion, is one that is repeated elsewhere. In central and southern Africa for example, taxes were imposed, necessitating sources of cash income and thereby 'encouraging' (actually, 'forcing') migration to work in mines or on settler estates (see Arrighi, 1970;

and also Raikes in Part Five). Scott analyses his material in terms of the idea of the 'articulation' (see the general introduction) of the developing capitalism of the sugar plantations with the pre-capitalist economy of the highlands. Other writers have made use of the concept of articulation, in demonstrating, for example, how pre-capitalist forms of production may contribute to reducing the costs of labour power for capitalism (see also Taussig's paper, in this volume). Labour migration is an especially important theme in southern and central African agrarian studies,[6] where the argument has been advanced that the survival of 'subsistence' production in many areas is intimately related to the reproduction of a pool of cheap migrant labour for mining operations. One aspect of this is the observation that landlessness and the existence of a large group of agricultural labourers is not just an Asian and a Latin American problem. In parts of Africa it is *different* because males migrate or go out to work while their families remain on land that may or may not be at all productive (so that the family does not get classed as 'landless'). There is a good deal of rural-rural migration as well as rural-urban migration, and there can be a substantial amount of wage employment on other people's farms and non-farm enterprises in areas where it is assumed that there is no landlessness and no agricultural labouring class.

Notes

1 Even Lipton (1974) is not above the charge of vagueness in this regard.
2 White's work was an early, and is still an important, exercise in the study of 'household economics', of a wider kind than in older, farm-centred research. See Binswanger *et al.* (eds.) (1980).
3 The concept of 'the informal sector' is discussed in papers in: Bromley (ed.) (1978); and Bromley and Gerry (eds.) (1979). The rationale of multiple occupations amongst the rural poor is well demonstrated by Saith and Tankha (1972). See also Elkan (1976); and Cleave (1974).
4 Lal (1976) reviews a number of articles regarding the trends in rural wage rates in India in which it is argued that real wages have not risen, in spite of growth in output. He discusses the

data base and the methodology of these studies and argues that the opposite conclusion may be drawn. See also the rejoinder to Lal by Jose (1978); and for a quite comparable debate with relation to Indonesia, see White (1979).

5 For studies of agricultural labour movements in Kerala see: Jose (1977); Mencher (1977); and Ommen (1971). Wider discussions of rural protest and peasant movements will be found in: Alavi (1965); Desai (ed.) (1979); Landsberger (1969); Scott (1976); and Wolf (1969).

6 See especially Palmer and Parsons (eds.) (1977) – together with the review article on this book by Ranger (1978) – and also Bundy (1979) and Wolpe (ed.) (1980).

References

The employment of the poor

Binswanger, H. P., *et al.* (eds.) (1980), *Rural Household Studies in Asia*, Singapore: Singapore University Press

Bromley, R. (ed.) (1978), 'The urban informal sector: Critical perspectives', *World Development*, 6, 9–10; and also Oxford: Pergamon Press, 1979

Bromley, R., and Gerry, C., (eds.) (1979), *Casual Work and Poverty in Third World Cities*, Chichester and New York: John Wiley

Chambers, R., Longhurst, R., and Pacey, A. (eds.) (1981), *Seasonal Dimensions to Rural Poverty*, London: Frances Pinter, and Totowa, NJ: Allanheld, Osmun Publishers

Cleave, J. H. (1974), *African Farmers: Labour Use in the Development of Smallholder Agriculture*, London: Praeger

Elkan, W. (1976), 'Africana: Concepts in the description of African economies', *Journal of Modern African Studies*, 14, pp. 691–5

Lipton, M. (1974), 'Towards a theory of land reform', in D. Lehmann (ed.), *Agrarian Reform and Agrarian Reformism*, London: Faber

Myrdal, G. (1968), *Asian Drama*, 3 vols., Harmondsworth: Penguin

Saith, A., and Tankha, A. (1972), 'Economic decision making of the poor peasant household', *Economic and Political Weekly*, annual number, February, pp. 351–60

Paternalism/Patron-client relations

Alavi, H. (1973), 'Peasant classes and primordial loyalties', *Journal of Peasant Studies*, 1, 1, pp. 22–62

Breman, J. (1974), *Patronage and Exploitation: Changing Agrarian Social Relations in South Gujarat, India*, Berkeley: University of California Press

Chambers, R., and Harriss, J. (1977), 'Comparing twelve South Indian villages: in search of practical theory', in, B. H. Farmer (ed.), *Green Revolution?* London: Macmillan

Clay, E. (1976), 'Institutional change and agricultural wages in Bangladesh', *Bangladesh Development Studies*, IV, 4, pp. 423–40

Collier, W. L., *et al.* (1974), 'Agricultural technology and institutional change in Java', *Food Research Institute Studies*, 13, pp. 169–94

Epstein, T. S. (1967), 'Productive efficiency and customary systems of rewards in South India', in R. Firth (ed.), *Themes in Economic Anthropology*, London: Tavistock

Van Hekken, P. M. and Van Velsen, II. U. E. Thoden (1972), *Land Scarcity and Rural Inequality in Tanzania*, The Hague: Mouton

Frankel, F. (1971), *India's Green Revolution: Economic Gains and Political Costs*, Princeton: Princeton University Press

Harriss, J. (1977), 'Implications of changes in agriculture for social relationships at the village level', in B. H. Farmer (ed.), *Green Revolution?* London: Macmillan

Scott, J. C. (1976), *The Moral Economy of the Peasant: Rebellion and Subsistence in S. E. Asia*, New Haven, Conn.: Yale University Press

Rural wages

Griffin, K. (1974), *The Political Economy of Agrarian Change*, London; Macmillan

Jose, A. V. (1978), 'Real wages, employment, and income of agricultural labourers', *Economic and Political Weekly*, XIII, Review of Agriculture, June, pp. A16–A21

Lal, D. (1976), 'Agricultural growth, real wages and the rural poor in India', *Economic and Political Weekly*, Review of Agriculture, June 1976, pp. A47–A61

White, B. (1979), 'Political aspects of poverty, income distribution and their measurement: some examples from rural Java', *Development and Change*, 10, 1, pp. 91–114

Rural labour movements and rural protest

Alavi, H. (1965), 'Peasants and revolution', *Socialist Register 1965*; reprinted in A. Desai (ed.) (1979)

Desai, A. (ed.) (1979), *Peasant Struggles in India*, Bombay: Oxford University Press

Jose, A. V. (1977), 'The origin of trade unionism among agricultural labourers in Kerala', *Social Scientist*, no. 71, pp. 1–20

Landsberger, H. A. (ed.) (1969), *Latin American Peasant Movements,* Ithaca: Cornell University Press

Mencher, J. (1977), 'Agricultural labour unions: some socioeconomic and political considerations', in K. David (ed.), *The New Wind: Changing Identities in South Asia*, Mouton: The Hague

Oommen, T. K. (1971), 'Agrarian tension in a Kerala district', *Indian Journal of Industrial Relations*; also published as Reprint no. 15, Sri Ram Centre for Industrial Relations, New Delhi

Scott, J. C. (1976), *The Moral Economy of the Peasant: Rebellion and Subsistence in S. E. Asia*, New Haven, Conn.: Yale University Press

Wolf, E. (1969), *Peasant Wars of the Twentieth Century*, London: Faber

The role of women

Boserup, E. (1970), *Women's Role in Economic Development*, London: Allen & Unwin

Deere, C. D. (1976), 'Rural women's subsistence production in the capitalist periphery', *The Review of Radical Political Economics*, 8, 1; and in R. Cohen, P. Gutkind, and P. Brazier, (eds.) *Peasants and Proletarians: The Struggles of Third World Workers*, Hutchinson: London

Hafkin, N. J., and Bay, E. G. (eds.) (1976), *Women in Africa: Studies in Social and Economic Change*, Stanford, Calif.: Stanford University Press

Meillassoux, C. (1975), *Femmes, greniers et capitaux*, Paris: Maspero; published as *Maidens, Meals and Money: Capitalism and the Domestic Community,* Cambridge: Cambridge University Press, 1981

Rogers, B. (1980), *The Domestication of Women: Discrimination in Developing Societies*, London: Kogan Page

Sharma, U. (1980), *Women, Work and Property in North-West India*, London: Tavistock

'Articulation' and proletarianization

Arrighi, G. (1973), 'Labour supplies in historical perspective: a study of the proletarianization of the African peasantry in Rhodesia', in G. Arrighi, and J. Saul (eds.), *Essays on the Political Economy of Africa*, New York and London: Monthly Review Press; and in *Journal of Development Studies*, 6, 3, pp. 197–234, 1970

Bundy, C. (1979), *The Rise and Fall of the South African Peasantry*, London: Heinemann

Cliffe, L. (1976), 'Rural political economy of Africa', in P. Gutkind, and I. Wallerstein (eds.), *The Political Economy of Contemporary Africa*, Beverley Hills and London: Sage Publications

Foster-Carter, A. (1978), 'The modes of production controversy', *New Left Review*, 107, pp. 47–77

Meillassoux, C. (1972), 'From reproduction to production', *Economy and Society*, 1, 1, pp. 93–105

Palmer, R., and Parsons, N. (eds.) (1977), *The Roots of Rural Poverty in Central and Southern Africa*, London: Heinemann

Post, K. (1978), *Arise Ye Starvelings! The Jamaica Labour Rebellion of 1938 and its Aftermath*, The Hague, Boston and Lodin: Martinus Nijhoff

Ranger, T. O. (1978), 'Reflections on peasant research in central and southern Africa', *Journal of Southern African Studies*, 5, pp. 99–133

Rey, P–Ph. (1973), *Les alliances de classes*, Paris: Maspero

Van Binsbergen, W. M. J., and Meilink, H. A. (1978), 'Migration and the transformation of modern African society', *African Perspectives*, 1, Leiden: Afrika–Studiecentrum

Wolpe, H. (1972), 'Capitalism and cheap labour power in South Africa: from segregation to apartheid', *Economy and Society*, 1, 4, pp. 425–56

Wolpe, H. (1980), *The Articulation of Modes of Production*, London: Routledge & Kegan Paul

13 Population, involution and employment in rural Java*

Benjamin White

Most post-war studies of the Javanese rural economy have pointed to Java's 'population problem' as an important component of present poverty and as a serious obstacle to future development. The prospect that Java, already one of the poorest and most densely-populated agricultural regions in the world, will double in population from 80 to 160 million within the next thirty-five or forty years is a natural if uncomfortable starting-point in considering the problems of improving (or some would say of even maintaining) levels of living in the Javanese countryside within the next few decades.

There is nothing necessarily alarming about projections of future population totals in themselves. As Missen reminds us, 'they are only meaningful, as with populations generally, when considered in terms of the capacity of the economy to absorb or use them, a principle which those brought up in the renewed neo-Malthusian fervour of the past few years should remember'.[1] Numerous observers have considered Java overpopulated since the early nineteenth century,[2] and one wonders what colonial officials may have thought after the census of 1930 (when the population was found to be 41.7 million) about the possibility of supporting almost double that number on Java by 1974. For those who now doubt the possibility of supporting a double population on this small and crowded island, there is perhaps some comfort in the fact that previous alarms have been consistently if only partially mitigated by the extraordinary resilience of the Javanese village economy in the face of population growth and innumerable other external pressures. We shall subject some aspects of this resilience to critical examination below, but its conventional formulation is well known: a combination of increasing internal complexity in the

---

*This chapter is taken from White (1976a).

distribution of land and labour opportunities, in the labour-intensive techniques of irrigated rice cultivation and in the distribution of the agricultural product, an extremely absorptive if ultimately self-defeating process whereby output per hectare increased with the growth of population while output per capita remained the same. These processes were called by Boeke 'static expansion', by Geertz 'agricultural involution' and by both authors 'shared poverty'.[3] Despite this resilience, however, there is evidence of declining real per capita incomes and levels of nutrition during the present century, and in recent years some authors have begun to suggest that the Javanese countryside is approaching the 'limits of involution': 'various pieces of contemporary evidence . . . indicate that during the period of independence the traditional elastic qualities of the Javanese village and indeed of rural Java as a whole [have] reached a point of extreme strain.'[4]

In considering the problems of population and poverty in rural Java it must be assumed at the outset that such strictly demographic measures as birth control and assisted out-migration are palliatives rather than solutions. We must also understand that given the already serious problems of overcrowding and unemployment in Java's rapidly growing urban populations, and the dismal labour absorption record of recent industrial development, the rural population cannot be viewed as a potential reserve of labour for urban industrial development. Solutions to rural poverty must therefore be sought primarily in the rural economy itself, in the opening-up of opportunities for the productive absorption of a growing rural labour force.

It thus becomes a matter of great importance to examine the existing structure of the Javanese rural economy, to determine what are the present barriers to the more productive use of labour and what kinds of changes might result in the removal of these barriers. Given the great variations that many researchers have noted even between adjacent villages in Java, this is clearly an enormous task, demanding research in many villages and on many levels before any answers or practical solutions can be confidently proposed. The purpose of this paper is to examine briefly two features commonly regarded as characteristic of 'population pressure' in Java: 'unemployment' or 'underemployment', and the general notions of 'involution' and 'shared poverty' mentioned above. Examples will be drawn from some recent studies and from my own field research in a Javanese village in 1972–3.

Population densities and population 'pressure'

'Overpopulation' or 'population pressure' are of course relative terms. Population pressure, or a population problem, can only be measured by relating crude population figures to a complex set of variables, some of which relate to the natural and some to the man-made environment. Of greatest importance are the land types available within a given area, and particularly the ratio of irrigated rice land (*sawah*) to unirrigated gardens (*pekarangan*) or other dry land (*tegalan*); the quality of that land, and of its water supply through rainfall or irrigation, and various other more external determinants of land use – for example, the presence or absence of government-imposed cultivation of sugar or other plantation crops, and the existence of specialized markets for the products of various agricultural or non-agricultural activities. Thus the proximity of large urban centres, or of roads leading to them, provides opportunities for many kinds of specialized crop production, for particular trades and crafts and for various kinds of wage labour away from home.

What then does population pressure mean in terms of its general effects on rural economy? Much of the literature goes little further than telling us what we would expect, that because of the pressure of people on resources landholdings are small, per capita incomes low, diets deficient in quantity and quality, employment opportunities scarce and so on. Such relationships (between people and food, people and land, and people and employment) are used by Bennett in his attempt to measure population pressure in East Java, from which he concluded that 'while each of the three scales... has indicated different degrees of population pressure, each emphasizes in quantitative terms the existence of far too many people for the existing technology'.[5] But these characterizations, however accurate, tell us little about the specific patterns of economic activity, the modes of gaining a livelihood, that we may expect to find in these villages where there are 'far too many people'.

Many village studies point also to the existence of large numbers of landless households and of uneven distribution of holdings among those who do own land. We should note (because this is not always made clear) that this feature of village life in Java is not an automatic consequence of high population : land ratios, in the sense that equal distribution of landholdings is quite compatible with situations of acute land scarcity even if it does not usually occur. Indeed, attempts to relate inequalities in landholdings to overall land/man ratios may meet with surprising results. Maurer, comparing four villages in Bantul (Yogyakarta) found that the proportion of landless households was highest in the villages with the best overall land/man ratios: 'one could say that in the village where the overall economic situation is the worst, the economic situation of a larger number of families is better than in the village where the overall economic situation is the best'.[6] Thus, although the economic structure of any Javanese village will reflect a combination of these two factors, it is important to distinguish the effects of absolute resource scarcity ('pressure of people on resources') from the effects of differential access to those resources ('pressure of people on people').

Population and employment

Myrdal in *Asian Drama*[7] complains that Western concepts of unemployment and underemployment do not adequately 'fit' the realities of Asian societies. Given the inappropriateness of Western categories of labour force analysis, and the inadequacy of official statistics on 'numbers of unemployed persons', etc. in Asian economies, Myrdal proposes a framework for the analysis of labour utilization in which the level of labour utilization is expressed as the product of three ratios: (1) the participation rate (the portion of the total labour force normally performing some work); (2) the duration of work among participants (in terms of average weeks per year, days per week, hours per day, etc); and (3) labour efficiency (level of output for a given number of work-hours). He deplores the general unavailability of this type of information and stresses that to obtain it, 'the labour utilization approach requires behavioural studies founded on observations of the raw realities'.[8]

It is highly instructive to compare conventional views of labour utilization patterns in rural Java with the few studies based on 'observations of the raw realities' that are available. According to the 'involution and shared poverty' approach, it is assumed that while the opportunities for productive labour are scarce, these opportunities are generally shared. Thus we might say that few individuals are unemployed, but the great majority are underemployed, or in Myrdal's terms, the 'participation rate' is high but the 'duration of work' is low.

When we examine some attempts to fill this picture with more detail it appears that the more directly observational the research methods, the more qualifications are needed in this conventional conception of labour utilization. Penny and Singarimbun in a recent study of population and poverty in the village of Sriharjo in Bantul (Yogyakarta)[9] devote a chapter to demonstrating that there are 'too many people for the work'. They substantiate this statement with a table showing the number of days of work (either self-employed or as a wage labourer) done per adult male in a random sample of 75 households over one 180-day rice season (rainy season 1969/70).[10] The data were collected in a survey in which people were asked at the end of this season to recall how many days or hours of work they had done in a variety of occupations; a 'full day' of work was considered to be six hours in rice cultivation and eight hours in other activities. The results are remarkable.

It appears that only a very small amount of working time was spent in rice cultivation (22 per cent of all actual working time, but only 10 per cent of all potential working time) and furthermore, that the adult males of this village spent only 78 of the 180 available working days doing work of any kind. If we take eight hours as the standard of potential daily working hours, then we must conclude either that this sample were unemployed for approximately 200 days per year, or that they were able to work for an average of only 3.3 hours per day. Thus their work-duration rate (whether in days per month or hours per day) was only about 41 per cent.[11]

The first of these conclusions is of great importance. By showing the small amount of the male population's time devoted to rice cultivation (in a village with a relatively normal amount of sawah – some 40 per cent of the total cultivable land) it suggests that the understandable preoccupation of rural economists and policy makers with Java's rice problem has led to a relative neglect of the study of possibilities for improved productivity in other areas of rural production. We shall return to this point later; for the moment, however, I wish to raise some doubts about the validity of the second conclusion, that less than half of available working time is actually spent in work of any kind.

In a study of 'land, food and work' in the three east Javanese villages previously used in Bennett's study of population pressure (see above), Edmundson[12] and his assistants followed the demanding procedure of accompanying 54 adult males during most of their waking hours, noting down their activities during the day and the amounts of time spent in each. Research of this intensity of course involves some risk that the methods of observation will influence the behaviour of the person observed; we have no way of knowing whether the subject is working more or less than normally because of the observer's presence. Edmundson found the average time spent daily in productive activities to be approximately 6.25 hours, and that once again a relatively small proportion of this time was spent in the cultivation of rice or other staple crops. He concluded: 'the Javanese villagers worked harder and perhaps spent a greater proportion of their time working than any comparable group of Western workers with whom I am familiar.[13]

Using different research methods in Kali Loro (Yogyakarta), I found daily work hours even higher than those reported by Edmundson. As part of a study of the economic importance of children, I and/or some local assistants made regular visits to a sample of households every six days and ascertained from the household members (both male and female, adults and children) how they had spent the 24-hour period immediately prior to the interview, and how much time was spent in each activity.[14] Altogether, more than 90 households were visited in this way but the data refer to a subsample of 20 households (104 individuals) for whom an entire twelve-month cycle of time-allocation data (60 visits per household) has been analysed. The material thus covers 6240 'person days' of activities, spread evenly over the year.

The sample of 20 households is approximately representative of the total village population in terms of access to land, with the exception that the 3.5 per cent of households who own more than one hectare of sawah (and who between them own 40 per cent of all the sawah in Kali Loro) are not represented. The sample of recorded days includes without bias holidays, days when individuals were sick, attending ceremonies or for other reasons doing less work than usual. The data show that adult men did a total of 8.7 hours of work per day throughout the year while adult women did 11.1 hours daily. If we exclude the work of household maintenance and childbearing and count only 'directly productive work', the men spent 7.9 hours daily in these activities and the women 5.9 hours. Although, as in Sriharjo, two crops of rice were grown on most of the sawah in Kali Loro, only 25 per cent of men's total working time (or 28 per cent of their total 'directly productive' work) was spent in rice cultivation.

Thus one of Penny and Singarimbun's conclusions (the small amount of time devoted to rice cultivation) is fully confirmed; but the other (the low average duration rates of annual or daily work) seems to be contradicted by both Edmundson's material and my own. If we again take eight hours as our standard of a full day's work, then Edmundson's sample of adult males appears to come quite close to, and mine to achieve, 'full employment' in terms of work-duration rates. Since the three studies mentioned cover only a total of five villages we obviously cannot conclude that one is correct and the others wrong; however, on methodological grounds alone there is justification for the view that the more direct .methods of observation will more closely approach Myrdal's 'raw realities'.

It may be noted in parenthesis that my own material is more complete in one respect than other studies of labour utilization in Java, in that it includes the female part of the adult labour force (who in fact outnumber their male counterparts in rural Java). Despite the five hours daily that women spent in housework, cooking, childcare, etc. in Kali Loro they also spent close to six hours daily in 'directly productive' activities. Examination of the income data collected by Ann Stoler for the same sample of households indicates the importance of both the amount and type of cash and real income contributed by women; the neglect of women's work is another aspect of much research on rural employment conditions which fails to do justice to reality.[15]

Occupational multiplicity, returns to labour and working hours

The employment situation in villages like Kali Loro is not characterized by low participation rates ('no work to do'), nor by low work-duration rates ('not enough work to do'), but by low labour productivity or labour efficiency, which for a landless or near-landless household means 'a lot of work to do, with very low returns'.

Much has been written about the low and possibly declining returns to labour in Javanese rice cultivation. Sajogyo for example, citing a study of three villages in Klaten (Central Java), estimates that the average level of labour productivity ranged from 0.8 kg of milled rice per man-hour (with local rice varieties) to 1.2 kg/man-hour (with new 'miracle rice' varieties).[16] For labourers, the real returns to their labour are of course lower than this, and they appear to have sharply declined during the last few years despite the higher yields made possible by the use of improved varieties, fertilizers and pesticides. Makali in an interesting study of twenty Javanese villages over the five-year period 1968/9–1972/3 shows that the real wage for a half-day's work (expressed as the amount of rice that can be purchased with it) has declined by about one-third during this period.[17] In Kali Loro in 1971 and 1972, a man's wage for a half-day in sawah would purchase ⅔ kg of rice and a woman's slightly less than ½ kg, but by late 1973 men's wages barely reached ½ kg and women's barely ⅓ kg. Women's lower wages (for transplanting) are compensated by their subsequent higher wages at harvest time; they are paid a share in kind (*bawon*) of the amount they harvest, varying from ⅙ or even more to ¹⁄₁₂ depending on their relationship to the farmer's household. Ann Stoler's research on harvesting in Kali[18] found the average wage for a harvester from a landless household (who has no harvesting opportunities to offer in return and is thus often paid a lower share) to be about 1.4 kg of milled rice per half-day, while for landowners the average wage was as much as 2.2 kg.

While it is generally stressed that returns to labour (for both farmer and wage labourer) are low in rice cultivation, it is not so often noted that they are even lower in most of the other productive activities in which most people spend the majority of their time. Table 4 shows approximate returns per hour of labour for selected activities available to a household with little capital, compared to those in rice cultivation. These estimates were made for early 1973, during which period the price of rice in Kali Loro market ranged from Rp. 50–70 per kg (Rp. 415 = US $1.00).[19]

The extent of any household's involvement in activities such as these in Kali Loro depends primarily on its access to sawah. Of the 478 households we surveyed 20 per cent had no access to sawah (as owners, share-croppers or renters) and a further 43 per cent cultivated less than one-fifth of a hectare. A household of average size in the village (4.5 persons), eating on average ⅓ kg of rice per person per day,[20] would require 540 kg of hulled rice per year; one-fifth of a hectare of sawah, if double-cropped, produces in average years just over 500 kg of unhulled rice once the costs of the necessary inputs (not counting unpaid family labour) have been subtracted. Thus over 70 per cent of the households in Kali Loro do not have enough sawah to attain even their annual rice requirement, let alone their other needs in food, clothing, school

Table 4   *Estimated returns to labour in various occupations at early 1973 wage and price levels**

Occupations	Returns to labour (rp./hour)
1 Rice cultivation	
(a) Owner-cultivator: 0.5 ha.	50
(b) Owner-cultivator: 0.2 ha.	25
(c) Sharecropper: 0.2 ha.	12½
2 Garden cultivation	25
3 Agricultural wage labour	
(a) Plough: own animals	70–90
(b) Hoe	9–11
(c) Transplant	6–7
(d) Weed	9–11
(e) Harvest	16–20
4 Non-agricultural wage labour	
(a) Carrying/construction	10
(b) Craftsman (carpenter)	15
(c) Weaving factory	7
5 Trade	
(a) Women on foot: capital = Rp. 1000	5–10
(b) Men on foot: capital = Rp. 1000	15
(c) On bicycle (Rp. 8000–12000): capital = Rp. 3000	20
6 Preparation of food for sale	
(a) Gula Jawa (coconut sugar): own trees	5–6
(b) Gula Jawa: sharecropping	2½–3
(c) Lontong (a cassava preparation)	3½
(d) Tempe (a 'biscuit' made from soya bean)	5
7 Animal husbandry	
(a) Ducks	5–12
(b) Goats	1–2
(c) Cattle: own	4–6
(d) Cattle on gaduhan (sharecropping) basis	2–3
8 Handicrafts	
(a) Tikar (pandans mats)	1½
(b) Kepang (split bamboo mats)	3

*Methods of estimation are discussed in White (1976), ch. 5.

fees, etc.[21] The great majority of households must therefore obtain a substantial part of their income (for 29 per cent of the households, all of their income) either from wage labour or from other activities of the kind described in Table 4, in which the returns to labour are much lower than in rice cultivation. As returns to labour decline, then obviously the number of daily hours of labour required to attain a given level of living must increase.

If we were to rank the various productive opportunities in order of their returns to labour (with harvesting at the top, mat-weaving at the bottom and so on) we would expect to find that households would whenever possible choose the available combination of activities with the highest total returns to labour. Thus, for example, women will often stop or reduce their trading or mat-weaving activity during harvest time to take advantage of the better returns in harvesting. Men may remain at home, cooking and babysitting to free their wives for the harvest; young children may herd livestock or cut fodder when there are wage-labour opportunities for their fathers, or they may cook and babysit while their father cuts fodder and their mother is planting rice, and so on. Mat-weaving is normally done only at times when there is no more productive activity available, particularly at night, or when one cannot leave the house (weaving, cooking and babysitting are often combined). It is hardly surprising that there are virtually no 'full-time' mat-weavers (exceptions are elderly women who can do no other kind of work), for at some times of the year when rice prices are high and mat prices low it would require twenty hours of weaving a day to provide an adult with rice.

Each household survives on a basis of extreme 'occupational multiplicity'[22] and a highly flexible division of labour among household members. Since the returns to labour in most occupations can barely support an adult let alone a whole household, the burden of subsistence is shared by men, women and children together. Each household's income is derived from a great variety of sources which constantly change in response to available opportunities according to the season, the state of the market and even the time of day; and each individual household member has normally not one or two occupations, but a great number in which he/she engages in differing combinations and for differing lengths of time in response both to his own opportunities and those of the other household members. An individual in Kali Loro may for example spend two hours collecting coconut sap, three hours in the sawah, two hours cutting fodder, two more hoeing the garden, two more weaving a bamboo mat and a few hours fishing in the dark, all in a single day; it would not be surprising therefore if retrospective employment surveys failed to achieve a realistic picture of work duration rates!

The slack periods in the rice cultivation cycle between each planting and harvest (approximately from January to March and from June to August during the years of my observations) are the lean seasons (*paceklik*) when prices are generally rising, labour opportunities in agriculture most limited and returns to labour in other occupations lowest. But the majority of households, without stores of rice or other savings during these periods, have no choice but to continue putting in long hours of work for lower returns, in order to survive. Thus we may expect that – contrary to conventional characterization of 'seasonal unemployment' – the agricultural cycle will be marked not by seasonal fluctuations in the total 'directly productive' work input per day, but rather by involuntary changes in the allocation of working time between agricultural and non-agricultural occupations. This is confirmed by observations in Kali Loro. Comparing the five markedly 'busy' and seven markedly 'slack' agricultural months for men and women, we find that while the percentage of total 'directly productive' working time devoted to agricultural work declines from 48 to 29 per cent (men) and 36 to 11 per cent (women), there is no significant change in the total daily input of 'directly productive' work for either sex. Like 'general' idleness, seasonal idleness is a luxury which most of the population of Kali Loro cannot afford.

One should of course be cautious in drawing general conclusions from this crude picture (based on a small sample of households, observed during one year in a single village) of rural employment and the variety of means by which household piece together a livelihood. However, if the conditions I have described are a general characteristic of Java's rural economy, then our conventional conceptions of rural employment, involution and shared poverty will require some modification. The 'pressure of people on resources' means not only that returns to labour in rice cultivation and agricultural wages are low, but also that the rural population as a whole is increasingly squeezed out of rice cultivation and into a large variety of other activities in which the returns to labour are even lower; the result in terms of average work duration is a longer, not a shorter, working day.

Some developments in the organization of rice production in recent years seem likely only to accelerate this process of channelling labour increasingly into less productive non-rice occupations. We may first mention the decline in real agricultural wages noted above, which makes other sources of income increasingly necessary to supplement those wages if levels of living are to be maintained. Secondly, several recent publications have documented the ways in which large farmers and landlords have recently begun to limit the number of harvesters in their fields or to reduce the wages given to them, particularly by the employment of a small number of male harvesters using sickles and paid a cash wage rather than larger numbers of women, harvesting with the small-bladed *ani-ani* and paid a share of what they harvest.[23] Similarly, the dramatic recent rise in the use of small machine rice-hullers, owned by wealthy villagers, to replace hand-pounding in the processing of the rice harvest has resulted in the loss of another relatively lucrative labour opportunity for women.[24] In Kali Loro the wage paid to women for hand-pounding (before the introduction of hulling machines in the late 1960s) was one-tenth of the amount hulled. Although many households still hand-pound their own rice for their daily needs, hand-pounding for wages (in which the returns to labour approached those of harvesting) has completely disappeared. One result of this change in Kali Loro was a dramatic rise in the number of women traders operating with tiny amounts of capital, consequent further saturation of the market system and presumably (although this is harder to document retrospectively) further diminution of their profits. In our 478-household sample, almost 40 per cent of women over fifteen years of age are now engaged in some form of seasonal or year-round part-time or full-time trading.

It has been suggested that these changes are evidence that involution and shared poverty have now reached their limit and are breaking down.[25] This question is difficult to approach in such general form, because there is room for doubt whether involution and shared poverty as Geertz defined them were ever adequate as characterizations of the political economy of Javanese village life. However, it is instructive to consider the more specific question why so many traditional labour arrangements in agriculture seem to be breaking down in recent years. All of the changes mentioned above serve the function for the wealthy farmer or landowner of cutting the costs of rice production, at the expense of smallholders and landless labourers. It is remarkable that these changes should have occurred within the space of a few years, and at a time when high-yielding varieties have opened the possibility of greatly increased returns to rice farming even without these cost-cutting measures. It seems on the face of it unlikely that these changes can be ascribed simply to population pressure; rather, we must recall the distinction made earlier between the effects of absolute pressure of people on resources and the effects of differential access to those resources, which is a matter of political economy.

The beginnings of the 'green revolution' in the late 1960s more or less coincided with major political and economic changes at the national level, whose consequences at the village level should not be underestimated. On the one hand we have seen the 'opening up' of the Indonesian economy, which has produced among other things an influx into city markets of expensive and mostly imported luxury consumption items (Hondas, radios, luxury textiles and so on) and a concomitant wave of 'consumerism' which has not failed to affect many wealthier villagers. On the other hand we have seen the 'closing down' of most forms of political activity at the village level,[26] so that powerful individuals in the village depend much less than before on the kinds of support which 'patrons generally need from their 'clients'; furthermore, the altered political climate makes much less likely the kinds of pressure from below which labourers have previously brought to bear in Java when, for example, traditional harvesting arrangements have been threatened.[27] For the wealthy villager, land and its produce are becoming less a source of local power through redistribution of wealth within the village (and consequent maintenance of a loyal following who will within limits protect their patron's power and privileges), and more a source of cash to be spent outside the village, on luxury items, on obtaining higher education and salaried jobs for their children, and so on. Borrowing the term used by Scott[28] in his analysis of the dynamics of South-east Asian patron-client relations, we may say that there has been a recent shift in the relative 'bargaining power' of richer and poorer villagers. These phenomena obviously require much more detailed analysis and have been described here too starkly and simplistically. In Kali Loro there are many wealthy landowners who still own no motorcycles or hulling-machines, who dress simply and give traditional harvest shares and other forms of security to those who depend on them; but there are larger numbers who spend more of their wealth than before outside the village and redistribute less than before to their fellow villagers.

We saw above that while the overall availability of productive opportunities in rice cultivation and in other activities may be seen as a function of population pressure on resources, we cannot understand the distribution of those opportunities among the population without reference to other factors. Similarly, it seems that shifts in the political economy of the Javanese village – particularly in the uses to which wealth is put, and in the relative bargaining power of richer and poorer villagers – offer more plausible explanations than population pressure of the recent cost-cutting changes in the behaviour of wealthy landowners.

Whatever the outcome of these and future changes may be, it is clear that rural development programmes must aim at improving the conditions of production both in and out of the sawah, and at providing not 'more work' but more productive work to those who need it most. These programmes require a better understanding of the existing 'raw realities' of labour utilization, and this understanding must be based on intensive research in which the basic units of observation are neither individuals nor 'occupations' but whole households. Finally, it is hard to envisage long-term improvements in the labour productivity and incomes of the majority of the rural population without a shift in attention from the 'pressure of people on resources' to the 'pressure of people on people'. While the former (largely irreversible) condition has reduced the average per household availability of sawah in Kali Loro to 0.2 ha, it is the latter condition, as manifested in the distribution of access to land and other resources, which determines the continuing inability of the majority of households, either singly or in co-operation, to achieve sustained increases in the productivity of their long day's work.

Employment and population

Thus far we have been concerned with the general effects of population pressure and some other factors on rural economy in Java. In conclusion it may be interesting briefly to reverse this focus and consider the possible effects of rural economy on population dynamics. We noted earlier that because of the generally low returns to labour, the burden of household subsistence must be shared by men, women and children alike. Thus while the 20-household sample is more complete than some other studies in that it includes women's work, our understanding of labour utilization in household economies – the basic 'atoms' of rural economy – is still incomplete if we do not consider also the contribution of children.

Table 5 shows for the same sample of 20 households, the

average work inputs of all children six years of age and over, according to age, sex and type of work, compared with those of adults. In this table, work inputs are expressed in hours per person per year. The contribution of children is clearly substantial, both in the work of 'household maintenance' (childcare, housework, firewood-collecting, etc.) which may free adults for more productive work, and in certain types of 'directly productive' work (especially handicrafts, animal care and agricultural wage labour for girls, and animal care for boys). We should remember also that the biologically-determined subsistence requirements of children are

Table 5   *Average annual work inputs by age, sex and type of activity, in hours per person per year, in a sample of twenty households, November 1972 – October 1973*

Sex	Female				Male			
Age group	6-8	9-11	12-14	15+	6-8	9-11	12-14	15+
No. in sample	7	4	6	33	6	7	10	31
1 Childcare	606	180	596	376	425	173	99	133
2 Housework	97	390	400	386	51	22	75	28
3 Food preparation	14	140	413	994	11	14	23	37
4 Firewood collection	95	100	28	32	218	285	332	75
5 Shopping	4	28	20	100	2	–	19	16
6 Handicrafts	35	657	958	847	–	–	37	163
7 Preparation of food for sale	–		38	151	11	2	1	125
8 Animal care/feeding	326	249	29	53	620	534	899	482
9 Trading	–	5	279	523	–	15	7	264
10 Garden (own)	6	2	8	39	4	38	45	267
11 Sawah (own)	18	78	134	151	7	13	84	689
12 Gotong royong	25	18	42	55	14	12	45	279
13 Wage labour (agricultural)	23	110	206	279	–	2	33	107
14 Wage labour (non-agricultural)	–	–	–	62	–	29	17	406
15 Other	3	–	4	11	5	53	53	102
16 Total 'directly productive work' (6–15):	436	1119	1698	2171	661	698	1221	2884
17 All work (1–15):	1252	1957	3155	4056	1368	1192	1769	3173

less than those of adults, as are their culturally-determined actual consumption levels (children in Kali Loro do not smoke or chew betelnut, or give *slametan* feasts, and their average expenses on clothing up to the early teens are less than those of adults), so that the productive value of children, relative to their drain on household income through consumption, is higher than the figures in Table 5 imply.

There is thus a possibility that under conditions of low labour productivity and extreme occupational multiplicity in the household economy, the economic advantages of large families lie not only in the provision of old-age security to parents (a factor recognized by many authors) but also in the economic contribution of children from an early age. I have given further consideration to this question in earlier papers[29] in which I suggested that both in the colonial period and at present, population growth in Java has not been the result of villagers' apathy or irrationality or of the non-availability of birth-control methods, but rather a response to an economic system imposing conditions of production on the household economy such that the economic advantages to parents of relatively high fertility outweigh the economic costs.

If high fertility is advantageous to successive generations of parents its results are the opposite for their successive generations of children, who must grow up in an increasingly crowded and under-productive economy in which working hours must become even longer if the meagre level of subsistence is not to decline. It is not surprising then that many of the children of Kali Loro when they reach adulthood decide to leave the village, and in many cases to leave Java. Measures of out-migration are difficult to obtain in the absence of adequate village records; however, some idea of the extent of out-migration from Kali Loro is obtained by examining the present place of residence of children of the older women (aged fifty and over) in our sample of 478 households. Of 465 children who have left the parental household, only 209 remained in Kali Loro; 31 had left the village but remained in the kabupaten (regency); 122 had left the regency but were still in Java, mostly in the cities of Jakarta and Yogyakarta or in smaller towns in Central and East Java; and 103 had left Java for Sumatra (with a few to Kalimantan and Sulawesi) in search of opportunities that might in some degree free them from this vicious circle of poverty, inequality, underproductivity and population growth.

Notes

1 Missen (1972), p. 257.
2 Some examples from the early nineteenth century are given by van der Kroef (1956), vol. II, p. 66.
3 Boeke (1953), Geertz (1956; 1963, chs 4–5).
4 Missen (1972), p. 259.
5 Bennett (1961), p. 106. See also Bennett (1957).
6 Maurer (1973), p. 8.
7 Myrdal (1968), vol. II, chs 21–23: vol. III, Appendix 6.
8 ibid., vol. II, p. 1027.
9 Penny and Singarimbun (1973).
10 ibid., p. 28, table 16.
11 Penny and Singarimbun note that if the few members of the sample who attended school are excluded, the average days of work rise from 78 to 82 days per person. They also note that they have underestimated the total amount of work done in rice cultivation by men, and that this has probably reduced their estimate of total days of all work by about 10 per cent; and that they have no information on work done in house gardens other than the tapping of coconut trees, but that probably little such work is done. Thus, when the relevant adjustments are made, it is unlikely that the total days of all work would be much over 90 days (i.e. a work duration rate of 50 per cent).
12 Edmundson (1972).
13 ibid., p. 143.
14 The validity of these research methods is discussed in White (1975).
15 See Stoler (1976a and 1976b), White (1976).
16 Sajogyo (1974), p. 39.
17 Makali (1974).
18 Stoler (1975).
19 Returns to nearly all the occupations mentioned are subject to great seasonal variability.
20 One-third kg of hulled rice per person per day (or about 120 kg per person per year) seems to be accepted both by villagers and researchers (e.g. Penny and Singarimbun, 1972, p. 83) as a reasonable average rice consumption requirement. It provides only 1200 calories per day.
21 This rice requirement is only one-half of the per capita total

real income officially defined as the 'poverty level' for rural Java (240 kg per person per year). A recent survey estimated that almost 60 per cent of rural Javanese households fail to attain this level (cited in UPGK 1974, p. 41).

22 'Occupational multiplicity' (the necessity for individuals or households to combine several economic activities in order to subsist) has been discussed in Comitas's (1973) study of Jamaican villages.

23 See for example Collier *et al.* (1973 and 1974a), Utami and Ihalauw (1973). At the time these reports were written, sickles were generally only used if the farmer/landowner had sold the standing crop to a middleman (*penebas*), often an outsider who recruited the harvesters himself. This disclaiming of responsibility by the farmer/landowner is some evidence of the great distaste with which the new practice is viewed by most villagers. However, visitors to the same villages a year later found that some wealthy villagers were employing sickle-harvesters without recourse to a *penebas* (William Collier, personal communication).

24 Collier *et al.* (1974b); see also Timmer (1973 and 1974). For a summary of labour displacements resulting from various technological innovations in rural Java, see Sinaga and Collier (1975).

25 Collier *et al.* (1974a).

26 Cf. Liddle (1973).

27 Wertheim (1964), p. 219. Collier *et al.* (1974a), p. 12, mention a recent case of angry harvesters beating up a *penebas*.

28 Scott (1972).

29 White (1973, 1975, 1976).

References

Bennett, Don. C. (1957), 'Population pressure in East Java', Ph.D dissertation, Syracuse University

Bennet, Don. C. (1961), 'Three measurements of population pressure in East Java', *Ekonomi dan Keuangan Indonesia*, March–April, pp. 97–106

Boeke, J. H. (1942), *The Structure of Netherlands Indian Economy*, New York: Institute of Pacific Relations

Boeke, J. H. (1953), *Economics and Economic Policy in Dual Societies*, Haarlem: Tjeenk Willink & Zoon NV

Collier, William L., Gunawan Wiradi and Soentoro (1973), 'Recent changes in rice harvesting methods', *Bulletin of Indonesian Economic Studies*, 9, 2, July, pp. 36–45

Collier, William L., Soentoro, Gunawan Wiradi and Makali (1974a), 'Agricultural technology and institutional change in Java', *Food Research Institute Studies*, 13, 2 (1974), pp. 169–94

Collier, William L., Jusuf Colter, Sinarhadi and Robert d'A Shaw (1974b), 'Choice of technique in rice milling on Java – a comment', *Bulletin of Indonesian Economic Studies*, 10, 1, March, pp. 106–20

Comitas, Lambros (1973), 'Occupational multiplicity in rural Jamaica', in L. Comitas and D. Lowenthal (eds.), *Work and Family Life: West Indian Perspectives*, New York: Doubleday-Anchor, pp. 156–73

Edmundson, Wade (1972), 'Land, food and work in three Javanese villages', Ph.D thesis, Department of Geography, University of Hawaii

Geertz, Clifford (1956), 'Religious belief and economic behaviour in a central Javanese town: some preliminary considerations', *Economic Development and Cultural Change*, 4, 2, January, pp. 134–58

Geertz, Clifford (1963), *Agricultural Involution*, Berkeley: University of California Press

Geertz, Clifford (1973), 'Comments on White', *Human Ecology*, 1, 3 (1973), pp. 237–9

van der Kroef, J. M. (1956), *Indonesia in the Modern World*, 2 32, 2, February, pp. 287–309

Liddle, R. William (1973), 'Evolution from above: national leadership and local development in Indonesia', *Journal of Asian Studies*, 32, 2, February, pp. 287–309

Makali (1974), 'Upah buruh tani pada tanaman padi dikaitkan dengan kenaikan produksi dan harga padi selama lima tahun di dua puluh desa sampel Intensifikasi Padi Sawah di Jawa' ('Relations between wages in rice agriculture, increased yields and rice prices over five years in twenty Javanese villages in the Rice Intensification Study sample'), Bogor: Survey Agro Ekonomi, Bogor

Maurer, Jean-Luc (1973), 'Some consequences of land shortage in four Kelurahan of the Kabupaten Bantul', mimeo, Yogyakarta

Missen, G. J. (1972), *Viewpoint on Indonesia: a Geographical Study*, Melbourne: Nelson

Myrdal, Gunnar (1968), *Asian Drama*, 3 vols., New York: Pantheon

Penny, D. H. and Masri Singarimbun (1972), 'A case study of rural poverty', *Bulletin of Indonesian Economic Studies*, 8, 1, March 1972, pp. 79–88

Penny, D. H., and Masri Singarimbun (1973), *Population and Poverty in Rural Java: Some Economic Arithmetic from Sriharjo*, Cornell International Agricultural Development, mimeo no. 41, Ithaca, New York

Sajogyo (1974), 'Modernization without development in rural Java', mimeo contributed to the study on changes in agrarian structures, organized by FAO of the UN, Bogor

Scott, James C. (1972), 'The erosion of patron-client bonds and social change in rural Southeast Asia', *Journal of Asian Studies*, 32, 1, November, pp. 5–37

Sinaga, Rudolf, and William L. Collier (1975), 'Social and regional implications of agricultural development policy', *Prisma, Indonesian Journal of Social and Economic Affairs*, 1, 2, November, pp. 24–35

Stoler, Ann (1975), 'Some socio-economic aspects of rice harvesting in a Javanese village', *Masyarakat Indonesia*, II, 2, November, pp. 24–35

Stoler, Ann (1976a), 'Garden use and household consumption patterns in a Javanese village', *Masyarakat Indonesia*, III

Stoler, Ann (1976b), 'Some economic determinants of female autonomy in rural Java', mimeo presented at the Agricultural Development Council RTN Workshop on 'Family labour force use in agricultural production', ICRISAT, Hyderabad, 2–3 February

Timmer, C. Peter (1973), 'Choice of technique in rice milling in Java', *Bulletin of Indonesian Economic Studies*, 9, 2, July, pp. 57–76

Timmer, C. Peter (1974): 'Reply to Collier *et al.*' (1974b), *Bulletin of Indonesian Economic Studies*, 10, 1, March, pp. 121–6

UPGK (1974), 'Usaha Perbaikan Gizi Keluarga (Hasil Survey Evaluasi Proyek UPGK 1973)', mimeo preliminary draft, Lembaga Penelitian Sosiologi Pedesaan, Institut Pertanian Bogor

Utami, Widya, and John Ihalauw (1973), 'Some consequences of small farm size', *Bulletin of Indonesian Economic Studies*, 9, 2, July, pp. 46–56

van der Walle, Etiene (1973), 'Comments on White' (1973), *Human*

Ecology, 1, 3, 1973, pp. 241–4

White, Benjamin (1973), 'Demand for labour and population growth in colonial Java', *Human Ecology*, 1, 3, pp. 217–36

White, Benjamin (1974), 'Reply to Geertz and van der Walle', *Human Ecology*, 2, 1, pp. 63–5

White, Benjamin (1975), 'The economic importance of children in a Javanese village', in Moni Nag (ed.), *Population and Social Organization*, The Hague: Mouton, pp. 127–46.

White, Benjamin (1976a), 'Population, involution and employment in rural Java', *Development and Change*, 7, pp. 267–90

White, Benjamin (1976b), 'Production and reproduction in a Javanese village', Ph.D dissertation, Columbia University

14 Peasants, proletarianization and the articulation of modes of production: the case of sugar cane cutters in northern Peru, 1940 – 69*

C. D. Scott

This paper is concerned with the possibility that 'Capitalism has different needs of pre-capitalist economies at different stages of development, which arise from specific historical circumstances, e.g. raw materials, land, labour power, and at crisis times, markets' (Bradby, 1975, pp. 128–9). More specifically, my aim is to show that the sequential evolution of the labour supply from the pre-capitalist highland sector of northern Peru to the capitalist plantation sector on the coast does not conform to the pattern suggested by dualist models, namely a movement from relative labour abundance to relative labour shortage. On the contrary, it is argued that first, it is necessary to redefine the concepts of labour abundance and scarcity to allow for temporary or seasonal migration, second, the sequential development of the labour market was the reverse of that predicted by dualism, namely a movement from labour scarcity to labour abundance,[1] and third, the consequence of labour abundance and concomitant unionization was the emergence of a different and specific type of 'duality' in the labour market for cane cutters.

The development of labour power as a commodity among the cane cutters of northern Peru may be understood in terms of a three-stage periodization.

*This chapter is taken from Scott (1976).

The author is grateful to the following persons and institutions for help in the collection of material and/or for comments on a previous draft of this paper: H. Rodriguez P. of the Centro de Documentacion Agraria, Lima; Personnel of the Oficina de Personal Obrero and of the Archivo de Servicios Urbanos of the Cooperativa Agraria de Produccion Casa Grande Ltda, No. 32, Peru; personnel of the Oficina de Campo, Cooperativa Agraria de Produccion Tuman, Ltda, No. 14, Peru; Colin Harding, Valpe Fitzgerald, Lewis Taylor, Harold Wolpe and Terry Byres. The research was financed by a grant from the Social Science Research Council, London.

Late nineteenth century to 1940s

The use of indentured and contract labour on the sugar plantations, first from China and then from Japan, was replaced by a system of debt bondage (*enganche*) for the recruitment of indigenous labour from the Andean highlands (*sierra*). Elements of extra-economic coercion were present at this stage, implying that labour power was not a wholly 'free' commodity, although most recruitment was formally contractual, and after the abolition in the 1920s of the payment system based on tokens, sugar workers were paid in money wages (Klaren, 1970, p. 49).

During the first four decades of the twentieth century, trade union organizations in the sugar plantations were generally weak, and plantation owners wished to decasualize and stabilize the labour force, because of the difficulties in recruitment. Therefore, proletarianization of the highland peasantry at this stage would have been in the immediate interests of capital on the coast.

1950s to early 1960s

Once an increased proportion of the plantation labour force became stabilized and permanently resident on the coast, the necessary conditions were fulfilled for the establishment of strong workers' organizations. However, it was not until the APRA party achieved a degree of formal political power at the national level after 1956 that the bargaining strength of the sugar trade unions became firmly established.

At this stage the system of *enganche* disappeared in all but a selected area of the Department of Lambayeque, due to changes in the state of the labour market caused by population growth in the *sierra*, increased development of capitalist relations of production in the Department of Cajamarca with consequent proletarianization of the peasantry, and heavy rural-urban migration from the highlands to the coast. Furthermore, a 'duality' appeared in the labour market for cane cutters. In both markets labour power had become a 'free' commodity divorced from its own means of production and exempt from extra-economic coercion. However, in one market labour was well organized in trade unions and enjoyed certain rights and benefits, while in the other, labour was deprived of the support of union organization owing to the legal status of temporary employment and to the presence of intermediaries in the labour market. Thus, plantation owners threatened by rapidly rising labour costs among their unionized labour force sought refuge either in the mechanization of sugar harvesting, or in a renewed reliance on temporary labour recruited from the growing pool of unemployed to be found in the slums of the coastal cities.

1970s

After the Agrarian Reform Law of June 1969, there was increased state intervention in agriculture both in the capitalist and pre-capitalist sectors. On the coast, the sugar plantations were transformed into production co-operatives which incorporated all permanent *macheteros* as members. Cane cutters classified as non-permanent were excluded initially, causing considerable labour conflict in the industry between this group, the co-operatives and various agencies of the state apparatus. As a result of this conflict, these *macheteros* succeeded in organizing themselves into a trade union, intermediaries were eliminated from the labour market, and large numbers of cutters obtained entry into the co-operatives as members. This change in economic, political and legal status of the labour power of a significant number of workers on the co-operatives threatened to undermine the commercial and financial viability of these enterprises, and has stimulated a new wave of mechanization of harvesting in the industry. Thus, within a period of approximately one hundred years, capitalism has created, developed and is now finally eliminating a proletariat of sugar cane cutters in northern Peru.

However, it is not possible in the space of a single paper to chronicle the history of labour power in the sugar industry throughout these three stages. Therefore, what follows is concerned with the transition from stage 1 to stage 2 in the above schema, and covers the period 1940–69. Most of the material is drawn from an archive at the Cooperativa Agraria de Produccion Casa Grande Ltda No. 32, in the Chicama Valley of the Department of La Libertad. This sugar complex was previously owned by the Gildemeister family under the name of the Empresa Agricola Chicama Ltda. It is the largest agro-industrial sugar complex in Peru, and reputedly the largest in the world.

The Peruvian sugar industry, 1940–69

The largest sugar plantations in Peru are concentrated in three valleys on the northern coast – Chicama, Zaña and Lambayeque, where they dominate the pattern of land use. Of the fourteen sugar mills on the coast listed by the National Agrarian Society (SNA) in 1940, twelve were still in operation by the late 1960s. In each case, the mill was owned jointly with an area of adjoining cane land, forming an agro-industrial complex. By the 1960s, over 90 per cent of Peruvian sugar output was produced by these twelve mills, which also instanced a high degree of geographical concentration.

The growth in output of the sugar industry between 1940 and 1967 may be divided into three periods. In the first, covering the 1940s, output was relatively stagnant, with cane and sugar yields fluctuating considerably. In the second, during the 1950s, output expanded rapidly due both to an increase in the area harvested and to increases in cane and sugar yields per hectare. Finally, the industry entered another period of stagnation in the 1960s, with output growing very slowly and sugar yields falling. Employment in the industry fell by approximately half over the period, that is to say from 46,197 in 1940 to around 24,000 in 1969.[2] This was a direct result of labour displacing technical change, particularly the mechanization of several major field operations such as cane cutting, cane loading and cane transport–the three activities which go to make up cane harvesting. During this period, the tonnage of cane milled at Casagrande represented approximately one quarter of the national figure and its labour force represented a similar proportion. The general movement of the output series for Casagrande followed the national series very closely. A final point of background is that, unlike most other sugar industries in the tropics, there is no marked season for cane harvesting in Peru. Cane cutting, like all other field operations, continues for ten or eleven months of the year, being interrupted only for the shutdown of the mill for repairs and maintenance work. This has important implications for the nature of the labour market for cane cutters.

The system of *enganche*

Since the end of the nineteenth century, when indigenous labour from the Peruvian highlands began to supplement and later replace the use of indentured labour from China and Japan in the Peruvian coastal plantations, the system of *enganche* (literally 'the hook') was the predominant method of recruitment of unskilled field labour, mainly cane cutters (*macheteros*) and cane loaders (*carreros*). Many of the violent labour disputes in the industry in the first three decades of the twentieth century were concerned with abuses inherent in early versions of *enganche* (Klaren, 1970, p. 55). At Casagrande, this method of recruitment functioned as follows. The *hacienda* had labour contractors (*agentes*) in the sierra (mostly in the Department of Cajamarca) who received cash advances from Casagrande through its Agency in the town of Cajamarca. These amounts were debited to the individual contractor's personal account at Casagrande. The agent then recruited peons with the money advanced, although certain individuals also used their own resources for recruitment. Once recruited, each peon signed a contract indicating the sum he had received, and was given in turn a paper slip by the agent showing the same amount (*papeleta*). Usually, the peons would make their own way to Casagrande, whilst on occasions it appeared as though transport was arranged by the agent. Once the peons arrived at the *hacienda* and were approved for employment (this involved checking their names against a 'black list' of 'undesirable elements', and submitting to a medical inspection), their paper slips were collected at the *hacienda* office (*Contrata Hacienda*). Every month the value of these slips corresponding to peons recruited by each agent was credited to his account. Thereafter it was the *hacienda's* responsibility to discount the sum advanced to each peon from his weekly earnings, which might amount to a deduction of one third or more. If a peon left the *hacienda* before cancelling his debt, then the agent was held financially responsible, being obliged to locate the absent peon or force his guarantor on the contract (*fiador*) to reimburse the sum concerned, or to work it off at Casagrande. In an earlier period some recruiting agents would themselves supervise the working off of the debts of the labour force in the sugar fields, and pay them either in cash or metal tokens only exchangeable at their own or the company's store. These were the true *contratistas* as opposed to the *socorredores de braceros* used by Casagrande at this date.[3] The *hacienda* employed more than a dozen agents in the *sierra* in the 1950s, and at least two of them (Vargas and Verastegui) had been working intermittently since the 1920s. In other cases, the occupation was handed down from father to son. These agents were recruited by Casagrande's agency in Cajamarca, which vetted likely candidates for their net worth and likely solvency, obtaining references from the banks to aid their judgment. As important as a man's economic assets was his standing in the local peasant communities. Thus, in a favourable comment on one individual who had offered his services as an agent to the agency, they wrote that he had

presence among the peasantry of Cajamarca, Huambocancha, and San Juan. The Credit Bank states he fulfils all his obligations to the letter. He is a good man, farmer and livestock breeder about forty years old, and for a long time has been in contact with peons, cattle traders and muleteers (Correspondence, 5.5.52).[4]

Indeed, many of the recruiting agents were cattle traders selling livestock to Casagrande. The *hacienda* obtained meat in much the same way as it obtained labour power, and for the agents, cattle trading and peon recruitment went well together. When Verastegui was short of cash, he would recruit peons by selling them animals whose value counted as a *socorro*. Conversely, peons sometimes paid off debts through selling him livestock, or even small plots of land.

Even without indulging in outright embezzlement of funds, the agents could earn significant sums from their activities. They were paid by means of two types of commission. The basic commission was payable per peon recruited for and arriving at Casagrande. The extra commission was calculated as a proportion of the value of the paper slips brought by recruited peons over the year. This percentage might vary from 5 to 10 per cent depending on the importance of the agent. However, the *enganchadores* were also penalized for peons who went absent from the *hacienda* before their debt was discharged. The absolute level of these fines was considerable and could wipe out completely the value of an agent's extra commission in a bad year.

Enganche as a stage in the development of the regional labour market

Here it is argued that in the time period and geographical area under consideration the system of *enganche* is most usefully seen as a historically specific stage in the development of the regional wage-labour market for cane cutters. This stage had one underlying

condition, two major features and a set of derived implications for
the social relations of production. The underlying condition was
the existence of a persistent shortage of labour in the market. The
two major features were as follows: potential workers were paid a
portion of their wages in advance, and these workers were
fundamentally migrant peasants seeking temporary off-farm wage
employment to increase their cash incomes. The set of derived
implications for the social relations of production included:
1 waves of temporary migration from the *sierra* to the coast were
established;
2 there were seasonal fluctuations in the supply of labour. At the
time of sowing and harvesting in the highlands, few peasants were
prepared to travel to work on the coast;
3 there was a high rate of turnover among the field-labour force;
4 the field-labour force (mainly *macheteros* and *carreros*), unlike
the mill-labour force, was not wholly proletarianized. The cane
cutters were 'free' in the sense that little or no extra-economic
coercion was exercised in their recruitment, but they were not
'free' in the sense that many of them still had access to land on the
coast or in the *sierra*.

Firstly, it is necessary to clarify certain analytical difficulties
inherent in the statement that there existed a wage-labour market
in the *sierra* at this date. The Agency in Cajamarca was quite clear
as to the forces at work when they wrote that 'the labour power of
the peon (*el trabajo del peon*) has become a commodity (*mercancia*)
like any other, subject to the laws of supply and demand'
(Correspondence, 6.5.52). However, the issuing of loans to the
peons may be thought of as a complication not provided for in
orthodox labour market analysis where supply and demand curves
are drawn up with respect to wage rates. In practice, the peasants
were faced by a package of economic inducements to work on the
coast, composed of a wage rate, bonuses, other benefits such as
free meals and subsidized food rations, an allowance for travel
costs and expenses, and a lump sum loan payment – the *socorro*.
Clearly the existence of fringe benefits does not invalidate the
concept of a labour market, any more than does the partial
payment of wage labour in advance of the work actually taking
place, although in the latter case the employer bears a risk that is
absent in more usual methods of payment (Correspondence,
3.1.44). A second point concerns the volition with which peasants
were recruited. The concept of a labour market does imply a

supply of labour willing to be recruited at given wage rates, levels of fringe benefits, etc. The evidence of the Casagrande correspondence suggests that in the 1950s most peons signed their written contracts with the *hacienda* freely and without interference. The difficulty, of course, is how exactly 'extra-economic coercion' is defined. Two examples may serve to illustrate this point. In 1944, under conditions of fierce competition for labour in Bambamarca at the time of conscription, Verastegui bought out the debts of a group of peons already recruited by Cayalti, and then advanced them cash to work in Sausal (a section of Casagrande). One is left wondering what pressures were brought to bear to persuade this group of peasants to change *haciendas* and end up owing money to both Verastegui and Casagrande. The second case concerns a variant of the system of *enganche* which was requested by the agents in 1952 and which had been suggested previously by the Agency in an attempt to reduce labour turnover on the plantation. This was to forward money in the *sierra* to the relatives of peons already working on the coast and thus bind them over to longer periods of employment. Clearly, such additional *socorros* could easily be presented to peons as a *fait accompli*, and they would simply have to fulfil the contractual obligation this implied, or risk leaving the *hacienda* prematurely and being hunted as a *profugo*. In any case, an element of coercion would seem to be involved. Nevertheless, even after making these qualifications, it is possible to argue that there existed a wage-labour market in the *sierra* of Cajamarca at this time and that the sugar *haciendas* of the coast played a dominant role in it.

Secondly, it is necessary to discuss the meaning, or meanings, of an underlying condition of a persistent shortage of labour. There are both 'strong' and 'weak' versions of this concept. Taking the 'strong' versions first, the most obvious reply is that the level of economic inducements to the *sierra* peons was below some hypothetical equilibrium level required to equate the supply of and demand for labour. For this reason, the demand for labour persistently exceeded the supply. To this the question immediately arises, why did the market not clear through competition between the *haciendas* and other enterprises bidding for labour which would push up the wage rate, levels of benefits, etc.? As it is, I believe that the market did clear in this way and that these 'strong' versions of 'labour shortage' are not wholly plausible. Certainly, there is evidence of collusion between *haciendas* in the setting of wage rates (e.g. in Bambamarca between Pomalca, Tuman and Cayalti in 1952) (Correspondence, 11.6.52), but there is no proof that such wage rate fixing gave rise to excess demand because set at a subequilibrium level. Nevertheless, there are three possible reasons why the wage rate might not rise to clear the market of excess demand. Firstly, there may have existed a backward-sloping aggregate supply curve of labour to the plantations *à la* Boeke-Berg (Berg, 1961; Boeke, 1953). If the *sierra* peasants came to the plantation to earn a target income, then to raise wages might only increase labour turnover without increasing the total labour supply. Indeed, the aggregate labour supply might fall if there were a more rapid turnover of a given number of peasants with few new entrants to the labour force being attracted by the higher wage. This assumes limited wants on the part of the peasants, which may have been more plausible earlier in the century when the *sierra* villages of Cajamarca and La Libertad were remote from road communications and enjoyed a high degree of economic self-sufficiency. Furthermore, evidence is given below that labour turnover fell rather than increased among cane cutters during the 1950s at Casagrande, while wage rates rose.

In addition, the *haciendas* may not have raised the wage to clear excess demand because they were all relying on their recruiting agents to invade new areas of 'natural peasant economy' to tap additional sources of labour supply. Again, such a presumption may have been plausible early in the century, but by the 1940s and 1950s at least the agents were aware they were playing a zero-sum game in the Department of Cajamarca. That is to say, one agent could only recruit a substantially larger number of peons at the expense of other agents.

Thirdly, it is possible that in a period of rapid expansion of output such as took place at Casagrande and in the industry as a whole during the 1950s, the rise in wage rates for cane cutters could lag behind the increase in demand for their services, thus giving rise to a type of dynamic disequilibrium.

However, evidence for this particular interpretation of labour shortage is slight. In April 1952 the Agency informed three of its agents that Casagrande would accept cane cutters from the middle of May, and asked them to send as many as possible because the plantation had increased the area of cane to be cut. No mention was made of any additional economic inducements with which to attract the peons. This incremental recruitment was clearly expected to be fulfilled by greater efforts on the part of the agents (Correspondence, 30.4.52). However, the cane cutters' wage had been increased by 20 per cent in November 1951, with the express purpose of recruiting a greater number of them (Agency Report, pp. 11–51).

The 'weak' versions of 'labour shortage' are generally more plausible than the 'strong' ones. The first of these concerns seasonal fluctuations in the supply of labour. Information for the two most important agents, Pastor and Vargas, shows a tendency for the number of arrivals of *sierra* peons to peak in March, with a trough occurring in May or June, when the mill was shut down for maintenance and repairs. The monthly production series for Casagrande approximately confirms this pattern. It is interesting to compare this seasonal movement in the departure of peons for the coast with the calendar of labour requirements in peasant agriculture in the Province of Cajamarca, as calculated by the Ministry of Agriculture (OSPA, 1970, pp. 41). This suggests that March is a relatively slack month in the *sierra* peasants' calendar. It comes after the harvest of the potato crop (November-January), after the sowing of the main types of cereal (oats, barley and wheat, which are sown between December and late February/early March) and before the busy harvest months of July and August for grains. Other evidence confirms that labour was simply not available in the *sierra* at certain peak periods of the peasants' agricultural calendar. Bardales, for example, reported on one occasion that it would be difficult to recruit peons because 'at this time of year, the people prefer to earn grain and not money (*ganar grano y no dinero*)' (Correspondence, 30.4.52). This suggests that, rather than a target income, peasants had a target number of days they were willing to spend down on the coast away from their families and land. Therefore, since the plantations used only one wage rate for cane cutters over the year, and if this wage rate tended to reflect the state of labour market when supply was most plentiful, then with labour in shorter supply, a labour deficit would appear at the going wage rate. Thus, in this version, labour shortage is character-ized as a persistent *seasonal* scarcity of labour giving rise to regular periods of excess demand.

The final 'weak' version of labour shortage to be considered is the simplest. This holds that while it is broadly true that Casagrande obtained the number of cane cutters it required at any one time in the 1950s at going wage rates, excepting perhaps seasonal shortages, the relatively rapid rate of turnover of these peons needed a constantly active recruitment effort in the *sierra* so as to maintain the required number of men in the plantation. In this version, the problem of labour shortage is effectively reduced to difficulties arising from a high rate of labour turnover, and to the high costs of recruitment associated with the *enganche* system which tied up a significant volume of working capital in the *sierra,* and involved the risk of loss of funds by the plantations to the recruiting agents. It is this meaning of 'labour shortage', together with the seasonal component described above, that is implied in the underlying condition of *enganche* as a historically specific stage in the development of the regional labour market.[5]

The mention of labour turnover raises several additional questions. First, it seems that during the 1940s and 1950s, if not earlier in the century, there developed in Casagrande a group of cane cutters who resided and worked on the plantation almost all the year round. These were the permanent or stable workers (*trabajadores permantes o estables*), who were to be distinguished from the seasonal or temporary migrants from the *sierra*. However, the exact basis of this distinction is not clear, although there is evidence for the existence of this duality in the labour market. In a set of demands placed before the *hacienda* in 1952 by three agents, the following request was included:

That when a peon has paid back his loan through working at Casagrande, and has returned to the *sierra*, then a new *socorro* advanced to him should be considered a new contract with the right to a commission, and he should not be defined as a stable, employee' (Correspondence, 6.6.52).

This suggests a first criterion for identifying this group of permanent cane cutters, that when they did return to the *sierra* and sought new loans, the agents did not earn a commission for recruiting them, as they were already considered as part of the plantation labour force. A second criterion is that they were listed on a separate payroll (*planilla*) on the *hacienda*, presumably because they had continued to work as 'unbonded' labour after their original loans were paid off. Thus, in 1956, Casagrande counted 300 cane cutters on its payroll, all of whom earned the same daily wage (S/.9.40), but who represented approximately one-third of the *hacienda's* daily requirements for *macheteros* (Fasshauer, 1973, p. 13). A third criterion of definition of this group is that, unlike the temporary migrant cutters, they were likely to be members of the trade union at Casagrande. The union was re-established formally in 1948, shortly before Odria came to power, then remained relatively dormant during his eight years of rule, only to become openly active again after 1956. Unfortunately, information is not available as to whether this group of cane cutters enjoyed higher wage rates or levels of indirect benefits than the migrant cutters. The evidence from the Lambayeque *haciendas* in the 1960s, where unionized and non-unionized cane cutters worked side by side, is that the permanent unionized workers did enjoy substantially higher real incomes than the temporary workers, although their daily productivity was lower. However, this information dates from a later stage in the development of the regional labour market, and it is likely that such discrepancies were not so great either in terms of earnings or of productivity in the 1940s and 1950s at Casagrande. Nevertheless, by the mid 1950s at least, there had emerged two categories of cane cutter with different statuses in the plantation, which suggests a certain duality in the labour market for this type of worker.

Secondly, there is the question of changes in the rate of turnover of the temporary cane cutters during the 1950s. The evidence suggests that Casagrande wished to increase the number of its permanent group of cutters and to reduce the rate of turnover of the '*socorridos*' up to 1957–8. This could be achieved in several ways. Higher average loans could be advanced and smaller proportions of a peon's weekly earnings discounted to pay the loan. Neither of these methods is mentioned in the correspondence, which is not to say that they were not used, but the first would have increased the financial risks run by the *hacienda*, while the second might have discouraged peasants from working at Casagrande at a time when recruitment was difficult enough anyway. Instead, bonuses for 'good attendance' were paid to cane cutters, and it is likely that after the agents' requests in 1952, *socorros* were made in the *sierra* to the relatives of peons already employed at Casagrande. Such measures seem to have had some effect, as preliminary calculations show that in the case of the two most important recruiting agents, the average length of time taken for a peon to work off his debt (assuming one-third of his weekly earnings was deducted for this purpose) rose from approximately two to four months between 1951 and 1957. Thus, this stage in the development of the regional labour market was characterized by a growing decasualization and stabilization of the cane-cutting labour force up until the late 1950s, when no additional workers were taken on the permanent payrolls of the plantations in the Chicama valley (Miller, 1967, p. 203) and the duality in the labour market was complete.

The transformation of the regional labour market and the disintegration of the *enganche* system

The system of *enganche* finally disappeared for the recruitment of cane cutters in the Departments of La Libertad and Lambayeque in the early 1960s. This section explores the reasons for the disappearance of this system and examines how it was replaced in one area by a new system of labour recruitment, and in another area by the mechanization of cane cutting. For a start, it is necessary to split the northern region into two zones, separating out on the one hand the La Libertad *haciendas* (Casagrande, Cartavio and Laredo) from the Lambayeque *haciendas* (Pucala, Tuman, Pomalca and Cayalti) on the other.

In La Libertad the first cause of the disintegration of the *enganche* system is to be found in the increased supply of labour in the market as a result of population growth, the proletarianization of the *sierra* peasantry and significant permanent migration from the *sierra* to the coast between 1940 and 1961. Census data shows that the provinces in the main catchment area of the La Libertad *haciendas* increased their populations by significant proportions over the 1940s and 1950s, as well as sustaining heavy outmigration. As a result, an increasing number of workers presented themselves for employment on the sugar *haciendas* in the late 1950s without passing through the channels of *enganche*. These were the *voluntarios* or unbonded labourers.

Population growth would lead to the subdivision and fragmentation of small landholdings, causing overcropping, the threat of erosion and a reduction in soil fertility and yields. Price inflation of purchased consumer goods also increased at a faster rate in the 1960s, thus putting a double squeeze on the highland *minifundia* as sources of income and employment. By the time of the agrarian reform, peasants in Cajamarca with fewer than five hectares (12.35 acres) received more than half their income from off-farm wage employment.[6] The growth of capitalist dairy farming in the valley and environs of Cajamarca to supply the PERULAC processing plant throughout the 1950s and 1960s may also have led to a reduction in employment opportunities, as land previously sown with foodcrops was turned over to natural pasture.

Secondly, as trade union power and organization grew in the Trujillo area during the 1960s, so the duality in the labour market for cane cutters was confirmed and hardened. After 1957–8 it became very difficult to pass from temporary to permanent status on the plantations. Furthermore, the unions included an ending to *enganche* as part of their collective demands, although this does not seem to have been pressed very hard. Thirdly, experiments with cane-cutting machines had been going on in the Chicama valley since 1955, when the prototype Duncan cane cutter was imported from Hawaii. These experiments had been stimulated by the falling labour productivity of the permanent cane cutters concomitant with sharp increases in money wages and indirect benefits. After ten years' experience with different types of cane harvester, the Chicama plantations opted for the system of cutting the cane with Push Rakes in 1965. This eliminated the labour market for manual cane cutters in the valley. The small areas of cane that continued to be cut by hand because of special soil conditions, etc., could be harvested by the sons of the permanent workers who were resident on the plantations.

In Lambayeque some of the same forces were in operation. Major recruitment areas such as Bambamarca and Chota increased their populations, despite flows of outmigration. In the coastal provinces of the Department the demographic explosion was much greater. The district of Chiclayo more than doubled its population between 1940 and 1961. As a result, the supply of labour to the *haciendas* increased significantly. By 1961 Tuman was employing unbonded labour in the field (*libres de campo*) and encouraging its agent in Chota to give preference to this type of labour over that recruited through the system of *enganche*. In the same year it withdrew its paid employee (*empleado*) from Bambamarca, and cancelled its *contrata* recruited by Verastegui, numbering only four persons by that date (Tuman, 12.9.61). However, there were important differences in Lambayeque compared to La Libertad. Trade unions were established there later than to the south. As a result, although duality in the labour market for cane cutters existed, it was not so rigid as in the Trujillo area. Wage levels in the sugar industry were also correspondingly lower in Lambayeque than in La Libertad. In Tuman, despite attempts in both 1946 and 1962, an official trade union was never recognized. Furthermore, in their attempts to ensure that no *sindicato* became established there in the 1960s, they followed a deliberate strategy of 'casualizing' the field-labour force, particularly in cane cutting. The permanent force of cane cutters was run down through natural wastage and transfer to other jobs, while increasing reliance was placed on outside contract labour (*trabajadores eventuales o contratados*) recruited through a legally established company (Contratistas Cañaveleros SA), who acted as an intermediary in the labour market. This labour was not recruited through the *enganche* system, and it was paid by the intermediary company, which also supplied at least two of the other four *haciendas* in the area, namely Pucala and Pomalca. Thus, in the case of the Lambayeque *haciendas*, the system of *enganche* was replaced by the use of unbonded labour employed through a different type of intermediary in the labour market. Cane cutting still has not been mechanized in this area. To sum up this new stage in the development of the labour market for cane cutters in Lambayeque, the same scheme can be used as was mentioned in the discussion of *enganche*. In this case the underlying condition is no longer a shortage of unskilled labour, but rather an excess supply of it. In the 'strong' versions the situation has been neatly reversed. As a result of legislation in the 1960s, the minimum wage for the area put a floor into the downward movement of wage levels. Thus, by the end of this period, it may not be an exaggeration to assume an unlimited supply of labour at the minimum wage. In contrast to *enganche*, the market did not clear because supply was chronically in excess of demand. The major features of this new stage are that workers were no longer paid a portion of their wages in advance, all cane cutting was carried out on simple piece rates paid at the end of each week, while many cane cutters could no longer be considered as fundamentally peasants. A growing proportion were an urban-resident, landless agricultural proletariat similar in many ways to the 'rural proletariat' described by Mintz in Puerto Rico (Mintz, 1956). The derived implications for the social relations of production became as follows:

1 the flow of temporary migration to the coast from the highlands for cutting cane dries up. The coast has become self-sufficient in unskilled labour;

2 seasonal fluctuations in the supply of cane-cutting labour to the plantations derived from the *sierra* peasants' agricultural calendar are less marked and of little relevance;

3 the rate of labour turnover is likely to have fallen, due to the

absence of alternative employment opportunities for the cane
cutters;
4 a higher proportion of the cane cutters have become effectively
proletarianized.

This growing disarticulation between the coastal capitalist mode
and the highland pre-capitalist mode of production during the
1960s had important political consequences. First, the secular
decline in demand for highland labour on the part of the sugar
plantations, at a time of accelerated population growth, coincided
with attempts by certain highland *haciendas* to dislodge tenants
and pasture-renters and to replace them with the use of wage
labour. This provided the essential dynamic behind the land
invasions and *hacienda-comunidad* conflicts in Cajamarca at this
time, which continue to cause problems for the execution of the
agrarian reform. Second, the pool of cheap labour in the area has
been transferred from the *sierra*, where it existed in rural form
with a dispersed settlement pattern, to the *barriadas* of coastal
towns such as Chiclayo and Ferreñafe, where this reverse army is
now highly concentrated on the very edges of the capital-intensive,
high-productivity sugar, rice and cotton estates. It is this startling
juxtaposition of rich and poor on the coast that threatens to
undermine the agrarian reform in the plantation sector as well,
and it has already led to land invasions on the sugar production co-
operatives.

Conclusion

In this paper I have attempted to show three things. First, I have
demonstrated how, at an abstract level, the capitalist mode of
production embodied in coastal plantation agriculture in Northern
Peru was articulated with the pre-capitalist peasant mode of
production in the *sierra* through the labour market between 1940
and the early 1960s. Second, I have explained how the specific
nature of this articulation operated through the system of *enganche*,
which corresponded to a historically contingent stage in the
development of the regional labour market. This stage was defined
by an underlying condition of labour shortage, while migrant
peasant workers received part of their wages in advance. A set of
derived implications for the social relations of production was also
identified. Third, I have outlined how after a process culminating
in the mid 1960s, the labour market was transformed by population
growth, proletarianization of the peasantry, internal migration and

labour-displacing technical change, which led to greater economic independence of coastal agriculture from the *sierra*. This may be termed provisionally a process of growing disarticulation of the two modes of production, implying a reduced degree of functional interdependence. This stage was defined by an underlying condition of excess supply of labour, while *macheteros* no longer received any portion of their wages in advance. In addition, a growing proportion of cane cutters had become an urban-resident, landless agricultural proletariat. Finally, a set of derived social relations of production was outlined which contrasted with that corresponding to the system of *enganche*.

Notes

1 For a similar argument in the case of Rhodesia, see Arrighi (1970).
2 The 1940 figure is from the Census of that year quoted in Hunt (n.d.). One source gave a figure of 'more than 20,000 workers' in the industry in 1970. See Sistema de Conduccion de la Reforma Agraria en los Complejos Agroindustriales (1970). The figure of 24,000 was quoted by the Central Office of the Sugar Co-operatives (CECO-AAP).
3 *Socorro* was the name given to the cash advance used in the recruitment of peons.
4 The 'correspondence' mentioned in the text refers to that between Casagrande and its Agency in Cajamarca. For simplicity of reference, I have identified letters by their dates. This material is filed in the archive of the CAP Casagrande Ltda.
5 It may be objected that it is in the nature of this type of source material that the *hacienda* administration, the Agency in Cajamarca, and the agents should all recount their various difficulties in labour recruitment and tend to exaggerate the extent of any labour shortages there may have been. There may be some truth in this argument, especially since most of the correspondence cited was written by the Agency in Cajamarca, which had to defend and justify its actions continually to the *hacienda* administration. Nevertheless, such an extreme view does ignore the significance of certain facts, such as the continual search for new recruiting agents and new labour catchment areas.
6 Personal communication from Lewis Taylor.

References

Agency Report (1951), *Informe Mensual de Anexos*, November, Agencia Cajamarca

Arrighi, G. (1970), 'Labour supplies in historical perspective: a study of the proletarianization of the African peasantry in Rhodesia', *Journal of Development Studies*, 6, 3, pp. 197–284

Berg, E. J. (1961), 'Backward sloping labour supply functions in dual economies – the African case', *Quarterly Journal of Economics*, 75, pp. 468–92

Boeke, J. (1953), *Economics and Economic Policy of Dual Societies*, Haarlem: Tjeenk Willink & Zoon N.V.

Bourricaud, F. (1961), 'Syndicalisme et Politique: le cas péruvien', *Sociologie du Travail*, 4, pp. 33–49

Bradby, B. (1975), 'The destruction of natural economy', *Economy and Society*, 4, 2, pp. 127–61

Correspondence (1927–55), Empresa Agricola Chicama Ltda, Cartas Confidenciales, Cajamarca y Agentes

Dobb, M. (1963), *Studies in The Development of Capitalism*, London: Routledge & Kegan Paul

Fasshauer, G. (1973), *Sistema de Cosecha de la Caña de Azucar*, Cooperativa Agraria de Producción Casa Grande Ltda, No. 32, Division Corte, Carguio y Transporte

Griffin, K. (1969), *Underdevelopment in Spanish America*, London: Allen & Unwin

Horton, D. (1973), 'Haciendas and cooperatives: a preliminary study of latifundist agriculture and agrarian reform in northern Peru', Research Paper no. 53, Land Tenure Center, University of Wisconsin

Hunt, S. (n.d.), 'Real wages and economic growth', unpublished draft, Princeton University, ch. 4

Klaren, P. (1970), *La Formación de las Haciendas Azucareras y los Origenes del Apra*, Lima: Instituto de Estudios Peruanos

Miller, S. (1967), 'Hacienda to plantation in northern Peru – the process of proletarianisation of a tenant farmer society', in J. H. Steward (ed.), *Contemporary Change in Traditional Societies*, vol. 3, Illinois

Mintz, S. W. (1956), 'Cañamelar: the subculture of a rural sugar plantation proletariat', in J. H. Steward, *et al.* (eds.), *The People of Puerto Rico*, Illinois

Oficina Sectorial de Planificacion Agricola (OSPA) – Mision

Iowa (1970), *Requerimientos Mensuales de Mano de Obra para la Agricultura por Hectaria, por Cultivo, por Provincias y gara la Actividad Pecuaria*, Año Base 1967, Lima: Convenio para Estudios Economicos Basicos

Prada, Luis G. (1945), *El Cultivo de Arroz por el Sistema de Transplante en la Zona Norte del Peru*, Lima

Scott, C. D. (1976), 'Peasants, proletarianisation and the articulation of modes of production: the case of sugar cane cutters in northern Peru, 1940–69', *Journal of Peasant Studies*, 3, 3, pp. 321–41

Sistema de Conducción de la Reforma Agraria en los Complejos Agroindustriales (1970), *Del Latifundio a la Cooperativa*, Lima

Tuman (1961), Letter from Manager (Lima) to *Hacienda* Administrator (Tuman), 12 September

Part Five

The state and the peasantry

Introduction

Several of the papers in previous parts of this book (Byres, Bernstein, and Taussig in his discussion of Rural Development in the Cauca Valley) draw attention to the fact that the activities of the state are profoundly influenced by what happens in rural society, and that the state in turn greatly affects processes of agrarian change. There is a long tradition of thought which conceptualizes 'the state' as existing 'outside of' or 'above society'; and in the line of this tradition there are a good many writers who treat the activity of 'Rural Development' as if it were conducted by 'the state' in the interests of 'the society' as a whole.[1] Taussig's paper in particular warns us that rural development programmes implemented by the state serve the interests of some groups and classes and not others, and that their real effects may be very different from what is claimed for them or from the rhetoric surrounding them.[2] The readings in this last part[3] are concerned with the state in relation to agrarian change, and with 'Rural Development' as part of the activity of the state. They take us back to the questions of strategy raised in Part One, and in doing so they confront again the debate over processes of change in agrarian societies which runs through this book.

An uneasy alliance of classes

In our first reading Raikes analyses the inter-relationships of the state and agrarian society – or more accurately the inter-relationships of the agrarian classes with the class controlling the institutions of the state – with reference to Tanzania. He shows how differentiation and the emergence of a rich peasantry have been encouraged, both directly and indirectly, by the policies of colonial and post-colonial governments of Tanzania; but he emphasizes the ambiguity in the relationship between the 'state class' and the rich peasantry. As he points out, there is a conflict

between the diverse and uncontrollable nature of rich peasant accumulation and the needs of the state class to extract surplus through the control of the channels for the disposal of produce. On the other hand, rich peasants are the class most likely to engage in productivity-raising innovations

– which the state class needs in order eventually to increase its revenues. (Washbrook, 1976; and Baker, forthcoming, similarly show the ambiguity in the relationship between the colonial governments of South India and the rural élites which they encouraged.)

The state versus the peasantry

In Tanzania there is an antagonistic relationship between the state class and the peasantry as a whole, for all the emphasis on 'socialism' in government statements. Hyden, in his study of state policy in Tanzania (1980), also detects this antagonism, though he disagrees with Raikes over the extent of the differentiation of the Tanzanian peasantry and argues rather, that in Tanzania as in much of sub-Saharan Africa, there is a distinct peasant mode of production, and that the peasantry remains 'uncaptured' by the market and the state. Hyden argues that development can only take place if the social autonomy of the peasants is removed by coercion, and he suggests that in view of the failures of capitalism seriously to undermine the autonomy of the peasantry, socialism will have to serve as the main agent of modernization. His work may be seen as a sustained apologia for the regime in Tanzania. The line of argument that he advances is strongly criticized by Williams in the second reading in this part.

According to Raikes the antagonism between the state class and the peasantry has arisen because the state must have revenue, and in an overwhelmingly agricultural country this must come primarily from agriculture. The state extracts surplus from the peasantry largely through its control of channels for the marketing of commercialized produce. Requirements for state revenue 'increasingly outstrip the development of production, necessitating the extraction of an increasing proportionate surplus and lowering the real price received by peasants for their produce'. This in turn has a depressing effect on the voluntary expansion of production so that increasingly there is resort to direct and coercive means to bring about such expansion, though this generally does not actually work very well. Much of the government's rural development programme – Raikes cites especially agricultural research and extension – is wrapped up in an ideology of 'modernization'. In practice many of the innovations and much of the advice which is offered is appropriate only for the richer cultivators. But their rejection by the ordinary cultivators – sometimes with protest – tends to reinforce the idea that the peasantry is 'resistant to change' and must be 'modernized', and thus to emphasize the need for still greater control to be exercised over them. Coulson's account of agricultural development policy in Tanzania (1977) provides a similar interpretation and more sustained discussion.

Raikes demonstrates both how state interventions influence agrarian change and how Rural Development policies and programmes may become instruments for the control of the mass of the peasantry with rather self-defeating, but still self-reinforcing, effects. It is this understanding of the (frequently) contradictory nature of what is done in the name of 'Rural Development' which leads Gavin Williams, in our next reading, 'to take the part of peasants' (in direct opposition to an argument like Hyden's). Peasants, Williams says, are the victims of the ideologies of modernization and development to which both many liberal and many Marxist economists adhere: 'Peasants are assumed to lack initiative and innovation. They are unable to develop. They must be developed.' He goes on to argue that peasants survive the development of capitalism and the expansion of commodity relations in a way which well summarizes for us the debates which run through this book. He argues that 'Inequalities are not sufficient evidence for the fundamentally capitalist tendencies of the development of the peasant economy'; that 'Wage employment, like inequality may be integrated into peasant production rather than become a feature of the "self-evident" transition from peasant to capitalist farming'; and that there are tendencies which 'contain social differentiation within the broad parameters of an unequal peasant society'. The peasantry is certainly not a homogeneous category for Williams, and he does not hesitate to recognize that 'there are cumulative advantages accruing to the better-off in a rural economy as in any other'; but he still argues that 'peasants survive the development of capitalism and the expansion of commodity relations [essentially] because of their ability to deliver goods to consumers at lower prices than capitalists' (see also our readings from Djurfeldt and Taussig in Part Two; and Vergopoulos, 1978). Williams goes on to explain why peasants often resist outsiders' plans for them, and why they may sometimes manage their agriculture more 'efficiently' when they are left alone. *But* 'Both capitalist and socialist development strategies require peasants to provide resources necessary for the development of the urban, industrial economy' and the state needs to control and to tax peasants (see Byres, in Part One, for a blunt statement of the necessity for this). Thus it is that in many African countries administrators continue to be attracted to irrigation and settlement schemes where farmers depend on the state – in spite of the fairly considerable evidence that such schemes are frequently disastrous even in terms of the objectives of the state (also see Raikes on this point). Williams's general conclusion is that 'The underdevelopment of peasant production is the condition for the development of capitalist and state production, in the interests of the state and its beneficiaries rather than the livelihood of the people.' (Corbridge, in his criticisms of Byres in Part One, implicitly takes this view also.) The onslaughts of the state are resisted by peasants, and this accounts for and underlines much of peasant political action.

A different approach

Finally Williams suggests that the only path of 'development' so far as the peasantry is concerned, is one like that described by Mao Tse-tung as 'walking on two legs', in which the development of peasant production is a condition for the development of industry: 'But the leg of agriculture cannot support the leg of industry until policies are no longer defined for peasants by their betters and when peasants stand up for themselves.'

The last reading in this part is a short extract from a recent paper by Mark Harrison, whom we have seen earlier to be a strong critic of the Chayanovian theory of peasant economy from a fairly orthodox Marxist standpoint (reading in Part Three). Yet he too would have us 'take the part of peasants'. The Marxist critique of the Chayanov school in the Soviet Union in the 1920s, and the modern critique of 'peasant economy', lacks a practical theory of socialist construction and thus 'carries within itself the possibility of becoming dangerously irrelevant to the material problems of the actually existing world'. In this passage Harrison refers to ideas and initiatives discussed in the Soviet Union in the 1920s, which were cut short by collectivization. His idea is not, as he says, to try to write a 'what might have been' history of the Soviet Union, but to indicate the roots of an alternative practical theory of 'rural development'.

Notes

1 Important discussions of the concept of the state are in: Laclau (1975); Miliband (1970, 1973); Poulantzas (1973). On the state in post-colonial societies refer to: Alavi (1972, 1975); Brett (1973); Freyhold, M. von (1977); Leys (1975, 1976); Moore (1980); and Saul (1974).
2 See the works listed under 'Critics of "Rural Development"' following the introduction to Part One.
3 This final part introduces further, important, aspects of issues referred to earlier, but it also serves as a conclusion to the book as a whole. Thus studies which have been listed earlier also relate to themes discussed here. See especially references listed under: 'The Russian Debates'; 'Land reform'; 'Critics of "Rural Development"'; and 'Critics of "Rural Development": towards a socialist agriculture' following the introduction to Part One.

References

Alavi, H. (1972), 'The state in post-colonial societies', *New Left Review,* 74, pp. 59–81

Alavi, H. (1975), 'India and the colonial mode of production', *Socialist Register 1975*; and *Economic and Political Weekly*, special number, August, pp. 1235–62

Baker, C. J. (forthcoming), *The Tamiland Countryside,* London: Oxford University Press

Bernstein, H. (1981), 'Notes on state and peasantry: the Tanzanian case', *Review of African Political Economy*, 21, pp. 44–62

Brett, E. A. (1973), *Colonialism and Underdevelopment in East Africa: The Politics of Economic Change 1919–1939*, London: Heinemann

Coulson, A. (1977), 'Agricultural policies in mainland Tanzania', *Review of African Political Economy*, 10, pp. 74–100

Freyhold, M. von (1977), 'The post-colonial state and its Tanzanian version', *Review of African Political Economy*, 8, pp. 75–89

Freyhold, M. von (1979), *Ujamaa Villages in Tanzania: Analysis of a Social Experiment*, London: Heinemann

Hyden, G. (1980), *Beyond Ujamaa in Tanzania: Underdevelopment and an Uncaptured Peasantry*, London: Heinemann

Laclau, E. (1975), 'The specificity of the political: the Poulantzas–Miliband debate', *Economy and Society*, 4, 1, pp. 87–110

Leys, C. (1975), *Underdevelopment in Kenya*, London: Heinemann

Leys, C. (1976), 'The "overdeveloped" post-colonial state: a re-evaluation', *Review of African Political Economy*, 5, pp. 39–48

Miliband, R. (1970), 'The capitalist state: reply to Nicos Poulantzas', *New Left Review*, 59, pp. 53–62

Miliband, R. (1973), *The State in Capitalist Society*, London: Weidenfeld & Nicolson

Moore, M. (1980), 'Public bureaucracy in the post-colonial states: some questions on "autonomy" and "dominance"', *Development and Change*, 11, 1, pp. 137–48

Poulantzas, N. (1973), *Political Power and Social Classes*, London: New Left Books

Poulantzas, N. (1976), 'The capitalist state: a reply to Miliband and Laclau', *New Left Review*, 95, pp. 63–85

Saul, J. S. (1974), 'The state in post-colonial societies: Tanzania', *Socialist Register 1974*

Washbrook, D. A. (1976), *The Emergence of Provincial Politics: The Madras Presidency 1880–1920*, London: Cambridge University Press

Williams, G. (1981), *State and Society in Nigeria*, Sheffield: Review of African Political Economy

Intervention by the state: exchange

(An area of intervention by the state which is of particular importance, is in exchange, as both Raikes and Williams in the papers in this part have suggested. Finally, we include some references to additional reading in this area.)

Harriss, B. (1980), 'Regulated foodgrains markets: a critique', *Social Scientist*, 8, 8, pp. 22–31

Krishnaji, N. (1975), 'State intervention in foodgrains prices', *Social Scientist*, 30–31, pp. 75–90

Onitiri, H., and Olatunbosun, D. (1974), *The Marketing Board System*, Ibadan: NISER

Panikulangara, V. (1976), 'Paddy procurement through producer levy: a case study of Kerala', *Social Scientist*, 4, 4, pp. 44–55

Raynaut, C. (1973), 'La circulation marchande et les mécanismes d'inégalité économique', Centre d'Etudes et de Recherches Ethnologiques, Université de Bordeaux, cahier no. 2

Raynaut, C. (1977), 'Circulation monétaire et évolution des structures socio-économiques chez les Haoussas du Niger', *Africa*, 47, 2, pp. 160–71

Subbarao, K. (1978), *Rice Marketing Systems and Compulsory Levies in Andhra Pradesh*, New Delhi: Institute of Economic Growth

Tiffen, M. (1976), *The Enterprising Peasant: Economic Development in Gombe Emirate, N. E. State, Nigeria*, London: HMSO

15 The state and the peasantry in Tanzania*

Philip Raikes

Introduction

Rural differentiation in Tanzania, as elsewhere, cannot be adequately studied in isolation from the development of commodity production, class formation and state form in the society as a whole. The purpose of this paper is to try to show the links between specific processes of differentiation and these more general processes. I am concerned not only to demonstrate the variety of paths to rural differentiation but the partially contradictory nature of some of these different paths and their relation to underlying contradictions in the overall social process. I shall also be concerned to demonstrate the importance of state form, structure and policy most especially as they affect effective possession of the access to the means of production, and the influence of the particular form taken by effective possession upon the process of accumulation (Hindess and Hirst, 1977).

This involves looking critically at those attempts which have been made to study and conceptualize these processes of differentiation. In the first place, there are those who, starting from the obvious fact that income distribution is less unequal in Tanzania than in most neighbouring countries, assume that rural differentiation is not significant. As will be shown this rests in part upon inappropriate selection and analysis of the available data. But more importantly, it rests upon a static analysis which considers only the level of differentiation in terms of measurable material wealth and ignores the processes involved. Since, as will be argued, these take the form of political consolidation and

*This chapter is taken from Raikes (1978).

In thinking about the various themes pursued here, I have been helped by discussion with (among others) Henry Bernstein, Jannik Boesen, Brighton Labour Process and Peripheral State CSE Groups, Michaela von Freyhold, Finn Kjaerby, Gary Littlejohn, Vicky Meynen, and Anne Whitehead. They should not be held responsible for the content of the paper.

preferential access to state resources as well as direct accumulation through investment and labour-hiring, such methods will evidently ignore many of the important factors.

On the other hand, many of those who have considered rural differentiation to be significant, myself included (Raikes, 1972), have tended to consider only one mode of differentiation and have so conflated two separate and partially contradictory processes. To be more specific, we have tended to consider only the 'classic' process whereby the peasantry becomes internally differentiated with the emergence of rich peasants or kulaks, gradually transforming themselves into capitalist farmers, accompanied by the extrusion at the lower end of landless labourers from the ranks of the poor peasantry. Other analysts, concerned rather with the processes by which African commodity production has been increasingly subordinated to the requirements of international capital, have proposed rather a process in which the peasantry as a whole is increasingly separated from control over the means of production and labour-process, thus becoming proletarianized even while they continue to own the land on which they cultivate (see Bernstein, Part Two of this volume). Such accounts tend to emphasize the development of increasingly tightly controlled 'schemes' for the production of export crops, often under the direct control of multinational corporations and for delivery to central processing plants. While I do not accept that such direct producers can be considered proletarians (a formulation which seems to me to gloss over some important differences between the two), there is no doubt that such developments are highly significant and substantially different from the 'classic' case. One important difference is that such schemes tend to be relatively undifferentiated internally, this being related to the more important factor of control over the production process. Not only is this normally worked out in sufficient detail that it precludes any diversification of accumulation into other activities and sectors, but the scope for accumulation is normally strictly limited by the scheme plan, which tends to limit the acreage and level of production of any individual producer in line with the quality control and technical criteria set by the scheme management. As Cowen (1976) has suggested, the aim of such schemes is to generate the development of an undifferentiated middle peasantry, producing high-grade export crops under controlled and increasingly technically advanced methods of production and to avoid the uncontrollable aspects of rich peasant differentiation. Certainly any study which aims to analyse the process of differentiation in Tanzania must distinguish between these two processes and place them in context.

The paper starts with a brief outline of the surface characteristics of the Tanzanian economy and society, aimed primarily at the reader who is not already familiar with these. The following section examines the proposition that rural differentiation is not a significant factor in Tanzania. This is followed by a brief outline of the development of commodity production in Tanganyika and Tanzania, indicating some important turning points and their relation to different processes of differentiation. This is followed by more detailed consideration of some of the specific processes, including the generation of migrant labour and labour-reserve areas, the inter-related development of rich peasants and an educated stratum especially in highland coffee-producing areas, the emergence of rich peasants in annual cropping areas, and the development of controlled schemes for the production of export crops (differentiation by sex is also considered in the article from which this chapter has been taken). Finally an attempt is made to relate all of these to the emergence and consolidation of control over the production process by the state and to consider more recent developments in the light of this increasingly centralized control.

Tanzania outline

Tanzania is a large, poor country, over 90 per cent of whose population, of some 15 million, live in the rural areas. The vast majority of these are peasants of one sort or another, producing both subsistence use-values and commodities for sale. The latter sphere of production is dominated by the production of export commodities, which is substantially greater by value than commodity production for the domestic market (though the degree to which this is the case is exaggerated by biases in the collection of official statistics).

Overall population density at about 44 per square mile is low, and the major concentrations of population are dispersed around the periphery of the country, mostly coinciding with areas of higher than usual rainfall. In most areas of the country, land is sufficiently plentiful not to have acquired a market value nor correspondingly to have generated substantial changes towards more intensive methods of cultivation. However, in some of the more advanced and densely populated export-crop producing areas intensification of land-use has been accompanied by renting and sale of land. These are at best quasi-legal since commercial transactions in land are limited by both 'customary law' (and its colonial codification) and post-colonial central legislation. Formally, the ownership of all land is vested in the state, and this has moved beyond formality in recent years with substantial compulsory movements of the rural population into villages, normally without compensation.

There is no landlord class as such. Current land leases tend to be short term, informal, and as often as not to involve the renting in of land by larger farmers (with mechanized equipment) from smaller.

In the pre-independence period 10 per cent of the cultivated area was controlled by foreign-owned estates and plantations, and produced up to 40 per cent of total marketed agricultural production. Since Independence in 1961, most of the estates and plantations have been nationalized and several new large parastatal farms and ranches have been set up.

The proportion of the rural population involved in wage-labour on large farms has declined since the mid 1950s, with mechanization of production processes and consequent stabilization of the labour force. There was a further substantial reduction in the plantation labour force during the mid 1960s, when the price of sisal (the major plantation crop) fell drastically.

Apart from this 'official' wage-labour force, which is subject to minimum-wage legislation and appears in statistical compilations, there is a substantial but unknown amount of casual seasonal migrant labour, both supplementing the official labour-force on the estates and, more importantly, working for rich peasants and African capitalist farmers.[1] The wages of these workers are typically well below the official minimum wage (in some cases one-third to one-half the level). Such labour-hiring is officially disapproved of by the government as being inconsistent with its 'socialist' policies and governmental restrictions have been imposed on it on occasion.

In this context, it may seem curious that mention of Tanzania's socialism has been deferred to this point, since for many people this is the country's best-known feature. While I would join those who reject Tanzania's claims to be socialist or moving towards socialism, it is clearly necessary to consider those claims.

There can be no doubt whatever of the extensive nature of state control of the Tanzanian economy. Some 70 per cent of fixed capital stock is under government ownership, while the proportion of gross fixed capital formation is similar. Nearly all major industrial companies are either owned outright by parastatal boards or have parastatal majority shareholding. This is also true of most of the large farm and ranch section. Prices throughout the country are controlled by the state, which also has monopoly control of almost all primary agricultural marketing, through co-operatives and parastatal marketing agencies up to 1976, and since then, with the abolition of the co-operatives, through the latter alone. In addition to this, there are the standard forms of state intervention through investment in infrastructure, provision of agricultural and other credit, agricultural research and extension and the various controlling activities of a large and growing bureaucracy. Finally, the state has attempted to change the whole basis of agricultural production in the past few years by moving the rural population into nucleated villages for the improved provision of services and more effective control over the process of production.

The Tanzanian state clearly has the means for considerable control over the internal operations of the economy; it has also laid great stress upon various policies to achieve 'socialism and self-reliance'. Apart from the nationalizations of 1967, the policy of *Ujamaa Vijijini* (socialism in the villages) was specifically intended to combat growing rural class-formation through the encouragement of largely automonous village producer co-operatives. 'Education for Self-Reliance' sought to move school education away from its current emphasis on academic studies, relevant only to the five per cent or so of the relevant age-group attending secondary school, towards more relevant subjects. Similar policies sought to achieve more rational and egalitarian patterns of health care and provision of social and economic services, while a major strand in the Arusha Declaration[2] forbade politicians and senior civil servants from the ownership of income-earning assets. Overall policy since 1967 has at least ostensibly been aimed at reducing the dependency of the economy upon primary exports and imports of foreign machinery, technology and skills.

This sounds an impressive policy slate, but achievements have been rather less spectacular. The proportion of foreign funds in the development budget, rather than declining since 1968, has in fact increased considerably, while foreign trade has not declined as a proportion of GDP. Industrial investment has been fairly rapid but has yet to tackle the problem of total dependency on foreign technology, skills, equipment and spare parts. Profitability in the parastatal industrial sector has been poor, the result of waste and misapplication of funds rather than its gearing to socialist goals. The hierarchy of command and system of production within the sector remains largely unchanged, with increasing repression of workers in recent years. All strikes are banned and the single official union is largely inactive on the workers' behalf.

Educational policy, although well-intentioned, suffered from the prevailing class distinctions and low status of agricultural labour in the society. Practical education in agriculture has turned out to be merely drudgery, largely unleavened by improvement in techniques. The students have usually gone to school in the first place as a means to escape from the agricultural sector, and where possible any sort of manual labour. This is not affected by the mouthing of slogans by teachers who do not mean them, especially since agricultural work is often used as punishment. Similarly, official policies have largely failed to shift the pattern of health care from curative services concentrated in the main towns, to rural-based preventive services, and the towns remain overwhelmingly better provided with all social services. Finally, *Ujamaa Vijijini* has rapidly developed from its initial statements as self-reliant, co-operative and democratic, into a programme, from which all pretence of socialism has been dropped, for the enforced nucleation of the rural population in 'development villages'.

It is not the purpose of this paper to argue that Tanzania's socialist policies were simply a fraud, perpetrated consciously by a bourgeoisie or petty-bourgeoisie for the consolidation of its own class position. Nevertheless, such consolidations more or less happened in practice and the combination of open class interest and self-mystifying ideology has assisted this process.

Degree versus process of differentiation

Certain observers of the Tanzanian scene have claimed, on the basis of available official statistics, that since the level of income inequality to be observed in rural Tanzania is less than in most surrounding countries, the phenomenon can be dismissed as insignificant[3] This is usually coupled with an attempt to demonstrate that Chayanovian 'demographic differentiation' is the only relevant process to be found. This viewpoint seems to me to be incorrect in every sense.

In the first place, it depends on a particular reading of unreliable data. Neither the Census of 1967, nor the 1969 Household Budget Survey,[4] the sources most often used, was collected with analysis of rural differentiation in view, a point readily demonstrated by the almost total lack of data compilations which allow its direct assessment. Both are concerned to provide aggregate and mean data, while differentiation is very obviously concerned with dispersion around the mean. Moreover, there is good reason to suspect the existence of bias in precisely those areas which do cover the phenomenon. Peasants are notoriously reluctant, the world over, to give accurate indications of their income or wealth to government snoopers – suspecting, and often justifiably, that such information will be used against them. But in Tanzania there were further specific causes for bias. Both the Census and the HBS relied on data collected after the Arusha Declaration, which had been forthright in its condemnation of labour-hiring by rich peasants as a form of exploitation, a point further hammered home by almost hourly quotations of slogans from the Declaration on the radio during the following year. Finally, since much of the rural wage-labour force in Tanzania is composed of cyclical migrants who also keep their own farms, many of them would have given their occupation as 'farmer' rather than wage-labourer.

But this is not the major point of criticism, for one can readily agree that differentiation in Tanzania is less far advanced than in most surrounding countries. What is of interest is not the stage which has been reached but the processes involved. As the account below should make abundantly clear, demographic differentiation, so far from being the most important of these, and an alternative to class-formation, is in fact a relatively minor factor and related to the process of class-formation.

This is not the place for a general criticism of Chayanov, which has recently been most ably performed by Gary Littlejohn (1977). Perhaps the central criticism of Chayanov is that, though he specifically mentions some of the links between peasant agriculture and the wider economy, these are assumed away for the bulk of the analysis, by a definition of peasant agriculture which ignores the social determination of the components of the 'labour-consumer balance'. Turning to the Tanzanian context, one finds that many of the implicit underlying assumptions of the theory are unfulfilled. There is no landlord class to obstruct or pre-empt opportunities for rich peasant development. Land is not generally in short supply and so not often subject to commodity transactions.

Technique, rather than being static, has in some cases gone from the hand hoe to the tractor and combine in the space of one or two decades. Family size depends, among other things, upon the number of wives a man has. This last indicates a major problem in the whole conceptualization of demographic differentiation. The point at issue is not whether income, farm size and family size are positively correlated or not. Here, as elsewhere, they tend to be. But Chayanov simply assumes demographic variables to be exogenous and determinant, where all the evidence available indicates that this is not the case. Certainly not in Tanzania, where a second marriage is often both a sign of wealth and financially restricted to the relatively wealthy.

Apart from this, there can be no doubt whatever that the extent of income differentiation in some of the more advanced commodity-producing areas extends far beyond what could possibly be expected on the basis of demographic differentiation, in addition to which a process of political consolidation can be observed which is certainly absent from the Chayanov model – whether or not such processes could have been observed in nineteenth-century Russia.

The final stand of this school of thought is to point out that the specific studies of differentiation, to be cited below, are concerned with relatively small areas, and may be considered 'exceptional'. Once again this misses the whole point of the argument, since the purpose is to study the processes rather than the state of play. Even at that, however, the point is considerably overstressed, since the areas covered include most of the major cash-cropping areas. Rich peasants themselves are, of course, virtually by definition, a minority of the population, though, in some cases, they are responsible both directly, and through the supply of contract services, for a substantial proportion of total commodity production. It seems reasonable thus to cease belabouring this dead horse and consider the processes concerned.

Colonialism and differentiation

As will be demonstrated, a number of different processes of differentiation and class-formation can be distinguished in Tanzania, each related in one way or other to the development of commodity production and to the economic, political and ideological forms generated in this process.

Colonial incorporation: the initial phase

The primary function of the colonial state in what became Tanzania, was the extraction of primary produce for the strategic and industrial requirements of the metropolis by the cheapest possible means. Alongside this, and in partial contradiction at certain points, was the requirement to secure the conditions of production and reproduction to the European colonists whose prior incursion had, to some extent, generated the German colonial venture in the first place.[5]

This implied the total restructuring of the regional economy to this purpose, destroying the pre-existing Indian Ocean trade links (which was rapidly achieved; see Lubetsky, 1971) and replacing existing internal commodity specialization and exchange with a pattern favouring primary product export. Destruction of petty commodity production of iron implements and cotton cloth (Kjekshus, 1977) provided a small market for metropolitan produce. More importantly it imposed a requirement for cash to purchase the imported replacements, which could only be met through wage-labour or export commodity production.

This in itself might well have been sufficient to generate a growing export production by peasants, though limited in pace by the low level of development of productive forces and lack of infrastructure. But the need for cheap labour not only required more direct methods of control but necessitated limitations on the development of peasant production lest it provide superior alternatives which would aggravate the difficulty of that task. In this respect, it must be stressed that the 'labour problem' was, between 1900 and 1955, the most serious and intractable problem facing successive colonial administrations. The means sought for its solution coloured every aspect of colonial policy during the period.

On this was imposed colonial agricultural policy. Mistaking the results of the disastrous process of decline and social disruption brought about by colonial methods for mobilizing labour for inherent laziness and incapacity, policies for development invariably stressed the regenerative qualities of hard work. Since these policies were implemented among populations from which many of the young men had already left for migrant labour, and given the declining fertility of the soil and the social impact of many years decline, their failure was not hard to predict. It only remains to state that this depressing saga continues to the present day. In some areas of western Tanzania, the tsetse-frontier continues to advance and population to decline, aggravated recently by renewed compulsory villagization. Still more depressingly, African administrators, in some cases, continue to attribute this to personal characteristics of 'backward' populations.

There can be no doubt that colonial labour policy contributed substantially to the obstruction of peasant commodity production in these areas, albeit, at least in part, unintentionally.

After the 1914–18 War, Tanganyika was mandated to Britain, as a relatively unimportant possession, to be run at low cost. This was achieved in part through reduced infrastructural expenditure and also through the introduction of 'indirect rule' which both reduced costs and the need for African education and further retarded the development of African commodity production to maintain the flow of cheap labour to the plantations. This resulted from efforts to retain the 'traditional' legal and authority structures, including restrictions on the ownership, transfer and hypothecation of land as security for loans (which were further restricted by law).

Colonial incorporation: development of commodity production 1945–61

A major change in direction occurred in the period 1945–61, though this was far from evident in the first few years of the period. The two single most important factors were the developments in productive technique and their impact upon labour requirements and a major upsurge in political consciousness among the African population. The first allowed the development of African commodity production at a different level, the second made it politically imperative for the colonial government.

The situation on the eve of Independence, resulting from changes in policy, may be summarized as follows.

Commercial agriculture was still heavily dominated by estates and plantations which produced some 40 per cent of monetary agricultural output by value. This sector continued to receive the bulk of all government resources invested in agriculture. Increased capitalization and the elimination of some of the more extreme structural inequalities, together with rising wages, was forcing this sector out of pre-capitalist into capitalist exploitation.

A class of African rich peasants was emerging which, though

still in its infancy, had already achieved a substantial degree of economic and political control at the local level, through improved access to resources related to its domination of the co-operatives and most other local administrative and decision-making bodies.

The state machinery was still overwhelmingly dominated by Europeans, but with rapidly increasing numbers of Africans rising through its ranks. No longer concerned with the provision of labour to the estates, its primary concern *vis-à-vis* African agriculture was the development of commodity production and of a rural 'middle class'. Against this, however, should be set the continuing need to control and channel this production into exports and through channels from which revenue could be extracted. As will be proposed later in the paper, there was to emerge a growing contradiction between this need for control and the increasingly uncontrollable activities of the rich peasants.

The ideological expression of this, and of the need to subordinate peasant production to international capital through technical innovation and direct control of the production process, was 'modernization', its major expression in the policy sphere at this time being 'close supervision'. Some insight into the ideological confusion surrounding this process can be gained from various policy statements about 'stalwart yeomen' being 'jealous of the fruits of the soil', etc. Such Arthur Youngian sentiments were singularly inappropriate to a situation in which the 'yeoman' could be expelled from 'his' land for contravention of the cultivation regulations.

Finally, there was the Party, TANU, a broad-based nationalist movement, encompassing all sections of the African population but largely dominated by members of the emerging educated stratum, by urban and rural traders and rich peasants. This did not, at the time, reflect conscious choice that this should be so. It was simply the reality of a situation in which education, funds and transport, elements necessary to national political organization and to the assumption of state power, were scarce and limited to these groups. The Party had relied heavily upon workers and all strata of the peasantry for the effectiveness of the Independence campaign. The outlawing of strikes and state control of unions, a few years after Independence, showed how easily trade union leaders could be detached from the rank and file and incorporated in the ruling strata. In a rather different way, progressive farmer policies and reliance on the rich-peasant dominated co-operatives showed similar signs for the rural areas.

But here the case was more complex, for TANU's populist ideology was not wholly in favour of rich peasants. Nyerere had already rejected the privatization and registration of land, in terms reminiscent of early colonial limitations. Settlement schemes, rather than individual rich peasants, were the major formal emphasis of early post-Independence policy. In the following years, the assumption of state power and the close interpenetration of party and bureaucratic hierarchies further reinforced an already strong implicit faith in government policy implementation as the means to development of the country.

Specific processes of differentiation

Highland areas: coffee, education and bureaucratic employment

The earliest development of African commodity production during the colonial period occurred in a few highland areas suitable for the production of coffee, notably Kilimanjaro, Bukoba and Rungwe. Not only were these areas of higher and more reliable rainfall than usual, but high population density in the pre-colonial era had already stimulated intensification of the system of production. In addition to this, their cool and pleasant climate encouraged the concentration of mission activities and thus education, in these areas. In all three areas, initial efforts at the introduction of coffee, conversion and education were concentrated upon the chiefs, and though they were by no means the only large farmers, they were certainly prominent among them.

Some African farmers were already hiring labour even before the War of 1939–45, but the high density of population together with customary limitations on the transfer of land, limited the opportunities for accumulation through increased landholding, and diverted surpluses into other channels. Pre-eminent among these were education for clerical employment and involvement in trade of various sorts. It is scarcely surprising that these should have been among the first areas to develop co-operative movements, nor that they should have been well poised to provide the bulk of the educated manpower for the civil service, church, teaching and other professions, with the approach of Independence. It is hard to document the impact of this upon the allocation of government resources between regions, especially since the impact of government spending upon the population of the region in which it is made varies very widely. For example, funds spent on the development of a state farm may have no local impact other than to take land which the inhabitants could otherwise use, while the same amount of money spent on schools, roads or dispensaries would have a substantially greater impact. There can be no doubt, however, that in terms of infrastructure, Kilimanjaro and Bukoba in particular are favoured in comparison with other parts of the country. In some cases, the impact of direct influence can be seen in rather curious forms. For instance, there is one, otherwise unremarkable, division of Bukoba District which has the highest incidence per square mile of post offices in the whole of East Africa.

Since established coffee is not a crop which uses large amounts of labour, the wage-labour requirements of larger farmers have been met by local poor peasants in Kilimanjaro and have thus resulted in extensive in-migration. In Bukoba, the situation is rather different since the pre-colonial hierarchy, and the existence of reserve areas close at hand have led to substantial migration of Rwandese workers to the coffee plots of large and even medium peasant coffee-producers. In addition to this, there has been an altogether different tradition of out-migration from Kilimanjaro and Rungwe to take advantage of both agricultural and trading opportunities in other parts of the country. Few towns worth the name in Tanzania are without the Kilimanjaro Bar. This, however, is less important than the dominance of the senior posts in the state and professions.

Regional inequality

Regional inequality cannot be considered as separate from or alternative to social differentiation and the formation of classes. Rather it has been a complementary process.

The most important regional differentiating factor has been the distinction between 'labour reserve' areas and those in which peasant commodity production was encouraged and developed. The main lines of this distinction were laid down during the German colonial period and have not changed very much since.

There has, however, been one very substantial change. With the change in labour organization and productivity in the estate and plantation sector which occurred in the 1950s, their demand for migrant labour has been static or even declining. To an increasing extent, African rich peasants took over the role of employers of such migrant labour, though since figures of this are both difficult to obtain and almost certainly inaccurate when obtained, the extent to which this has proceeded is hard to assess. Its major significance for the labour-hiring areas relates to the development of the class structure there. In very few of the richer commodity-producing areas are the majority of wage-labourers poor peasants from those areas; rather they tend to be migrants from the depressed areas of the south and west. Where locals are employed for wages, they tend to occupy the more skilled and permanent jobs, and those with better opportunities for advancement. They may even employ migrant labourers on their own farms. This in turn reflects the fact that there are relatively few areas in Tanzania where land is in such short supply that families cannot obtain access to enough to meet their subsistence requirements. This is even true of most Tanzanian migrant labourers who lack not land but rather the means to cultivate it, this itself being largely due to the absence of men for migrant labour. The major exception to this rule are migrants from Rwanda and Burundi, where land shortage is far more intense. Characteristically, Rwandese and Burundians, who normally cannot get access to land for themselves in Tanzania, are among the worst paid and treated labour force in the country.

Annual cropping areas: cereals and cotton

Another significant series of processes started in the period after 1945 and mainly concerned areas producing grains and cotton. The development of maize production in Ismani, Iringa Region, is the best known example. In the space of a few years, a group of tractor-owning African farmers emerged, cultivating areas of several hundred acres each and accumulating substantial wealth which was reinvested both in maize production and in a variety of other trading and business ventures.[6]

The development of wheat production in north-central Tanzania followed a not dissimilar pattern (Raikes, 1945); a rather similar process has been documented by Kjaerby (1976) for Hanang District, some 100 miles to the south, and similar developments could be seen in several parts of north-central Tanzania based variously on the production of wheat, maize and beans. A similar, though less dramatic process, is documented by Branner Jespersen (1973) for the development of paddy production in the Usangu Plains of Mbeya Region, this time based on the opening and cultivation of new land with oxen. Without doubt similar developments could be found elsewhere, though probably on a somewhat smaller scale.

The development of cotton production in the area south and south-west of Lake Victoria shows certain similarities; and there seems little doubt that comparable processes could be detected, though at a less advanced stage, in many other areas of the country. Van Velzen (1973) has recorded the emergence of a consolidated and locally dominant group of rich peasants in one of the less developed areas of Rungwe District (outside the coffee zone). He showed that their emergence was considerably assisted by favourable treatment by local officials of the government and privileged access to government resources. In fact, almost every detailed rural study which has bothered to look for signs of the emergence of rich peasants has found them. Where it is not documented this is normally because the process has been ignored and the questions left unasked.

Some of the main features of this emergence of rich peasants may be summarized briefly. For the most part, unlike the developments in the highland areas, it dates from the 1950s and 1960s, although the individuals involved would often have been among the wealthier local inhabitants previously. This was the period in which government policy was most concerned to encourage 'progressive farmers' with improved and more relevant advice and almost all of the growing agricultural credit. Since the system of land tenure continued to preclude most forms of private credit, almost all of this came from the state. Thus one of the noteworthy aspects of rich peasant development was that they rapidly consolidated themselves politically, at the local level, in order to ensure the continuation of this preferential access, not only to credit but to such infrastructural facilities as feeder roads and water supplies. Control of both marketing co-operatives and a variety of local committees were the major channels through which such access was achieved.

The patterns of production which emerged were to some extent dependent on the requirements of the crop and the prior development of the area. That is, mechanized cultivation was most important in north-central Tanzania, which had been a major focus of European farming and where tractors had been introduced by Europeans before the 1939–45 war. The production of wheat could be, and was in many cases, mechanized to the extent that one African farmer in North Iraqw cultivated some 800 acres and ran a transport business with the labour of his three sons and two drivers. Otherwise he hired casual labour intermittently for bird-scaring and carrying bags at harvest time. Even in northern Tanzania, the cultivation of maize was far less mechanized, as it was usually planted, weeded and harvested by hand. This necessitated substantial wage-labour, usually by migrants, which was to emerge as a major bottleneck when some of these farms were turned into *ujamaa* villages and the hiring of such labour stopped. Cotton again required considerable hand-labour for cultivation, weeding and harvesting, once again mostly performed by migrants from the poverty-stricken areas surrounding the main cotton-producing zone, though with some migrants coming from Rwanda and Burundi. Rwandese also provided the main labour force on the coffee farms of Bukoba, the poverty and overcrowding of these two countries leaving their populations particularly open to exploitation in its most naked form.

But if one studies the patterns of accumulation a certain unity emerges in the very diversity of the investment patterns encountered. In North Iraqw, the economic activities of rich peasants included: production of cash crops other than wheat (beans, onions, maize), transport of produce, sale of produce unofficially and smuggling across the Kenya border, operations of shops, bars and 'hotels', tractor, vehicle and bicycle repair, grain-milling, beer-brewing and illegal distillation of liquor. No doubt the list could have been extended. North Iraqw is by no means one of the larger areas of rich peasant development (merely the one in which I happened to do field work) and similar trends have occurred elsewhere.

The implications of this pattern of investment are significant, for it was certainly intended as a hedge not only against climatic risk but against the efforts of the state to extract a greater proportion of the surplus through marketing charges and taxation. Not only did the substantial degree of black-marketing directly reduce state revenues, but the diversity of production patterns reduced dependency on any one crop by increasing the opportunities for response to changes in relative prices by shifting between different economic activities. In short, it reduced the level of control by the state at the point of realization.

Controlled export crop production schemes

The introductory section of this paper mentioned the process by which peasant producers have been increasingly subordinated to international capital through the development of directly controlled schemes for the production of export crops, normally for a nucleus processing plant. There have been a number of schemes in Tanzania which have followed broadly this pattern, though normally controlled by government or parastatal bodies rather than international firms, and with significant differences relating to this. There have also been a number of other state initiatives aimed at the achievement of direct control over the peasant productive process, notably tractor-hire schemes and the current villagization programme.

The significance of this development of direct control over the peasant production process is considered in the concluding section of the paper. For the present, attention is confined to impact upon rural differentiation.

All of the settlement schemes initiated in the period between 1955 and 1965 had as one primary aim the development of a class of peasant producers substantially better-off than the majority of rural dwellers. This was stated specifically in a number of policy statements, replete with statements about the sterling qualities of land-owning yeomen and their attachment to the soil. That these were somewhat inappropriate to a situation in which the peasant could be expelled from 'his' land for failure to follow the cultivation rules appears not to have occurred to these ideologues.

That at least the virginia tobacco schemes did lead to substantial differentiation and the emergence of rich peasants is not in doubt, but the programme was very far from fulfilling the government's expectations. In the period immediately after Independence, and with the strong backing of the World Bank, the vast bulk of government resources for the rural sector were directed to the 'transformation' of the system of production for a small minority through the development of 'village settlements'. These were schemes for the production of cash crops (mainly for export) under the control of externally appointed managers. These latter were given powers ranging from fines to expulsion with which to enforce their control of the production system, this being generally specified in considerable detail and being based on the requirements of 'modern farming' (i.e. mechanization). These schemes did assure to their members a substantially higher standard of living than that of the average peasant, but since 'modern' methods turned out, with few exceptions, to be uneconomic, this had to be achieved through government subsidization. For the most part, the schemes were of fixed size geographically, and did not envisage a continuing process of accumulation for their members. This the latter remedied in some cases by using scheme resources to develop their own farms outside the schemes. The schemes themselves were considered by most of the settlers to be government farms, and with considerable justification, since control of their incomes was entirely in the hands of the manager, who could decide how the gross receipts should be divided between loan repayment, scheme investment and settler incomes. Although it had been proposed in the First Five Year Plan that 'transformation' should continue to take the bulk of resources for the rural areas until one million people were living in village settlements by 1980, the programme was terminated in 1965, after the disastrous experience of a few pilot schemes.[7] Most of the schemes already in existence continued, however, many of them constituting a continuing drain on public funds. The tobacco schemes continued to expand and a number of schemes for the satellite peasant production of tea were later initiated. These latter, funded by the World Bank, have been perhaps the closest approximation in Tanzania to the 'classic' concession-company type of scheme, having been modelled closely on a successful scheme of this nature in Kenya.

Thus closure of the village settlement programme did not imply any overall retreat from the policy of increased direct control over the peasant production process. One favourite theme to account for its failure, which was to recur in relation to *ujamaa*, was that 'socialism and agriculture don't mix', though in retrospect it is hard to discern what aspects of the programme could possibly have been so termed. One suspects that the 'experts' concerned equated socialism with 'government interference' which had undoubtedly been a component of the programme.

Post-colonial developments: a brief summary

From 1961 to 1967, the government followed a fairly orthodox 'post-colonial' development policy, stressing the need to increase export crop production, attract foreign investment and educate manpower for the Africanization of the bureaucracy. European agriculture was not discouraged, but the major emphasis was on 'village settlement' and a variety of similar schemes for irrigation, block-farming and tractor hire; though this emphasis died down somewhat with lack of success and the closure of the village settlement programme in 1965. Individual rich peasants took advantage of the much increased availability of credit and its distribution, after some years, through the co-operatives on which they had increased their hold. The co-operatives took over the vast majority of primary marketing from Asians and acted as semi-official organs of government policy, as for example in the tractor-hire programmes. Their expansion from the relative security of export crops like coffee into the complexities of domestically marketed crops like maize posed major problems, especially since the rich peasants who largely controlled them were among the first to sell their crops illegally outside the co-operative monopoly, reducing through-put and increasing costs. Development of export crop production during this period was fairly rapid, although the general price level was well below the peak of the mid 1950s, with the exception of sisal, whose price fell drastically after 1964.

By 1967, the Party, and expecially the President, was becoming concerned at the direction development was taking. The reluctance of foreign capital to invest in Tanzania meant little growth in industry and none at all in employment. This latter was partly due to the near collapse of the sisal industry, which also prevented the achievement of export targets. The emphasis on education and Africanization was producing growing urban income disparities and the emergence of a separate educated class, beginning to branch out into private profit-making ventures, aided by its preferential access to government resources. Progressive farmer policies and such settlement schemes as succeeded at all were producing a similar class formation in the rural areas.

The Arusha Declaration proposed a move away from concern with export dependency, based on production for local needs and reduction of imports. It forbade 'leaders'[8] to engage in private business activities. A number of foreign firms, banks and insurance companies were nationalized, including the major import-export houses. The document castigated those who lived by the work of others, stressed the virtues of pre-colonial African culture and society and enjoined leaders to remember their obligations to the people, somewhat in the spirit of the 'public school ethic' inculcated at Tabora Government School.[9] Thus private firms and businesses (mainly European and Asian) and to a lesser extent rich peasants were to be considered exploiters and enemies. The mass of the rural population was assumed to possess the 'traditional' virtues, although the context in which communal work and mutual assistance had developed was fast disappearing. Most significantly, leaders were the chosen instrument of government socialist policy, and not being direct exploiters were considered to be susceptible to moral injunction.

The evolution of agricultural and overall policy thereafter is somewhat complex. The country was already self-sufficient in basic food-crops, and in the absence of any clear plan for industrialization based on local raw materials, crop priorities continued as before. That is, export crop production was stressed except in times and places where food shortages emerged. A policy aimed at improving the rather poor level of nutrition would have required a major change in the whole pricing and distribution system, to say nothing of the production process, and nothing so drastic was envisaged. Credit, agricultural research and extension, and infrastructural investment continued to favour the export crop areas and rich peasants for some years.[10] Crop marketing was already almost entirely in the hands of co-operatives and behind them, marketing boards, both operating under statutory monopolies. The system had been operating rather poorly and at high cost and continued to do so. A series of commissions and foreign consultants recommended narrowing the functions of the co-operatives to primary marketing, but since they were conceived as broad-based organs of government policy this was hardly feasible. Tractor-hire programmes died out for a while but soon began again, while the co-operatives took control of processing plants in many areas. It was the nationalization of importing that had the first major impact, since a combination of determination to reduce imports and poor organization led to recurrent shortages of various commodities, unfortunately by no means always or even mostly luxuries. A fairly rapid increase in government investment kept imports rising, as, after 1969, did foreign aid and investment.

The *ujamaa* programme started slowly and gradually gathered momentum. A few genuinely voluntary villages were started, and rather more at government initiative, through promises of material goods and services, like tractors or piped water. On occasion there may have been some over-enthusiastic 'encouragement', but this was largely hidden from view since most of the early villages were in poorer areas of the country and widely dispersed. However *ujamaa* was government policy to be implemented and the implementation assessed. Every increase in the size of *ujamaa* programmes encouraged others to follow suit and increase the bidding, so that while the first years had seen programmes for individual villages, these were followed by group programmes and then programmes for whole Districts. Obviously as the size of programme increased, the scope for explanation steadily decreased and the rising cost of providing material incentives engendered a move to more forceful methods of 'persuasion'.[11] In this process the co-operative element, never dominant, was increasingly reduced, the communal village plot became increasingly vestigial and the nucleation of the rural population in compact villages came to be overwhelmingly the dominant aspect. By late 1973, after a series of District and Regional 'Operations' (the military analogy being increasingly apt), the President reversed the previous official policy to bring it in line with reality and made it compulsory to live in villages within three years. This led to a renewed acceleration in the number and forcefulness of the operations and the movement of huge numbers of people. By May 1976, it was officially estimated that 12 million people, or about 85 per cent of the population, were living in some 8000 villages (Tanzania, 1976, p. 3). Even allowing for optimism this is an enormous change from the estimated 8 per cent of the mid 1960s (Georgulas, 1967).

Obviously, change of this order could be expected to have far-reaching implications throughout the economy. Already in 1971 there had come the first confrontation with rich peasants, in the expropriation of the Ismani maize growers to make way for *ujamaa* villages. But this was an isolated case and it was not until 1973 that compulsory villagization first began to hit the major commodity-producing areas. Even after the villagization order, few of the rural areas of Bukoba or Kilimanjaro were affected, though 1974 saw a continuous stream of senior officials through Bukoba, making sure that their own home villages were untouched. By this time, the allocation of credit had shifted substantially towards *ujamaa* villages, though a substantial proportion still went to tea and tobacco villages. Rich peasants owning tractors were in many, but not all cases, experiencing difficulties in getting spares and maintaining their equipment.

On the other hand, *ujamaa* and villagization, together with associated developments, provided opportunities for accumulation by rich peasants. Sender (1973) gives an example where rich peasants used the *ujamaa* rubric to gain government acceptance of their encroachment into catchment forest in the Usambara Mountains. A number of similar examples of sharp practice could be cited, mostly from northern Tanzania, notably Kilimanjaro, where it might be harder to find examples which did not follow this general pattern. Kjaerby (1976) notes a variant in which a rich peasant cultivated his own previous land on behalf of the *ujamaa* village which had taken it over. The costs of this were paid by the government, which was very considerably overcharged. Another sort of opportunity arose from increasing problems in the marketing system. This stemmed in part directly from corruption and the misuse of co-operative tractors. But this helped to widen the gap between official and illegal black-market prices for crops, while the increasing divergence of the Kenya and Tanzania shillings offered further lucrative opportunities for those who had access to transport for smuggling. Such activities must however be clearly distinguished from the productive accumulation which had previously characterized at least some aspects of rich peasant growth. In the earlier period, a proportion of the rich peasant's revenues might come from corruption, but tended in most cases to be invested in expanded production. With this opportunity now usually lost through villagization, almost the only channels left for investment and profit-making are corrupt and illegal transactions. At least one source of these was removed in 1976 with the closure of the marketing co-operatives. What the real impact of this has been I have been unable to find out, since in many cases, the co-operative buildings and employees continue to perform their previous functions. But it does seem likely that this not only strikes at the local power of the rich peasants, but was specifically intended to do so. In this, it is merely the most recent in a series of changes which have reduced local political autonomy. Starting with the replacement of local taxes with central government grants in 1968, this continued with the so-called decentralization of 1972, and after. This in fact simply involved the posting of more central government personnel to the regions, a further reduction in the elective element in local committees, and a planning process which gives very little financial autonomy even to senior civil servants posted locally.

Notes towards a class analysis

It remains to attempt some conceptualization of the processes involved and try to arrive at some coherent picture. I shall not venture into the question of how the classes concerned should be categorized, avoiding this, for the present, by using the merely descriptive labels 'state class', 'rich peasantry' and 'international capital'.

What I am trying to describe here in the simplest terms possible, is the playing out of an antagonistic relationship between the state class and the peasantry as a whole, in the context of Tanzania's overall subordination to international capital. In this process, the relationship of the rich peasantry to both 'sides' has been and remains ambiguous.

The state class has a virtual monopoly of centralized coercive power and extracts surplus mainly from the peasantry through control of the means of appropriation (i.e. channels for the disposal of commercialized produce). This has increasingly been supplemented by the assumption of direct control over the productive process, both to increase the level of production, but especially to increase the proportion which is channelled through official markets. One of the reasons for this is that requirements for state revenue increasingly outstrip the development of production, necessitating the extraction of an increasing proportionate surplus and lowering the real price received by peasants for their produce. This discourages the voluntary expansion of production so that increasingly direct and coercive means have to be applied to achieve this end. But this increase in control is of an ambiguous nature for besides the direct and coercive methods of pre-capitalist exploitation, which have re-appeared in recent years, it is also much concerned to increase productivity through the use of purchased inputs; that is the analogue in terms of state-peasant relations of relative surplus-value exploitation.

It is here that one aspect of the ambiguity of relations between the state class and the rich peasantry enters. On the one hand, there is a definite conflict between the diverse and uncontrollable nature of rich peasant accumulation and the needs of the state class to extract surplus through the control of channels for the disposal of produce. On the other hand, rich peasants are the class most likely to engage in productivity-raising innovations. Here, of course, lies one of the reasons for the continuing favour given to schemes for the controlled development of export-crop production by relatively undifferentiated middle-peasants. Control over the production process is aimed not only to produce the requisite quality of produce, but perhaps more importantly, to channel labour into the production of export crops with 'modern' methods, limiting the diversification of activities. In reality, with the exception of a few producing high-valued crops, the schemes failed to produce incomes comparable with those open to individual rich peasants, except where they were subsidized. In both of these cases, the schemes tended to be used by the settlers as stepping-stones to individual accumulation outside the schemes, thus defeating their own purpose (or at least this one purpose). This was facilitated by the relatively easy availability of land in Tanzania.

This points to one essential characteristic of rich peasant accumulation, which to some extent counteracts the control by the state class over the means of realization and political domination. The basic objective, accumulation of surplus by whatever means are to hand, is well-defined but flexible. This contrasts with the ideology and policy of the bureaucracy, which is diffuse and partially contradictory, combining lack of a clear overall direction with a rigid specificity in particular cases. This rather important point may perhaps be confusing without further explanation and examples.

At the very simplest, the distinction which I am trying to make can be described as follows. Rich peasants tend to follow capitalist principles and to invest in those lines which bring the greatest return (allowing for the spreading of risk); they are, in short, concerned with exchange-value. The state class tends rather to define its 'policies' in specific projects and programmes, whose underlying purpose is, in many cases, not solely the maximization of productive revenue. Thus one finds projects which are blatantly unviable economically (i.e. in terms of western economics) justified and pursued on a number of grounds: they are 'in line with (overall) government policy', they are 'socialist', they promote 'development', they will produce some material result required (ignoring whether this end could better be achieved in some other way). This could be described as determination in terms of use-value. This does not, however, get one very far, since the concept of use-value is very broad and since it leaves open the vital question: what are the use-values desired? Put another way: how is the commensuration of different use-values achieved, given that this is not through the market and exchange-value? Leaving this question unanswered, except to note that it certainly does not preclude some form of determination in accordance with the requirements of international capital as mediated through the operations of the local state, it may be worth giving a brief example since this may help to clarify.

Government policies in the agricultural sphere, that is projects, programmes and extension campaigns, are invariably concerned with quite specific material products and labour processes. In most cases this specification is-performed in very simple and rigid terms. A certain crop is to be produced, with given inputs, planted on a given date, weeded on another, spaced, pruned, fertilized, etc. in specified set ways. Not only do these instructions fail to take account of variations in soils, climate, water-availability, etc., but they ignore the overall production process within which the given set of operations is to be situated. Normally, the labour-process advocated is assumed to be the only one in consideration, thus ignoring the competing demands for land, labour, and cash of other activities, many of which may be of equal or greater importance to the peasant farmer. This is notably the case with respect to labour, since the research performed on government research stations tends to assume the existence of 'spare' labour on the peasant farm. This in turn relates to the way in which such research is performed: on one crop at a time, and in the presence of all the requirements (labour, machinery, biological-chemical inputs) for the achievement of a technical 'optimum' (maximum yield per acre).

Take, for example, the production of coffee in Bukoba. This is mostly produced interplanted with bananas, and for the very good reason that since land is short, there is no other way it could be produced without going short of the staple food (bananas or more precisely plantains). Once again, no great agricultural expertise is required to understand that recommendations for the production of pure-stand coffee will be different than for inter-planted coffee, since the bananas take a considerable amount of nitrogen and water from the soil and also shade the crop to a large degree. For the past twenty to thirty years, the agricultural extension service has based its advice to the farmers of Bukoba upon experiments performed on pure-stand coffee. The advice is thus relevant only to that small and wealthy minority of the rural population which has sufficient land to separate bananas and coffee. For as many years as they have been giving this advice, extension officers have been complaining about the conservatism, laziness, etc. of the Bukoba coffee-growers who have failed to adopt 'improved' methods. Nor is this an isolated case; it could be duplicated from almost every corner of Tanzania.

Before considering the implications of the fairly obvious contradictory elements of such policies, the point must be made that there is a clear element of class bias in them. The rich peasant cultivates under conditions much closer to those of the research station than does the mass of the rural population, and to that extent, the advice is likely to be more relevant to him. More importantly, perhaps, the social context in which the rich peasant encounters the extension agent is far more likely to encourage discussion and the fruitful application of the latter's expertise; besides which he is far more likely to encounter the more skilled personnel who have any expertise to offer.[12]

Returning to the general process as it affects the mass of the peasantry, tracing its implications offers some partial insight into its derivation, for it is intimately linked at various points to the ideology of 'modernization'. Innovations, generated from outside the peasant farming system (in this case on the research station), are to be diffused into a peasantry characterized as 'traditional', that is, ignorant, conservative and 'resistant to change'. The innovation itself, being 'modern', is not subject to critical scrutiny. Its rejection by the peasants when, as is so often the case, it is irrelevant, merely justifies the initial hypothesis of their 'resistance to change'. The 'modernization' hypothesis has the further implication that it is useless to reason with the peasantry since they are not rational, and this points to the use of coercion as a means of implementation. Even if successful in achieving the direct result required, this will also tend to generate evasion by the peasantry, thus justifying a further stereotype of slyness and laziness. In many cases, it will also generate forms of 'passive resistance' as the peasants try to demonstrate that the innovation is not worthwhile by applying it incorrectly. (For example, to give actual cases, by frying cotton-seed before planting or by planting cassava cuttings upside down.) This only gives further confirmation to the official of the abject stupidity of the peasants and the need for greater control.[13]

The process described above is concerned with agricultural extension and grossly oversimplified at that. But it can, I think, be used with caution, to provide analogies for larger processes. For one thing, it shows how the ideology is justified through the actions and policies which it generates – notably, in this case, the confusion between class position and personal characteristics, and the need for coercive action on the part of the dominant. But the significance of the justification of control extends beyond simply the vindication of exploitative action. On the one hand it provides the justification for the activities of a specifically state class. On the other, it links directly to the twin needs of the state class and international capital. The former needs to channel labour for the production of specific use-values (export crops and others which pass through official marketing channels) from which a surplus can be extracted. International capital has similarly specific requirements, for export ·crops and for production processes which allow the maximum degree of control through 'technical' subordination. That is, in the second case, processes which are maximally dependent upon mechanical, chemical and biological inputs whose technology is ultimately controlled by international capital. This may seem to prefer a conspiracy theory where the productivity of the inputs advocated provides an adequate and simpler explanation. In the first place, I am no more concerned to attribute this to simple conspiracy than I am concerned to do this in the case of the extension agent. This would assume ideology to be conscious fraud and propaganda, which to my mind grossly oversimplifies the concept.[14]　But secondly, an argument from productivity simply will not suffice. Space does not permit detailed elaboration and the provision of firm evidence, but the accounts of both extension advice and settlement schemes above indicate that the most 'modern' techniques of production are by no means necessarily the most productive. Of course, this raises the question of how productivity is to be defined, but if one considers the most productive technique to be that which contributes to the most rapid sustained development of the productive forces, the unproductiveness of these policies seems fairly clear.

This brings one to the conditions for the reproduction of the classes concerned and the relations of these to international capital. The state class extracts surplus through its control over the means of realization of the product, by means of which it sets the terms of exchange facing the rural producer. The contradiction inherent in the process is that development of the forces of production within the framework of capitalist commodity production necessarily implies the emergence of a rich peasantry and eventually a class of capitalist farmers. Not only are the productive activities of this class harder to control and 'tax', but its developing economic power is accompanied by increasing control of local state decision-making bodies, as, I think, was happening in Tanzania from 1955 to 1967. On the other hand, tight control over the realization and even production processes may achieve an increase in the surplus extracted over a short period (through greater proportionate exploitation), but at the cost of failing to develop the forces of production.

The reproduction and development of a rich peasantry and capitalist farming class *as such* depends upon the development of the property and legal relations of generalized commodity production, these implying a reduction in the level of direct control over production and realization. In the absence of these conditions, the accumulation of this stratum tends to be channelled increasingly into forms relating to bribery, the use of licensing and monopoly and mediation between the state class and the mass of the peasantry. In short, a symbiotic relationship develops in which the rich peasantry reproduces itself as a stratum, while changing its class character. At least to some extent, this seems to me to be what has been happening in Tanzania over the past decade since 1967.

Notes

1 To avoid subsequent misunderstanding it may be worth specifying how these categories are used here. I make no strong distinction between rich peasants and African capitalist farmers, since even the largest of the latter (with up to 1000 acres or even more) follow a diversified and short-term profit-oriented investment pattern, imposed (as indicated below) by the fragility of legal property relations and the high profits to be made in a number of agency, mediatory and other interstitial transactions. Both rich peasants and capitalist farmers are assumed to be accumulators, without this necessarily implying any 'classical' pattern of 'productive' accumulation confined to agriculture. Middle peasants, by contrast, are taken to be those who maintain living standards without recourse to outside labour but without accumulating, even though they may in some cases hire labour.

2 The Arusha Declaration of 1967 was the major policy statement which outlined Tanzania's 'move to the left' (Nyerere, 1968, pp. 231–50).

3 As an example of this viewpoint, see Gottlieb (1972).

4 The Tanzania Population Census of 1967, has been published in six volumes, variously dated, by the Government Printers, Dar es Salaam. The relevant volume of the Household Budget Survey (United Republic of Tanzania, 1972) is 1 , dealing with income and consumption.

5 For accounts of the pre-colonial and early colonial periods, see Iliffe (1969), Kimambo and Temu (1969) and Kjekshus (1977).

6 On Ismani see R. Feldman (1970) and Awiti (1975).

7 For a description of the settlement schemes, see Cliffe and Cunningham (1973).

8 'Leaders' means senior government and party officials.

9 This was the school which trained the sons of chiefs (including Nyerere) in leadership, during the colonial period.

10 In 1970, 90 per cent of loans were still allocated for export crops and 70 per cent went to the nine richest regions; see Loxley (1975), p. 281. There is no way of telling which farmers in those areas received the credit, since it was distributed from the regional level by the co-operatives, and no records were published.

11 Coulson (1975) outlines the chronology of this development. Freyhold (1973) and Raikes (1975) present analyses. Freyhold (1979) presents a number of articles on *ujamaa*.

12 For examples see Raikes (1972), Thoden van Velzen (1972).

13 The processes so briefly and inadequately sketched here are treated at greater length in Raikes and Meynen (1972).

14 Considered very simply and in this specific context, an ideology can be seen as a class-based, partial and self-serving 'version of reality' but not one which is necessarily consciously fraudulent. Indeed, since its major function is both to justify and to inform class action, in part by closing the gap between subjective good intentions and exploitative class practice, it can scarcely be wholly cynical and perform this function. Most particularly is this the case with respect to a class such as the state class of Tanzania, which appears actually to be foregoing material benefits (in comparison with its Kenyan counterparts for example) through adherence to the ideology outlined above.

References

Awiti, A. (1975), 'Ismani and the rise of capitalism', in Cliffe *et al.* (1975), pp. 51–78

Cliffe, L., and Cunningham G. L. (1972), 'Ideology, organization and the settlement experience', in Cliffe and Saul (1972), vol. II, pp. 131–40

Cliffe, L., and Saul J. S. (eds.) (1972), *Socialism in Tanzania*, 2 vols, Nairobi: East African Publishing House

Cliffe, L., Lawrence, P., Luttrell, W., Migot-Adholla, S., and Saul J. S., (eds.) (1975), *Rural Cooperation in Tanzania*, Dar es Salaam: Tanzania Publishing House

Coulson, A. C., (1975), 'Peasants and bureaucrats', *Review of African Political Economy*, 3, pp. 53–8

Cowen, M. P., (1976), 'Capital, class and peasant households', mimeo Nairobi

Feldman, R., (1970), 'Custom and capitalism: a study of land tenure in Ismani, Tanzania', ERB Paper 71.31, mimeo, Dar es Salaam

Freyhold, M. von, (1973), 'Government staff and Ujamaa villages', *Proceedings*, East African Social Science Conference, mimeo, Dar es Salaam

Freyhold, M. von (1979), *Ujamaa Villages in Tanzania: Analysis of a Social Experiment*, London: Heinemann

Georgulas, N., (1967), 'Settlement patterns and rural development in Tanzania', mimeo, Syracuse, New York

Gottlieb, M., (1972), 'The process of differentiation in Tanzanian agriculture and rural society', *Proceedings*, East African Social Science Conference, mimeo, Nairobi

Hindess, B., (ed.) (1977), *Sociological Theories of the Economy*, London: Macmillan

Hindess, B., and Hirst, P. (1977), *Mode of Production and Social Formation*, London: Macmillan

Illiffe, J., (1969), *Tanganyika under German Rule*, London and Nairobi: Cambridge University Press

Iliffe, J. (1971), *Agricultural Change in Modern Tanganyika: An Outline History*, Nairobi: Historical Association of Tanzania, Pamphlet no. 10

Jespersen, C. Branner (1973), 'Paddy in Usangu Plains', mimeo, Mbeya

Kimambo, I., and Temu A. J. (eds.) (1969), *A History of Tanzania,* Nairobi: Heinemann International

Kjaerby, F., (1976), 'Agrarian and economic change in northern Tanzania', unpublished Magister Konferens Thesis, mimeo, Copenhagen

Kjekshus, H., (1977), *Ecology Control and Economic Development in East African History,* London: Heinemann

Littlejohn, G., (1977), 'Peasant economy and society, in Hindess (ed.) (1977)

Loxley, J. (1975), 'Rural credit and socialism: a critique of rural credit policy in Tanzania', in Cliffe *et al.* (1975)

Lubetsky, R. (1972), 'Sectoral development and stratification in in Tanganyika 1890–1914', *Proceedings,* East African Social Science Conference, mimeo, Nairobi

Nyerere, J. K., (1968), *Uhuru na Ujamaa/Freedom and Socialism,* Dar es Salaam: Oxford University Press

Raikes, P. L. (1972), 'Differentiation and progressive farmer policies', ERB Seminar Paper, mimeo, Dar es Salaam

Raikes, P. L. (1975), 'The development of mechanized commercial wheat farming in North Iraqw, Tanzania', unpublished Ph.D. Thesis, Stanford University, California

Raikes, P. L. (1978), 'Rural differentiation and class formation in Tanzania', *Journal of Peasant Studies,* 5, 3, pp. 285–325

Raikes, P. L. and Meynen, V. (1972), 'Dependency and the diffusion of innovations: a critique of extension theory and practice', *Proceedings,* East African Social Science Conference, mimeo, Nairobi

Sender, J. (1973), 'Some preliminary notes on the political economy of rural development in Tanzania, based on a case-study in the Western Usambaras', ERB Seminar Paper, mimeo, Dar es Salaam

Thoden van Helzen, H. U. E., (1972), 'Staff, kulaks and peasants ', in Cliffe and Saul, (eds.) (1972), pp. 153–79

United Republic of Tanzania (1972), *1969 Household Budget Survey,* vol. 1, *Income and Consumption,* Dar es Salaam

United Republic of Tanzania (1976), *Hali ya Uchumi wa Taifa kaika mwaka 1975–6,* Annual Economy Survey, Dar es Salaam: Government Printers

16 Taking the part of peasants*

Gavin Williams

Modernization and development represent the achievements of advanced, industrial societies and define the objectives of backward, non-industrial societies. Modernization refers to the adoption of complex forms of social organization of production and administration. Development refers to the capacity of advanced technology to increase the productivity of labour. By contrast, 'peasant' denotes cultural and technological backwardness. Peasants are assumed to lack initiative and innovation. They are unable to develop. They must be developed.

Peasants are expected to contribute to development by providing the resources for others to develop the urban industrial economy. Alternatively, they are required to give way to capitalist producers or state farms. Either alternative requires the ruthless application of violence against peasant communities (Marx, 1974, pp. 671–715; Lenin, 1907, pp. 273–5; Moore, 1966). Peasants have fought to maintain their access to the management of their own resources. They have refused obstinately to concede their limited measure of autonomy to the plans for a future society devised by their betters (see Raikes, Part Five of this volume). Modernization and development have been achieved only on the backs and over the dead bodies of peasants or by the liquidation of peasants as a class (see Taussig, Part Two of this volume). The recalcitrance of peasants to outsiders' conceptions of progress and the peasants' place in it defines the peasants as backward and delineates the peasant problem.

*This chapter is taken from Williams (1976).

I am indebted to Sara Berry and to the members of the Political Economy Group, Durham, for debates which stimulated this paper and to Kay Frost and Philip Corrigan for comments on a previous draft. I am indebted to the Social Science Research Council and the University of Durham Research Fund for supporting my research in Nigeria and the United Kingdom. I am indebted to the farmers of Ibadan for teaching me about the 'peasant problem'.

Peasant economics

Despite the great difference in their ideologies and policies, states such as Nigeria and Tanzania (see Raikes, this volume) have defined peasants as a problem. They share the assumption of capitalist and socialist economists who identify progress with the replacement of peasant production by capitalist or state forms of production, characterized by the application of advanced technology and increasing division of labour within the productive enterprise.

One view of the peasant problem defines the peasant as 'traditional man'. Peasants are allegedly bound by tradition, suspicious of individual betterment, and confined by a lack of imagination and resistance to innovation. They have limited wants or are just plain lazy. They prefer to defend a traditional way of life rather than adapt to market incentives. From the 'formal' viewpoint of neo-classical economics, such conduct leads to a suboptimal allocation of resources, which should therefore be removed from the control of peasants and placed in more responsible hands (see Ruthenberg, 1968).

By contrast, Jones (1960) defines the rural producer in Africa as 'economic man' – that is, as 'rational man'. Rural producers are redefined as 'capitalists', whose decisions are assumed to be based on a utilitarian calculation of the relative costs and returns to allocating scarce resources to alternative ends. Thus Hill (1970, pp. 21–9; cf. Berry, 1975a) argues that Ghanaian cocoa farmers are 'rural capitalists' in that 'they have always regarded cocoa growing as a business'. They have bought land according to commercial criteria, have mobilized savings and credit, have reinvested part of their profits in the acquisition of new land, have financed public facilities such as roads, and have taken a long-term view in deciding on investments. Jones (1960, p. 133) argues that, since rural producers will adjust supply to match changes in price, their own well-being, along with the well-being of everyone else, will be secured if the economy is not 'state directed', but rather is 'economically free', so that 'all members of the society are assured equal access to markets, to resources, and to knowledge'. This may be a satisfactory theorem in the imaginary world of general equilibrium theory. In the real world, it only legitimates the subordination of the peasant to the unfree and unequal relations of the capitalist world market.

Both schools of thought identify progress with the adoption of the rationality characteristic of capitalist profit-making. The only question between them is whether African farmers are 'traditional peasants' who must be reformed or replaced or whether they are budding 'capitalist farmers' who only need to be integrated into 'the market' for all to be well.

Chayanov (1966) contrasted the social organization of peasant production with capitalist production (see Djurfeldt and Harrison, this volume). In capitalist enterprises, the producer does not own the means of production, but is employed as wage-labour. The worker is free from servile obligation. He has neither land nor tools with which to meet his needs and is forced to seek employment (Marx, 1874, p. 174). Peasant agriculture is conducted ideally by the family labour unit, working its own land with its own equipment. Since the producer does not pay either himself or his family a wage, we cannot apply the capitalist category of net profit to the operation of the farm. The peasant is unable to treat the family farm as an enterprise 'for reinvestment and business, looking on the land as commodity and capital' (Redfield, 1956, pp. 18–19). The farm is rather his source of livelihood.

'Peasants' are defined by their relation to overlord, market, and state. The 'peasant economy' cannot therefore be analysed as a self-sufficient 'natural economy', independently of its relation to commodity exchange.

In 'feudal' society, peasant production meets the demands of the landlord for tribute in labour or kind and meets the subsistence needs of the family. Landlords may exchange the proceeds of tribute in a market and may even come to commute it for payments in cash, thus adapting 'feudal' claims to the requirements of commodity exchange. Alternatively, peasants may free themselves from servile obligation and organize production for the market themselves. Lenin analysed these two adaptations to commodity production as representing two alternative transitions to capitalist production: 'the Prussian path', in which the 'feudal' Junkers became capitalists, and the 'American path', in which peasants themselves became capitalists. Peasant production is 'subordinated to the market'. This creates within the peasantry:

all those contradictions which are inherent in every commodity economy and every order of capitalism: competition, the struggle for economic independence, the grabbing of land (purchasable and rentable), the concentration of production in the hands of the proletariat, their exploitation by a minority through the medium of merchant's capital and the hiring of farm labourers. (Lenin, this volume, p. 130)

Peasants are differentiated into a 'rural bourgeoisie or ... well-to-do peasantry', from among whom 'a class of capitalist farmers is created', and a 'rural proletariat ... of *allotment-holding wage-workers*'. A precarious 'middle peasantry' is progressively eliminated by the advance of commodity relations and the consequent differentiation of the peasantry. Differentiation is retarded by the perpetuation of such features of precapitalist economies as 'bondage, usury, labour-service, etc.' The elimination of the landlord economy in favour of peasant landholding leads to the more rapid development of the forces of production and of capitalist social relations in the countryside (Lenin, this volume).

For both Lenin and the Bolsheviks on the one hand and Stolypin and the Tsarist state on the other, this 'general picture of the dynamics of peasant society ... was firmly established as a piece of self-evident knowledge, i.e., it had become part of the prevailing ideology not only in the normative but also in the cognitive sense' (Shanin, this volume, p. 223).

Lenin's revolutionary achievements have established the self-evident correctness of these propositions for subsequent Marxists. Thus Cliffe (n.d.) suggests that the above quotation from Lenin 'seems admirably to sum up the kind of changes whose occurrence among the Tanzanian peasantries we have been trying to document'. Nyerere (1969, pp. 343–4) argues that scarcity of land, in the absence of socialist intervention, must lead to the creation of 'a farmer's class and a labourer's class'.

Commodity production by family farms is thus interpreted as one of the ways in which capitalist production assimilates pre-capitalist modes of production to itself, by identifying inequality and wage employment as features of the transition from the peasant economy to capitalist production, rather than as features of the peasant economy *per se* (Lenin, 1969, pp. 71–92).

Numerous studies in different societies have established varied but significant inequalities among peasants in access to the whole range of sources of income. Wealthier farmers not only own more land than others, but usually command more family labour and more and better tools with which to cultivate it. They are more likely to employ hired labour and can do so at lower average costs than poorer farmers. Their farm production is better organized and is more likely to take place at the best time of year. They grow more food crops per family member or per working man than others and are more likely to diversify production into one or more lucrative cash crops. They are more likely than others to purchase land or to rent land, and they do so on better terms than poorer farmers. Income inequalities from non-farm employment – trading, money-lending, manufactures, and salaries – are usually even greater than inequalities from agricultural production. Wealthier farmers can market their crop more cheaply and expeditiously and may be in a position to store grain for profitable resale to the less fortunate. They are likely to be recognized by the authorities and by other farmers as the proper representatives of their communities, and they have far greater access than others to credit, extension services, sprays, and fertilizers (see Raikes and Bharadwaj, both this volume; and Lenin, 1969, pp. 138–43; Hill, 1970, p. 152; Galetti, 1956, pp. 145, 151–3, 285, 459; Essang, 1970; Gottlieb, 1972, p. 24; Boesen, 1972; Madsen, 1972; Thoden van Velzen, 1973). The extent of differentiation is greatest in areas of land abundance, where settlement has been more recent. In such areas, the cultivation of land may be initiated by capitalist farmers who can finance the opening of large tracts of land with machines and hired labour (Lenin, 1969, p. 142; Awiti, 1972).

Inequalities are not sufficient evidence for the fundamentally capitalist tendencies of the development of the peasant economy. Class relations, not inequality as such, define production as capitalist. Classifications based on the extent of landholdings are inevitably somewhat arbitrary, even when they are controlled for size of family household and labour force. Consequently, they tend to reflect the conclusion that the researcher wishes to establish rather than distinctions among modes of production and relations among distinct classes. Lenin, (1969 pp. 72, 77, 132–5) and Awiti (1972, pp. 17, 25) both reduce the number of 'middle peasants' by assigning to the categories of 'poor peasants' and 'rich peasants' or 'capitalist farmers' some producers whose activities are clearly similar to those of 'middle peasants' rather than the 'allotment-holding wage-workers' and 'capitalist farmers' with whom they are identified at either extreme. Shanin (1972), pp. 170–4) and Gottlieb (1972) present evidence which shows that in Russia and Tanzania the 'middle peasants' made up the vast majority of peasant households. As Lenin (1969, p. 69) himself declared, 'Only in proportion as [labour power] is transformed into a commodity does capitalism embrace the entire production of the country.'

With the expansion of commodity production, and the availability of opportunities for wage employment outside the peasant household, labour-time itself acquires a cash value. Conventional arrangements for the mobilization of labour break down, and neighbours and strangers are employed for wages to supplement family labour. For their part, the employees may supplement the products and incomes from their own farms by wage employment. Thus we are no longer dealing with Chayanov's ideal peasant-farm, from which the very principle of wage-labour is excluded. Nor are we dealing with Marx's and Weber's free wage capitalism in which the producer has no access to his own means of production (see Lenin, 1969, p. 181).

Employment for wages, both within and outside the rural economy, may provide a source of cash income and of savings which are then reinvested in the establishment of peasant holdings. Migrant workers may be able to earn cash incomes in periods when their labour is not required on their home farms (Feldman, 1969, p. 109; Berry, 1975b). Migrant cocoa farmers in Western Nigeria finance the purchase of land and the hiring of labour to establish their own farms with savings from wage employment on others' farms (Berry, 1975b). Boesen (1972), and Madsen (1972) show how, during a specific period in their life cycle, young men are faced with demands for cash income to pay both for daily necessities and for such investments as a dowry (the main means of acquiring farm labour) and the land on which to establish their own cash crops. Young men who have completed periods of apprenticeship as craftsmen earn wages to purchase the equipment necessary for their business. Thus the use of wage labour does not necessarily presuppose the existence of a landless proletariat or even of allotment-holders tied for a lifetime to wage employment because of the lack of other sources of income. Aggregate figures for Russia, before and after the Revolution, as well as for contemporary Tanzania, reveal few proletarians outside plantations and state farms. This is not incompatible with periods of wage employment by peasants, especially younger men (Lenin, 1969, p. 160; Shanin, 1972, pp. 170–1; Gottlieb, 1972). Wage employment, like inequality, may be integrated into peasant production rather than become a feature of the 'self-evident' transition from peasant to capitalist farming. The 'self-evident' nature of this transition stems from the identification of the 'forces of production' with 'technology' (Cliffe, n.d.; see also Li, 1973). It is assumed that larger units of production can take advantage of economies of scale over a range which extends beyond the size of the largest peasant landholdings. This enables wealthier farmers to take advantage of advanced technology and of a more complex division of labour in the organization of production. For this reason, 'efficient' capitalist producers are assumed to be able to displace 'backward' peasants, and the reorganization of production along co-operative lines is assumed to offer unquestionable advantages to peasant producers (Lenin, 1969, p. 140; Nyerere, 1969, p. 345; Tanzania, 1969, p. 26; Nigeria, 1973).

Undoubtedly there are cumulative advantages accruing to the better-off in a rural economy as in any other. As we have already seen, wealthier farmers have greater access on more favourable terms to the whole range of productive resources than do the rural poor. They apply these resources more effectively and market their products on more favourable terms. There are also evident advantages in co-operation in certain productive activities. The opening up of new land for settlement demands either the employment of machines and hired labour by capitalist farmers or the co-operation of settlers in clearing land and establishing settlements. Co-operative labour can build roads and other public facilities. Co-operation may offer economies of scale in storage, marketing, and access to public resources. The range over which such economies exist will vary for each activity (Feldman and Feldman, 1969).

Nevertheless, peasants survive the development of capitalism and the expansion of commodity relations because of their ability to deliver goods to consumers at lower prices than capitalists. They have adapted production to take advantage of new opportunities and to integrate changes into the peasant economy. Peasants benefit from their knowledge of the local environment. They are able to combine the production of different crops with symbiotic ecological features and complementary requirements for labour and other inputs. They are knowledgeable about the availability and relative costs, including opportunity costs, of local resources and can adapt decisions to the requirements of particular farms and localities. Labour is provided by family members at no marginal cost, except in additional drudgery to the household, and by temporary employment of hired labour for peak periods (Chayanov, 1966; Jones, 1960).

Innovations can be integrated into existing patterns of production. Existing social institutions can be used to acquire cash funds, labour, and land and to regulate the provision of these resources (Berry, 1975a, 1975b). The introduction of new crops and methods may be combined with older, tried methods for the production of subsistence crops, thus enabling farmers to experiment with new possibilities while ensuring their own security (Ruthenberg, 1968, pp. 245, 331–2, 344; Madsen, 1972, p. 38; Feldman, 1969, pp. 105–6). Unlike wage earners who rely on their employers to provide their means of subsistence, peasants must save out of their income and invest that saving in order to sustain their own source of livelihood. Thus contrary to the prejudices of many economists, peasant producers have high marginal and average rates of savings. (see Galetti, 1956, pp. 471–5, 595–7; Upton, 1967, p. 42; Okurume, 1969, pp. 91–2; Warriner, 1939, p. 163).

The management of capitalist and state farms and of state schemes for settlements and co-operative cultivation incurs high costs for items which are not required by peasant households or met more cheaply within them. High salaries are paid to officials, managers, and technicians, and the wages are paid in advance of the sale of the product of labour. Settlers on state schemes are paid a subsistence allowance to tide them over until the first, or even subsequent, harvests. The provision of housing and of social facilities, often the major incentive to settlers, is a further prior charge on the future income of the enterprise. Outsiders have all too often misunderstood local conditions and sought to apply rules and examples without due regard for the advice of peasants, the availability and complementarity of local resources, and the burden of labour on the prospective returns to innovation. It is not financed out of earnings, as in peasant communities (see Wood, 1950; Frankel, 1953; Baldwin, 1957; Olatunbosun, 1967; Wells, 1967; Laurent, 1968; Ruthenberg, 1968; Cliffe and Cunningham, 1973; Raikes, 1975).

Mechanized inputs, whose superior yields are held to justify more authoritarian forms of labour organization, are often too costly to justify the improved returns they bring, if any. Equipment, spare parts, and repairs must be paid for; skilled workers must be employed to operate and maintain machines; and complementary inputs of unskilled labour must be employed to prepare land for ploughing and to weed lands (Wood, 1950; Frankel, 1953; Baldwin, 1957). Other costs may include the exclusion of intercropping of other crops, the expense of fertilizers to maintain soil fertility, and the loss of both topsoil and the cover for the land. Capitalist farmers tend to treat the land as a source of profit, which can be reinvested in other activities, so that they may have less incentive than peasants to maintain soil fertility (Awiti, 1972; see also Warriner, 1939, pp. 149–150). Wage earners do not share the peasant's commitment to his work since they do not own the product. Peasants regard state-managed settlements and co-operatives as 'government farms' and consider work on these schemes as work for the government, and subsistence allowances to settlers as low wages (Baldwin, 1957; Freyhold, 1973).

Peasants have initiated a variety of co-operative activities. These have usually been undertaken for specific tasks, over specific periods, to supplement household production or to develop resources for household use. Communal systems for allocating resources have been widely used, but as a means of regulating access to resources among individual households. Plans for co-operative labour flounder when no clear relation can be established between an individual's earnings and the effort and efficiency of his work (Hill, 1963; Feldman, 1969).

Co-operation imposed from above has rarely recouped its administrative costs in increased output. In some cases, the more powerful members of a community have turned it to private advantage. It has rarely enhanced the well-being of its members. Usually it has subjected peasants to outside direction and confirmed peasant suspicion of state plans. Peasants resist outsiders' plans to change the countryside not out of an obtuse conservatism, but because of a clear and comprehensible preference for a way of life which allows them the freedom to manage their own resources. They will not welcome schemes for co-operation without clear evidence that the schemes will bring material benefits and improve their way of life, rather than destroy it.

Studies of social mobility (Chayanov, 1966; Shanin, 1972; Hill, 1970; Berry, 1975a; Boesen, 1972) within and between generations in peasant communities have revealed tendencies which counteract 'short-term spirals of relative affluence or poverty' (Hill, 1970, p. 152) and contain peasant social differentiation within the broad parameters of an unequal peasant society.

Accumulations of wealth in one generation are rarely passed on to the next in the form of large landholdings. A wealthy farmer tends to have several wives and many sons, none of whom inherits the whole of his property or household including the ability to command and organize the labour of its members. While larger households tend to divide, smaller households may merge (Shanin, 1972; Hill, 1970; Berry, 1975a). Extreme poverty within rural communities is attributed to the individual misfortunes to which poor people are always vulnerable. Lack of family labour is the most common circumstance cited in a Russian study and a Nigerian study. This in turn may be occasioned by illness or natural disasters. The downward spiral into extreme poverty involves the isolation of the individual from a household – and by the same token the extinction of the household (Shanin, 1972, p. 172; Hill, 1970, p. 147).

The size of peasant households tends through division, merger, and extinction to regress to the modal size. This is not just a product of rules of inheritance and the imperative of cultural tradition. It reflects the limited advantages of expansion of scale beyond the means of the peasant household, which do not outweigh the benefits of an equitable division of household resources that is essential to co-operation in developing the household economy.

The process of merger and division also depends on the relative advantages of employment, income, and profit in the urban economy relative to farming. Poor farmers will migrate to seek opportunities elsewhere if either land or wage employment is available. Wealthier men will seek to educate their children to give them access to the benefits of salaried employment or will establish themselves or their children in trade. Both salaried employment and trading offer opportunities for monopolistic advantages to those who can get access to formal education at a relatively high level or can corner trading opportunities. Such advantages can only be established in farming if peasant farmers can be forcibly excluded from access to the land. State taxes and spending tend to transfer resources and thus opportunities out of the rural into the urban areas. Thus rich peasants may not pass on proto-capitalist farming enterprises to their sons, but they can pass on access to education and to commercial opportunities, so that their sons can become bureaucrats and urban entrepreneurs. Capitalist farming can only be introduced to develop new areas of cultivation, often at the cost of pastoralists and the expansion of peasant cultivation or by measures to eliminate peasant competition. Socialist programmes for the proletarian management of agricultural estates require expropriation of peasants or landlords and the exclusion of peasants from the seizure of landed estates. (See Lenin, 1960–70, 13, pp. 430–1.) It may be easier to leave the business of agricultural production in peasant hands, and exploit them rather than overcome peasant resistance.

Both capitalist and socialist development strategies require peasants to provide the resources necessary for the development of the urban, industrial economy (Helleiner, 1966, p. 140; Preobrazhenskii, 1965). Peasant households control and manage their means of production, thus allowing them a measure of autonomy *vis-à-vis* other classes. This autonomy must be broken down if peasant production is to be adapted to the requirements of urban, industrial capital formation and state development planning. Peasants must be made dependent on external markets and powerholders for access to the resources which come to be necessary to their way of life, or they must be coerced into organizing production to meet external requirements.

The surplus value of peasant labour can be appropriated by control of the exchange relations through which the value of the product is realized. Peasants can limit the rate of exploitation to the extent that they can switch production from one crop to another and from production for exchange to direct consumption, and they can seek out alternative buyers and sellers of commodities. State marketing monopolies allow the state to determine the rate of exploitation according to its own priorities. State monopolies reflect an authoritarian belief in the virtues of state regulation of commerce and production and state direction of resources and opportunities—a belief common to colonial administrators and their successors and shared with the bureaucrats of Tsarist Russia and Stalin and his successors. State monopolies have been used as instruments of exploiting peasants, just as the Tsarists used the imposition of redemption payments and Stalin used the machine tractor stations to tax peasants. State control can be enforced on corporate communities more effectively than on isolated farmers. In Tsarist Russia the redemption payments were exacted from communes; Stalin collectivized the farmers to enforce grain procurement on villages. In Tanzania, peasants have been resettled into villages so that the state can provide amenities, impose taxes, and supervise production more easily. But it lacks instruments for enforcing the compulsory delivery of crop quotas (Raikes, 1975). Conformity with official priorities and directives and provisions of economic plans can be imposed more easily when the state controls access to land, irrigation, and other resources necessary to production. Hence the continued attractions to bureaucrats, despite repeated disasters, of settlement schemes where farmers are dependent on the state for their livelihood, isolated from their communities, and subordinated to the supervision and control of officials. Coercion needs to be supplemented by incentives. Incentives are relative and may depend on the state's ability to limit alternative sources of income (Ruthenberg, 1968, pp. 347–52). The model for all subsequent settlement schemes, the Gezira, depends on management's monopoly of irrigated land to enforce the delivery of cotton from tenants (Barnett, 1975).

Capitalist and socialist strategies of so-called 'primitive accumulation' either displace peasant producers to make way for capitalist or state farms or impose institutions to force peasant agriculture to deliver its tribute to the powers of advanced mechanical, social, and military technology. The underdevelopment of peasant production is the condition for the development of capitalist and state production, in the interests of the state and its beneficiaries rather than the livelihood of the people.

Peasant politics

The first priority of the colonial state was to establish itself as the ultimate source of legitimate power and to remove any rulers who failed to give it full recognition. The state ruled through local intermediaries. In return for their loyalty and the carrying out of administrative tasks the government supported them, not only in exercising authority, but in their claim to land rights, political jurisdiction, and favours for themselves and their clients (Beer and Williams, 1975; Iliffe, 1969).

When government policy shifted towards institutional reform and economic development, colonial rulers and their successors used the 'progressive' elements, identified by their education, wealth, and outlook to promote 'modernization' among their communities. Officials formed an alliance with local community leaders based on control of access to the resources within their respective arenas: on the one hand, there was access to the patronage, credit, office, and plain graft of public institutions (including the state, the co-operatives, and the party), and, on the other hand, there was access to land, ready cash, and influence among the community (Essang, 1970; Beer and Williams, 1975; Thoden van Velzen, 1973).

Peasants will normally adapt to the realities of institutional power and public status. Their opposition to unpopular officials and resentment toward local notables may take such forms as witchcraft accusations or campaigns for the removal of particular individuals from office, with the support of their rivals among the local élite. Objectionable state directives are met by various strategies, from sullen obedience and a formal show of co-operation to dumb insolence (see also Raikes, this volume).

Peasants have resisted the exactions of the state, landlords, and capitalist farmers when such exactions have threatened to deprive them of the resources necessary to maintain their way of life, especially by denying them access to land and by imposing excessive and arbitrary taxation. 'Middle' peasants control their own means of production and form the backbone of peasant society. They are most committed to the conservation of the peasant way of life and are the most militant in its defence (see Alavi, 1965; Wolf, 1969; Beer and Williams, 1975). In Africa, rural communities have resisted their subordination to the administration of the colonial state, and they have resisted state measures that force them into cash-crop cultivation, enforce labour service, and coerce them into wage employment. Successive Nigerian risings have opposed extortionate exactions by state agents and the extension of taxation in periods of worsening terms of trade for rural producers. Tanzanians and Nigerians resisted the imposition of agricultural regulations by colonial authorities. Peasant hostility was directed against government agents, notably court officials, agricultural officers, and the ubiquitous sanitary inspectors, and against government institutions, courts, offices, even railways and schools. They also attacked local rulers, who were seen to support their masters rather than speak for their people, and they have attacked their local allies, usually wealthier farmers and traders (Post, 1972; Beer, 1975; Beer and Williams, 1975; Iliffe, 1969).

Conflicts within peasant communities did not arise out of the internal differentiation of peasant society. They arose out of the primary contradiction between peasants and the state, and the resistance of peasants to state exactions which threatened their way of life. Local rulers, traders, and wealthy farmers were attacked and even killed because in such conflicts they were loyal ultimately to their protectors, the state, rather than to their own communities.

Peasants' resistance has been able to redress specific grievances, such as excessive taxation on agricultural regulations. Peasants have not ended their dependence on external markets and subordination to the state, but they have imposed limitations on their own exploitation. Nor have peasants ended the domination of rural communities by a 'bloc' of officials, traders, and farmers, or intervened effectively in the routine process of resource allocation, except as clients of influential patrons (Beer, 1975).

Peasants have not usually sought to transform their society either along lines of their own choosing or on the lines willed for them by socialist intellectuals. They have sought to defend their gains within the frontiers of peasant society, but have not acted of their own accord to seize state power and thus control the instrument of their own exploitation. This is not because of their lack of imagination or their inability to acquire an appropriate political consciousness. It stems from two sources. First, peasants lack any clear evidence that a transformation of their way of life along capitalist or socialist lines will ensure their security, improve their well-being, and extend their independence – and they find considerable evidence to the contrary. Second, not only do they lack the resources necessary to conquer the state; they even lack the means of gaining access to its administration. In particular, African peasants lack access to the literate culture through which the contemporary state is administered and legitimated. They do not command the technology with which industrial production, together with many of the exchange and marketing activities necessary to the prosperity of the rural economy, are carried out. They do not wish to withdraw from the market economy and bring into being a vision of a pre-capitalist community. They therefore remain committed to the institutions which are the means of their exploitation and oppression.

Peasants will stand up for themselves when they are forced to reject external domination and to unite with an urban revolutionary movement which is forced to rely on the peasants for the prosecution of the revolutionary struggle. As Cabral (1969, p. 70) directed his comrades in Guinea: 'Always bear in mind that the people are not fighting for ideas, for the things in anyone's head. They are fighting to win material benefits, to live better, and in peace, to see their lives go forward, to guarantee the future of their children.'

Mao Tse-tung (1974, pp. 61–83) argued that the development of heavy industry as the leading sector of the economy can only be built on an agricultural foundation. He argued for increasing investment in agriculture and light industry, lightening of the burden of agricultural taxation, and establishment of favourable prices for agricultural in relation to industrial goods. The development of agriculture and light industry provides markets for heavy industry and also accumulates investment funds for heavy industry more rapidly than heavy industry itself. But most importantly, agriculture and light industry produce the daily necessities of the people's livelihood, which is essential if the creative and productive abilities of the people are to be mobilized to increase production. The development of agricultural production is not achieved by the development of the technical forces of production in urban industry and the donation of technical improvements to agriculture. Rather, the development of peasant production is a condition for the development of industrial production. The economy needs to 'walk on two legs'. But the leg of agriculture cannot support the leg of industry until policies are no longer defined for peasants by their betters, and when peasants stand up for themselves.

Cabral (1969) recognized that revolutionary victory may give the 'petty bourgeoisie' control of the institutions of state power which they alone are capable of directing, thus ending their reliance on the masses. Hence the need to avoid taking over the institutions of a centralized colonial state, with its capital, presidential palace, concentrated ministries, and authoritarian chain of command. In economic policy, the priority must he given to raising food production. This cannot be achieved by state direction of peasant producers, but only by encouraging peasant initiative based on their own experience and improving their own material well-being, and defending their own gains against the demands even of the revolutionary state.

References

Alavi, H. (1965), 'Peasants and revolution', *Socialist Register*

Awiti, A. (1972), 'Class struggle in the rural society of Tanzania', *Maji-Maji*, 7, pp. 1–39

Baldwin, K. D. S. (1957), *The Niger agricultural project*, Oxford: Blackwell

Barnett, A. (1975), 'The Gezira scheme: production of cotton and the reproduction of underdevelopment', in I. Oxaal, T. Barnett, and D. Booth (eds.), *Beyond the Sociology of Development*, London: Routledge & Kegan Paul

Beer, C. E. F. (1975), *The Politics of Peasant Groups in Western Nigeria*, Ibadan: Ibadan University Press

Beer, C. E. F., and Williams, G. (1975), 'The politics of the Ibadan peasantry', *African Review*, 5, pp. 235–56

Berry, S. S. (1975a), 'Export growth, entrepreneurship and class formation in rural western Nigeria', R. E. Dummett and L. Brainherd (eds.), *Problems of Rural Development*, Leiden: E. J. Brill

Berry, S. S. (1975b), *Cocoa, Custom and Socio-economic Change in Rural Western Nigeria*, Oxford: Clarendon Press

Boesen, J. (1972), *Development and Class Structure in a Smallholder Society and the Potential of Ujamaa*, Copenhagen: Institute for Development Research

Cabral, A. (1969), *Revolution in Guinea*, London: Stage 1

Chayanov, A. V. (1966), *The Theory of Peasant Economy*, trans., D. Thorner *et al.*, Homewood, Ill.: Richard D. Irwin

Cliffe, L. (n.d.), 'The method of political economy and socialist practice in rural Tanzania', unpublished MS

Cliffe, L., and Cunningham, G. L. (1973), 'Ideology, organisation and the settlement experience in Tanzania', in L. Cliffe and J. S. Saul (eds.), *Socialism in Tanzania*, 2 vols., Nairobi: East African Publishing House

Essang, S. M. (1970), 'The distribution of earnings in the cocoa economy of western Nigeria', unpublished Ph.D thesis, Michigan State University

Feldman, D. (1969), 'The economics of ideology', in C. Leys (ed.), *Politics and Change in Developing Countries*, London: Cambridge University Press

Feldman, D. and Feldman, R. (1969), *Co-operation and the Production Environment*, no. 69:12, Dar es Salaam: Economic Research Bureau

Frankel, S. H. (1953), *The Economic Impact on Underdeveloped Societies*, London: Oxford University Press

Freyhold, M. von (1973), 'Government staff and ujamaa villages', paper presented to the East African Universities Annual Social Sciences Conference

Galetti, R., *et al.* (1956), *Nigerian Cocoa Farmers*, London: Oxford University Press

Gottlieb, M. (1972), 'The extent and character of differentiation in Tanzanian agriculture and rural society, 1967–1969', paper presented to the East African Universities Annual Social Sciences Conference

Helleiner, G. K. (1966), *Peasant Agriculture, Growth and Economic Development in Nigeria*, Homewood, Ill.: Richard D. Irwin

Hill, P. (1963), *Migrant Cocoa Farmers of Southern Ghana*, London: Cambridge University Press

Hill, P. (1970), *Studies in Rural Capitalism*, London: Cambridge University Press

Iliffe, J. (1969), 'Tanzania under German and British rule', in L. Cliffe and J. S. Saul (eds.), *Socialism in Tanzania*, 2 vols., Nairobi: East African Publishing House

Jones, W. O. (1960), 'Economic man in Africa', Food Research Institute Studies, 1, pp. 107–34

Laurent, C. K. (1968), *Investment in Nigerian Tree Crops*, East Lansing and Ibadan: CSNRD 18

Lenin, V. I. (1960–70), *Collected works*, 45 vols., Moscow: Progress Publishers

Lenin, V. I. (1969), *The Development of Capitalism in Russia*, New York: Beekman Publishers

Li Cheng (1973), 'Theory of productive forces', *Peking Review*, 30, 11–15 November

Madsen, B. S. (1972), *A Preliminary Report on Socio-economic Patterns in an Urbanised Rural Area and the Response to Planned Development*, Copenhagen: Institute for Development Research

Mao Tse-tung (1965), *Selected Readings*, Peking: Foreign Languages Press

Mao Tse-tung (1974), *Mao Tse Tung Unrehearsed*, ed. S. Schram, Harmondsworth: Penguin

Marx, K. (1963), *Selected Writings in Sociology and Social Philosophy*, Harmondsworth: Penguin

Marx, K. (1974), *Capital*, London: Lawrence & Wishart

Moore, B. (1966), *Social Origins of Dictatorship and Democracy*, Boston: Beacon Press

Nigeria (1973), *Guidelines for the Third National Development Plan, 1975–80*, Lagos: Government Printer

Nyerere, J. K. (1969), *Freedom and Socialism*, Nairobi: Oxford University Press

Okurume, G. E. (1969), *The Food Crop Economy in Nigerian Agricultural Policy*, East Lansing and Ibadan: CSNRD 31

Olatunbosun, D. (1967), *Nigerian Farm Settlements and School Leaver's Farms*, East Lansing and Ibadan: CSNRD 9

Post, K. W. J. (1972), '"Peasantisation" and rural political movements in western Nigeria', *Archives Européenes de Sociologie*, 13, 2, pp. 223–54

Preobrazhenskii, E. A. (1965), *The New Economics*, trans. B. Pierce, Oxford: Clarendon Press

Raikes, P. (1975), 'Ujamaa vijijini and rural socialist development', *Review of African Political Economy*, 3, pp. 33–52

Redfield, R. (1956), *Peasant Society and Culture*, Chicago: University of Chicago Press

Ruthenberg, H. (1968), *Smallholder Farming and Smallholder Development in Tanzania*, Munich: Weltforum Verlag

Shanin, T. (1972), *The Awkward Class*, Oxford: Clarendon Press

Tanzania (1969), *Five Year Development Plan, 1969–74*, Dar es Salaam: Government Printers

Thoden van Velzen, H. (1973), 'Staff, kulaks and peasants', in L. Cliffe and J. S. Saul (eds.), *Socialism in Tanzania*, 2 vols., Nairobi: East African Publishing House

Upton, M. (1967), *Agriculture in South Western Nigeria*, Reading: University of Reading Department of Agricultural Economics

Warriner, D. (1939), *The Economics of Peasant Farming*, Oxford: Oxford University Press

Wells, J. C. (1967), *Government Agricultural Investment in Nigeria*, Ann Arbor and Ibadan: University of Michigan and NISER

Williams, G. (1976), 'Taking the part of peasants: rural development in Nigeria and Tanzania', in P. Gutkind and I. Wallerstein (eds.), *The Political Economy of Contemporary Africa*, London: Sage Publications

Wolf, E. R. (1969), 'On peasant rebellions', *International Social Science Journal*, 21, pp. 286–93

Wood, A. (1950), *The Groundnut Affair*, London: Bodley Head

17 Towards a practical theory of agrarian transition*

Mark Harrison

In the 1920s the only school of Soviet thought which was rooted in solving practical problems of agricultural production was the Chayanov school of 'Peasant Economy'. It was Chayanov's colleagues and adherents, not Marxists, who largely staffed the agricultural academies and planning, co-operative and agronomic agencies in the USSR at the beginning of the 1920s. At the same time Bolshevik leaders were aware of the urgent necessity of developing Marxist work.[1] Consequently the task of educating the new generation of Marxist intellectuals fell to the Chayanov school.[2]

This younger generation of 'Agrarian-Marxists' led by L. Kritsman developed their outlook in strong reaction against their mentors. As they began to organize their own independent work, they directed it against both the theoretical conceptions and the forms of knowledge produced by the Chayanov tradition. However, they were unable to match the Chayanov tradition's breadth of scientific endeavour. Consequently in their own work they sought to reduce the area of scientific controversy to one subject – the nature of 'Peasant Economy' and the capitalist differentiation processes at work within the Soviet peasantry.[3] They sought to expose the apologetic foundations of 'Peasant Economy', the reality of growing relations of exploitation in peasant farming, and the part played in encouraging capitalist differentiation processes by the practices of the Chayanov school.

At the same time they failed to develop their own practical theory, and could not construct an alternative, socialist mode of rural intervention. Caught between a world which was not going their way, and a dominant practice which accentuated class divisions, they abandoned the search for the Marxist intellectual function combining theory with practice, and became mere critical theoreticians.

*This chapter is taken from Harrison (1979), pp. 94–8.

How could such a school encompass the destruction of Chayanov's 'Peasant Economy' school in 1929? Their victory was only superficial. It was not won by the 'Agrarian Marxists' on their own account, but by the intervention of the Stalinist political state. The state put an end to the Chayanov school primarily because the state was also finishing with the world of peasant smallholding economy to which the school's theory and practice related. But the Agrarian-Marxists had no relationship to practice at all; they had as little to say about solving the problems of collective farm organization as they had found to meet the needs of peasant production. There was no room for them in the new world either, and they did not survive their 'victory' for long.

The modern critique of 'Peasant Economy' has relived much of the experience of the 'Agrarian-Marxists'. It carries within itself the possibility of becoming dangerously irrelevant to the material problems of the actually existing world, and a similar vulnerability to demands for 'relevance' which are coercive at heart.

Roots of a Marxist practice in the 1920s

In the course of Bolshevism's struggle to escape some of the limitations of its origins it also threw out many fresh and creative impulses. In relation to the peasantry we find these expressed firstly by Lenin, who wrote just before his death of the possibility of establishing direct links between the town and country in order to serve the 'cultural needs' of the latter, the possibilities of a cultural revolution and of a co-operative path to socialism.[4] These incomplete and fragmentary themes were further developed by Bukharin in the middle 1920s.[5] They remained primitive and underdeveloped, especially because the political conditions did not exist for their practice to take root. However, we can identify a series of points relevant to intervention in the actually existing world of the Soviet peasantry in order to advance it towards socialism. Bukharin conceived of this advance as necessitating the construction, with the peasantry, of a new Soviet village 'culture', rooted in new civil institutions, embracing new kinds of practical theory.

This use of the word 'culture' is strange enough to us today to be worth emphasizing. It was distinct from the kind of 'culture' found only in museums and opera houses, because of its intrinsic relationship to practical tasks, including economic practices. But it was also distinct from the 'culture' of Stalin's and Mao's 'cultural revolutions', because it was defined in terms of the voluntary relations of civil society, not of revolution 'from above'. This usage made culture stand for the 'natural' way of solving practical problems, uniting both production and popular politics.

Therefore, neither Lenin or Bukharin saw the actually existing village as culture-less. Lenin emphasized the dangers inherent in the traditional 'bureaucratic culture or serf culture.'[6] Bukharin added to this the element of the existing 'kulak culture': literate, technically progressive, rooted in the productiveness of kulak farming, capable of bringing large sections of the village (including the under-financed Soviet institutions) into dependence upon the rural bourgeoisie. Consequently Bukharin saw the development of co-operatives, and of other democratic voluntary organizations, as potential arenas of struggle against both capitalist and serf-bureaucratic practices.

Bukharin saw the organizers of this struggle not as armed men in jackboots but as 'cultural invaders' (*kulturtregery*) – educators bearing practical theory – working with the peasantry to construct a culture capable of meeting the productive and social needs of the whole peasantry, not just of the richer sections, and capable of developing the civil community to a point where it could bring under control the coercive, centralizing and bureaucratic forces within the Soviet state.[7]

This distinguishes the Bukharin tradition from other approaches. Unlike the Chayanov school of 'Peasant Economy' he recognized the existence of different classes and class perspectives within the peasantry. Thus, while in his heart Chayanov may have supported Bukharin, it seems wrong to me to portray Bukharin as an adherent of Chayanov. Chayanov saw co-operative, agronomic and extension officers as organizers of production; Bukharin saw them as organizers of class struggle as well. But Bukharin also differed from the Marxists who rejected the possibility of participating in this struggle from within, and saw the rural services personnel as organizers of capitalism. On the contrary, Bukharin saw the role of co-operative, agronomic and extension officers as potential organizers of new elements of socialist productive forms, not just as unconscious agents of capitalist differentiation.

What light does this throw upon rural practice in the actually existing countryside of the USSR in the 1920s? In reality, to have been an agronomist, co-operator or extension officer could not have meant a purely technical, apolitical role free of contradictions or of political choice.

An agronomist confronted by a locality where tens of thousands of farms are experiencing mass economic problems must learn to distinguish between problems. On one farm, the problem is not enough to eat; this is a poor peasant farm. Without enough to eat, the family cannot even stay in the neighbourhood, let alone improve the household economy. Its members must go and work for others, or even sell up and leave. On another farm, the problem is that the soil shows signs of exhaustion, and with the changing pattern of prices the existing pattern of activities has resulted in declining incomes. Should the farmer adopt a fresh rotation, or rent additional land? What about new outbuildings, and additional livestock and what about additional workers? This is a rich peasant farm. The problem is completely different.

Yet both these different types of problem required solution, not only to secure agricultural prosperity but also to secure the basis for socialist industrialization. Solving these problems simultaneously was not – and could not have been – merely a technical responsibility. The set of solutions involved a political choice, between the different individual and co-operative frameworks for the application of new technologies and resources. In slightly different words, the resolution of such problems required the introduction of elements of new social relations of production. But of what kind, and who (of our dramatis personae) will play the determining role?

Again, an agronomist confronted by a locality where tens of thousands of farms are experiencing mass economic problems must make decisions over the channelling of resources. One can organize resources in such a way that a minority of farms (the minority best placed to benefit) can be visited, reorganized and improved). This creates only individual, capitalist solutions. Alternatively one can innovate means of organizing resources to make them accessible to the mass of households. In this case there may be no solutions because the organization is too rickety and inadequately staffed, the resources cannot meet the demands placed upon them, and the servicing operation breaks down. The only strategic response to such a situation is a political response which seeks to change the system of control over the allocation of resources, and the criteria which decide who is to benefit. In this process the agronomist's relationship to his clients must be transformed.

The stratum of intellectuals whose role was to intervene in peasant production had, therefore, a role which was both political and technical. The politics of this role was bound up with the possible paths of agrarian development and roads to socialism. It was a wide-open politics not mechanically identified with any one strategy or social class interest. It would be an important historical project, therefore, to examine the exercise of this role, the forces to which it responded, and the different options exercised in the field. However, for Marxists to do so, requires developing new kinds of practical theory, relating agricultural production, peasant enterprise and the intervening agencies. It may, of course, be difficult to believe in the possibility of such a project. The space for it is bounded by the hegemony of social democratic practice on one side, and subordinate Marxist criticism on the other. Traditionally, this space has been extremely narrow – a kind of no man's land between the trenches, shelled and undermined from both sides.

In thinking why we should trace out the alternative practices and strategies of the twenties, I am not trying to rewrite history, or to construct some better alternative with which reality may be unfavourably compared. In reality the political options of the twenties were not particularly wide open, and the political and technical resources with which a more consensual cultural revolution might have been pursued were extremely limited. In the Stalinist collectivization of agriculture at the end of the 1920s, it was the old serf-bureaucratic culture which actually prevailed, and which decided the form of socialization. This too had been predicted by Bukharin when he had described how a politically victorious working class which lacks 'culture' (practical theory) may in turn be defeated by the culture of the politically vanquished class enemy.[8] However this was not the only potential outcome present in the 1920s. From this point of view the historian's task is to present the options which were discarded – in all their incompleteness and lack of finish – as well as the one actually undertaken.

In conclusion I hope this will contribute to a more strategic discussion of the concepts of 'Peasant Economy' and the problems of peasant agriculture.

Notes

1 Bukharin (1924b).

2 What followed is described in a new and valuable account to which this chapter owes a great deal: Gross Solomon (1977).
3 ibid., pp. 110, 115–52.
4 Reference is made to Lenin's *Last Letters and Articles* (1964), written in the spring of 1923.
5 See Cohen (1974), chs. VI and VIII.
6 Lenin (1964), p. 47.
7 Bukharin (1924b), pp. 22–3.
8 Bukharin (1924a), pp. 237–8.

References

Bukharin, N. (1924a), *Ataka: Sbornik teoreticheskikh statei*, Moscow

Bukharin, N. (1924b), 'O nekotorykh zadachakh nashei raboty v derevne', *Bol'shevik,* 7–8, pp. 21–2

Cohen, Stephen F. (1974), *Bukharin and the Bolshevik Revolution*, New York: Wildwood House

Gross Solomon, Susan (1977), *The Soviet Agrarian Debate: A Controversy in Social Science, 1923–1929.* Boulder, Colo.: Westview Press

Harrison, Mark (1979), 'Chayanov and the Marxists', *Journal of Peasant Studies,* 6, 1, pp. 94–100

Lenin, V. I. (1964), *Last Letters and Articles*, Moscow

Index

This index is intended primarily as a guide to themes dealt with in the text. Only those authors are listed whose work is described in detail or discussed at some length.